Care in a Time of Humanitarianism

Humanitarianism and Security

General Editor:
Antonio De Lauri, Chr. Michelsen Institute

Amid the growing convergence between the politics of aid and policing, emergency and military governance, securitization and the production of collective fear, this series examines humanitarianism and security as both ideology and practice. To this end, it offers ethnographic and theoretical analyses that contribute to the development of critical approaches at the intersection of anthropology, sociology, geography, international relations, and other disciplines.

Volume 5
Care in a Time of Humanitarianism: Stories of Refuge, Aid, and Repair in the Global South
Edited by Arzoo Osanloo & Cabeiri deBergh Robinson

Volume 4
Humanitarian Shame and Redemption: Norwegian Citizens Helping Refugees in Greece
Heidi Mogstad

Volume 3
The UNHCR and the Afghan Crisis: The Making of the International Refugee Regime
Giulia Scalettaris

Volume 2
Continental Encampment: Genealogies of Humanitarian Containment in the Middle East and Europe
Edited by Are John Knudsen and Kjersti G. Berg

Volume 1
Rethinking Internal Displacement: Geo-political Games, Fragile States and the Relief Industry
Frederick Laker

CARE IN A TIME OF HUMANITARIANISM

Stories of Refuge, Aid, and Repair in the Global South

Edited by
Arzoo Osanloo & Cabeiri deBergh Robinson

berghahn
NEW YORK · OXFORD
www.berghahnbooks.com

First published in 2024 by
Berghahn Books
www.berghahnbooks.com

© 2024 Arzoo Osanloo & Cabeiri deBergh Robinson

All rights reserved. Except for the quotation of short passages
for the purposes of criticism and review, no part of this book
may be reproduced in any form or by any means, electronic or
mechanical, including photocopying, recording, or any information
storage and retrieval system now known or to be invented,
without written permission of the publisher.

Library of Congress Cataloging-in-Publication Data

Names: Osanloo, Arzoo, 1968- editor. | Robinson, Cabeiri deBergh, editor.
Title: Care in a time of humanitarianism : stories of refuge, aid, and repair in the
  Global South / edited by Arzoo Osanloo & Cabeiri deBergh Robinson.
Description: New York : Berghahn Books, 2024. | Series: Humanitarianism and
  security ; Volume 5 | Includes bibliographical references and index.
Identifiers: LCCN 2024013291 (print) | LCCN 2024013292 (ebook) | ISBN
  9781805394907 (hardback) | ISBN 9781805394914 (paperback) | ISBN
  9781805394938 (epub) | ISBN 9781805394921 (adobe pdf)
Subjects: LCSH: Humanitarian assistance—Developing countries. | Refugees—
  Services for—Developing countries. | Forced migration—Developing countries.
Classification: LCC HV555.D44 C37 2024 (print) | LCC HV555.D44 (ebook) |
  DDC 361.2/5091724—dc23/eng/20240516
LC record available at https://lccn.loc.gov/2024013291
LC ebook record available at https://lccn.loc.gov/2024013292

British Library Cataloguing in Publication Data
A catalogue record for this book is available from the British Library

ISBN 978-1-80539-490-7 hardback
ISBN 978-1-80539-491-4 paperback
ISBN 978-1-80539-493-8 epub
ISBN 978-1-80539-492-1 web pdf

https://doi.org/10.3167/9781805394907

The electronic open access publication of *Care in a Time of Humanitarianism* has been
made possible through the generous financial support of the Mellon Foundation.

This work is published subject to a Creative Commons
Attribution Noncommercial No Derivatives 4.0 License.
The terms of the license can be found at https://creative-
commons.org/licenses/by-nc-nd/4.0/. For uses beyond
those covered in the license contact Berghahn Books.

CONTENTS

List of Illustrations — viii

Acknowledgments — x

Introduction. Care in a Time of Humanitarianism: Stories of Refuge, Aid, and Repair in the Global South — 1
Arzoo Osanloo and Cabeiri deBergh Robinson

Part I. Refuge, Law, and Empire in the Global South

Chapter 1. Patriation: Conceptualizing Migration after Empire — 35
Pamela Ballinger

Chapter 2. Quezon's Hospitality: Transitional Asylum and Humanitarian Intimacies during Philippine Decolonization, 1935–1941 — 51
James Pangilinan

Chapter 3. Burma Evacuees: R. Sanyassiah, Postwar Return, and Displacement in Modern South Asia — 68
Emma C. Meyer

Chapter 4. Khao-I-Dang Refugee Camp: Local Hosts and Hauntings of the Third Indochina War in a Transit Zone — 84
Khathaleeya Liamdee

Chapter 5. A "Lucky Escape": Ethnic Cleansing and What Happens When International Humanitarianism Fails — 98
Kathie Friedman-Kasaba

Chapter 6. Benevolent Arts: The Persistence of Mercy in Humanitarian Logics — 112
Arzoo Osanloo

Part II. Aid, Intimacy, and Humanitarian Praxis

Chapter 7. Humanitarian Departures: Reflections of a
Refugee Aid Worker   131
    Ilana Feldman

Chapter 8. Quiet Aid: Barbara Schöfnagel's Private
Humanitarianism in the Socialist Gray Area (and What Else
the Global East Can Teach Us)   145
    Cristian Capotescu

Chapter 9. Yūsuf's Struggle: Negotiating Development and
Charity in a Palestinian Refugee Camp   161
    Gözde Burcu Ege

Chapter 10. "They Are *Muhajir*, We Are *Ansar*": Godforsakenness
at the Myanmar-Bangladesh Border   176
    Tanzeen Rashed Doha

Chapter 11. "We're All Humanitarians": International Humanitarian
Organizations, Islamist Service Societies, and the Practice of
"*Humanitariyan Jihad*" in Kashmir   189
    Cabeiri deBergh Robinson

Part III. Repair in a World of Care

Chapter 12. Red Coat, Denim Shirt: Conceptualizing Displacement
across Generations   207
    Rawan Arar

Chapter 13. The Barrette: Unlikely Humanitarian Images and
Practices of Repair   222
    Jenna Grant

Chapter 14. Memoir and a Sinking Ship: Reconstituting
Humanity through Refugee Narratives   238
    Megan Butler

Chapter 15. The Gift of Food: An Islamic Ethics of Care   254
    Amira Mittermaier

Chapter 16. Mothering the Dead: Care beyond Life in Kurdistan   268
    Mediha Sorma

Chapter 17. Unintended Consequences: Debating the Protection
of Cultural Heritage during Humanitarian Crises   284
    Stephanie Selover

Conclusion. Closing Conversation: Lessons in Humanitarianisms
from the Global South   298
  Arzoo Osanloo and Cabeiri d≤Bergh Robinson

Appendix. Pedagogical Supplement: Thematic Pairings of Chapters
for Teaching Modules   307
  Arzoo Osanloo and Cabeiri d≤Bergh Robinson

Index   311

ILLUSTRATIONS

☻-☻-☻-☻-☻

Figure 1.1. "Torneremo," 1943.	45
Figure 2.1. "A Home for the Persecuted," 1940.	61
Figure 3.1. Evacuee letters and petitions, circa 1950.	77
Figure 4.1. Aunt Fang showing her Khao-I-Dang photo album, 2018.	91
Figure 6.1. Poster advertising the play *Manus*, 2017.	114
Figure 9.1. A wall on the rooftop of al-Ḥayāh association, Amman, 2018.	165
Figure 11.1. Women's health unit of the Jamaat-ul-Dawa Mobile Medical Camp, Muzaffarabad, AJK, November 2005.	191
Figure 11.2. Model military-civilian field hospital, Chakoti, AJK, November 2005.	192
Figure 12.1. The author as a child, sitting on a swing with her father and grandmother (teta), Amman, Jordan, circa 1987.	208
Figure 12.2. Panel display of Mama's denim shirt with Palestinian emboidery, circa 1993.	215
Figure 13.1. *Untitled* by Elizabeth Becker, Phnom Penh, 1978.	223
Figure 13.2. *Untitled* by Elizabeth Becker, 1978.	229
Figure 13.3. *Untitled* by Elizabeth Becker, Takeo, 1978.	230
Figure 14.1. "Stop the Boats," 2013.	243
Figure 15.1. Sayyida Zaynab mosque in Cairo, 2020.	255

Figure 16.1. Still from the short movie *7 Days, 7 Nights* by Ali Bozan, 2018.   269

Figure 16.2. Online news coverage of Emine Cagirga standing in front of the freezer where she kept her daughter's dead body for six days, 2022.   275

ACKNOWLEDGMENTS

We came to this project through dialogue and discussion, and even a bit of debate, starting in the heady pre-pandemic days of the fall of 2018. In those conversations, we agreed that too little attention was being paid to the vast networks of local humanitarian care in the global South, where the majority of the world's forced migrants have been, and remain, for well over a century. The project that emerged, *Humanitarianisms: Migrations and Care through the Global South*, was intended to be our exploration of the myriad traditions of humanitarian care through a series of talks at the University of Washington.

None of this would have been possible, however, if it weren't for the encouragement and support of Kathleen Woodward, the director of the University of Washington's Simpson Center for the Humanities, which, together with the Andrew W. Mellon Foundation's Sawyer Seminars, funded much of this project over the course of three years. Once our project found shape, Woodward gave us the full backing of the Simpson Center's various resources. We also had the support of the Sawyer Seminar Advisory Board: Eva Cherniavsky, Danny Hoffman, Selim Kuru, Christian Novetzke, Vicente Raphael, an eclectic inter- and multidisciplinary group with whom we were able to bounce around ideas and seek advice. Our conversations and much of the planning took place during the rather innocent days of pre-pandemic life. We had envisioned a completely different set of outcomes for our project, including in-person presentations and a conference at our university. Over the course of months, however, when the pandemic spread unabated throughout the world, we realized we had to change tack.

The shift to remote learning, as it happened, gave us two advantages: an enduring internet presence and global accessibility, both for us and for our audience. Over the course of nine months (Fall 2020–May 2021), we broadcasted our events to some sixteen hundred viewers in forty-four countries. Caitlin Palo, the Simpson Center's program and events manager, made much of this happen with her abounding tech savvy and creativity. The professional quality of our videos is a testament to her skill and imagination.

Our conversations with our then-postdoctoral fellow Cristian Capotescu allowed us to develop our ideas and translate them into action. It is Cristian who built and for some time maintained our wonderful project website.[1] Two amazing then-doctoral students, Gözde Burcu Ege and Mediha Sorma, helped with every aspect of the Sawyer Seminar, including appearing on camera to lead conversations, even while conducting their own research and writing for this project. Early on in the inception phase of this project, we had the opportunity to work with Parijat Jha, our then-graduate assistant, who brought immense creativity and a spirit of innovation to the project.

We all had to overcome being camera shy and work out our very own world of production—"green rooms," show notes, intro and outro music—and we even had some fun utilizing Zoom's appearance-enhancing tools in lieu of makeup artists, of course. But it was our amazing speakers who brought their astute insights, challenges, and provocations to the finer intellectual questions we had raised. For that, and for the fact that they agreed to have their presentations recorded and permanently disseminated, we are immensely grateful and the better for it. For this we thank (in the order of their presentations) Anne McNevin, Pamela Ballinger, Ilana Feldman, Jessica Whyte, Emma Meyer, Elena Fiddian-Qasmiyeh, Amira Mittermaier, Sienna Craig, Basit Iqbal, China Scherz, Sinan Antoon, Cristian Capotescu, Dean Spade, Nermeen Mouftah, and Juno Salazar Parreñas, who made up the core speaker series that inspired many of the conversations that led to this volume.

Those conversations were aided by the tremendously engaged and enthusiastic working group that convened alongside the speaker series. Amid the wreckage of the pandemic, we managed to maintain an intellectually engaging rhythm of conversation throughout the Sawyer Seminar and two workshops that followed, our only sustenance being our provocative conversations and curated care packages. Most of our speakers and working group members ended up writing articles, some for this volume and others for their own projects. We are so grateful to the members of our very active working group.

Julie Stovernik and Rachel Arteaga at the Simpson Center were also indispensable for navigating the University of Washington's bureaucracy. Erin Gilbert and Megan Ward were wonderful copy editors, who helped tackle the finer details of producing a volume as unwieldy and complex as this one. Two anonymous peer reviewers gave us the best kind of feedback—at once critically engaged and supportive. At Berghahn, Anthony Mason and Tom Bonnington gave superb advice while helping to shepherd this project to fruition, while Ryan Mastellar smoothed out the manuscript considerably.

The resulting volume grew out of a sustained and engaged dialogue in which we, the volume's editors, shared the conceptualization, writing, and revising equally. Similarly, we accept equal responsibility for any errors, however inadvertent.

Note

1. For more information, visit https://www.humanitarianisms.org.

Introduction
Care in a Time of Humanitarianism
Stories of Refuge, Aid, and Repair in the Global South
Arzoo Osanloo and Cabeiri deBergh Robinson

In these times, a reader perusing any newspaper will quickly encounter stories of forced migration, displacement, and flights from persecution. Contemporary depictions of forced migration call up the bodies of children washed up on European shores, while examples of humanitarian care portray relief workers delivering supplies to desperate women and children baking under the Mediterranean sun in makeshift refugee camps. Yet, as we witnessed the flight of Ukrainian civilians across Europe's internal borderlands, numerous others, forcibly displaced from their homes and seeking refuge, remained within the Middle East, North Africa, and South and Southeast Asia. The vast majority of these forced migrants are denied the welcoming embrace of Europe, North America, and Australia.

As two anthropologists of the global South—Iran and Pakistan, respectively—working on complementary but divergent topics, ranging from Islamic law to women's and refugee rights and political violence, we were puzzled over this vivid, sympathetic, and sensorial attention to the need for aid accompanied by vocal and self-congratulatory praise for a culture of hospitality found in wealthy countries of Europe, North America, and Australia. One reason for our continued surprise at the dominance of narratives and visual representations of humanitarian care administered to suffering displaced people in these regions was that in 2017, these countries hosted just 15 percent of the world's forced migrants and refugees. The remaining 85 percent sought refuge and remained in the global South, mostly for protracted periods, often generations.[1] We also noted that much contemporary scholarship on humanitarianism portrays patterns of forced migration as linear flows north and westward, for which Western philosophies of care serve to construct migrants as subjects of compassion and aid. One of the effects of framing the practices of care in this way is that the global South is relegated to being a region that produces refugees and a place refugees migrate *from* rather than *to*. Yet, the stark reality is that the vast majority of migrants, displaced persons, stateless people, and refugees continue to seek shelter and stay in the global South.[2]

For decades, the top host countries of the world's refugees have been in the global South; Columbia, Iran, Jordan, Lebanon, Pakistan, Türkiye, and Uganda are frequently named in the top five.[3] Additionally, 13 percent—9.4 million—of forcibly displaced people who are now "of concern" to the United Nations High Commissioner for Refugees (UNHCR) are in the Asia and Pacific region. They include 4.2 million refugees, 2.7 million internally displaced people, and 2.2 million stateless people, of whom the majority originate from Afghanistan and Myanmar.[4] In 2016, the top six destination countries for forced migrants (Jordan, Türkiye, Palestine, Pakistan, Lebanon, and South Africa) hosted approximately 50 percent of refugees, asylum seekers, and forcibly displaced people but commanded only 1.9 percent of the world's cumulative GDP. The six richest countries (Germany, France, China, the United States, UK, and Japan) made up 56.6 percent of the world's cumulative GDP but hosted only 8.8 percent of forced migrants.[5] The 2021 collapse of the Afghan government resulted in a small rise in Afghan hosting by countries of Europe and North America, but the vast majority fled to neighboring Pakistan and Iran.[6] The outpouring of refugees from Russia's unprovoked attack on Ukraine in 2022 added to these numbers but also elicited a greater welcome by countries in North America and Europe.

If we give due consideration to the actual scale and duration of relief and aid projects that these statistics invoke about responses to the forced migrations of the global South, then we must also rethink our understanding of the normative claims of the global humanitarian project. The humanitarian sites that were intended to deliver temporary refuge and aid are actually intertwined with protracted living in nominally temporary conditions. The conditions we outlined above are not exceptions to ideal global humanitarian practices or aberrations of the principles of global humanitarianism. In actuality, displaced people, the places they inhabit in short-term or long-term rehabilitation, and the representatives of host governments and local relief agencies also produce the field of humanitarian experiences. As it stands, depictions of humanitarianism have largely written the global South out of the accounts of its historical origin, philosophical foundations, legal apparatus, and expert practices, except as the recipient of aid. One of the enduring features of this framing of humanitarianism has been to exclude from this master narrative an account of the experiences, knowledge, and values about care from other parts of the world. In an attempt to include these previously excluded forms and accounts of care, we refer to *humanitarianisms*, in the plural, in an effort to invoke the multiplicity of forms of humanitarian care.

In contrast, the overarching argument of *Care in a Time of Humanitarianism* is that the global humanitarian project will be better understood if we look at it as developing out of hybrid formations of the management of care, which include local and vernacular practices. The hosting practices of any nation-state are a combination of many factors—geopolitical, social, cultural, and economic. Thus, care work, one of the central inquiries of this volume, presents itself in myriad forms and practices. Through this exploration, humanitarian care emerges as possessing multivalent properties of historical, cultural, and religious traditions of caring for distant others, all of which shape humanitarianisms in practice in the global South. We argue that the spaces and practices of humanitarian care in the global South do not stand outside of or as exceptions to normative global humanitarian practices but are integral to it as it is practiced in reality.

The critical chapters in this collection decenter the normative rhetoric and understanding of humanitarianism by examining the histories of forced migration and practices of humanitarian care both for "conventional" and "humanitarian" refugees that developed outside of Europe and North America. Our contributors examine alternative historical trajectories of humanitarianism. They explore important conceptual categories that organize regional humanitarian practices, such as the figure of the refugee, what caring for others looks like, and what kinds of suffering, beyond that of humans, is worthy of repair. Our approach to understanding contemporary humanitarianism is both comparative and focused from the ground up. We start by examining practices and spaces where care is offered in the global South as examples of humanitarian engagement. From there, we seek to reveal the ethical systems, logics, and rationalities of care that underlie everyday practices of crisis management, charity, hospitality, and caring labor across cultural and religious traditions in the Middle East and North Africa, the southern Mediterranean, South Asia, Southeast Asia, and Eastern Europe.

Each chapter offers an illustrative story that serves as a departure point from which each author offers a layered interpretation of the story. While the chapters emphasize grounded humanitarian practices over their philosophical genealogy, ideology, or legal apparatuses, the authors also show readers how they think with and through expert frameworks to understand the work of care in a time of humanitarianism. Through the telling of the story, each contributor highlights how their ethnographic and humanistic research into refuge making and sustaining, care work, and material and therapeutic practices of repair in the global South reshapes understandings of humanitarianisms writ large.

What Is "the Global South"?

At this juncture, it is useful to consider the question: What is the global South? And further, why do we claim that the global South is an important concept to use to understand forced migration and care in the contemporary world?

The term "global South" now has a substantial history with several different meanings and implications. In its most simple invocation—and one that we are not using here in this volume—the "Global South" (with both words capitalized) is a term that developed in the 1990s to replace the concept of the "Third World."[7] For many nongovernmental organizations, including those involved in providing humanitarian aid, the term "refers to countries classified by the World Bank as low or middle income that are located in Africa, Asia, Oceania, Latin America, and the Caribbean."[8] However, beyond this nation-state and development-paradigm definition is a conceptually richer and, we think, analytically more useful meaning of the term. This conception of the "global South" (with the mixed capitalization that we use here) draws on critiques of the ongoing global structures of inequality and subjugation, particularly those created by colonial legacies and by neo-imperial geopolitical relationships. This articulation of the global South is not exclusively territorially defined, and indeed, in this conceptualization, "there are Souths in the geographic North and Norths in the geographic South."[9] Instead, this concept of the global South has created a very important domain of dialogue for scholars and activists who articulate connections between struggles that appear localized and global power structures that have enduring historical impacts and spatial connections that sometimes contradict contemporary geopolitical realpolitik.[10]

We are particularly inspired by Mukoma Wa Ngugi's discussion of the value of the concept of the global South as one that requires that we dare to do away with classic colonial and imperial theories of cultural and political centers and peripheries. Instead, the concept requires that we think in nonhierarchical ways of the interactional production of all forms of knowledge and expertise and the composite nature of identity. He credits the origins of global South thinking to the process of decolonization and its theorization and to the dynamics of the postcolonial world, in which "knowledge becomes a multiple lane highway in which all sorts of exchanges, some of them equal and others exploitative, take place."[11] He further suggests that the West Indian poet and intellectual Édouard Glissant's concept of being "in-relation" is a good way of expressing horizontal, circular exchanges that abolish the concept of center and periphery. As Ngugi argues, "Other ways of knowing and relating have always been there—that is to say, they are historical and at the same time ongoing, and to ignore them is to approach the world with one intellectual hand tied behind our backs."[12] In this task, he argues, "the goal is not to sublimate or ignore the West—far from it. . . . The goal is to be in-relation with the West as with everyone else."[13]

We draw from Ngugi's use of "the global South" because it has a critical edge that we find helpful in thinking about the global production of humanitarian conditions in new ways that go beyond decentering these geographic South-to-North images of forced migration. The "Global South" is too often relegated to being a site in which Enlightenment humanitarianism operates and as the place refugees migrate *from* rather than *to* and *within*. As a result, much contemporary scholarship, journalism, policy analysis, and public culture representation of forced migration depict migrant flows as linear, northward, and westward, for which Western philosophies of care ultimately make the migrants visible only as depoliticized subjects of compassion and aid. Allowing "the North" to occupy the center stage for understanding humanitarian norms and practices inevitably obscures forms of humanitarian engagement as enacted and experienced by vast numbers of people in various parts of the world.

More significantly, however, by thinking in dynamic, horizontal, circular, and "in-relation" ways, we recognize that there are diverse rationalities and forms of expertise that underlie practices of care, aid, relief, and repair among the bulk of the world's refugees and forcibly displaced people. From a purely geopolitical perspective, a focus on host countries and societies in the global South, which have been and remain the primary hosts of displaced peoples since World War II, would reorient our attention to the spaces of caregiving and of living in extended precarious conditions. Hosts in the global South—and this means host countries, host communities, and refugees who host other refugees—are sources of knowledge and producers of expertise in humanitarian care; they are not its passive recipients, beneficiaries, or conduits for external donor agencies. Moreover, these spaces and practices are not exceptions to global humanitarianism. Rather it is in these spaces, in the global South, that multiple historical, cultural, and religious traditions of caring for others shape humanitarianism in practice. It is to these relations that we turn our attention.

Humanitarianisms "in-Relation"

As we have noted, the Europe-centered depiction of the origins of humanitarian law and the international refugee regime, the foundations of humanitarian reason, and the basis of professional expertise has largely written the global South out of its genealogy, except as the beneficiary or recipient of care. This master narrative excludes accounts of the experiences and knowledges about care from other parts of the world—what we, joining a critical community of scholars call, *humanitarianisms*.[14] We revisit the limiting assumption that rules of care and the management of suffering during wartime and other crises emerge from Western political thought and ethical traditions. We examine the production and management of humanitarian care in the global South by shifting our focus to practices, knowledges, and traditions of care to those parts of the world that are empirically responsible for hosting most of the world's forced migrants, displaced persons, stateless people, and refugees. We also note that these humanitarian practices draw not only from philosophical and cultural traditions but also from regional legal apparatuses that may not have become globally dominant but have nonetheless left traces; their logics are evident and their effects impact the implementation of relief or aid administration in local contexts. We argue that the resulting hybrid or composite *humanitarianisms* have had an impact on the global humanitarian project as it expanded and made ever broader claims to universalism. It is the recognition of the importance of these multiple ways of coming to understand care work that ultimately motivates our attempt to understand humanitarianism "in-relation."

To look at humanitarian encounters in this way—as *humanitarianisms*—we must examine the foundations of important conceptual categories that organize humanitarian practices, such as the figure of the refugee, what caring for others looks like, and what kinds of human suffering are deemed worthy of care. Legal and administrative regimes, particularly, purport to have a natural, self-evident reality, but they are, themselves, products of cultural and political struggles.[15] Indeed, the epistemological ordering—the process of defining categories—of displacement is a project that arranges political relations by assigning different values to dislocation experiences.[16] Thus, when a category is represented as nonpolitical and possessing self-evident boundaries of inclusion and exclusion, it has already become naturalized. It is important to remember this about all of the regulatory apparatuses that guide policies on forced migration and to clarify distinctions between categories of migration—including labor migration, family reunification, human trafficking, and internal displacement.

Humanitarian Logics

In this section, we seek to unpack some of the diverse but conflated strains of thought, law, and practice that make up understandings of humanitarianism across academic fields and in the popular media. We do not seek to narrow the term to one superior understanding but rather to trace the numerous domains from which the idea of humanitarianism has emerged and gains purchase and meaning.

Often when reporters or scholars speaking across disciplines speak of "humanitarianism," a number of different ideas and concepts are conflated. Humanitarianism may refer to a philosophy about a common humanity that serves as the basis for the ideal that all humans, regardless of race, nationality, gender, or social class, are equal and deserving of liberty and security. Or, it may invoke the notion of humanitarian law, which emerges from centuries-old laws of war and a more direct expansion of the Fourth Geneva Convention (1949). These laws provide for the protection of civilians during armed conflicts. Additionally, there is a separate but related area of regulation: international refugee laws, which are composed of international agreements regarding the treatment of civilians forced to flee their home countries.

In what follows, we hope to underscore the importance of understanding these distinctions, but also note that by the end of the twentieth century, these concepts had come to be used more or less interchangeably. In other words, Enlightenment logics and philosophical ideals about a common humanity and notions about protection of civilians in times of war have come to overlap with logics of providing safe haven for refugees and forced migrants.

Indeed, humanitarianism, as a concept for organizing practices of care, has deep roots in diverse religious traditions of love, compassion, charity, mercy, hospitality, and also cosmopolitanism. But later influences evolved beyond faith and philosophy to include social and political movements, including the abolitionist movement, the emergence of social work, the politics of anticolonialism and national liberation, and other moral movements, faith-based and non-faith-based alike. Many of these practices later became professionalized, and even if faith-based in their conception, they often came to appear secular amid wider bureaucratic and regulatory approaches to humanitarianism.

Thus, discussions of humanitarianism often index discursive traditions that mingle all these meanings and concepts. These are not simple misunderstandings or conflations that need to be disentangled. Instead, humanitarianism, once flattened and thus obscuring the multiple traditions of care and processes of humanitarian management, possesses its own productive power. We believe that it is this ensuing power that scholars must examine more methodically.

Philosophical Humanitarianism, the Laws of War, and the Refugee Conventions after World War II

Most contemporary genealogies of humanitarianism emphasize its historical emergence through a Western canon, especially the philosophical traditions grounded in the European Enlightenment. In this understanding, humanitarianism begins with European moral sentiments and, at its core, is a project oriented around preserving life and relieving human suffering near and far.[17] These life-preserving measures, as indexed in a European context, were also connected with Christian moral values, notably charity, hospitality, and love and compassion.[18]

The origins of the laws of war are often linked to the traditions that by the late eighteenth century came to emphasize a common humanity of all people, regardless of social ties, race or ethnicity, gender, socioeconomic status, or creed, if not in practice, at least in discourse.[19] This specific humanitarianism grew out of a broader movement in seventeenth-century Europe to establish the rule of law between nation-states. The principles emerging from this, over centuries, addressed states' conduct during warfare and other emergencies in order to regulate the treatment of civilians caught in zones of conflict or disaster.

In this context, contemporary understandings of humanitarianism trace their origins to the Genevois social activist, Henri Dunant. In the mid-nineteenth century, Dunant, who witnessed the ravages of war firsthand, cofounded the International Committee of the Red Cross (ICRC) in 1863.[20] After the Battle of Solferino, Italy, in 1859, Dunant sought to establish a permanent wartime voluntary relief network to protect soldiers, albeit initially for Christians only. While Dunant likely meant unpaid labor, a more contemporary understanding of voluntarism includes the "selflessness" of humanitarian workers who willingly accept a dangerous mission in order to serve others. However, Dunant's colonial interests were part and parcel of these organizations' missions.[21] Today, these critiques have been folded into their broader aid and relief works.

Sometime later, the ICRC's Jean Pictet, a Swiss lawyer and later vice president of the ICRC, was instrumental in drafting the 1949 Geneva Conventions for the protection of victims of war and negotiating the 1977 Additional Protocols I and II. Pictet also proposed the ICRC's seven Fundamental Principles adopted in 1965: Humanity, Impartiality, Neutrality, Independence, Voluntary Service, Unity, and Universality, the first four comprising the core of humanitarianism. These humanistic projects derive from and delve into how European forbearers valued the lives of distant others and encountered their suffering and how public mourning indexed the differential values accorded to human lives.[22] They further underscore that humanitarian aid practices are political processes even as they aim to address human suffering.[23]

Of course, humanitarian organizations are far from the only sources of aid or relief for human suffering. In the aftermath of World War II, international laws to protect the right of forced migrants to seek protection emerged as a domain distinct from international humanitarian law (or the laws of war). The 1951 Convention Relating to the Status of Refugees defined a refugee as a person outside of their country of nationality or habitual residence and who is unwilling or unable to return due to a well-founded fear of persecution. The persecution must be causally linked to their race or ethnicity, religion, nationality, membership in a social group, or political opinion. This convention was adopted largely in response to displacements caused by World War II and was limited to people displaced as a result of events occurring prior to 1 January 1951 and who were fleeing Europe. The 1967 Protocol Relating to the Status of Refugees removed the geographical and temporal constraints to the refugee definition. Today, 149 countries have ratified one or both of these treaties.

Some forty years after the ratification of the 1951 Convention, human rights scholar Louis Henkin wrestled with the shortcomings of the convention and protocol, noting that while they afforded forced migrants a right to seek asylum, they offered "the right to leave, not a right to be received, to enjoy a haven or to resettle," and thus amounted to "half a right."[24]

A World of Refugees, Looking beyond the "Conventional" Definition

Yet even in this critical reflection, Henkin was still thinking about Europeans, not about the millions of people across the global South who had been displaced because of World War II and the period of postcolonial nation formation that followed. For, in the years immediately following World War II, as the Refugee Convention was being negotiated, forced displacement was a truly global phenomenon, driven as much by wars that were fought in Africa, the Middle East, and the Asia-Pacific region as in Europe. Displacement was also driven by the pressures of decolonization and postcolonial nation-state formation. In addition to those displaced across Europe, tens of millions of displaced persons emerged from conflicts in East Asia, the Middle East, and Africa. In South Asia, during the Partition of British Colonial India between 1947 and 1951, over fourteen million people were registered as legal refugees, and approximately ten million were accommodated in official state refugee camps.[25] In China, the total number of people who were forcibly displaced during the Sino-Japanese War of 1931–45 reached over sixty million. Due to Japanese efforts at imperial expansion in the Asia-Pacific during World War II and decolonization immediately after, displacements from Korea, Indochina, and the Pacific islands meant that the overall scale of forced migrants who were recognized by regional authorities in East Asia as refugees between 1937 and 1950 was over ninety-five million.[26]

In 1951, Nehemiah Robinson, the Israeli delegate to the Geneva Conference of Penitentiaries, which drafted the final version of the Convention Relating the Status of Refugees, observed, "For the purposes of the Convention, there were practically no refugees in the world other than those coming from Europe."[27] Indeed, while the representatives who drafted the Refugee Conventions aspired to produce a useful definition of "refugee" that would transcend the politics of states, the actual minutes of the drafting committee show that many representatives who participated in writing the definition thought that it did not represent the universal aspirations of the Charter of the United Nations.[28] Still, nearly as soon as the politically negotiated definition of the "refugee" as a person who "crosses international borders" due to "fear of persecution" was adopted in 1951 and entered into force in 1954, this conventional definition quickly came to dominate categorial recognition of refugees and became hegemonic on a global scale. Indeed, already by 1953, Jacques Vernant, in his global refugee survey for the UNHCR, concluded that there were "no refugees" in Asia.[29]

Colonial-era legal categories impacted who could be seen as a refugee worthy of care, even in those foundational moments when the Refugee Convention was being drafted. Moreover, even at the edges of Europe at the end of World War II, large numbers of people were written out of refugee recognition. Therefore, the alleviation of human suffering related to forced migration in practice became intricately linked with practices of national or ethnic identification and, often, forced repatriation.[30] These legacies have regrettably been written out of many accounts of humanitarianism's genealogies.[31]

In the Middle East and North Africa, for example, displacement after World War II was handled as a problem of national repatriation and, in the case of displaced and dispossessed Palestinians, marked off as a separate problem that would be administered by distinct agencies.[32] This treatment was in part a legacy of the treaty agreements that developed in the nineteenth and early twentieth centuries to handle mass forced displacement between and within the Ottoman Empire and European colonial territories. It also derived from the institutional and administrative practices applied by the League of Nations after the dissolution of the Ottoman Empire and during the interwar years. Refugee recognition as applied in this region was developed to reduce conflict and also to legitimize new territorial borders. Over time, in the spaces of short-term and long-term rehabilitation, the representatives of voluntary charitable organizations, host governments, and relief agencies fundamentally shaped the field of humanitarian experience and expectation.[33]

The examples of East and Southeast Asia further highlight how a distinction between labor and economic migration, tied to practices of compelled displacement and forcible resettlement by the alliances between global trading companies and colonial governments, was codified in legal distinctions during the global colonial era and then taken up by international relief organizations in the interwar and postwar years.[34] Indeed, comparatively speaking, international law and politics from the seventeenth and eighteenth centuries, which sought to create a legal basis by which colonial authorities could compel individuals and populations to move in order to engage in "productive labor," influenced contemporary categories of migration.[35] These cases underscore that forms of structural violence—economic, labor, or environmental—have historically been written out of analyses of forced migration, in part because national governments (such as the Chinese nationalist government) operating near or on the edges of areas of colonial influence (such as Hong Kong) also had vested interests in retaining the ability to make its citizenry mobile through dispossession.[36]

Development and Transformation of the Figure of the Refugee

During the Cold War, another category of recipient of protection emerged, that of the "humanitarian refugee," who was a subject of aid and intervention as the United Nations expanded the scope of refugee recognition to deal with what it refers to as "refugee-like" situations. The expansion of the normative legal category of the "refugee" shifted the work of refugee identification from the realm of legal adjudication to one of sociopolitical representation. The "humanitarian refugee" emerged as a subject of aid and intervention as the United Nations sought to provide assistance to displaced people who were not juridical recipients of relief in a strict reading of the refugee conventions. By the 1980s, this "new humanitarian" approach to people in such "refugee-like" situations had become firmly established.

One impetus for this new approach was a need to respond to the suffering produced by famines, environmental disruptions, and conflict-driven migration, which were not covered by the conventions. In the 1970s, groups such as Oxfam and Save the Children worked with governments to launch large-scale relief projects in Africa, seeking to address the structural causes of starvation.[37] United Nations relief projects also began to operate on a development paradigm, and the United Nations High Commissioner for Refugees became a central coordinator of seemingly paradoxical "relief-development" projects.[38]

Another motivation was political turmoil and conflict that displaced large numbers of people *within* state borders. The emergence of the internally displaced person (IDP) was one way of classifying who was eligible for this kind of humanitarian response.[39] Yet another factor was the emergence of a "rights-based humanitarianism" and the practice of offering temporary protection to people who could be shown to be victims of human rights violations, a shift that became one of the core ethical, philosophical, and practical questions of humanitarian practice in the post–Cold War era.[40] In the international mobilization of philanthropic funds by International Non-Governmental Organizations (INGO), for example, the visual and discursive representations of women and children became "embodiments of refugeeness" and reflected institutional expectations of refugees' helplessness in order to draw donations. This also produced refugees as dehistoricized and depoliticized "speechless emissaries," whose experiences were represented as separate from the geopolitical and postcolonial conflicts that had displaced them.[41] These depictions similarly drew on representations of women as inherently innocent and less political than men. This attitude is expressed in the humanitarian domain through the fact that boy children become, as they grow into men, a "problem" for humanitarian projects in a way that girl children do not.[42]

Yet, more recent studies have argued that the figure of the refugee is, itself, a subject-making category. Building on foundational philosophical works, such as those in the post–World War II period by Hannah Arendt (1951) and in the contemporary period by Giorgio Agamben (2000), newer scholarship has examined the conditions of the camps as well as urban integration, whose spatial and temporal dimensions create new conditions of possibility for refugees.[43] At the same time, some scholarship has begun to question the adequacy of the current legal framework to resolve the vast flows of forced migrants in the world.[44] Indeed, many of the distinctions that vex our ability to apply these terms today—for example to those who have had to migrate due to environmental degradation and require us to ask the question: Is there such as thing an environmental refugee?—are determinations that in turn subject people to very different treatments and contain traces of global power relations.

Scholars regularly reference these European origins of humanitarianism and the management practices that have served to standardize and professionalize the care of the afflicted.[45] Such a focus treats the spread of these ideas and practices around the world as the progression of an enlightened reason, fraught though it may be, rather than as the product of processes of erasure and appropriation—the elimination of other values, rationalities, and practices of care—from the narrative of humanitarianism.

Rather, the representatives of host governments and local relief agencies produce the very field of humanitarian experiences, and it is in these spaces that multiple historical, cultural, and religious traditions of caring for distant others shape humanitarianism in practice. Through engagement with the practices that govern the care of forced migrants in the global South, we look beyond the Euro-American canon to investigate how refugees and forced migrants, as privileged subjects, make visible diverse genealogies, theories, and practices of humanitarianism. As such, this volume explores how these forms of knowledge and practices of care enter into this humanitarian canon.

Logics and Philosophical Grounds of Other Humanitarianisms

In order to better understand humanitarianism "in-relation," we need to consider the multiple sources of knowledge that underwrite logics of care. Some of these we have acknowledged already—including legal categorial thinking and Enlightenment moral reasoning. Here, we need to engage with the concept of moral reasoning outside of Enlightenment frames.

The traditions and philosophies that provide sources for such moral reasoning include orthodox religious systems, and a significant body of inquiry establishes these connections through examination of faith-based aid networks.[46] Other values, such as service, hospitality, gift giving, or mercy, preceded and influenced such moral reasoning. They underlie and legitimate practices of care that operate as part of the daily experiences and ethical ideals of both caregivers and care-receivers. It is thus worthwhile to consider these practices as part of a repertoire of humanitarian care rather than assuming they stand apart from "real" humanitarianism, which is known, regulated, and evaluated by standards set through Euro-American norms.

During the Sino-Japanese War across China, relief for armed-conflict wounded and displaced persons was organized primarily by grassroots civilian groups and religious orders. These groups became more formal voluntary societies after the end of the war and provided the first models of organized and standardized collective action for refugee relief fundraising and material provisioning as they tapped into international social networks.[47] These resources were important as local governments took up some of their practices—for refugee identification, aid distribution, and resettlement policies after international governmental organizations (such as the UNHCR) refused to recognize the war-displaced of Asia as "refugees."[48] In the Middle East and South Asia as well, the functioning of emergent relief regimes depended on making distinctions about who would receive what kind of aid, a process in which nongovernmental voluntary organizations, missionary societies, and national militaries participated, alongside of United Nations relief agencies.[49] This dynamic is particularly significant in contexts where state agencies and international organizations take over refugee-hosting practices initiated by local communities, a process that continues into contemporary times. This does not always occur willingly, such as in the case of Acehnese fishermen, who invoked the right of offering hospitably in their homes and brought displaced Rohingya, stranded on the Andaman Sea, onshore in direct resistance to government authorities. Their actions forced the hand of the Indonesian government, whose attempted solution to the problem of boat refugees had been to prevent them from landing.[50]

Faith-based groups working around the world drew on models of charity that were imbued with religious values of "responsibility for others."[51] The origin of many humanitarian practices across traditions can be traced to such values. In India, Hindu communities created a new form of domestic humanitarian work by connecting gift giving with voluntary service work.[52] Many early humanitarian INGOs were founded by organized Christian groups, which brought specific sectarian values and conventions of network organizing into early humanitarian practices, especially in the nineteenth and early twentieth centuries. Examples include the role of Calvinists in establishing the Red Cross Federation and the Society of Friends (Quakers), the latter of which was prominent in the founding of both Oxfam and Amnesty International.[53]

Throughout this volume, we engage understandings of humanitarian and care practices from the ground up. We thus pay close attention to the practices of care that emerge in Muslim-majority countries. The literature on humanitarianism, however, has marked Islam as an exception to care, and as having distinct logics, such as a *compulsion* to charity that, for some, challenges the possibility of an authentic concern for the suffering of others.[54] This creates a conceptual paradox because there is an important connection between Islamic charitable organizations, as institutions of funding, dispersal, and aid management, and conceptions and values of service, hospitality, and the human right to be cared for by others in many contemporary predominantly Muslim societies.[55] This characterization, however, misses a key component in an intellectual exploration of Islam: that it is not charity but rather an ethical sensibility to build a more just and compassionate society that defines Islam's theory of care, one that emphasizes equity not equality.[56] So, engaging with the concept of Islamic humanitarianism is an interesting way to take up the challenge to think "in-relation" about humanitarianisms. This is not only because Türkiye, Jordan, Lebanon, Iran, Pakistan, and Bangladesh, hosts that have taken in a large portion of the world's refugees, are predominantly Muslim-majority countries, but also because several of these countries are not parties to either the 1951 Convention Relating to the Status of Refugees or the 1967 Protocol, and thus have no legal duty to take in refugees. As five of the six top host countries for forced migrants are Muslim majority, we examine how people articulate Islamic values as both a force of faith and as a source of intellectual knowledge that underwrites logics of care.

We do not aim to search or exhaust the corpus of non-Western traditions to find common ground and are not attempting to forge humanitarian dialogue.[57] Instead, we are engaging understandings of humanitarian and care practices from the ground up to illustrate the myriad forms they take and how they operate in-relation to other processes and forms of care. Ultimately, these comparisons allow us to illuminate how values and reasoning, beyond those of the Western Enlightenment, constitute the objects of suffering, practices of care, and who or what qualifies as the object of that care.

Care in a Time of Humanitarianism

Possibly one of the boldest assertions in this volume comes from our claim that we are examining care in a specific temporal moment, in a *time of humanitarianism*. In the next few paragraphs, we elaborate on what we mean by this, noting that we advance this claim as an offering for how to understand our current zeitgeist. The protections ostensibly offered to humans in the post–World War II regime of human rights and humanitarian care, simply by virtue of their humanity, have been found to be unfulfilled. It remains that states confer protection through citizenship or some other legal category of personhood. In lieu of full recognition, we are witnessing a wider range and new forms of care, aid, and relief to serve the basest of human needs.

We see these forms of care increasingly spread beyond the "marginal" figure of the refugee to categories of people living in precarious conditions. As we have noted, these forms of care have their roots in emergency—and are thus *intended* to be temporary. These frameworks of humanitarianism, however, have come to settle into our lifeworlds as more than temporary and have themselves become the forms-of-life through which millions of forced migrants, and many others who have had their rights and liberties diminished, seek to survive. Thus, we argue, we are living in a period in which humanitarian and other forms of care are life defining and demarcating for us all (not just forced migrants). That this is an era of humanitarianism, moreover, becomes clear once we account for both the scale and duration of this formerly-seen-as-temporary problem and reckon with the fact that care, in the form of charity, aid, and relief, no longer exists only for those living in or fleeing from active war zones but for millions of others as well.

As of this writing, more than one hundred million forced migrants are wandering the globe seeking shelter, asylum, solace, and succor from innumerable catastrophes, whether their underlying causes are human conflict or climate disaster. The secretary general of the Norwegian Refugee Council, Jan Egeland, reflected, "Indeed, we have broken that ceiling that I didn't believe we would break, I hoped we would never break in my lifetime, which is well over 100 million people now displaced by violence and conflict in the world. You go back ten years and it was 45 million; now it is 110 million."[58] While this volume attends to the kinds of care work wrought by these emergencies and disasters, we take seriously the meaning-making effects of these enduring and protracted regimes of humanitarianism and understand care work in the context of this temporal dimension.

Taking "care in a time of humanitarianism" seriously begins with the recognition that the drafters of the 1951 Refugee Convention construed the need for refugee protection as a temporary problem. The UNHCR has provided three durable solutions to the temporary problem of forced migrants: repatriation, local integration, and resettlement in a third country. Yet only about 3 percent of forced migrants have recourse to these (according to UNHCR statistics, in the past few years, anywhere between 1 and 3 percent are resettled, while only about 2 percent return voluntarily). And while these stated solutions are desired, they have no binding legal basis in international refugee law. As a result, the vast majority of forced migrants remain in the liminal spaces of temporary camps. This "zone of indifference" to which they are relegated makes up the constitutive outside of today's nation-state.[59] But our point is not simply about the numbers of people that remain in temporary and isolated camps. To add to this consideration, we also need to take note of the fact that these forced migrants, 85 percent of which remain in the global South, are also in what the UNHCR defines as *protracted conditions*. The UNHCR defines protracted conditions as twenty-five thousand or more people in a camp for five or more years in refugee situations. Today's average for protracted situations is a whopping twenty-six years! And 78 percent of the world's refugees are currently living in such conditions. These statistics do not necessarily account for the world's internally displaced or those who are in what we referred to earlier (as defined by the UN) as refugee-like conditions. These are people whose circumstances do not fit the very narrow definition of a refugee according to the international laws.

In 1943, Hannah Arendt wrote that refugees "represent the vanguard of their peoples."[60] What made them the vanguard? The fact that the refugee is only a figure with rights when it has the recognition and thus protection of a nation-state, but refugees remain subject figures and have the potential to comprise a political community outside the boundaries of a nation-state. However, without recognition as subjects with rights in the nation-state polity, refugees remain dependent on charity.[61] At a time at which the nation-state was in decline, as Arendt saw it, refugees could form a new kind of assemblage of peoples, rethink political categories, and, in doing so, reshape relationships between states and societies.

Italian philosopher Giorgio Agamben later found resonance with Arendt's argument and sought to extend it to the contemporary era.[62] Agamben noted that the refugee, although "formerly regarded as a marginal figure," had now become an enduring and disquieting one: enduring because of the quality of this exclusion through which "growing sections of humankind are no longer representable inside the nation-state," a fact that contests the nation-state's very foundation.[63] The plight of so many forced migrants is ultimately a disquieting concern because it disrupts the ordering capacity of the nation-state. The presence of refugees challenges the nation-state's ability to define itself through the creation, categorization, and distinction between citizens and non-citizens and to give meaning to life, itself, by defining categories that include some in the polity and others outside of it. Thus, this state of ever-increasing precarity, characterized by myriad struggles for mere biological survival in which forced migrants find themselves, is no longer simply an exceptional situation. Rather, now, the exceptional figure of the refugee, in its enduring and increasingly widespread forms, has become a normative and defining personage of our present.

In order to think this through, we look beyond the definition of a refugee or laws of war or the immediate post–World War II era and shift our thinking to the *humanitarian conditions* through which countless groups, not just refugees, are living. Ever-increasing numbers of people are living in precarious situations, characterized by diminishing, little, or no state protection. Without a state's acknowledgment of their personhood, the rights of such people, which are vested in legal recognition, have been subverted and overtaken by forms of charity, aid, care, refuge, and repair—in a word, humanitarianism.

Humanitarian Conditions and Humanitarian Governance

Scholars have been tracing this shift away from refugees as subjects of political exclusion to refugees as recipients of care. For instance, Feldman's work on Palestinians examines refugees in principle, but the generational study reveals the persistence and transference of forms of care from village to village, camp to village, people to people, and generation to generation.[64] Similarly, Fiddian-Qasmiyeh has emphasized that this dual identity of displaced people living as both refugees, recipients of aid and care, and also as hosts, serving as expert care workers and providers of aid, is a defining feature of protracted refugeedom in the global South.[65] Scholars increasingly examine care as politics and what the politics of care look like in a world in which the struggle for mere survival has overtaken the (now) bold claims to civil and political rights, that is, political recognition.[66]

Thus, care or care work, which is our focus here, has become an enduring and expansive legacy of humanitarian governance.[67] Yet, as we show in this volume, these forms of care are not or are no longer limited to the figure of the refugee, or forced migrants, or other displaced people relegated to live their lives in nominally temporary camps. The practices of aid NGOs in the African Sahel during the Cold War also show that international humanitarian organizations spread new forms of governmental practice that undermined newly developing independent postcolonial states.[68] As aspects of their humanitarian labor, Catholic activists in the trans-Mediterranean deploy theories of charity and hospitality to critique, undermine, and work around state practices of asylum processing and administrative detention.[69] Gendered migration between Southeast Asia and the Middle East raises questions as to whether humanity has become a category of juridical protection from which the domestic field of careworkers are excluded.[70]

At the same time, the politics of a global economy have engendered *humanitarian conditions*, even where humanitarian crises as we know them have not manifested. We can see this in the context of the neoliberal restructuring in societies—through which millions of people have been made to live under precarious conditions—such as Chile, Greece, or even the south side of Chicago.[71] We can also see humanitarian conditions emerge as a result of protracted regimes of international sanctions in, say, Cuba, Haiti, Iran, and Iraq.[72]

Increasingly, questions about care and caring for others relate to entities beyond the living or even human. We might, moreover, need to understand the demands by the already dead for rights recognition and intervention, as described by Claire Moon in her analysis of "forensic humanitarianism" in Latin America.[73] And, of course, in this era of climate change, care for animals has become an important nodal point in questions about climate governance.[74] Thus, while the refugee represents, perhaps, the most vulnerable of the categories of personhood that have become dependent on forms of care, ever-increasing numbers of people are becoming refugees or find themselves in refugee-like situations. We observe these latter refugee-like conditions as an extension of care, akin to humanitarian care to populations that ostensibly fall *within* the sanctified, if not protected, realm of the nation-state.

Drawing from these points, we add that the extensiveness, attractiveness, and ubiquity of forms of care for forced migrants have multiplied and spread so much that they have become normalized. They are overwhelmingly the taken-for-granted forms of claims that people now make. The state of exception has been extended to include the members of the polity. Here we agree with Agamben, who notes that "so-called sacred and inalienable human rights are revealed to be without any protection precisely when it is no longer possible to conceive of them as rights of the citizens of a state."[75] That is, this resort to aid, charity, and relief takes place even within a nation-state system; this political era is a time of humanitarianism.

Organization of the Volume: Stories of Refuge, Aid, and Repair

We begin this section with a note on the tone and voice of this volume as we seek to reorient audiences to the conceptual basis for and importance of story-based chapters. The chapters in this volume are empirically grounded and theoretically informed but are communicated through stories and the first-person voices of the researchers. The story-forward emphasis of these chapters is intentionally distinct from other writings on humanitarianism. By "story forward," we mean that each story holds at its core an illustrative person, place, or thing that carries the story to its conclusion. Each story leads readers into the complex worlds of humanitarianisms, but without the jargon that requires scholarly specialization. We invite instructors who are interested in incorporating some of these chapters into their courses to make use of the appendix to this volume, in which we offer thematic pairings among the volume's contributions for teaching on topics related to these critical issues of our time.

The motivation underlying our storytelling methodology is to animate and highlight the lived experiences and lifeworlds of forced migrants and of recipients of humanitarian care rather than contend with primarily scholarly issues in historiography, law, or even the formation of institutional categories. Here, our story-forward approach permits a reorienting and even questioning, if subtly, of the underlying taken-for-grantedness of categories. Our scholars' positionality and choice of person, place, or thing to explore humanitarian lifeworlds exposes the hidden assumptions underlying seemingly fixed categories. At the same time, the authors' embeddedness within the narratives and their commitment to sharing how they come to their interpretive interventions allows them to show the myriad ways their interlocutors may be positioned in-relation to history, law, or the formation of categories as objects of care.

The chapters in this volume emphasize the care work being done in the global South, including its motivations, methods, and manners. They focus geographically on South and Southeast Asia, the Middle East and North Africa, and socialist Eastern Europe, areas of the world that have been historically and epistemologically underrepresented in studies of humanitarian care. These regions have been conceptually marked off from the understanding of the development of humanitarianism but have been and continue to be the hosts of the bulk of the world's refugees and forcibly displaced people since World War II. At the same time, we are not attempting to represent every understudied area.[76]

The authors of these stories are scholars sharing encounters and interpretations of being in-relation with interlocutors and objects and ideas. It is through these interactions that they interpret the contingent historiography, the taxonomies of legal apparatuses, and the conceptual frameworks that people draw on in orienting themselves to their lived experiences of humanitarian care. Our researchers do not claim the authority to write as refugees or as humanitarian workers, but instead work to center global South perspectives *in-relation* as the starting point to understanding the importance of the stories they tell in a period of expanded and protracted humanitarian contingency.[77]

We present the chapters in *Care in a Time of Humanitarianism* in three parts. In part 1, "Refuge, Law, and Empire in the Global South," the chapters examine the foundations, contingencies, and elisions of international humanitarian law. In part 2, "Aid, Intimacy, and Humanitarian Praxis," the authors explore how humanitarianism operates in distinct and different contexts. In part 3, "Repair in a World of Care," we provide chapters that seek to understand how care work may contribute to healing after conflict in what we claim is a new era that privileges charity and aid over rights.

Part I: Refuge, Law, and Empire in the Global South

In the first part of the volume, our story-based chapters explore and question the international legal apparatus that shapes humanitarianism and produces categories of forced migrants, including refugees, displaced people, stateless persons, and asylum seekers. Our contributors challenge the status of the laws and legal framework as the sole source of humanitarian legitimacy. By examining other legal, bureaucratic, and institutional structures created for managing forced migration and mitigating suffering, their stories reveal the contingent nature of this legal framework. These other structures draw their force from legal forms that did not internationalize but still carry weight in local or regional contexts. These stories also show the limits of the law as a means to protect individuals, provide them with relief, and offer a sense of belonging. The chapters in this section include investigations into how the new postwar legal order codified certain inequalities while consolidating and maintaining power, especially after World War II.

This section also considers the contingency of the refugee definition; it examines its taxonomies and who and what were written out of recognition as well as who was recognized in the moment the Refugee Convention emerged as the legal codification of protected classes of migrants. It also emphasizes the colonial legacies of these taxonomies and their underlying legal structures. Denaturalizing these nomenclatures is a part of understanding humanitarianisms in the global South, as is recognizing how they shaped the greater global humanitarian order.

The chapters speak to and offer unique global Southern considerations, impacts, and reactions to the new postcolonial legal order. Thus, each chapter here explores the unspoken or hidden aspects of the world order created by the decolonial movements in the immediate postwar period. This is why the focus on the global South as a site of humanitarian production, not just its object, is such a crucial intervention.

Pamela Ballinger's story explores debates over how to classify newly arrived European migrants (Italian nationals) to Italy who were forced to leave Libya at the end of colonial rule and in the immediate postwar era when the 1951 Refugee Convention was being finalized. Her chapter illustrates that evaluations of language, race, and cultural identity underlie distinctions between "refugees" and "repatriating migrants" and justify new legal structures for citizenship recognition that in turn begin to map out a (postcolonial) global South domain.

James Pangilinan's story examines *Quezon's Game* (2019) for its filmic representation of the Philippine leader Manuel Quezon's humanitarian gesture of offering "Filipino hospitality" to Jewish refugees during the interwar years. Pangilinan considers the film's representation of how the Filipino government shored up resources to deliver relief to displaced European Jews at a time when the domestic context allowed the president to showcase a nationally distinctive conception of care as a method of state building.

Emma Meyer's chapter tells the story of how one of the founders of the Burma Evacuees Association influenced the development of refugee relief practices of modern India. The chapter links the classification of the "evacuee," a legal category for forcibly displaced people in South Asia during World War II and thus before independence, both to the colonial legal structure and the organizational moment of the international refugee system.

Khathaleeya Liamdee's chapter focuses on the story of Khao-I-Dang (KID) Transit Center, a representative of camps along the Thai-Cambodian border that shelter those who escaped armed conflict and political turmoil during the

Cold War era. The story of border refugee camps highlights the continuation of postcolonial regional conflicts in Cambodia's ongoing transition to peace.

Kathie Friedman-Kasaba's chapter examines the story of a Bosnian refugee who encountered a legal "architecture of repulsion" alongside idiosyncratic access to humanitarian protection. Her chapter examines the importance of personal interactions and experiences, which one refugee calls moments of "luck," in making it possible for forced migrants to access the bureaucratic processes that lead to relief in a global postcolonial world of intrastate conflict.

Finally, Arzoo Osanloo's chapter examines how a play, produced in Iran—both a major host country and a site from which refugees flee—reflects the circulation of knowledge about international humanitarian norms. Her story about cultural production explores the enduring relationship between premodern modalities of benevolence and contemporary humanitarianisms and suggests that appeals to care have overtaken rights-based demands in a world in which humanitarianism has become a normative mechanism of governance.

Part II: Aid, Intimacy, and Humanitarian Praxis in Comparative Context

In the second part of the book, our contributors highlight the different logics at work in humanitarianism. Understanding the forms of humanitarianism in the global South requires a willingness to engage with humanitarianism not as an ideology but rather as a praxis with multiple agents. These chapters also emphasize that practices which are different from the mainstream ideology are not to be treated or viewed as failures to live up to an idea but as the actual core of what humanitarianism is. These chapters examine how humanitarian practices become sites of agency for so many actors involved in this work. They also reveal the deeply intimate qualities of care work. Thus, as our authors show, care work and humanitarian engagement emerge from multiple sources.

Examining humanitarian praxis in the global South shifts the perspective away from states as managers of temporary relief operations, including material aid, repatriation, and asylum—and thus whether forced migrants are deserving of relief. The attention then turns to the actual long-term, often multigenerational, reality of living and working as a refugee. Our contributors, thus, examine the new practices of humanitarian management, refugees themselves as experts in delivering humanitarian assistance, and caring labor as a particular domain of work that has governance aspects to it.

Ilana Feldman's story about a refugee aid worker shows how, in the spaces of short- and long-term rehabilitation, the representatives of voluntary charitable organizations, host governments, and relief agencies shaped the field of humanitarian experiences and expectation. Here, Palestinian aid work serves as a testimony to the "double position" of being simultaneously aid worker and refugee—a common phenomenon in protracted refugee situations.

Cristian Capotescu's chapter tells the story of a young Viennese woman moved by a catastrophic flood in Romania in 1970 to mount a relief effort to aid victims of the disaster. Through this story, Capotescu shines a light on humanitarian work across the Iron Curtain, especially among socialist Romanian aid workers, and considers the role of private aid networks in socialist societies. The story illustrates how relations of informality in private aid giving combined both cultural and material forms of care across boundaries that were impenetrable to institutionalized humanitarian organizations.

Gözde Burcu Ege's chapter examines generational support mechanisms through the story of a refugee aid worker in a Jordanian refugee camp. Ege considers the intricacies and complexities of doing aid work in one's own community as refugees aspire to shape a long-term care regime for an intergenerational community while humanitarian organizations paradoxically persist in pursuing crisis-oriented care even while those organizations take on governance roles within the camps and incorporate refugees into their labor force.

Tanzeen Doha's story is an ethnographic meditation on the dynamic interactions between Islamists of the South Asian Deobandi tradition and Rohingya refugees from Myanmar in Cox's Bazar, Bangladesh. Doha recounts how these encounters, which re-historicize classical Islamic stories into the present, also displace the taken-for-granted categories of humanitarian "volunteers" and "refugees" within the logics of secular humanitarianism.

Lastly, Cabeiri Robinson's chapter explores the shift from militancy to humanitarian care work in the face of disaster. She tells the story of an Islamic militant fighting in the Kashmir Jihad who demobilized after a disaster and became a relief worker and organizer of humanitarian assistance. His acceptance as a "humanitarian" by the local community began when he performed care work, including recovering dead bodies and offering specialized medical care to the least privileged segments of society.

Part III: Repair in a World of Care

In the third part of the book, our contributors explore the effects of care in light of the prevalence and persistence of humanitarianism as a global norm and ethos of our contemporary moment. The stories in this section demonstrate that care is multivalent; it is material, psychological, environmental, and social. At the same time, care work is not limited to attending to innocent "victims" but rather extends to active agents, maybe even those who are morally compromised. Indeed, humanitarian care is not solely human focused, and hosts in the global South do not necessarily limit their ideas of relief, material aid, protection, or reparation to the human subjects of liberal humanitarianism.

Our contributors highlight the deeply intimate relations care work produces. They also examine emotional repair, especially in protracted humanitarian conditions in which generations of forced migrants find common cause—and each other—through layered memories attached to what might otherwise be seen as trivial objects. Our contributors' attention to the many facets of care also highlights the politics of that care. They do so by exploring the restorative work that goes into developing memorials or archives of tragedy, crafting cultural productions intended for social critique or reflection or developing databases for what counts as cultural heritage worthy of preservation.

Rawan Arar's story considers how a denim shirt she wore during interviews with refugees signals a sensorial realm in refugee life sparking a sense of enduring attachment and fraught nostalgia. Arar's denim shirt, first worn by her own mother a generation earlier, emphasized her relational link to Palestinian displacement after 1948 and demonstrates that objects are imbricated with memories that produce intergenerational affective relationships.

Jenna Grant tells the story of a photograph and its enduring memory. She demonstrates that care may focus on reparative strategies proposed by art and artists who engage with an archive of photographs of daily life under an authoritarian regime during a time of genocide. Her chapter offers a different vision of what it means to engage in care work after humanitarian crisis by attending to the persistent psychic effects of violence that are left unmet by emergency relief.

Megan Butler's chapter examining a memoir by Kurdish-Iranian intellectual Behrouz Boochani conveys how an asylum seeker experienced the sea voyage and arrival at Manus Island Prison as a forced migrant seeking to access the liberal promises of protection from persecution. Butler's story underscores how writing serves not only as an archive of inhumane policies but also as a space of the refugee's sovereignty and agency.

Amira Mittermaier's story details the efforts of a devotee who provides food to the homeless, displaced, and other visitors of a Sufi shrine in Cairo. She describes the breadth of *khidma* or service in a space of giving that is situated outside of the logic, infrastructure, and rhetoric of humanitarianism. In doing so, Mittermaier explores the margins of humanitarianism and reflects on the possibilities of care that exist in a time of humanitarianism, but which are not centered exclusively on humans as their sole object of attention.

Mediha Sorma focuses on Kurdish mothers' embrace of their dead children in order to examine unconventional forms of care work that emerge from resistance to the Turkish state. Her story illustrates that intimate care work extends to the nonliving but ultimately serves as a form of political expression, even resistance to state violence. Here, mothers', not humanitarian experts', work of "rescuing the dead" extends the boundaries of the object of caring beyond the living.

Finally, Stephanie Selover's story considers the protection of cultural heritage during the Syrian Civil War and the role of international aid and intervention. Starting with the destruction of archaeological sites in Syria from 2011 to the present, Selover evaluates international initiatives to protect cultural heritage in the Middle East. Through the Syrian case, Selover considers the effects of these initiatives to determine which objects are deemed worthy of protection and the consequences of such determinations. Ultimately, Selover boldly situates the history of intervention in the destruction/protection binary of cultural heritage care work.

Conclusion: Humanitarianisms in-Relation

The stories in this volume demonstrate that care is always multivalent with psychological, environmental, and relational-social as well as material aspects, and that aid is also best understood as a form of caring labor. Our contributors' attention to the praxis of humanitarianism and caring, rather than its ideology, makes room for recognizing cultural, religious, or ethical values other than those of the Enlightenment tradition—values that actually guide and organize principles of refuge, aid, and repair in multiple contexts in the global South. They also show that there are rich national and regional legal regimes that developed to manage forced migration or to alleviate the impact of armed conflict. These alternative definitions left political traces, and, we contend, these definitional practices impact how global humanitarianism is understood and operationalized on a global level.

Each story, ultimately, disrupts the conventional narratives about suffering told by the humanitarian aid industry. Our overall aim is to add depth and nuance to the meaning of the figure of the refugee, to reconsider the kinds of suffering that seem worthy of care, and to reevaluate what caring for others looks like once we open our investigations beyond—albeit not independent of—the global North: thus, to think always of humanitarianism as a project "in-relation."

Arzoo Osanloo is professor in the Department of Law, Societies, and Justice at the University of Washington. She is a legal anthropologist and has previously worked as an immigration and refugee attorney. She is the author of the award-winning *Forgiveness Work: Mercy, Law, and Victims' Rights in Iran* (Princeton University Press, 2020), and *The Politics of Women's Rights in Iran* (Princeton University Press, 2009).

Cabeiri deBergh Robinson is associate professor of international studies and anthropology at the University of Washington. She is the author of *Body of*

Victim, Body of Warrior: Refugee Families and the Making of Kashmiri Jihadists (University of California Press, 2013), which won the Bernard Cohn Book Prize in 2015. She is coeditor of *Forced Migration In/ Of Asia: Connections and Convergences*, a special issue of the *Journal of Refugee Studies* (2018), and of *The Palgrave Handbook of New Directions in Kashmir Studies* (Palgrave, 2023).

Notes

1. UNHCR, *Global Trends*, 2017.
2. UNHCR, *Global Trends*, 2022, citing 76 percent of refugees and others in need of protection are hosted in low- and middle-income countries, while 70 percent remain in neighboring countries.
3. UNHCR, *Global Trends*, 2017, 2018, 2021, 2022.
4. UNHCR, *Global Trends*, 2017.
5. Oxfam 2016.
6. UNHCR, *Global Trends*, 2021.
7. Clarke, "Global South"; Kloß, "Global South as Subversive Practice." This usage became especially prevalent after the 2003 "Forging a Global South'" initiative of the United Nations Development Program.
8. Clarke, "Global South."
9. Mahler, *From the Tricontinental*. 32. Mahler and other scholars working within an orientation to the global South that starts with a critique of deterritorialized political economy and the concept of "internal colonization" draw inspiration from Antonio Gramsci's notes on "Some Aspects of the Southern Question" (1926).
10. Clarke, "Global South."
11. Wa Ngugi, "Rethinking the Global South," 1–2.
12. Wa Ngugi, "Rethinking the Global South," 8–9.
13. Wa Ngugi, "Rethinking the Global South," 8–9.
14. There are several ways that multiple scholars have sought to engage with this empirical condition that they have observed in their research. Some have talked about "hybrid humanitarianism" to acknowledge the merging of legal or administrative apparatus. Some used the phrase "alternative humanitarianisms" to highlight systems of ideas and practices that drew on sources other than the Western cannon but had long regional traditions. Others used the term "vernacular humanitarianism" sometimes in this way, but sometimes more specifically to refer to locally organized efforts that drew on global humanitarian practices but were run by private voluntary groups. And still others noted that the tension between "Islam" and "Western modernity," which has historical colonial origins, led to forms of humanitarian practices that, while locally distinct, shared some features that warranted their own terms, either "Islamic humanitarianism" or "Muslim humanitarianism." We believe this experimentation with terms at that time emerged from multiple engaged scholars and practitioners responding to the need to decenter the idea that global North humanitarianism could adequately explain the lived experience of care—or knowledges, expertises, practices, and legacies—in the global South. See, for example, Brković, "Vernacular #Humaniarianisms"; Mostowlansky, "Muslim Humanitarianism."
15. For an extensive discussion of this point, see Mazower, "Strange Triumph."

16. Malkki, "Refugees and Exile"; Zolberg, "Formation of New States."
17. Feldman, *Life Lived in Relief*.
18. Albahari, *Crimes of Peace*.
19. Fassin, *Humanitarian Reason*. Some defend these Western origins. See, for example, Slim, *Humanitarian Ethics*.
20. Dunant, *Memory of Solferino*.
21. Whyte, "'Dangerous Concept of the Just War.'"
22. Butler, *Precarious Life*. The trope of the distant other as the object of humanitarian action should not be understood solely in terms of proximity. See, Fechter, "Helping Distant Strangers"; Chatterjee, "Introduction," 2.
23. Whyte, "'Opposite of Humanity.'"
24. Henkin, "Refugees and Their Human Rights," 1079.
25. Robinson, "Too Much Nationality," 345.
26. Gatrell, *War and Population Displacement*; Muscolio, *Refugees, Land Reclamation*; Lary, *Chinese People at War*.
27. Bem, "Blank Cheque," 662.
28. For a discussion of objections made on behalf of Kashmiri, Indian, Arab, Greek, and Chinese displaced peoples' exclusion from the "refugee" definition in 1950, see Robinson, "Too Much Nationality," 345–46.
29. Vernant, *Refugee in the Post-War World*.
30. Ballinger, *World Refugees Made*; Mayblin and Turner, *Migration Studies and Colonialism*.
31. Mayblin, *Asylum after Empire*, 32.
32. Tejel and Öztan, *Forced Migration and Refugeedom*.
33. Feldman, *Life Lived in Relief*; Ballinger, *World Refugees Made*.
34. See Ho and Robinson, "Forced Migration in/of Asia."
35. Peterson, "Sovereignty International Law."
36. Muscolio, *Refugees, Land Reclamation*.
37. De Waal, *Famine Crimes*.
38. Loescher, *UNHCR and World Politics*.
39. Barnett, "Humanitarianism with a Sovereign Face."
40. Barnett, "Humanitarianism with a Sovereign Face"; Chandler, "Road to Military Humanism."
41. Malkki, "Speechless Emissaries," 388–89.
42. Robinson, *Body of Victim*, 140–43.
43. Turner, "What Is a Refugee Camp," 144; Mayblin, Wake, and Kazemi, "Necropolitics," 110.
44. Behrman, "Legal Subjectivity," 2; Benhabib, "End of the 1951 Refugee Convention," 79.
45. Barnett, *Empire of Humanity*; Fassin, *Humanitarian Reason*; Feldman and Ticktin, *In the Name of Humanity*.
46. For a full discussion, see Fiddian-Qasmiyeh and Horstmann, "Introduction"; Barnett and Stein, *Sacred Aid*.
47. Lincoln, "Fleeing from Firestorms"; Henriot, "Beyond Glory"; Dillon, "Politics of Philanthropy," 190–91; Nedostup, *Superstitious Regimes*, 61–64.
48. Madokoro, "Surveying Hong Kong"; Lopes, "Impact of Refugees."
49. Feldman, "Difficult Distinctions"; Robinson, "Humanitarian Internationalism"; Zamindar, *Long Partition*.
50. McNevin and Missje, "Hospitality as a Horizon of Aspiration."
51. Benthall and Bellion-Jourdan, *Charitable Crescent*.

52. Bornstein, *Disquieting Gifts*.
53. See Dromi, *Above the Fray*, and Feldman, "Quaker Way."
54. Calhoun, "Imperative to Reduce Suffering."
55. Benthall, *Islamic Charities*.
56. Osanloo, "Measure of Mercy"; Osanloo, *Forgiveness Work*.
57. Our goal here is not to trace the genealogy of the term *humanitarianism* through multiple linguistic traditions to create parallels or draw distinctions, although there are some excellent resources for this approach (see, for example, Moussa, "Ancient Origins, Modern Actors"). Instead, we acknowledge that the concept and terminology of humanitarianism is wrapped into global discursive traditions in ways that are constantly evolving and changing. Understanding the power of these discursive forms requires understanding their multiple meanings in global and local settings and in circulation as they evolve. See Davies, "Continuity, Change and Contest," for scholarly discussion, and de Lauri, *Humanitarianism: Keywords*, for a compendium of contemporary terms that emerge from this approach.
58. Egeland, "End the Occupation."
59. Agamben, *Means without End*, xi.
60. Arendt, "We Refugees," 77.
61. Arendt, "Decline of the Nation-State," 296.
62. Agamben, *Means without End*, x.
63. Agamben, *Means without End*, 21.
64. Feldman, *Life Lived in Relief*.
65. Fiddian-Qasmiyeh, "Shifting the Gaze."
66. See de Lauri, *Politics of Humanitarianism*; Fassin and Pandolfi, *Contemporary States of Emergency*; Feldman and Ticktin, *In the Name of Humanity*.
67. Practitioners and scholars began using this term in the early 2000s to trace changes in the humanitarian field that were evident after the mid-1990s. For an overview of the origins of the term, see Aalen, "Governance." For a full discussion of its incorporation into current scholarly analysis of contemporary humanitarianism, see Barnett, "Humanitarian Governance."
68. Mann, *From Empires to NGOs*.
69. Albahari, *Crimes of Peace*.
70. Tadiar, *Remaindered Life*.
71. Han, *Life in Debt*; Varoufakis, *And the Weak Suffer*; Walley, *Exit Zero*.
72. Alejandro, "Economic Impact of US Sanctions"; Garfield and Santana, "Impact of the Economic Crisis"; Osanloo, "Entangled Lives"; Gordon, *Invisible War*.
73. Moon, "Human Rights, Human Remains."
74. Parreñas, *Decolonizing Extinction*; Govindrajan, *Animal Intimacies*.
75. Agamben, *Means without End*, 19.
76. Readers seeking a focus on Latin America or Africa will find that recent studies do heavily emphasize these regions of the world.
77. See Kloß, "Global South as a Subversive Practice," 12, 14.

References

Aalen, Lovise. "Governance." In *Humanitarianism: Keywords*, edited by Antonio de Lauri, 84–86. Leiden: Brill. 2020.

Albahari, Maurizio. *Crimes of Peace: Mediterranean Migrations at the World's Deadliest Border*. Pennsylvania Studies in Human Rights. Philadelphia: University of Pennsylvania Press, 2015.

Agamben, Giorgio. *Means without End: Notes on Politics*. Translated by Vincenzo Binetti and Cesare Casarino. Minneapolis: University of Minnesota Press, 2000.

Alejandro, Pavel Vidal. "El impacto económico de las sanciones estadounidense a Cuba, 1994–2020" [The Impact of Economic Sanctions on Cuba, 1994–2020]. Working Paper, *Real Instituto Elcano*, January–July 2022.

Arendt, Hannah. "The Decline of the Nation-State and the End of the Rights of Man." In *The Origins of Totalitarianism*, 267–302. New York: Schocken Books, 1951.

———. "We Refugees." *The Menorah Journal* 31, no. 1 (January 1943): 69–77.

Ballinger, Pamela. *The World Refugees Made: Decolonization and the Foundation of Postwar Italy*. Ithaca, NY: Cornell University Press, 2020.

Barnett, Michael. "Humanitarianism with a Sovereign Face: UNHCR in the Global Undertow." *International Migration Review* 35, no. 1 (2001): 244–77.

———. *Empire of Humanity: A History of Humanitarianism*. Ithaca, NY: Cornell University Press, 2011.

———. "Humanitarian Governance." *Annual Review of Political Science* 16, no. 1 (2013): 379–98.

Barnett, Michael, and Janice Stein. *Sacred Aid: Faith and Humanitarianism*. New York: Oxford University Press, 2012.

Behrman, Simon. "Legal Subjectivity and the Refugee." *International Journal of Refugee Law* 26, no. 1 (2014): 1–21.

Bem, K. "The Coming of a 'Blank Cheque'—Europe, the 1951 Convention, and the 1967 Protocol." *International Journal of Refugee Law* 16, no. 4 (1 December 2004): 609–27.

Benhabib, Seyla. "The End of the 1951 Refugee Convention? Dilemmas of Sovereignty, Territoriality, and Human Rights." *Jus Cogens* 2 (2020): 75–100.

Benthall, Jonathan. *Islamic Charities and Islamic Humanism in Troubled Times: Islamic Charities and Islamic Humanism in Troubled Times*. Manchester: Manchester University Press, 2016.

Benthall, Jonathan, and Jerome Bellion-Jourdan. *The Charitable Crescent: Politics of Aid in the Muslim World*. 2nd ed. London: I. B. Tauris, 2008.

Bornstein, Erica. *Disquieting Gifts: Humanitarianism in New Delhi*. Stanford, CA: Stanford University Press, 2012.

Brković, Čarna. "Vernacular #Humaniarianisms." Allegra Lab: Anthropology for Radical Optimism, September 2017. https://allegralaboratory.net/category/thematic-threads/humanitarianisms/.

Butler, Judith. *Precarious Life: The Powers of Mourning and Violence*. London: Verso, 2006.

Calhoun, Craig. "The Imperative to Reduce Suffering: Charity, Progress, and Emergencies in the Field of Humanitarian Action." In *Humanitarianism in Question: Politics, Power, Ethics*, edited by Michael Barnett and Thomas Weiss, 73–79. Ithaca, NY: Cornell University Press, 2008.

Chandler, David. "The Road to Military Humanitarianism: How the Human Rights NGOs Shaped a New Humanitarian Agenda." *Human Rights Quarterly* 23, no. 3 (2001): 678–700.

Chatterjee, Deen K. "Introduction." In *The Ethics of Assistance: Morality and the Distant Needy*, edited by Deen K. Chatterjee, 1–8. New York: Cambridge University Press, 2004.

Clarke, Marlea. "Global South: What Does It Mean and Why Use the Term?" *Global South Political Commentaries*, 2018.
Davies, Katherine. "Continuity, Change and Contest: Meanings of 'Humanitarian' from the 'Religion of Humanity' to the Kosovo War." London: Overseas Development Institute, 2012.
de Lauri, Antonio, ed. *The Politics of Humanitarianism: Power, Ideology, and Aid.* London: I. B. Taurus. 2016.
———. *Humanitarianism: Keywords.* Leiden: Brill. 2020.
de Waal, Alexander. *Famine Crimes: Politics and the Disaster Relief Industry in Africa.* Bloomington: Indiana University Press, 1997.
Dillon, Nara, and Jean Chun Oi, eds. *The Politics of Philanthropy: Social Networks and Refugee Relief in Shanghai, 1932-1949.* At the Crossroads of Empires: Middlemen, Social Networks, and State-Building in Republican Shanghai. Stanford, CA: Stanford University Press, 2008.
Dromi, Shai M. *Above the Fray: The Red Cross and the Making of the Humanitarian NGO Sector.* Chicago: University of Chicago Press, 2020.
Dunant, Henry. *A Memory of Solferino.* Washington, DC: American National Red Cross, 1959.
Egeland, Jan. "End the Occupation: Norwegian Refugee Council Warns Israeli Elections May Empower Extremist Parties." Online Interview, 1 November 2022. https://www.democracynow.org/2022/11/1/jan_egeland_israel_election_november_2022.
Fassin, Didier. *Humanitarian Reason: A Moral History of the Present.* Berkeley, CA: University uf California Press, 2012.
Fassin, Didier, and Mariella Pandolfi. *Contemporary States of Emergency: The Politics of Military and Humanitarian Interventions.* New York: Zone Books. 2010.
Fechter, Anne-Meike. "Helping Distant Strangers? Proximity and Distance in Everyday Humanitarianism." *EASA Anthropology of Humanitarianism Network*, 2020.
Feldman, Ilana. "Difficult Distinctions: Refugee Law, Humanitarian Practice, and Political Identification in Gaza." *Cultural Anthropology* 22, no. 1 (2007): 129–69.
———. "The Quaker Way: Ethical Labor and Humanitarian Relief." *American Ethnologist* 34, no. 4 (2007): 689–705.
———. *Life Lived in Relief: Humanitarian Predicaments and Palestinian Refugee Politics.* 1st ed. Oakland: University of California Press, 2018.
Feldman, Ilana, and Miriam Ticktin, eds. *In the Name of Humanity: The Government of Threat and Care.* Durham, NC: Duke University Press, 2010.
Fiddian-Qasmiyeh, Elena. "Shifting the Gaze: Palestinian and Syrian Refugees Sharing, Making and Contesting Space in Lebanon." In *Refuge in a Moving World*, edited by Elena Fiddian-Qasmiyeh, 402–14. London: UCL Press, 2020.
Fiddian-Qasmiyeh, Elena, and Alexander Horstmann. "Introduction: Faith-Based Humanitarianism in Contexts of Forced Displacement." *Journal of Refugee Studies* 24, no. 3 (2011): 429–39.
Garfield, R., and S. Santana. "The Impact of the Economic Crisis and the US Embargo on Health in Cuba." *American Journal of Public Health (1971)* 87, no. 1 (1997): 15–20.
Gatrell, Peter. "War and Population Displacement in East Asia, 1937–1950." Oxford: Oxford University Press, 2013.
Gordon, Joy. *Invisible War: The United States and the Iraq Sanctions.* Cambridge, MA: Harvard University Press, 2012.

Govindrajan, Radhika. *Animal Intimacies: Interspecies Relatedness in India's Central Himalayas*. Chicago: University of Chicago Press, 2018.

Han, Clara. *Life in Debt: Times of Care and Violence in Neoliberal Chile*. Berkeley: University of California Press, 2012.

Henkin, Louis. "Refugees and Their Human Rights." *Fordham International Law Journal* 18, no. 4 (1994): 1079–81.

Henriot, Christian. "Beyond Glory: Civilians, Combatants, and Society during the Battle of Shanghai." *War & Society* 31, no. 2 (2012): 106–35.

Ho, Elaine Lynn-Ee, and Cabeiri deBergh Robinson. "Introduction: Forced Migration in/of Asia—Interfaces and Multiplicities." *Journal of Refugee Studies* 31, no. 3 (2018): 262–73.

Kloß, Sinah Theres. "The Global South as Subversive Practice: Challenges and Potentials of a Heuristic Concept." *The global South* 11, no. 2 (2017): 1–17.

Lary, Diana. *The Chinese People at War: Human Suffering and Social Transformation, 1937–1945*. New Approaches to Asian History. New York: Cambridge University Press, 2010.

Lincoln, Toby. "Fleeing from Firestorms: Government, Cities, Native Place Associations and Refugees in the Anti-Japanese War of Resistance." *Urban History* 38, no. 3 (2011): 437–56.

Loescher, Gil. *The UNHCR and World Politics*. New York: Oxford University Press, 2001.

Lopes, Helena F. S. "The Impact of Refugees in Neutral Hong Kong and Macau, 1937–1945." *Historical Journal* (2022): 1–27.

Madokoro, Laura. "Surveying Hong Kong in the 1950s: Western Humanitarians and the "Problem" of Chinese Refugees." *Modern Asian Studies* 49, no. 2 (2015): 493–524.

Mahler, Anne Garland. *From the Tricontinental to the Global South: Race, Radicalism, and Transnational Solidarity*. Durham, NC: Duke University Press, 2018.

Malkki, Liisa H. "Refugees and Exile: From 'Refugee Studies' to the National Order of Things." *Annual Review of Anthropology* 24 (1995): 495–523.

———. "Speechless Emissaries: Refugees, Humanitarianism, and Dehistoricization." *Cultural Anthropology* 11, no. 3 (1996): 377–404.

Mann, Gregory. *From Empires to NGOs in the West African Sahel: The Road to Nongovernmentality*. African Studies. Cambridge: Cambridge University Press, 2014.

Mayblin, Lucy. *Asylum after Empire: Colonial Legacies in the Politics of Asylum Seeking*. Lanham, MD: Rowman & Littlefield, 2017.

Mayblin, Lucy, and Joe B. Turner. *Migration Studies and Colonialism*. Cambridge: Polity Press, 2021.

Mayblin, Lucy, Mustafa Wake, and Mohsen Kazemi. "Necropolitics and the Slow Violence of the Everyday: Asylum Seeker Welfare in the Postcolonial Present." *Sociology* 54, no. 1 (2020): 107–23.

Mazower, Mark. "The Strange Triumph of Human Rights, 1933–1950." *Historical Journal* 47, no. 2 (June 2004): 379–98.

McNevin, Anne, and Antje Missbach. "Hospitality as a Horizon of Aspiration (or, What the International Refugee Regime Can Learn from Acehnese Fishermen)." *Journal of Refugee Studies* 31, no. 3 (2018): 292–313.

Moon, Claire. "Human Rights, Human Remains: Forensic Humanitarianism and the Human Rights of the Dead." *International Social Science Journal* 65, no. 215-16 (2014): 49–63.

Mostowlansky, Till. "Muslim Humanitarianism." Allegra Lab: Anthropology for Radical Optimism, July 2019. https://allegralaboratory.net/category/thematic-threads/humanitarianisms/.

Moussa, Jasmine. "Ancient Origins, Modern Actors: Defining Arabic Meanings of Humanitarianism." London: ODI Humanitarian Policy Group, 2014.

Muscolino, Micah S. "Refugees, Land Reclamation, and Militarized Landscapes in Wartime China: Huanglongshan, Shaanxi, 1937–45." *Journal of Asian Studies* 69, no. 2 (2010): 453–78.

Nedostup, Rebecca. *Superstitious Regimes: Religion and the Politics of Chinese Modernity*. Harvard East Asian Monographs, no. 322. Cambridge, MA: Harvard University Asia Center, 2009.

O'Hagan, Jacinta, and Miwa Hirono. "Fragmentation of the International Humanitarian Order? Understanding 'Cultures of Humanitarianism' in East Asia." *Ethics and International Affairs* 28 (2014): 409–24.

Osanloo, Arzoo. "The Measure of Mercy: Islamic Justice, Sovereign Power, and Human Rights in Iran." *Cultural Anthropology* 21, no. 4 (2006): 570–602.

———. *Forgiveness Work: Mercy, Law, and Victims' Rights in Iran*. Princeton, NJ: Princeton University Press, 2020.

———. "Entangled Lives: Enduring under Sanctions." *Journal of Humanity* 14(2): 264–281, Summer 2023.

Oxfam International. *A Poor Welcome from the World's Wealthy*. 18 July 2016. Retrieved 14 December 2022 from https://oi-files-d8-prod.s3.eu-west-2.amazonaws.com/s3fs-public/a_poor_welcome_-_embargoed180716.pdf.

Parreñas, Juno Salazar. *Decolonizing Extinction: The Work of Care in Orangutan Rehabilitation*. Experimental Futures: Technological Lives, Scientific Arts, Anthropological Voices. Durham, NC: Duke University Press, 2018.

Peterson, Glen. "Sovereignty, International Law, and the Uneven Development of the International Refugee Regime." *Modern Asian Studies* 49, no. 2 (2015): 439–68.

Reeves, Caroline. "Lost in Translation: Local Relief Provision and Historiographical Imperialism." *New Global Studies* 12 (2018): 277–92.

Robinson, Cabeiri deBergh. "Too Much Nationality: Kashmiri Refugees, the South Asian Refugee Regime, and a Refugee State, 1947–1974." *Journal of Refugee Studies* 25, no. 3 (2012): 344–65.

———. *Body of Victim, Body of Warrior: Refugee Families and the Making of Kashmiri Jihadists*. Berkeley: University of California Press, 2013.

———. "Humanitarian Internationalism and Funding Relief for Refugees from Jammu and Kashmir in Pakistan, 1947–1951." In *The Handbook of New Directions in Kashmir Studies*, edited by Haley Dushinski, Mona Bhan, and Cabeiri Robinson, 333–50. New York: Palgrave MacMillan, 2023.

Slim, Hugo. *Humanitarian Ethics: A Guide to the Morality of Aid in War and Disaster*. London: Hurst & Company, 2015.

Tadiar, Neferti Xina M. *Remaindered Life*. Durham, NC: Duke University Press, 2022.

Tejel, Jordi, and Ramazan Hakkı Öztan. "'Forced Migration and Refugeedom in the Modern Middle East' towards Connected Histories of Refugeedom in the Middle East." Special issue, *Journal of Migration History* 6, no. 1 (February 17, 2020): 1–15.

Turner, Simon. "What Is a Refugee Camp? Explorations of the Limits and Effects of the Camp." *Journal of Refugee Studies* 29, no. 2 (2015): 139–48.

UNHCR. *Global Trends Forced Displacement in 2017*, 25 June 2018. https://www.unhcr.org/media/unhcr-global-trends-2017.

UNHCR. *Global Trends Forced Displacement in 2018*, 20 June 2019. https://www.unhcr.org/media/unhcr-global-trends-2018.

UNHCR. *Global Trends Forced Displacement in 2021*, 16 June 2022. https://www.unhcr.org/media/global-trends-report-2021.

UNHCR. *Global Trends Forced Displacement in 2022*, 14 June 2023. https://www.unhcr.org/global-trends-report-2022.

Varoufakis, Yanis. *And the Weak Suffer What They Must? Europe's Crisis and America's Economic Future*. New York: Nation Books, 2016.

Vernant, Jacques. *The Refugee in the Post-War World*. New Haven, CT: Yale University Press, 1953.

Wa Ngugi, Mukoma. "Rethinking the Global South." (Blog) The Global South Project. Retrieved 12 December 2022 from http://www.globalsouthproject.cornell.edu/rethinking-the-global-south.html.

Walley, Christine J. *Exit Zero: Family and Class in Postindustrial Chicago*. Chicago: University of Chicago Press, 2013.

Whyte, Jessica. "The 'Dangerous Concept of the Just War': Decolonization, Wars of National Liberation, and the Additional Protocols to the Geneva Conventions." *Journal of Humanity* 9, no. 3 (2018): 313–41.

———. "'The Opposite of Humanity': Anti-colonial Challenges to International Humanitarian Law." 3 December 2020. https://www.humanitarianisms.org/.

Zamindar, Vazira Fazila-Yacoobali. *The Long Partition and the Making of Modern South Asia: Refugees, Boundaries, Histories*. New York: Columbia University Press, 2007.

Zolberg, Aristide. "The Formation of New States as a Refugee-Generating Process." *ANNALS of the American Academy of Political and Social Science* 467, no. 1 (1 May 1983): 24–38.

PART I

REFUGE, LAW, AND EMPIRE IN THE GLOBAL SOUTH

CHAPTER 1

Patriation

Conceptualizing Migration after Empire

Pamela Ballinger

Where and how do concepts and categories originate, derive their power and resonance, and develop over time? Such a broad question has provoked many types of answers, ranging from the philosophical to the cognitive to the historical. In this chapter, I address the question in much more concrete terms, offering an account of an intellectual journey centered on specific classifications—those of the displaced—rather than any sort of theory of concepts. I examine how the refugee label came into existence through a narrowing of eligibility criteria for humanitarian care and relief and a series of systematic exclusions. In the critical period between the end of World War II and the promulgation of the 1951 Geneva Convention on Refugees, these exclusions from the international refugee category included not only most non-European displaced persons (notably those from former European empires) but also those European populations who became classified as "national refugees."

This chapter explores such exclusions through a telling of my own scholarly efforts to reconstruct the making of the legal category of the (international) refugee and its consolidation after 1945. In focusing my research on the experiences of individuals who migrated to the Italian peninsula from the Italian possessions lost after fascism's defeat, I continually came up against the inadequacy—in legal, political, or conceptual terms—of the "refugee" label to capture their status and condition. Such dilemmas remain salient, as many individuals today displaced by environmental, economic, and political forces do not acquire the label of official refugee.

When confronted with the challenges of offering an alternative term to capture the processes of displacement experienced after World War II by so-called national refugees, I finally settled upon the notion of "patriation." The story I recount here of these conceptual struggles illustrates how scholars often produce theory in multilayered and extended conversations with other scholars, as well as policymakers and the subjects of theory themselves (in this case, displaced persons). The conceptual impasses that blocked me at different moments in this journey reflected how accounts of the international regime of refugee relief that arose after World War II relied upon problematic compartmentalization of the global North and global South, as well as of empire and nation. As my account here reveals, the complex history of refugee migrants to the Italian peninsula from its lost empire complicates any such easy distinctions.

I aim here to highlight the kinds of conversations that inform all scholarly work and that necessarily reflect the historical and cultural contexts in which they take place. This reminds students that when they read and write about issues such as refugees, they likewise participate in those conversations and debates. Readers of this volume do so in a charged moment in which there predominates what sociologist Lucy Mayblin has deemed a "myth of difference" distinguishing "genuine" refugees from the global North from those from the global South, with many of the latter coming from former European colonial spaces. As Mayblin and the contributors to this volume demonstrate, this myth of difference "discredits non-Western asylum seekers through both a blurring and reinforcing of the boundaries between economic migration and forced migration."[1]

By restoring the history of key definitional debates that established this boundary, I build upon the extensive critique of the 1951 convention's Eurocentric nature, given the temporal and geographic limits put upon the original refugee definition in Article 1 that effectively restricted refugees to Europeans displaced before 1 January 1951. Yet the Italian case also underscores just how particularistic this refugee regime was even within a European context, given that the convention's refugee definition also excluded many European displaced persons from recognition. Ignoring refugees produced by decolonization like the Italians I have studied helped perpetuate a false division between the postwar "European" refugee problem associated with World War II and its aftermath, on the one hand, and the globalization of the refugee question with decolonization, on the other.[2] Such pernicious distinctions became mapped spatially (North/South) and temporally (1945–60/1960–present). In light of the enduring consequences of the refugee as legal category, it took me many years to see beyond the blind spots created by much of the scholarship around the refugee.

A Series of Puzzles

In 2020, I published *The World Refugees Made*, a study of Italian decolonization after World War II and the migrations to the metropole it generated, in particular those of former settlers and/or Italian nationals.³ In the 1940s and the 1950s, many of these individuals came to bear the designation of "national refugees." These migrants came from a wide range of territories with distinct statuses that included formal colonies (Eritrea, Ethiopia, and Somalia, fused together as Africa Orientale Italiana), departments or "possessions" (Libya, the Dodecanese Islands), and protectorates (Albania). Also included in this group and subject to the same juridical status were an estimated 180,000–200,000 persons migrating out of the former Adriatic lands that had been integral parts of the Italian state and were ceded to Yugoslavia between 1947 and 1954. This diverse and varied population of national refugees stood in contrast to international or bona fide refugees recognized for eligibility under the emerging refugee regime centered around the United Nations and its intergovernmental agencies.

The differentiation between national and international refugees and the critical question of who would provide for their care and maintenance reflected the consolidation of the belief that "national" refugees were merely returning to their home country and thus did not require the humanitarian protection of the UN, as their home states should and would provide for them. This rested on a fiction that in "going home," such migrants had not crossed an international border, one of several key criteria for refugee status according to Article 1 of the 1951 convention.⁴ As Cabeiri Robinson notes, "The idea that refugees are 'deprived of their nationality' had the effect of excluding displaced people who could be argued to have multiple claims of nationality [and *home*]—effectively, people displaced by post-war decolonization."⁵ Today such an idea appears so commonplace and obvious as to have become naturalized, enshrined in more recent vocabularies that differentiate refugees from internally displaced persons, or IDPs, as well as from voluntary or economic migrants.

In the Italian case, this walling off of supposedly distinct types of migrants was heightened by the ways in which the experiences of Italian nationals displaced from the colonies and overseas possessions had been kept apart and distinct from the histories of those who migrated out of the Adriatic territories severed from the Italian state between 1947 and 1954. Thus, in the Italian case at least, even the very category of national refugees remained poorly defined beyond a legal standpoint and had received little scholarly attention as a classification.

My initial interest in these intertwined migration histories developed out of anthropological research I conducted in the mid-1990s with self-styled *esuli*, or exiles, individuals who had left Italy's Istrian and Dalmatian territories when they passed under Yugoslav control after World War II. On the one hand, the voluminous body of memoirs, poetry, and journals produced by these migrants either stressed the uniqueness of their experience or located it within a logic of "ethnic cleansing" supposedly inherent to the Balkans and wider Eastern Europe.⁶ On the other hand, in casual conversations and oral histories I collected, individuals sometimes mentioned living in refugee camps in Italy alongside Italians who had come from other lost territories, such as Libya or Eritrea. Sometimes, these Italian exiles from the eastern Adriatic had also shared camps with "foreign" refugees, mostly from Central and Eastern Europe. How to account for the lack of discussion in these groups' commemorative practices or the silence in historical work about such shared experiences?

As I began to conduct initial research in the archives of intergovernmental bodies such as the United Nations Relief and Rehabilitation Administration (UNRRA) and the International Refugee Organization (IRO), as well as in various Italian state repositories, I encountered skepticism over my plan to write a broad history of Italian national refugees embedded within an account of the making of the postwar international refugee order. Fellow scholars in Italy and my exile interlocutors alike cautioned me about putting together "apples and oranges," warning of the dangers of seeing Italians displaced out of a formerly integral part of the Italian state like Istria through the same prism as those coming from a colony like Italian East Africa. Given that the Yugoslav socialist regime under Tito had deemed Italians "colonizers," thereby erasing a centuries-long history of Venetian administration, settlement, and culture along the Adriatic coast, most exiles were not eager to be lumped together with former Italian settlers repatriated from colonies like Somalia or Ethiopia. These *esuli* insisted upon their deep roots in the Adriatic territories, indeed their autochthony or "nativeness," in contrast to Italian settlers who could boast at most a few generations in the former colonies. The very premise of Italian claims to territories like Istria, Trentino, and Alto Adige (all of which became part of the Italian state after World War I) was that these were historically and ethnically Italian lands, artificially separated from the motherland and in desperate need of "redemption." Hence the birth of the term *irredentism* to describe the political claim for the "return" of territories to the motherland.

Yet the postwar history of assistance by the Italian state to its own "national" refugees—who shared common experiences upon coming to Italy as displacees, even if their histories *within* the territories lost by Italy after the war often differed dramatically—also revealed to me the all too real political stakes at work in disentangling the histories of Italy's colonial and irredentist lands. In making claims upon the state based on their losses, Italian refugees during the 1940s and 1950s had established a hierarchy (albeit a contested one) among themselves. As some of the former colonial repatriates I interviewed noted with bitterness, the Adriatic refugees had managed to prioritize their claims and suffering. This became even more pronounced in the 1990s, when the dissolution of Yugoslavia and the introduction of the term "ethnic cleansing" provided exiles with a narrative that worked to distance the fate of the eastern Adriatic territories from the brutality of fascist rule. At that point, a presumed "Balkan" tendency toward ethnic cleansing made exile claims that they had paid for the "sole crime of being Italian" compelling and persuasive.

Beyond the Italian context, I encountered skepticism from other scholars about the logic of putting national and international refugees in the same frame. At one presentation, a colleague who works on the Adriatic region asked a pointed question about the title of my book. *The World Refugees Made* alluded to the work of several different authors, including migration scholar Peter Gatrell, and to Eugene Genovese's pioneering 1974 study *Roll, Jordan, Roll: The World the Slaves Made*.[7] One of Genovese's signal contributions lay in how he restored agency and humanity to enslaved African Americans by demonstrating their creativity and resilience in resisting oppression. In referencing Genovese's landmark study in my title, I sought to underscore how the refugee regime was produced through asymmetric negotiations between those who administered and classified the displaced and the displaced themselves. Though structurally disadvantaged, the displaced possessed agency and exercised it at various points, particularly when their condition of displacement did not receive "official" recognition. Yet my colleague rightly reminded me that in the Italian context I was studying, many of those who became "national refugees" had enjoyed positions of relative privilege and authority in relation to local populations in the colonies or non-Italian ethnic groups in the former irredentist lands. Indeed, the type of paternalism that convinced slave owners in the American South that their slaves would not rise up against them similarly worked to blind some Italian settlers to the inherent violence of colonialism and irredentism. How to square the fact that these settlers and repatriates had been privileged in one setting and disadvantaged in another, thereby working against common notions of refugees as (merely) dispossessed victims?

Similar questions arose in other discussions with colleagues. At another presentation I gave, an audience member pressed me, assuming that by talking about these two types of displacees together I was arguing that they should be seen as synonymous. I rather lamely replied that my point was that legal categories should not constrain or delimit the categories that scholars employ. But, at that point, I *was* struggling to articulate my own position on where I thought the national refugees belonged in the frame of what Peter Gatrell has called "refugeedom."[8]

In this, my own puzzlement mirrored the historical picture in the 1940s and 1950s, when questions about the eligibility of Italians displaced from former Italian territories for forms of international refugee assistance were persistent. The question of how to classify these migrants preoccupied not only UN personnel but also officials in the Vatican, the British Military Administrations that temporarily governed former Italian possessions in Africa and the Aegean, the Italian government, and the Intergovernmental Committee on European Migration, among other actors.

As I researched my book over more than a decade, I heeded the suggestion of legal specialists like James Hathaway to take both historical and "real account" of the context in which the 1951 Geneva Convention on Refugees coalesced. For Hathaway, this entailed exploring debates among the convention's framers alongside "evidence of contemporary factual challenges to the treaty's effectiveness."[9] As a historian, my method and my understanding of context operated differently. Rather than focus on the intentions of the architects of the convention, I toggled between classifications on paper and in practice and their implications in the realm of actual humanitarian relief. This meant moving between the debates over eligibility within the UN agencies that preceded and informed the convention debates and that took place in an often ad hoc manner and among the displaced themselves. These displaced often challenged the categorizations applied to them as they navigated emerging worlds of relief and rights. Some of those considered national refugees requested that they be considered international refugees, for example. Furthermore, the very idea of national refugees as *repatriates* merely engaging in a "return" migration thus prompted a whole series of questions about what homeland and belonging meant for these migrants, a knot of questions that I only began to untangle in *The World Refugees Made*.

After the book came out, I gave another series of presentations, most of them in virtual formats due to the pandemic. While discussing the book with colleagues from Ohio State University, my host historian Theodora Dragostinova pressed me on my critique of the inadequacies of the term "repatriation." Professor Dragostinova has grappled with similar questions in her research on ethnically Greek migrants from Bulgaria who moved to Greece in a series of supposedly voluntary population exchanges.[10] The presence of "Greeks" (a term that indexed both language and religion) in what became the Bulgarian state after 1878 reflected the deep histories of imperial formations in Southeastern Europe—those of the Ottomans, Habsburgs, and Romanovs—characterized by multilinguistic, multiconfessional, and multiethnic populations. The series of ethnic unmixings that transformed the region in the period stretching from between the Balkan Wars through the Cold War rested on fictions of moving back to a homeland not dissimilar to those operating in the case of Italian decolonization. And in these varied instances, these fictions were employed not only by state authorities and national activists but also by agents of humanitarianism who often, whether unwittingly or wittingly, contributed to the reinforcement of nation-state logics.

My own research highlighted how the idea of a "return" or a "reverse" migration obscured the complexities of such flows and of the identities of residents in the former Italian possessions. I asked just what exactly constituted home for migrants said to be making a return to their *patria* with the advent of decolonization? And what, in turn, did their "Italianness" consist in? Some of the migrants who became recognized as national refugees had been born in the Italian possessions and had never been to the Italian peninsula prior to decolonization. A subset of these came from families of diasporic "Italians" living in the territories of other European colonial powers, notably French Tunisia and Algeria or British Egypt, who subsequently moved to the Italian possessions. Another subset had lived in territories such as Libya or the Dodecanese Islands prior to Italian rule and had acquired protection as Italian protégés under the system of extraterritorial citizenship that existed for "Europeans" within the Ottoman Empire. The ties of such protégés with Italy—including their linguistic affiliations—were often tenuous at best. At times, this ambiguity was mirrored in the juridical statuses held by these former protégés within the former Ottoman lands now under Italian control, as some individuals received a kind of demi citizenship (such as the *cittadinanza egea* in the Dodecanese Islands) in contrast to those who became (or remained) Italian in juridical terms.

Yet even for those who had merely engaged in a migration back to the Italian peninsula after a relatively short period of time in the possessions and whose citizenship never came into question, such returns often proved anything but straightforward or simple. Indeed, I have characterized the migrations involved in Italian decolonization as multidirectional since some individuals displaced during the war pressed the relevant authorities, notably the British who temporarily administered the former Italian possessions in Africa and the Aegean, for permission to repatriate *back* to Libya or Rhodes or Asmara after 1945. When denied the possibility, some turned to clandestine migration. This became a particular point of contention for the British Military Administration governing Libya, which sometimes deported Italians intercepted at drop-off points along the Libyan coastline where they had been smuggled on small fishing boats from Sicily. Such stories underscore how, in affective terms, home for many of these migrants was not Italy proper but the place in Africa or the Balkans that they called *casa*. This sense of home is reflected in the memoirs of such former settlers, who often refer nostalgically to the scents, sounds, and flavors of the places they considered home.

Some such "Italians" did not view a distant metropole as either welcoming or homey, choosing instead to migrate directly from the former possessions to traditional destinations of Italian immigration. And some, in turn, took the path of migration after a period spent in the Italian peninsula, often living in a refugee camp. Given these many wrinkles and complexities, I elaborated at length in *The World Refugees Made* on why the vocabulary of repatriation—together with an associated set of "re" prefixes (return, reverse, reflux, regurgitate)—proved inadequate at the level of either description or conceptualization.[11] What, however, to put in its place?

Toward a New Concept

In merely critiquing the notion of repatriation, I had failed to replace it with a constructive category that better captured and expressed its complexities. I had thus committed a classic error of failing to practice what I preach, given that I always remind my students that it is much easier to deconstruct and critique than to offer something fresh, and consistently urge them to aim for the latter. When Professor Dragostinova first posed her query, I replied that the most accurate term was likely that of "nationalization." By this, I meant to refer to a process by which these migrants were fashioned into proper national (that is, Italian) subjects. A nagging voice in my head reminded me of the problems with this term. In places like Italy's lost territories on the eastern Adriatic, nationalization had been a popular term during the 1940s to decry the factors prompting migration out of Istria, Kvarner, and Dalmatia. "Nationalization" in these contexts often signified heavy-handed policies of ethnic engineering, standing in for what would later be deemed *genocide* after the term's introduction by Raphael Lemkin in 1948 or *ethnic cleansing* after it became part of the lexicon in the 1990s. Even in its more benign usages, nationalization implied highly directed projects of identity building. Usually spearheaded by state authorities, these nationalization processes aimed at turning the proverbial peasants into Frenchmen, that is, homogenizing languages and cultures in the name of the nation.[12]

In the weeks that followed the OSU seminar, I came to realize that a more suitable term to describe the complicated, ambivalent, and often incomplete processes of migration and integration after decolonization was that of *patriation*. This left in place the notion of the *patria*, an Italian term that simultaneously indexes and elides home, homeland, and country. The word *paese* similarly can signify home, town, or country in Italian. Conversely, the Italian term *spaesato* signifies a feeling of being lost or disoriented, that is, of literally not feeling at home in the world. Patriation, to my mind, captured the ways in which migrating to a supposed homeland actually required a complex process of *becoming* Italian, both in terms of self-ascription and external ascription. And, paradoxically, the process of patriation continually marked out the difference of these Italians who had come from outside the peninsula by making them visible objects of state-sponsored forms of humanitarianism (housing, subsidies, compensation for losses).

With its prefixal *patr-*, patriation also gestured toward the patrilineal bias in Italian citizenship, a largely consanguineal notion designed from almost the beginning of Italian statehood to facilitate the retention or easy reacquisition of Italian citizenship by members of the diaspora. Though in some instances there existed debate or ambiguity around their legal status, most of the national refugees were citizens of the country to which they migrated (Italy), and this—

above all else—distinguished them from international refugees recognized by the 1951 convention. The process of migration out of the former colonies also embedded an implicit association of whiteness with Italianness, excluding most former colonial subjects from Italian territories from either citizenship or assistance from the postwar Italian state. Nor was this experience unique to Italy, as seen in the case of the *retornados* or colonial settlers in Portugal who came to the metropole from Africa, Goa, and East Timor in the mid-1970s.[13] Portugal's 1975 Nationality Law actually instated the principle of *jus sanguinis* or belonging through descent/blood, replacing a nearly centuries-long tradition of citizenship based on *jus soli* or birthright citizenship. A 1981 law further entrenched this form of citizenship, facilitating the "return" to the metropole of persons of Portuguese descent while tightening the possibilities for migration to or metropolitan citizenship by former Portuguese subjects.[14]

In the Italian case, by contrast, the citizenship regime had rested on the principle of blood and descent from almost the beginning of Italian statehood, a reality that reflected not only an oft-cited "protective" impulse toward members of the expansive Italian diaspora abroad but also the politics of colonial expansion and racial exclusivity. While the end of empire ushered in profound transformations in citizenship in Italy, it happened mostly through very particular legal processes rather than a complete overhaul of the citizenship law, which marked the Portuguese case. The citizenship "option" in Article 19 of the 1947 Peace Treaty with Italy, for example, laid out the terms under which individuals in the areas of Venezia Giulia ceded to Yugoslavia and the Dodecanese Islands awarded to Greece could either retain their Italian citizenship or acquire that of the respective new states. Retaining or (re)acquiring Italian citizenship rested on several key criteria, notably domicile in the ceded territories on or before 10 June 1940 (the date of Italy's entry into World War II) and "language of customary use." Interpreting what the latter meant in practice created a host of complications, raising pointed questions about language and its capacity to signify formal belonging or reinforce feelings of homeliness or, conversely, alienation. The notion of Italian as a *madrelingua* or "mother tongue" connecting members of the far-flung diaspora to the *patria* or fatherland also underscores how visions of home and homecoming become shot through with understandings of gender, domesticity, and rootedness.

Although the vocabulary of the citizenship option in the peace treaty suggests that individuals could simply "choose" their citizenship according to their preferences, in practice Italian authorities saw such procedures as tools through which to sharpen the state's newly redrawn boundaries of both territory and citizenship. Throughout the Cold War, for example, authorities within Italy argued that the fragile new democracy—confronted by the challenges of its own national refugees and continued problems of surplus population—could not become a permanent home for foreign or international refugees. This included non-Italian migrants from Italy's former colonies, with the exception of a small population of mixed-race children who had been recognized by their Italian fathers and could thus make claims to Italian citizenship. Addressing the humanitarian concerns of "national refugees" and drawing boundaries around who could be the recognized object of such patriation thus became an important means by which an Italian state shored up its still fragile sovereignty in the transition out of empire, war, and fascism.

The Paradoxes and Limits of Patriation

What critical work does the notion of "patriation" do? While scholars are often accused of loving jargon and "theory for theory's sake," concepts serve to illuminate broader patterns. And a theory, by definition, merely provides an explanation of some sort. What patterns or processes does patriation help us see? In addition to bringing out the complexities of Italian identity and belonging among migrants themselves and the central role of citizenship/statelessness in understandings of refugees, it highlights the efforts required of states like Italy to "patriate" their repatriated citizens. For individuals who "come home" to their putative ethno-national state (even if for the first time), patriation also must act as a counterweight against powerful sentiments of nostalgia for the places they have left behind and sometimes for the previous state formations (colonialism, fascism) that made life in such lost homes possible. Such nostalgia operates in tandem with more future-oriented understandings that may nourish dreams of an eventual return to the place from which they migrated.

In the case of the Italian empire, patriation competed with dreams of returning to the lost colonial homeland and older dreams of "returning" to the irredentist territories. The fascist regime sponsored such dreams until its bloody end in 1945. Despite having lost military control over East Africa by 1942 and Libya by 1943, for example, the regime nourished unrealistic hopes, as given expression in this 1943 propaganda poster promising Italians, "We will return." (see figure 1.1). Tellingly, the colonial settlers looking longingly toward Africa pictured here are a small boy and his grandfather (the father presumably off fighting the war), highlighting the patrilineal and *patriarchal* biases of fascist citizenship.

The previous regime worked hard to convince those displaced settlers that their move was a temporary one and that they would return to Africa after eventual Italian victory in the war. The democratic Italian Republic reestablished on the rubble of fascism had to convince these Italians that their true home lay in the Italian peninsula and the democratic state. But this only came after a decade of diplomatic wrangling over the fate of the African colonies and proposals for some form of continued Italian control. In the case of So-

Figure 1.1. • "Torneremo," 1943. Photo by David Almeida and designed by Giulio Bertoletti; published by Studio Tecnico Editoriale Italiano, Rome; and printed by Ind. Grafiche N. Moneta, Milan. Display card, "Io so, io sento che milioni e milioni di Italiani soffrono di un indefinibile male che si chiama il male d'Africa. Per guarirne non c'è che un mezzo: tornare. E torneremo" (I know, I feel that millions and millions of Italians suffer from an indefinable malady, known as the Africa sickness. There is only one means of recovering: to return. And we will return), 1943. Published with the permission of the Wolfsonian-Florida International University (Miami, Florida).[15]

malia, Italy would administer a UN trusteeship over its former colony for a decade (1950–60). This marked the formal end of Italian decolonization and the extinguishing of any realistic hopes for hanging on to colonial possessions. Yet this reminds us that there may exist many versions or understandings of "return" and *patria* that may directly conflict with one another.

In going beyond the Italian case to search for broader trends, we find other state-directed projects of patriation. For example, anthropologist Andrea Smith's research on repatriates of Maltese origin who left Algeria for France reveals a case marked by a high degree of success in the French colonial project to nationalize settlers, first in the colony and then through the process of decolonization and repatriation. These individuals of Maltese background numbered among the estimated one million *pieds-noirs* (the term used to denote European settlers in Algeria) who departed Algeria for France en masse in 1962 with Algerian independence. Malta never entered the migrants' minds as a potential destination upon their departure. Indeed, most *pieds-noirs* of Maltese origin had no memories of Malta and rarely spoke of life in this "homeland."[16] Born and raised in what became a department of France in 1848, these *colons* or colonists possessed French citizenship and had been educated in a system that stressed speaking French.[17] As Smith puts it, for these former colonial settlers, "There is no question in their minds about their French nationality: they speak French, sometimes only that language, and certainly not Maltese. They attended French schools, and most of the men served several long years in the French army during World War II. To them, their 'Frenchness' is unquestioned and unquestionable."[18]

The French language thus became a powerful engine of assimilation for Maltese, whose native language—a Semitic variant mutually intelligible with Arabic—had placed them close to the bottom of the European hierarchy within Algeria.[19] Before repatriation, this hierarchy put limits on assimilation by keeping ethnic and racial markers in place that demonstrated Maltese difference from other Europeans. The act of migrating to France helped obviate such distinctions, given that despite their differences, all *pieds-noirs* were "labeled by French state officials *rapatriés* and the migrations *rapatriements*, or repatriations, terms that are still used today."[20] Yet the process of successful patriation eliminated neither the suspicions of some metropolitan French about the genuine Frenchness of the *pieds-noirs*—indeed, the very term "black feet" indexed a sense of alterity and inferiority—nor the sense among some Maltese *pieds-noirs* that they possessed multiple homelands.

In the 1990s, some of these very Frenchified *pieds-noirs* nonetheless became interested in their ancestral homeland, making journeys of discovery to Malta. Trips to Malta by Maltese Algerian clubs, however, triggered memories of another *patrie*—Algeria, as sights (the built environment, plants such as prickly pear cactus), sounds (the Maltese language, which resembles Arabic), and smells (the cooking of grilled sardines) temporarily emplaced these *pieds-noirs* in a specific landscape that they had never before experienced.[21] In this re-emplacement, the *pieds-noirs* no longer sat at the bottom of the colonial settler hierarchy nor were viewed suspiciously by their fellow citizens of France. Rather, "Malta became Algeria and the Maltese themselves [i.e., those encountered by the former settlers] stood in place of indigenous Algerians."[22] This example underscores the complex routings of home and homeliness together with the limits of patriation as a totalizing or monopolistic project. It also hints at the utility of patriation of a concept beyond the Italian case I have studied.

Conclusion: The Power of Categories and Concepts

This chapter has charted my thinking about how displaced persons become sorted into particular categories and my progressive understanding that the conceptual walling off of types of migrants from one another—economic versus political, voluntary versus forced, national versus international refugees—developed out of the processes by which persons displaced in the 1940s were classified and by which responsibility for humanitarian assistance was divvied up. In practice, migrations display aspects of both voluntary and forced movement, thereby blurring categorical boundaries. Such ambiguities suggest it is more productive to talk about the migration processes in which individuals participate and through which they move; that is, it is more useful to think of the act of migration as a verb (to migrate) than of migrants as a noun. Nonetheless, the 1951 Refugee Convention with which we still contend today continues to define refugees as fixed subjects rather than as actors moving through varied processes of displacement, and this results in a whole host of definitional and operational problems.

Scholars have the luxury, however, of not being constrained by legal taxonomies, and the histories I have detailed here point to alternative understandings of the refugee. Indeed, the chapters collected in this volume highlight the multiplicity of understandings of what it means to be a refugee and what assistance entails. Yet, even as they offer suggestions for thinking about potential future legal meanings of displacement, the fact that most such understandings never became normative at the level of international law serve as poignant reminders of the asymmetries of power that privilege some legal regimes over others, then and now. Exploring histories like those of post-1945 national refugees also remind us that exclusions made in the 1940s and 1950s—particularly the exclusion of decolonization refugees and *non-European* displaced persons—entailed deliberate and conscious choices and were not mere oversights or compromises. These exclusions reflected the ongoing salience of colonialism, as anticolonial activists and representatives from states like India and Pakistan pointed out at the time.²³ Such exclusions continue to reverberate despite the formal end of colonialism.

Italians displaced with the loss of empire, together with those advocating for their inclusion within the emerging international refugee regime, critiqued from *within* what was essentially a European refugee regime that became normative at the international level. For the most part, though, these Italian critics did not question the colonial order of things, reminding us of my colleague's trenchant observation about the *relative* privilege of these colonial displaces. Rather, these national refugees questioned the marginality of a postcolonial Italy within the emerging postwar international order, one in which the "myth of difference" between political refugees from the global North and economic migrants from the global South would only sharpen over ensuing decades. Italy, in particular, has become a front line in Europe's ongoing migration "emergencies." Yet since the very beginning of its statehood, Italy has figured as a place that sits uneasily at the intersection of North ("Europe") and South ("Mediterranean," "Oriental"), rendering it a valuable observatory post from which to question a whole series of categorical boundaries around displacement. The story of Italy's own national refugees thus offers the possibility to rethink our own conceptualizations and vocabularies in service to changing the conversation.

Pamela Ballinger is professor of history and the Fred Cuny Chair in the History of Human Rights in the Department of History at the University of Michigan. She is the author of *History in Exile: Memory and Identity at the Borders of the Balkans* (Princeton University Press, 2003), *La Memoria dell'Esilio* (Veltro Editrice, 2010), and *The World Refugees Made: Decolonization and the Foundation of Postwar Italy* (Cornell University Press, 2020).

Notes

1. Mayblin, *Asylum after Empire*, 31.
2. According to this problematic periodization, decolonization and the rise of the global refugee then necessitated universal instruments of protection. See Gallagher, "Evolution of the International Refugee System," 583.
3. Ballinger, *World Refugees Made*.
4. For a discussion of how Partition refugees were considered as not having lost the protection of their home states, giving rise to a regional refugee regime distinct from that of the UN, see Robinson, "Too Much Nationality," 345–46.
5. Robinson, "Too Much Nationality," 346.
6. For details, see Ballinger, *History in Exile*.
7. Gatrell directs attention to "the world that refugees made, not just the world that has been made for them." Gatrell, "Refugees," 179; Genovese, *Roll, Jordan, Roll*.

8. Gatrell's concept of refugeedom highlights a "specific category of humanity" together with "the changing manifestations of a 'refugee regime,' taken to mean the principles, rules and practices adopted by government officials and others to manage refugees, and the protection gaps in the system." Gatrell, "Refugees," 178.
9. Hathaway, *Rights of Refugees*, 74.
10. Dragostinova, *Between Two Motherlands*.
11. The "re" prefix rehearses many of the same issues inherent in the classification "post" and its implications of having moved beyond a particular condition or state; see Chari and Verdery, "Thinking between the Posts."
12. On the classic formulation, see Weber, *Peasants into Frenchmen*.
13. On this and for a comparative perspective: Buettner, *Europe after Empire*. The volume *L'Europe Retrouvée* represents an early and pioneering work on colonial repatriations "back" to Europe. Miège and Dubois eds, *L'Europe Retrouvée*.
14. Kalter, *Postcolonial People*, 52–53.
15. The Mitchell Wolfson Jr. Collection, XB1992.2392. The original poster is 13-3/8 x 9 inches (34 x 23 centimeters).
16. Smith, "Place Replaced," 336–37.
17. This resulted from the citizenship law of 1889, which provided for mass naturalization of European settlers not of ethnic French origin on the grounds of *jus soli*. Smith, *Colonial Memory and Postcolonial Europe*, 106–7.
18. Smith, *Colonial Memory and Postcolonial Europe*, 18.
19. Smith, "Place Replaced," 337–38.
20. Smith, *Colonial Memory and Postcolonial Europe*, 163.
21. Smith, *Colonial Memory and Postcolonial Europe*, 167; Smith, "Place Replaced," 344–45.
22. Smith, "Place Replaced," 350.
23. Mayblin, *Asylum after Empire*; see also Robinson, "Too Much Nationality," 346.

References

Ballinger, Pamela. *History in Exile: Memory and Identity at the Borders of the Balkans*. Princeton, NJ: Princeton University Press, 2003.

———. *The World Refugees Made: Decolonization and the Foundation of Postwar Italy*. Ithaca, NY: Cornell University Press, 2020.

Buettner, Elizabeth. *Europe after Empire: Decolonization, Society, and Culture*. Cambridge: Cambridge University Press, 2016.

Chari, Sharad, and Katherine Verdery. "Thinking between the Posts: Postcolonialism, Postsocialism, and Ethnography after the Cold War." *Comparative Studies in Society and History* 51, no. 1 (2009): 6–34.

Dragostinova, Theodora. *Between Two Motherlands: Nationality and Emigration among the Greeks of Bulgaria, 1900–1949*. Ithaca, NY: Cornell University Press, 2011.

Gallagher, Dennis. "The Evolution of the International Refugee System." *International Migration Review* 23, no. 3 (1989): 579–98.

Gatrell, Peter. "Refugees—What's Wrong with History?" *Journal of Refugee Studies* 30, no. 2 (2017): 170–89.

Genovese, Eugene. *Roll, Jordan, Roll: The World the Slaves Made*. New York: Vintage, 1976.

Hathaway, James. *The Rights of Refugees under International Law*. Cambridge: Cambridge University Press, 2005.
Kalter, Christoph. *Postcolonial People: The Return from Africa and the Remaking of Portugal*. Cambridge: Cambridge University Press, 2022.
Mayblin, Lucy. *Asylum after Empire: Colonial Legacies in the Politics of Asylum Seeking*. Lanham, MD: Rowman and Littlefield, 2017.
Miège, Jean Louis, and Colette Dubois, eds. *L'Europe Retrouvée: Les migrations de la décolonisation*. Paris: L'Harmattan, 1994.
Robinson, Cabeiri Debergh. "Too Much Nationality: Kashmiri Refugees, the South Asian Refugee Regime, and a Refugee State, 1947–1974." *Journal of Refugee Studies* 25, no. 3 (2012): 344–65.
Smith, Andrea. "Place Replaced: Colonial Nostalgia and *pied-noir* Pilgrimages to Malta." *Cultural Anthropology* 18, no. 3 (2003): 329–64.
———. *Colonial Memory and Postcolonial Europe: Maltese Settlers in Algeria and France*. Bloomington: Indiana University Press, 2006.
Weber, Eugen. *Peasants into Frenchmen: The Modernization of Rural France*. Stanford, CA: Stanford University Press, 1976.

CHAPTER 2

Quezon's Hospitality
Transitional Asylum and Humanitarian Intimacies during Philippine Decolonization, 1935–1941

James Pangilinan

In 2014, the United Nations High Commissioner for Refugees encouraged the Philippines to prolong a storied "tradition" of hospitality by accommodating recent refugees.[1] The UNHCR cited Section 47(b) of the Philippines' Immigration Act of 1940, which permitted the president to "admit aliens who are refugees for religious, political and racial reasons for humanitarian reasons, and when not opposed to public interest."[2] This law appeared precocious, as it preceded by eleven years the 1951 Refugee Convention, which codified definitions for *refugee* and *persecution*. While the UNHCR cites this asylum clause to advance "burden sharing" by strategically localizing refuge in the global South, the claim that the Philippines set a precedent obscures a messier story of hospitality in the Philippines shaped through shifting relations of imperial rule and attempted decolonization.

A more critical reader of the UNHCR's rhetoric might ask, "What is missed by conveniently citing the 1940 Immigration Act's asylum clause as exemplifying a 'tradition' of Filipino hospitality?" Nevertheless, we may still consider why this storied tradition remains attractive to international and Filipino audiences alike. The recent film *Quezon's Game* (2019) has popularly memorialized Filipinos' "tradition" of hospitality by circulating an imaginative story of how welcoming Jewish refugees factored into the shaping of Philippine independence from 1935 to 1941. In this period, American and Filipino elites negotiated not only independence but also the curious potential for Filipino nationalism to be refashioned through hosting displaced European Jews, when most European-American states rejected refugees. Undoubtedly, there existed a domestic landscape of conflicting interests and some Filipino nativism. But the popular framing of *Quezon's Game* usefully narrates the humanitarian potential of refuge in the global South as an anticolonial undertaking. Instead of underlining a legal precedent (as the UNHCR emphasizes), *Quezon's Game* provocatively asks, why did the Philippine president Manuel Quezon welcome refugees as a national cause advancing decolonization? This chapter details the circulation of *Quezon's Game* and the transitional context that the film popularizes through an accessible depiction of colonial Filipinos attempting to make humanitarian history even before achieving independence.

Dramatizing Filipino Hospitality

Centering an unlikely footnote in the interwar history of the Philippines, Matthew Rosen's Philippine-filmed, ABS-CBN-produced *Quezon's Game* opened to popular and critical acclaim in May 2019. Featuring performances from Raymond Bagatsing as Manuel Quezon and Rachel Alejandro as Aurora Quezon, the film's release quickly became the talk of the town. For a moment, it even competed with Hollywood blockbusters—no small feat in a market still dominated by American films.

The unlikely humanitarian story of Quezon's hospitality brings to light the considerable domestic negotiations and international maneuvering enabling refugee rescue even prior to the Philippines' independence. On the one hand, this humanitarian gesture played well internationally: Quezon took a morally distinctive, symbolic upper hand against the Philippines' American colonial rulers, who mostly rejected displaced Jews. On the other hand, this gesture also embodied Philippine society's inequalities, which formed through shared colonial connections among Philippine-American elite. In other words, these colonial relations provided the fraught historical conditions for the Philippines' refugee hospitality.

Yet the popular rendering of Filipinos' transitional receptiveness to host refugees has also reentered domestic Filipinos' consciousness through a series of parallel media stories and popular films recently released and transnationally circulated.[3] Filmic depictions and journalistic reception have generally conveyed a heroic account equating the Philippine president to a colonial Oskar Schindler.[4] But actual emphasis must also be placed on Manuel Quezon's intimate ties with diasporic Jewish organizers and US colonial officials, who together effectively shaped refuge in the sovereignty-aspiring Philippines. Of all the popular, memorializing accounts of the Philippines' transitional hospitality, what I find most fruitful is the way in which these relations of hospitality between US and Filipino elites comprise the narrative focus of Matthew Rosen's film *Quezon's Game*. Socializing with the likes of US commissioner Paul McNutt, Dwight Eisenhower, and prominent, Manila-based Jewish entrepreneurs Alex and Herbert Frieder, Quezon came to devise alternative aid while simply enjoying informal parlor games. Such intimate spaces, wherein Quezon served as host to American and Jewish diasporic refugee advocates, were also pivotal in shaping the Philippines' transition to independence. By suggestively juxtaposing Filipinos' larger drive to independence with Quezon's political gamble of responding to refugees, *Quezon's Game* offers an imaginative story that provides the Filipino "nation" a kind of moral self-depiction exemplified by Manuel Quezon's reputedly "exceptional" response. Such presentations of the Philippines' hospitality appear even more "heroic," for Filipino viewers, because this humanitarian response preceded independence and served as an expression of emergent sovereignty on an international stage.

Although *Quezon's Game* suffers from uneven performances by relatively A-list Filipino actors paired with rather underwhelming B-list American talent, the film dramatically captures the peculiar manner that the charismatic Filipino president Manuel Quezon sought to balance the strategic dance toward independence while struggling to convince US officials and fellow Filipinos to mount a humanitarian response to increasing Jewish displacement from Europe. Sympathy for dislocated Jews was rarely acted on during this period. American unwillingness to help refugees is outlandishly exemplified in the film by the US State Department's counsel general Lawrence Cartwright. Portraying the anti-Semitism prevalent even among US bureaucratic circles of the era, Cartwright (played by Paul Holmes) questions the wisdom of hosting displaced Jews during Filipinos' independence drive. For Cartwright, even though he held no affinity for Nazism, his discrimination against Jews colors his appraisal of Quezon and his collaborators' proposal of Jewish resettlement. Upon hearing of Quezon's requests for additional visas to facilitate Jewish migration to the Philippines, Cartwright expresses repugnance at the prospect of introducing Jewish refugees by going so far as claiming that Jews are worse than African Americans, who in Cartwright's racist language and anti-Black logic at least seem easier to segregate according to phenotypic difference (unlike European Jews). For Cartwright, Jewish resettlement thus seemed to offer only further political risks by injecting a new racial question during an uncertain transition to Philippine independence.

While Cartwright outlandishly plays the spoiler to Quezon, Paul McNutt, and Herbert and Alex Frieder's rescue plans, much of *Quezon's Game* is more generatively devoted to sharper, suggestive dialogue among Filipino elites expressing their somewhat more subtle misgivings at refugee resettlement. As we shall see, opposing Filipino nationalists generally favored prioritizing independence and Filipino welfare as opposed to charity for racialized Jews.

Philippine-American War veteran Emilio Aguinaldo and fellow Nacionalista Party member Sergio Osmeña appear in the film as influential domestic voices contrasting Quezon's moral concern. Unlike the power-hungry Quezon caricatured in the era's American press, Raymond Bagatsing's Quezon is depicted as positioned morally above the political fray. Quezon even appears heroically sacrificial, insofar as he is willing to risk his political fortunes by tethering Jewish rescue to the very possibility of independence. Thus, the film accentuates the narrative drama of how Quezon broke from his party and prioritized Jewish rescue even after becoming weakened by a relapse of tuberculosis. Eventually, his deteriorating health and the backlash resulting from his refugee support threaten to undo everything he sought to accomplish. In a word, *Quezon's Game* spares no intrigue. Such drama is fictionally heightened when an SS officer is stationed in Manila. With these high personal stakes and embodied risks, planning even a modest rescue mission would have to be undertaken surreptitiously—lest Nazis intercede from afar.

Hospitality as Transitional Exchange

Just as scholars of colonialism have shown how domestic politics, empire, and geopolitics play out through intimate interactions, *Quezon's Game* exhibits how seemingly everyday scenes of hospitality provide the generative basis for Jewish rescue as an outcome of Filipinos' aspirational renegotiation of American colonial rule. But as a far-flung part of America's overseas empire, the Philippines seemed to factor curiously into international responses to Europe's Jewish "refugee problem." Under the suspecting eyes of Cartwright and German onlookers, negotiations had to take place within informal spaces where Quezon frequently entertained guests over poker, cigars, and brandy. The day's legislative affairs, requests for state favors, and even refugee aid were all similarly shaped within intimate spaces of political collaboration and elite homosocial camaraderie. In this way, *Quezon's Game* offers an immediate representation of Filipino hospitality in practice. At the same time, the film lends useful insight on the substantial impact of smaller, intimate spaces for conceiving state policy, geopolitics, and specifically humanitarian efforts.[5]

To appreciate why this US territory offered refuge, one must examine how Philippine-American political relations in the 1930s centered around a collaboratively staged "decolonization." Under an ostensibly "benevolent" American colonial rule, elite Filipinos were subjected to liberal educational programs and thereby recruited as local protégés trained to gradually replace US colonial officials.[6] Through this tutelary process, Filipino nationalists also competed among one another to satisfy the hierarchical standards of the "capacity to responsibly exercise power in the colonial state."[7] Rivalries among Filipino elites often led to inconsistent positions shifting between confrontation and collusion with American colonial rule. In other words, "decolonization" was refashioned according to elite political partnerships, strategic contingencies, and individually pursued redefinitions, including Quezon's attempts to tie Philippine independence to Jewish rescue.

Quezon's response to Jewish humanitarian advocacy followed this pattern of distinction-making and competition against the contrasting ambitions of his domestic and American colonial rivals. The necessity of welcoming refugees proved to be a matter of considerable debate even for members of his own party. In a pivotal scene, following a botched attempt to bribe the German ambassador to obtain the refugees' exit visas, his former rival Sergio Osmeña furiously questions why the Philippines must receive refugees. Faced with Osmeña's criticism that not even the United States is willing to accommodate more refugees (in reference Jewish refugees from the MS *St. Louis* who were kept from docking on the US mainland), Quezon asserts he cannot "wait and sit around for another country to do something. I'm not going to turn away those in need when I should have the power to save them. I am not like Roosevelt!" A distraught Osmeña retorts, "This is not a pissing contest" playing out with Quezon's willingness contrasting with Roosevelt's humanitarian limitations.

On the one hand, the Philippines' receptiveness presented a moral contrast to American hesitance regarding Jewish migrants. On the other hand, Quezon touted the additional benefits of welcoming Jewish refugees to counter discontent. When Osmeña exhorts Quezon to "save some of that bravado for our Filipino peasants, who need your service just as much as those refugees," the latter deflects this zero-sum framing of citizen-bounded responsibilities with a win-win counterargument. For Quezon, even Filipino peasants would benefit from injecting the skilled labor of Jewish refugees into the nascent Philippine national economy. Journalism from the period echoed Quezon's counterargument. On 24 April 1940, the *Philippines Herald* reported that any "Policy on Jews" formulated by Quezon's administration would be based on the "Hospitality of P.I. [Philippine Islands] To Harassed Race."[8] As Quezon asserted, "Filipinos are going to realize that in allowing these few refugees to come ... we are not only performing a humanitarian act, but we are, in the end, going to profit from this humane act as is always the case." Any relief for displaced Jews promised future returns, especially since displaced Jews were selected from asylum petitions by "doctors, lawyers, engineers, scientists, etc." Economic benefits were expected by inviting Jewish professionals and active contributors, as seemingly attested by existing diasporic enterprises like the Frieder brothers' Helena Cigar Company.

Alex and Herbert Frieder's pragmatic friendship with Quezon arose from existing Filipino "cultures of hospitality" and colonially espoused "cultures of Filipino-American sociability" recounted by American commentators following the Filipino-American War.[9] Civil spaces of shared intimacy were important in easing tensions and inviting Filipino elites within the colonial project of postwar state building. In the later ten-year transition as a US commonwealth (1935–45), similar spaces of hospitality were centered by Filipino elites to showcase their elevated status as hosts aspiring to sovereign control. Filipinos thus sought to reverse imposed subordination as pupils and guests to imperially defined, racially hierarchical liberalism under American rule. In contrast to the hierarchies of the early American colonial period, Filipino elites during the Commonwealth era could now serve as hosts to anyone they so pleased, including refugees.

But acting as nearly sovereign hosts also articulated with Filipino elites' designs for continued domestic dominance. Indeed, the elite political dynamics and patronage practices established under colonial democracy would shape the trajectory for the Philippines' "independence without decolonization."[10] These conservative patterns for forming enduring relationships serving Filipino elites is evidenced in *Quezon's Game* when McNutt and Alex Frieder try recruiting Manuel Quezon into finding a way to convince the German ambassador to provide exit permits for eligible refugees. To avoid drawing unwanted attention from the SS officer stationed at the German embassy, Quezon suggests that they throw a presidential ball as an amicable interface with the ambassador. Through the extension of social graces and liberally poured brandy, Quezon is thus depicted as skillfully exhibiting Filipinos' refigured position as hosts who can even skirt the wary eyes of Nazis and US officials. Quezon's manner of hosting even opposed parties is framed to exhibit his ability to renegotiate and reposition the Philippines under continued yet waning foreign control. Extending protection to Europe's racial others could signal an end to US colonial rule according to terms laid out by Quezon and allied Filipino elites.

Approximating Independence

Even prior to governance under American occupation, native elites in the Philippines were accustomed to creating relationships of political dependence, hospitality, and indebtedness with foreign actors in order to renegotiate imperial intrusion and foreign rule in their own land. Existing accounts attempt to explain the emergence of the Commonwealth's asylum offer as the sole project of US high commissioner Paul McNutt.[11] But limitations arise from a biographically driven narrative that individually centers US colonial leaders while overlooking American dependence on Filipino elites. By turning American control over migration to and from the Philippines into an issue for Filipinos to rally around, *Quezon's Game* vividly depicts how responding to Jewish displacement offered the ailing Manuel Quezon a gesture and avenue to pursue "decolonization" on elite Filipinos' own terms.

Put conversely, Quezon's efforts to reshape Philippine "independence" provided the mixed grounds for Filipinos' expression of qualified solidarity with Jewish refugees. Although from the very onset, "Filipinization" was the operative logic of US colonialism in the Philippines, where power was gradually delegated to US-trained Filipinos, the Commonwealth period from 1935 to 1945 evidenced how political power remained entrenched in the hands of a national elite and a handful of political parties. Basically, only a few factions of Filipino elites competed among themselves by voicing vacillating demands for independence or American retention, statehood, or dominion status.[12] Quezon's Nacionalista Party figured as one of usually two parties since 1898 that rhetorically championed claims to independence (immediate or otherwise) while privately or publicly questioning the timing and terms of "decolonization."

Quezon's Game places the independence question as central to how Quezon thought of refugees by maintaining his hold on domestic politics. Indeed, historian Aruna Gopinath apologetically contends that Quezon gambled prospects of Filipino independence by undercutting, delaying and redirecting independence legislation advanced by his main rival Sergio Osmeña so as not to appear to be "playing second fiddle" to Osmeña.[13] The film hints at lingering competitions between Osmeña and Quezon, even though they share cordial scenes where Osmeña and his fellow emissary Manuel Roxas are scheduled to visit Washington to lower excise taxes on Philippine crops. But, pivotally, Quezon's "real play" is to renegotiate scheduled independence sooner, "during [his] lifetime."

While this aspiration is portrayed as intensifying with Quezon's tuberculosis relapse, Quezon also sent Osmeña and Roxas to reconsider the independence timeline for political reasons. It served as a move in the "power game" Quezon sought to play "with the intellect and skill of a master strategist."[14] For political gain, Quezon undermined his rivals' claims to secure independence by organizing opposition to the initial independence framework—the Hare-Hawes-Cutting Act formulated during Osmeña and Manuel Roxas's 1933 mission to Washington. Under pressure to scrap this bill, the Philippine Assembly rejected their proposal. Yet their bill provided the blueprint for Quezon's preferred 1934 Tydings-McDuffie Act. Burnishing his anticolonial credentials before the Commonwealth's 1935 elections, Quezon himself went to Washington to nominally renegotiate independence phased in after ten years. "Staking his political future on one great gamble," Quezon struck a coup by triumphantly returning from Washington with "the same old act but for a change of some fifty words."[15] These nominal revisions reinforced Quezon's dominance over rivals including Osmeña, Roxas, and Emilio Aguinaldo. Such power grabs led some commentators, such as socialist Pedro Abad Santos, to warn of imminent descent into a dictatorship—a palpable fear given the era's fascism.

With growing fears of a dictatorship, Nacionalistas resorted to "populist" strategies of welfare and social relief. Quezon's concern for refugees echoed this stylization as both the "friend of the poor" and the "warrior-hero needed to lead them to the promised land of independence."[16] Returning from Washington with a recycled independence framework, Quezon also came back with New Deal–inspired "social justice" projects intended to appease "forgotten" Filipino "masses" through pursuing development initiatives across the whole archipelago.[17] But "Social Justice" reinforced his patronage networks instead of amounting to actually equitable reform. In Quezon's intimately conceived view, "Social Justice or its equivalent has always been *an urge in me*. As President ... I had fought with all vigor for the rights and welfare of the working man."[18] Quezon's social justice struggle amounted more to a reciprocal transaction of debt between capital and labor: "When I declared in my inaugural address ... I did not hesitate to declare that Labor is more essential to Capital because the factory of all wealth in this world is an indebtedness to Labor ... [which] is entitled to a latitude of fairness because the security of the State depends upon it." Debt and reciprocal obligation—not dispossession and capitalist exploitation—are the ties that bind capital and labor in Quezon's vision. In other words, "social justice" articulated with Quezon's politics of intimate collaboration with business leaders or American officials.

Foreign yet Domestic Refuge

Focusing on this personal collaborative dynamic, *Quezon's Game* highlights the way that solidarity with refugees can become entangled—while simultaneously increasing tension—with domestically focused social justice. Much of this tension is depicted through dialogue that relays how Quezon's moral concern conflicts with rival preoccupations voiced by his counterpart Sergio Osmeña. While the latter sought to prioritize domestic poverty over refugee needs, Quezon suggests that Jewish misery exceeds even Filipinos' mundane needs: "Our people have rights ... the Jews do not. Our people need our help to prosper. The Jews need my help to escape slavery, torture, execution." These conflicting duties and needs arose in a moment when the Philippines' political transition coincided with intensifying Jewish persecution following the 1935 Nuremberg laws, Germany's March 1938 invasion of Austria, *Kristallnacht* in November 1938, and the annexation of Poland in 1939. These events outraged Filipinos even from afar. Yet unlike other Filipinos, Quezon's immediate outrage was prompted by a visit to Paris and Berlin in 1937 to promote Philippine interests abroad.[19] According to the president's grandson Manuel L. Quezon III, the hostile appearance of Nazi soldiers "shook" Quezon's wife Doña Aurora Aragon to her core.[20] Not surprisingly, Quezon came under considerable pressure to respond to this dark turn.

Condemnation of Jewish persecution grew following the publicized violence of *Kristallnacht*. Even as Jewish social economic dislocation had existed for some time, outrage in the Philippines solidified following *Kristallnacht*. A major "Indignation Rally" convened at the Ateneo University, where Jewish and Christian leaders joined "civil society" and more radical opposition groups, including the Philippine Independent Church founded by Gregorio Aglipay.[21] While some remained wary of involvement in the Jewish refugee question, Filipinos visibly expressed sympathy for Jewish refugees through early Filipino editorials, public rallies, and even some Americans' appreciation of the Philippines as a potential refuge.[22] In this way, *Quezon's Game* rearticulates the positive appraisal of Philippine refuge through recirculating popular international encouragement of localized accommodation of the displaced in the global South.

Yet the film underscores limitations in the way Filipinos' willingness to accommodate refugees conflicted with Americans' salient anti-Semitism, which buttressed the colonial metropole's distancing of Jewish refugees. On the one hand, Quezon could act as a strong-handed host, whose mostly uncontested dominance over domestic and international Philippine affairs allowed the larger game over independence, trade, and refugee aid to play out smoothly. On the other hand, this did not always play out without friction expressed by his fellow Filipino politicians. As *Quezon's Game* dramatically conveys, one issue, which complicated Quezon and the Frieder brothers' rescue plan, was the way American and European racial inequalities did not fully resonate. There existed some disharmony between Filipinos' experience of US colonialism and the racial persecution of European Jews. Before the film nears some narrative resolution, announcing an "Open Door" policy for Jewish asylum-seekers, Osmeña still voices exasperation with Quezon, who refuses to put aside his seeming obsession with the Jewish question over what could be best for the Nacionalista Party. For Osmeña, Quezon's stance risks additional vulnerability to their domestic rival Emilio Aguinaldo, who wields the refugee issue against them. Dismayed by Osmeña's advice to cease offering asylum, Quezon colorfully suggests, "When you go to the White House, use their toilet." A surprised Osmeña asks, "Are you joking?" Quezon insists, "Use their toilet, Osmeña, for your countryman." Osmeña questions why he would have to go to separate facilities: "I know how Americans treat the Negros, but I am not a Negro!" But Quezon highlights, "It doesn't say 'Negro,' it says 'Colored.' As in not white. That's you, me, and every one of your countrymen. We are only allowed in the White House because we have seventeen million votes behind us." While anti-Black racism and American colonialism are mutually reinforcing, it takes some insistence to forge resonance between Filipinos' colonial subjection, Jewish persecution, and anti-Black segregation. After Quezon insists on a racial analogy and alignment against the kind of racist hostility prolonging US colonial rule, Osmeña quietly relents and finally agrees to renegotiate independence with the aim of enabling Filipinos to set their own immigration policy as a key point of contention. As Quezon reasons, the juxtaposition of Filipinos' potential hospitality for Jewish refugees with Americans' mundane racial hostility underlines the need for placing the Philippines under sovereign Filipino control. Being able to welcome anyone thus becomes imaginatively imbued with anticolonial possibilities in *Quezon's Game*, because hosting refugees could elevate Filipinos' position against the subordinations of US colonialism and racial liberalism.

By reframing the stakes of Philippine independence, welcoming refugees offered more than merely another one of Quezon's self-serving attempts to appease elites and working Filipinos, as was the case with Quezon's banking on "the emotional capital of the independence issue."[23] Rather, the film dramatically suggests that Quezon's increasing awareness of his mortality necessitated a legacy of redemptive benevolence beyond self-aggrandizement. *Quezon's Game* reaches its dramatic arc when Quezon delivers a rousing televised speech resembling his February 1939 "Open Door" policy proclamation. The film concludes by suggesting that the stakes extend beyond the technical challenge of the Philippines seeking to control its own immigration and borders through a new immigration law. Rather, Filipino hospitality could serve as a rallying cry advancing actual independence.

Quezon's Dramatic Entry at Évian

Quezon's Game presents a memorializing story that recalls actual depictions circulated during the fraught prewar period. Before Quezon's "Open Door" policy announcement, American president Franklin Roosevelt organized an ambitious thirty-two-nation conference to coordinate refugee relief. The 1938 Évian Conference has been widely panned as failing at delivering an adequate response.[24] One reason for this failure was agreement from the start that resulting assistance had to conform with states' existing immigration laws in a period of considerable immigration restriction exemplified by the stringent US quota system in place since 1921. With Depression-era labor pressures, increasingly restrictive sentiment in Europe and the United States led to official and popular pressure to situate Jewish resettlement elsewhere. Latin America presented one alternative landscape for receiving displaced Jews during a period when immigration to Palestine was limited by the British Colonial Office.[25] While Zionist-leaning scholars suggest that the reason Évian failed was because Palestine remained off the table of options, considered non-Zionist Jewish advocates including the Frieder brothers of Manila and the New York–based Joint Distribution Committee collectively sought out alternative havens beyond "Zion." Sidelining Palestine from Évian's geography of possible settlement could not alone explain the overall failure of European and American states to mount an effective refugee response, even following *Kristallnacht*.

Against this international backdrop of limited refuge, Quezon grandly signaled Philippine support for Jewish refugees.[26] In December 1938, news broke from Évian that the Philippines welcomed refugees. In so doing, Quezon suggested the Philippines could prove to be more generous than Western states and most of Latin America—except for Santo Domingo—which mostly rejected Jews.[27] Claiming some moral high ground compared to the Philippines' colonial and geopolitical hegemons, Quezon's staging of Filipino hospitality offered a "means of expressing and reversing a pattern of domination" upheld by Euro-American refugee rejection (see figure 2.1).[28]

However, like other alternative settlement offers in the Dominican Republic, British and Dutch Guyana, Australia, and Bolivia, the Philippines offered a limited option. Each settlement project only conceived of accommodating no more than a few hundred refugees.[29] However limited, these few options were nevertheless seriously considered by the Intergovernmental Committee on Refugees (IGC), Évian's successor forum. Struggling to manage German demands of externalizing its Jewish population through overseas "resettlement," IGC negotiators sought to avoid setting a precedent for other European states

Figure 2.1. • "A Home for the Persecuted," Alfonso Torres, Manila, 1940. Courtesy of the Franklin Delano Roosevelt Library.

contemplating a fix to their "ethnic" problems by pursuing policies "compelling political, religious or 'racial' minorities to flee as refugees."[30] Given these overlapping concerns, any option for Jewish settlement necessitated careful framing, advocacy, and considerable persuasion. Proposals for refugee settlement were often framed as advancing asylum countries' "development" needs. For states emerging from colonial dominance and political economic exploitation, like the transitional Philippines, refugees were positively cast as populations who could offer specialized labor for a newly independent national economy. However, in the rhetoric invoked by Quezon and the rescue plan's publicists, these contributions took on moral terms as expected reciprocation for offered hospitality.

Quezon's Protection and Patronage

Balancing Filipinos' material demands with moral imperatives to assist refugees presented challenges and symbolic possibilities. Quezon rhetorically sought to translate humanitarian motives into filial terms of paternal protection, hosting, and indebting intimacy. Such reframed reasons were similar to the terms mobilized in his "Social Justice" gestures. In the popular press, Quezon similarly tried circulating a depiction of the Philippines as a welcoming "home for the persecuted."[31] Upon visiting an early refugee-run farm in the Marikina Valley, Alfonso R. Torres, a journalist from *Philippines Free Press*, relayed the storied suffering and resilience attested by refugees.[32] Morris Grimm stood out to Torres for his remarkably toothless appearance. In the Philippines, Grimm would finally receive dental help after losing his family and teeth at the hands of Nazi concentration camp guards. Morris was one of several hundred refugees welcomed at Marikina Hall, a model refugee farm built on Quezon's own land north of the new capital Quezon City. Not only was a new "home" in the Philippines at the invitation of the Jewish Refugee Committee of Manila on offer in Marikina, but the "Jews at Marikina Hall" also became grateful beneficiaries of Manuel Quezon's accumulation of power and capital.

Put simply, refuge in the Philippines came at the behest of Quezon, whose land and shaping of Philippine independence appeared to benefit even non-citizen displaced Jews. Popular stories of Filipino hospitality, such as *Quezon's Game*, incompletely detail and thus hint at the manner that formerly persecuted refugees became the beneficiaries of Quezon's intimate and paternal accumulation of power. Unlike contemporaneous criticism of Quezon's increasingly strong-handed rule, his offer of protection lent a compassionate veneer to the Philippines' international image.[33] Ironically, when asked of their opinion of Quezon, one refugee at the Marikina model farm observed, "Herr

Quezon strikes me as fatherly, a leader who is inclined to be paternalistic in his ways. As for Hitler, let's not talk about the blankety-blank." A peculiar irony of Quezon's hospitality is that he shared the totalitarian tendencies of Hitler. Yet, although the Philippine president appreciated the fascist leader's style of nationalist leadership amid the trials of 1930s upheaval, Quezon's authoritarian inclinations could be put to other uses.[34]

Protected by "Fatherly Herr Quezon," Jewish refugees expressed gratitude for his hospitality and "freedom" from racial violence. As Torres observes, though this early stage of the "Jewish refugee experiment . . . is rich in idealism, but virtually lacking in cash," refugees at Marikina Hall appeared optimistic, and "the general feeling that prevails among them is one of gratitude, gratefulness for the opportunity to live free among their fellow men."[35] But, even if accommodations outside Manila were certainly freer than in Germany, hospitality under Quezon's sovereign protection entailed ambiguities and asymmetric expectations expressed through giving, gratitude, and reciprocation. Anticipated returns included morally and symbolically burnishing Quezon's international image. In this symbolic manner, refugee accommodation tied to Philippine decolonization remained marred by the same political and social inequities that Quezon and his allies sought to preserve.

Rereading the Final Scenes of Decolonization and Jewish Refuge in the Philippines

Celebratory narratives of refuge in the global South can overlook historical complications and the tensions of colonialism setting uneven grounds for refuge, as evidenced by the transitional Philippines' welcoming of Jewish refugees. The reproduced series of international rhetoric, such as the UNHCR's, and popular depictions, such as *Quezon's Game*, present stories that dramatize, and potentially exaggerate, the humanitarian potential of hospitality in the global South.

Nevertheless, there are valid reasons for tracing popular humanitarian depictions of national hospitality, distinctive care for refugees, and the moral benevolence of anticolonial elites. Studying how such stories circulate enables us to appreciate the way national constructions of humanitarian memory and reputed "lessons learned" remain entangled with the complications of colonialism and the ambivalent attempts that even elite colonial subjects make to reshape imperial relations through humanitarian action. *Quezon's Game* memorializes and turns one of the interwar period's rare rescue plans into an accessible narrative of the Filipino nation formed through hosting otherwise rejected refugees. By serving as hosts, Filipino elites translated and rewrote colonial relations into a renewed story of national hospitality and receptivity to displaced others—others who would nevertheless be subjected to the messy, fraught, and implicating processes of American colonialism and elite-framed decolonization.

Through the sensational story of Jewish rescue, Quezon's dramatized generosity underscores how humanitarian memories can be reimagined through the moral fantasies of the nation and how such fantasies can overlook asymmetric grounds of colonial intimacies and imperial relations lasting beyond formal decolonization. With Jewish exiles and American officials newly positioned as guests to Quezon's nearly independent nation, intimate gatherings could occasion less plausible promises of hosting even more Jewish refugees than previously imagined. While the film maintains restraint in keeping with the early negotiations over settling refugees in Manila, in fact, at a luncheon with McNutt and the Frieders, Quezon's vision for potential Jewish settlement mushroomed into inflated prospects for "resettling as many ... refugees as we cared to in Mindanao ... [which] is big enough to support as many people as Luzon ... we could settle a million refugees in Mindanao."[36] With Quezon's dramatic flair, such "lavish hospitality" was neither wholly disinterested nor unparalleled by contemporary undertakings, for instance, by his Dominican contemporary Rafael Trujillo.[37]

The eventual failure and eclipse of Quezon's rescue efforts were not entirely forgotten through the unfortunate course of World War II. Hinting at postwar complications of decolonization in the Middle East and Mindanao, Filipino journalist Alfonso Torres asserts that Jewish refugees in the Philippines had another "big task before them." This comprised settling "unpopulated" spaces with the same steadfastness as "their brethren who revitalized Palestine and established it, after years of noble sacrifice, on a sound economic footing."[38] Doubtless, these expansive visions of "virgin" lands overlooked Indigenous communities, as was the case in Palestine. Comparisons were palpable for Alex Frieder, who reported after his luncheon with Quezon, "If refugees want to settle in Mindanao, it will be a bigger project than Palestine. The land is more fertile than Palestine, there are more minerals, timber ... it is the richest land in the Philippines."[39] Clearly, trafficking in comparisons and racial stereotypes of Jewish hyperproductivity remain excessive and questionable. And as with other long-distance depictions of the nation, such expansive fantasies of diasporic abundance and Global South refuge would go on to have far-flung significance beyond the Philippines itself. As late as November of 2019, *Quezon's Game* would be played at Philippine embassies abroad, cinemas in Israel—from Tel Aviv to Jerusalem—and even at the United Nations.[40] While presenting this film serves as a strategic reminder in the face of Israeli campaigns to deport Filipina caregivers, this wider circulation of Quezon's humanitarian collaboration with diasporic Jewish advocates has helped sustain compelling moral fictions of Filipinos' potential for care far and near.

James Pangilinan is a PhD candidate in human geography at the University of British Columbia. His work focuses on diasporic humanitarianism, decolonization, and transnational asylum politics arising relationally through the Philippines. He is currently completing a dissertation entitled *Filipino Hospitality and Transpacific Spaces of Humanitarian Practice*.

Notes

1. Kerblat, "Most Urgent Story"; Penamente, "Nine Waves of Refugees."
2. *Philippines Star*, "Filipinos Helping Refugees."
3. Rosen, *Quezon's Game*; Hodge and Scott-Johnson, *Rescue in the Philippines*; Hernandez, *Last Manilaners*.
4. *San Diego Reader*, "Quezon's Game"; Quismorio, "House to Honor People."
5. Pain and Staeheli. "Introduction."
6. Kramer, *Blood of Government*, 191.
7. Kramer, *Blood of Government*, 192.
8. *Philippines Herald*, "Quezon's Policy on Jews," 24 April 1940, NARA, RG350, box 1388, folder 2.
9. Kramer, *Blood of Government*, 188–89.
10. McCoy, "The Philippines."
11. Kotlowski, "Breaching the Paper Walls."
12. McCoy, "The Philippines"; Kotlowski, "Independence or Not?"
13. Gopinath, *Manuel L. Quezon*, 17–21.
14. Gopinath, *Manuel L. Quezon*, 72.
15. Gopinath, *Manuel L. Quezon*, 74.
16. Gopinath, *Manuel L. Quezon*, 21.
17. Friend, "What Kind of Nationalist Was Quezon?"
18. Mistica, *Manuel L. Quezon*, 97.
19. Kotlowski, "Independence or Not?" 886.
20. Kotlowski, "Independence or Not?" 886.
21. *Philippines Herald*, "Local Condemnation of Nazi Action Voiced at Meeting," 21 November 1938, Franklin and Eleanor Roosevelt Library, NARA, RG350, box 1338, folder 2, no. 28943.
22. *Graphic Magazine*, "Wandering Jews," 21 July 1938; *Philippines Herald*, "Indignation Rally" 19 November 1938, NARA, RG350, box 1338, folder 2, no. 28943; *Manila Daily Bulletin*, "As American Editors See Us: Jews to the Philippines," 16 September 1938, NARA, RG350, box 1338, folder 2, no. 28943.
23. Friend, "What Kind of Nationalist Was Quezon?" 89.
24. Smith, "Silence and Refusal."
25. Feingold, *Politics of Rescue*, 31–33; Wells, *Tropical Zion*, 31.
26. *Manila Bulletin*, "London Hears of Quezon's Plan to Open Up Mindanao to Jews," 14 February 1939, Jorge Vargas Scrapbooks, vol. 26 (January–March 1939), Vargas Museum and Library.
27. Wells, *Tropical Zion*.
28. Herzfeld, "'As in Your Own House,'" 79.
29. Rovner, *In the Shadow of Zion*.

30. Walter Adams, "The Evian Conference July 1938: Provisional Memorandum in the Future of Assistance to Refugees," James G MacDonald Papers, Columbia University, box 31, folder 5.
31. Torres, "Home for the Persecuted."
32. Torres, "Home for the Persecuted."
33. Rovner, *In the Shadow of Zion*.
34. Rovner, *In the Shadow of Zion*.
35. Torres, "Home for the Persecuted."
36. Letter from Henry Frieder to Bruno Schachter, Refugee Economic Corporation, 8 December 1938, box 8, folder 2, Myron C. Taylor Papers, Franklin and Eleanor Roosevelt Library.
37. Quezon feared being upstaged by Dominican Republic dictator Rafael Trujillo. Harry Woodring to Cordell Hull, "Translation of Radiogram," 3 December 1938, NARA, RG59, box 6 folder 11.
38. Torres, "Home for the Persecuted."
39. Letter from Henry Frieder to Bruno Schachter, Refugee Economic Corporation, 8 December 1938, box 8, folder 2, Myron C. Taylor Papers, Roosevelt Library.
40. Salaverria, "DFA to Remind Israel"; Marquez, "PH Film 'Quezon's Game' Premiers"; Pangilinan, Peralta, and Attewell, "Between Caregiving and Soldiering."

References

Feingold, Henry. *The Politics of Rescue*. New Brunswick, NJ: Rutgers University Press, 1970.
Friend, Theodore. "What Kind of Nationalist Was Quezon?" *Philippine Historical Association Historical Bulletin* 22 (1978): 86–92.
Gopinath, Aruna. *Manuel L. Quezon: The Tutelary Democrat*. Quezon City: New Day, 1987.
Hernandez, Nico, dir. *The Last Manilaners*. Documentary. Philippines: iWant, 2019.
Herzfeld, Michael. "'As in Your Own House': Hospitality, Ethnography, and the Stereotype of Mediterranean Society." *Honor and Shame and the Unity of the Mediterranean* 22 (1987): 85–89.
Hodge, Russell, and Cynthia Scott-Johnson, dirs. *Rescue in the Philippines: Refuge from the Holocaust*. Documentary, Dreamscape Media, 2013.
Kerblat, Bernard. "The Most Urgent Story of Our Time." *UNHCR Philippines*, 20 June 2014. https://www.unhcr.org/ph/10715-urgent-story-time.html.
Kotlowski, Dean. "Breaching the Paper Walls: Paul V. McNutt and Jewish Refugees to the Philippines, 1938–1939." *Diplomatic History* 33, no. 5 (2009): 865–96.
———. "Independence or Not? Paul V. McNutt, Manuel L. Quezon, and the Re-examination of Philippine Independence, 1937–9." *International History Review* 32, no. 3 (2010): 501–31.
Kramer, Paul. *The Blood of Government: Race, Empire, the United States, and the Philippines*. Durham: University of North Carolina Press, 2006.
Marquez, Consuelo. "PH Film 'Quezon's Game' Premiers in Tel Aviv, Israel." *Philippine Inquirer*, 15 November 2019. https://globalnation.inquirer.net/182090/ph-film-quezons-game-premieres-in-tel-aviv-israel.
McCoy, Alfred. "The Philippines: Independence without Decolonization." In *Asia—The Winning of Independence*, edited by Robin Jeffrey, 23–62. Hong Kong: Macmillan, 1981.

———. "Quezon's Commonwealth." In *Philippine Colonial Democracy*, edited by Ruby R. Paredes. Quezon City: Ateneo de Manila University Press, 1989.

Mistica, Sergio. *Manuel L. Quezon, a Character Sketch*. Manila: UST Press, 1948.

Pain, Rachel, and Lynn Staeheli. "Introduction: Intimacy—Geopolitics and Violence." *Area* 46, no. 4 (2014): 344–47.

Pangilinan, James, Christine Peralta, and Wesley Attewell. "Between Caregiving and Soldiering: Filipina Non-citizens and Settler Militarisms in Israel." *Amerasia Journal* 46, no. 2 (2020): 183–99.

Philippines Star. "Filipinos Helping Refugees: A Noble Tradition, a Way to Give Back." 24 August 2015.

Penamente, Laurice. "Nine Waves of Refugees in the Philippines." UNHCR, 7 June 2017. https://www.unhcr.org/ph/11886-9wavesrefugees.html.

Quismorio, Ellson. "House to Honor People behind Highly Acclaimed Filipino Film 'Quezon's Game.'" *Manila Bulletin*, 2 December 2019.

Rosen, Matthew E., dir. *Quezon's Game*. Philippines: Star Cinema, Kinetek, 2019.

Rovner, Adam. *In the Shadow of Zion*. New York: New York University Press, 2014.

Salaverria, Leila. "DFA to Remind Israel of PH Rescue of Jews in Quezon's time." *Philippine Inquirer*, 20 August 2019. https://newsinfo.inquirer.net/1155565/dfa-to-remind-israel-of-ph-rescue-of-jews-in-quezons-time.

San Diego Reader. "Quezon's Game: Filipino Schindler's List?" 23 January 2020. https://www.sandiegoreader.com/news/2020/jan/23/movie-review-quezons-game-filipino-schindlers-list/.

Smith, Neil. "Silence and Refusal: Refugees, Race and Economic Development." In *American Empire: Roosevelt's Geographer and the Prelude to Globalization*. Oakland: University of California Press, 2003.

Torres, Alfonso. "A Home for the Persecuted." *Philippines Free Press*, 4 May 1940, 2. Franklin Delano Roosevelt Library, National Archives of America (RG350 B1388 F2. 28943).

Wells, Allen. *Tropical Zion: General Trujillo, FDR, and the Jews of Sosúa*. Durham, NC: Duke University Press, 2009.

CHAPTER 3

Burma Evacuees
R. Sanyassiah, Postwar Return, and Displacement in Modern South Asia

Emma C. Meyer

In August 1948, R. Sanyassiah wrote a letter to the Government of India on his observations of migration patterns from south Indian ports to Burma (Myanmar), which lay across the Bay of Bengal.¹ By his own account, Sanyassiah had lived his life split between India and Burma. Before World War II, Sanyassiah had spent thirty years in prewar Burma conducting business and employing laborers there as a stevedore contractor.² After Japanese military forces began a takeover of British-held Burma in December 1941, he became one of approximately five to six hundred thousand people who evacuated from Burma to relative safety in colonial India.³ The majority of those who left Burma for India came from among the large communities of Indian descent that had established themselves in Burma from the second half of the nineteenth century onward.⁴ These displaced individuals frequently referred to themselves as "Burma Indian evacuees" or, simply, "Burma evacuees."

Upon arriving in India in 1942, Sanyassiah served for several years as the president of the Visakhapatnam District Burma Evacuees Association located in the town of Yellamanchili, Visakhapatnam District, in southern India.⁵ He and the other leaders of this organization claimed to represent the interests of approximately six thousand evacuees living locally.⁶ After the war, Sanyassiah offered his insights to the Indian national government in Delhi, presenting himself as an expert due to his past in Burma and his experience as a displaced person and an organizer of evacuees. As his letter detailed:

Evacuees ... are at present returning to Burma indiscriminately and without due regard to their own interests whether there is hope of employment in Burma or not. Either on account of the economic conditions obtaining now in India or their anxiety to go back to serve in their familiar surroundings, evacuees both skilled and unskilled are very eager to return to Burma at any cost and they leave no stone unturned to achieve their purpose.[7]

Due to the calamitous evacuation and its financial impact, most Burma Indian evacuees spent the war years in India, often separated from family members, employment, and properties that they had been forced to leave behind. While there, they became the subjects of relief efforts organized by the colonial government, local Indian charities and benefactors, and aid associations formed by the evacuees themselves. As the war ended and Allied forces reoccupied colonial Burma in 1945, the prospect of returning to Burma to regain their lives and livelihoods became tantalizingly possible for many evacuees who had reached India in 1942.

Writing in August 1948, Sanyassiah demonstrated in his comments on the "craze among evacuees" to return to Burma that, even three years after the end of World War II, a long-term solution to the disruptions wrought by the war had yet to be found for many Burma Indian evacuees. Sanyassiah's observations were made during an important transitional moment in India's and Burma's histories. Both were in the process of decolonizing: India had won its political independence in 1947, and Burma's independence arrived in January 1948 after years of struggle. Even as both India and Burma broke away from British colonial rule, however, relations between the two fledgling governments of these neighbors still needed to be arranged.

An important part of ongoing negotiations was the discussion over what would happen to the millions of people, including hundreds of thousands of Burma evacuees, who had fled their homes and places of residence to seek safety during the war. The colonial administration of India and the various charitable organizations regularly referred to those who escaped from Burma in late 1941 and 1942 as "evacuees" and even "refugees." Administrators and aid workers perceived evacuees, in part, as victims of the war needing assistance to cope with their displacement. However, as World War II ended and political independence loomed, a different set of questions about the Burma evacuees arose. Namely, how would their lives and patterns of migration shift when both India and Burma were independent countries? Many evacuees of Indian descent had been born in India before migrating to Burma in the prewar era, though a sizeable number counted Burma as their birthplace. Some had established lives there long term, while others sought to come and go, working for a few years and saving money. Did these evacuees now belong in India, or was Burma their native or adopted homeland? In addition, would evacuees be allowed to travel freely between India and Burma, or would they be expected to stay put in one country or the other?[8]

Part of understanding how and why South and Southeast Asian decision-makers acted in the ways that they did requires historically specific contextualization. Policies and procedures for responding to displacement did not grow out of a vacuum but were created in response to the pressures of decolonization and nation making that were happening concurrently. In addition, bureaucrats, politicians, and evacuee representatives were forced to consider existing laws and agreements governing migration, many of which dated from before the war. Therefore, the arrangements made for Burma Indian evacuees as displaced people were emerging out of a postwar moment of decolonization but also were rooted in existing colonial-era policies. Instead of imagining the postwar treatment of the Burma Indian evacuees as part of the global rise and spread of an international refugee regime, this chapter will help uncover a separate—and largely unfamiliar—history of regional and local responses to displacement.

In addition to the decision-making efforts of Indian and Burmese politicians, administrators, and bureaucrats, many people who evacuated from Burma sought to make themselves heard regarding matters related to postwar India-Burma migration policy. Through their organized campaigns and their everyday choices—to attempt the return to Burma and recoup what they had lost during the war or remain in India—Burma Indian evacuees questioned and challenged developing policies meant to settle their displacement and to govern future India-Burma migration patterns.[9] Though evacuees' campaigns were not always successful, the appeals and arguments they posed helped shape the terms of regionally focused debates over the proper treatment of displaced people and migration policy across the mid-twentieth century.

Burma Indian Evacuees and Refugee Histories

The 1940s and 1950s were an important time for the emergence of what scholars often refer to as the international or global refugee regime. The term "international refugee regime" is shorthand for the historical development of norms, practices, and procedures that determined which people experiencing displacement were classified as refugees and how those populations would be treated.[10] As is now widely recognized, these midcentury attempts to enshrine rights and protections for refugees were often limited, in effect only applying to a portion of the total number of displaced people around the globe.[11] The relatively narrow limits placed on who would be considered a refugee, including chronological and geographical stipulations, meant that the plights of millions of displaced people in Asia, Africa, the Middle East, and other regions around the globe were overlooked or dismissed.[12]

The Burma Indian evacuees discussed in this chapter composed one small segment of the global populations of displaced people who received only limited attention or care from the "international community." Though they remained outside the purview of practices and policies created by international decision-making bodies, Burma Indian evacuees became the subjects of ongoing debates between administrators and politicians in the late colonial and early independence-era governments of India and Burma (Myanmar). Therefore, their histories of displacement and the details of the treatment they received during and after the war provide a convenient entry point to better understand the development of regionally specific responses to displacement.

In this chapter, I examine the debates of Indian and Burmese politicians, bureaucrats, and administrators who were deeply engaged with the question of what to do with Burma evacuees in the postwar era. I also explore letters and petitions produced by Burma Indian evacuees such as R. Sanyassiah during the late 1940s and early 1950s as they sought to negotiate their position in the changed circumstances wrought by the war. Burma Indian evacuees had already been displaced by wartime bombings, firefights, and the fear of invasion. With the war's end, however, evacuees found themselves facing new barriers to a return to their prewar lives, including migration policy, documentation requirements, and shifts in regional transportation networks.

To begin understanding these debates, this chapter will review the findings of the 1944 subcommittee appointed by the Standing Emigration Committee of the Government of India. The subcommittee was made up of Indian politicians, prominent members of Burma Indian communities, and businessmen, many of whom had evacuated from Burma to India in 1942. Its members' discussions and commentary provide insight into the most pressing issues of the day, including their attempts to determine how *laboring* evacuees (otherwise referred to as "unskilled" laborers or by more pejorative terms) would be classified and treated. The crux of these debates was a disagreement over whether evacuee laborers—who comprised the majority of all evacuees of Indian descent—should be seen as the victims of war and therefore offered some advantage on the basis of humanitarian grounds. In the context of Indian and Burmese intergovernmental relations in the late 1940s and early 1950s, the advantage at stake was the right to return to Burma and to take up the livelihoods and patterns of mobility that had structured their prewar lives. The countervailing argument was that laboring evacuees should be viewed predominantly as a body of displaced migrant workers, and therefore be made subject to existing migration policies, including restrictions placed on their ability to repeatedly traverse the India-Burma border.

As R. Sanyassiah's writings also reveal, however, Burma Indian evacuees had their own ideas about the legislation and policies that directly affected their lives and livelihoods. Their eagerness to return to Burma, as Sanyassiah described, showed that evacuees were not passive recipients of government policy and procedures. In southern India, where large numbers of evacuees had settled, they organized into associations and relief organizations and repeatedly opened dialogues with Indian provincial and national government administrations by organizing delegations and letter-writing campaigns in the 1940s and early 1950s. These demonstrations often expressed the concerns that evacuees had about their living conditions, difficulty finding work, and inability to reclaim their prewar lives, livelihoods, and mobility.

Prewar Migration and the Evacuation

British colonial forces ruled Burma and designated it as a province of British India from the late nineteenth century into the early decades of the twentieth century. The demands of British-ruled Burma's colonial economy, concurrent developments in transportation networks, and the lure of jobs and higher wages in Burma helped create booming migration patterns between India and Burma. In addition, episodic "push" factors, including harvest failures, cyclones, floods, and droughts, led to further short-term boosts in rates of Indian emigration.[13] Migrants moving from India to Burma during this period were largely seasonal, circular migrants who worked in Burma for a few years before returning to their homes in India. Many undertook this journey multiple times in their lives. A smaller but still significant number of migrants from India settled in Burma longer term or permanently, establishing it as their main residence and starting families and businesses there.[14] Altogether, between 1846 and 1940, an estimated twelve to fifteen million passages took place from India to Burma.[15]

The large-scale population movements that had characterized the late nineteenth and early twentieth centuries would not last, however. Beginning with the shocks of the Great Depression felt across the Bay of Bengal in the early 1930s, the long-standing pattern of Indian migration into Burma was reversed, with more Indian migrants leaving the province than arriving from India for the first time in several decades.[16] In addition, the economic tumult of the Depression years and the strengthening of Burmese nationalist movements in the 1930s led to intense debates about immigration and more uncertainty for people of Indian descent living in Burma.[17]

Once Burma split away from India to become a separate Crown Colony in 1935, some Burmese politicians increasingly called for an end to unrestricted migration from India. However, it was not until 1941 that the first major effort to curb Indian immigration to Burma came into effect. The Indo-Burma Immigration Agreement of 1941 proposed new controls on immigration (especially targeting the free movement of Indian laborers into Burma) and a tiered visa system.[18] The 1941 agreement was never fully implemented due to its unpopularity among Indians and the sudden arrival of World War II in Burma in December 1941. Despite the war's interruption, however, the Indo-Burma Immigration Agreement would lay the groundwork for postwar negotiations between India and Burma on border enforcement, Indian immigration policy, the return of the evacuees after the war, citizenship in Burma, and other related issues.[19]

The eruption of World War II in colonial Burma (Myanmar) in late 1941 led to the evacuation of thousands of people of Indian descent who had settled in Burma prior to the war. Japanese imperial forces bombed Rangoon in December 1941 and took over the remainder of the colony in the following months, which ended with the fall of Myitkyina in northern Burma on 8 May 1942.[20] These attacks prompted millions of Burma's inhabitants to leave behind their dwellings: while some migrated internally, others sought to leave Burma altogether and seek refuge in neighboring territories. Approximately six hundred thousand people, the clear majority of whom were of Indian descent, set out westward toward the neighboring colony of British India, traveling by steamship, by aircraft, or on foot.[21] Evacuees faced harsh conditions and ongoing skirmishes and air raids on the trek. They often lacked supplies such as food and potable water, leading to high death tolls. Though estimates of the number of people fleeing to India varied, roughly five hundred thousand evacuees survived the ordeal and remained in India for the duration of the war.[22]

The Question of Return

Although they had sought refuge in India due to the war's advance, many evacuees desired to return to Burma once hostilities ceased to pick up the lives that they had left behind. From 1942 onward, evacuees based in India sought reassurance from the colonial administration that they would be allowed to go back, assuming that Allied forces were victorious.[23] One of the most extensive debates occurred in mid-1944 as the Government of India appointed a subcommittee of ten members, including representatives from multiple Burma Indian communities, Indian politicians, and businessmen. Subcommittee members included Raza Ali, Hriday Nath Kunzru, Dr. R. S. Dugal, S. N. Haji, S. A. S. Tyabji, A. M. M. Vellayan Chettiar, A. Narayana Rao, Dr. M. A. Rauf, M. A. Master, and R. N. Banerjee. Several of the members had evacuated from Burma during the war. The subcommittee was to respond to a draft of the Government of Burma's position on Indian immigration to Burma, including the questions of whether and how Burma Indian evacuees would return to Burma after the war.[24]

In addressing these issues, the subcommittee had to weigh both historical precedents and the pressures of the moment. Many of the subcommittee's discussions rehashed debates that had begun in the 1930s and early 1940s in the lead-up to and aftermath of the India-Burma partition. These included older determinations about cross-border migration and the composition of the India-Burma border, such as the 1935 Government of Burma Act and the 1941 Indo-Burma Immigration Agreement. The war had temporarily delayed any definitive answers to the issues of Indian immigration and the path to establishing domicile for Burma's Indian residents, but these matters had not been forgotten. Despite engaging with the past, delegates clearly were aware that their decisions would have an impact on India and Burma's futures as colonies and, eventually, as independent nation-states.

Both the Government of Burma and the subcommittee members acknowledged the special challenge posed by Burma Indian evacuees. Those who had evacuated during the war seemed to have a strong claim to return to Burma, both because of their history in that colony as well as their appeals made as the victims of war. However, even recognizing that evacuees had suffered and lost homes, family members, and sources of income during the war, there were mixed opinions on whether all evacuees should be allowed free access to come and go to Burma once the war had ended.

Since the majority of evacuees were manual laborers, it was unclear whether they would be allowed to return to Burma. The last major immigration agreement passed between the two governments had been the 1941 Indo-Burma Immigration Agreement that, among other innovations, had placed an embargo on the immigration of "unskilled," or manual, laborers from India. Though this unpopular agreement had never been fully implemented and the war had stifled migration across the Bay of Bengal, Burma's government was considering reviving the immigration agreement for the postwar era. The Burmese administration was therefore ambivalent about the return of Burma Indian evacuees, which would be providing a back-door entry through which "unskilled" Indian laborers could reenter Burma.

The subcommittee's appointees, however, argued that evacuees had left Burma "for reasons completely beyond their control. The rapid expansion of the Far Eastern war to Burma resulting in the Japanese occupation of the country . . . were events for which the [Burma] Indian community was ill prepared." As the committee's report further stated, "But for the turn the war took, almost all of these Indians would have remained in Burma today." As such, the committee felt that there should be no barrier to evacuees' return. They also pushed against a return of the 1941 ban, stating that laboring evacuees should be allowed to return freely as they were just a subsection of the larger body of the displaced:

> It will be quite unfair, if not inhuman, to place any obstacles in the way of their safe and automatic return to and rehabilitation in, the country of their adoption which is

the only home of many of them. We are of the definite and considered opinion that the question of their return should not even admit of any dispute and we must insist on, and secure, their unconditional return to Burma.[25]

Despite the committee's call for "unconditional return," the majority of the committee recognized that evacuees' return to Burma would need to be gradual due to "military exigencies and shortage of shipping and other means of transport." Each group of evacuees would "have to take their turn according to the urgency of the functions they would be called upon to perform in the post-reoccupation economy of Burma." One Burma Indian evacuee committee member named S. A. S. Tyabji dissented from the majority position on the evacuees' right of return. Tyabji belonged to a prominent family of Indian descent and had been a well-known figure in prewar social and civic circles among Burma Indians in Rangoon (Yangon). In his statements, Tyabji argued that "the unskilled elements" among the evacuees should not have unregulated access to Burma. Tyabji believed that evacuees who conducted manual labor for a living would not be able to find employment in the changed postwar landscape of Burma. He therefore felt that the "unskilled" evacuee workers should only be allowed to return when there was a specific labor demand or a quota set by the Burmese government.[26]

Despite these caveats and objections, however, the subcommittee's findings were notable in part because they suggested strongly that evacuees, including manual laborers, should not be treated as a subset of Indian migrants to Burma. As they summarized, "We do not consider that the evacuee Indians' right to return to Burma—after the reoccupation of the country—is necessarily intertwined with the general question of Indian immigration into Burma." The subcommittee's efforts to distinguish evacuees as a separate category of migrants sought to set them apart from the general body of people wanting to travel between India for business, family ties, work, religious or cultural pursuits, or leisure. Instead, their proposition to disentangle the Burma evacuees' return to Burma from the general debate over migration was clear recognition of evacuees' suffering during the war as well as their history with and past residence in Burma.[27]

The 1944 subcommittee did not have the final say, however, and their opinions formed only a part of a wider conversation between the administrations of Burma and India.[28] As the combined Indian and British military forces retook Burma in 1945, the question of how the two governments would deal with evacuees and migrants of Indian descent remained unanswered. Still, the subcommittee's debates are important because they foreshadowed the developments of the next several years.

Beginning in December 1945, the Government of India, in cooperation with Burma's administration, arranged a distinct "repatriation" program for evacuees. According to a pamphlet published by the Government of India

Press in the same year, "It is a principle accepted by both the Government of Burma and the Government of India that all [evacuees] should be enabled to return to Burma before others who had no previous connections with that country."[29] All evacuees wishing to return to Burma could register themselves and apply for evacuee identity certificates, which were simple, passport-like documents that would serve as both proof of identity and as travel documents for evacuees. Each evacuee family was to fill and submit forms that would provide the colonial government with demographic information and details about their postwar plans.[30] The Indian administration used this information to prioritize evacuees according to their circumstances: Indians who had left behind families in Burma would have top priority for returning to Burma, followed by landholders and merchants wanting to look after their possessions.[31]

Despite these preparations to equip Burma Indian evacuees with travel documents, a large-scale return of the displaced never materialized. The war had wrought extensive damage in Burma, leading to transportation, food, and accommodation shortages and considerable destruction within Burma's infrastructure and industries. The war had taken a heavy toll, and repatriation programs stalled due to concerns that the large-scale return of evacuees would exacerbate difficult conditions in Burma.

Even without a formal, functioning government repatriation program, however, many evacuees continued to attempt to cross the Bay of Bengal into the late 1940s. As the following section will explore, evacuees migrating regionally faced a number of changes regarding their access to transportation networks, bureaucratic offices, and paperwork regimes from the late 1940s to the early 1950s. For instance, steamships that had frequented the northern Andhra coastline prior to the war no longer visited Visakhapatnam and other, smaller ports in the region. At the same time, Burmese diplomatic offices in Visakhapatnam that had outfitted intending passengers with the correct paperwork closed due to a decline in traffic by 1950. Due to these changes, multiple small ports closed altogether, further limiting travel options for those hoping to reach Burma (as well as other destinations). Finally, during the same period, the Evacuee Identity Certificate was discontinued as a valid travel document, replaced by other paperwork requirements.

These discontinuations of the late 1940s and early 1950s did not occur without opposition, and sustained campaigns arose to either reverse these changes or find alternative ways to allow evacuees to cross the Bay of Bengal. Letters and petitions on these matters provide insight into how those claiming evacuee status sought to keep hold of older patterns of movement (see figure 3.1). By coming forward to local offices to sign their names or affix their thumbprints to letters and petitions, Burma Indian evacuees were laying claim to privileges that were theirs through tradition and seeking to produce connections of accountability and responsibility between the government and themselves.

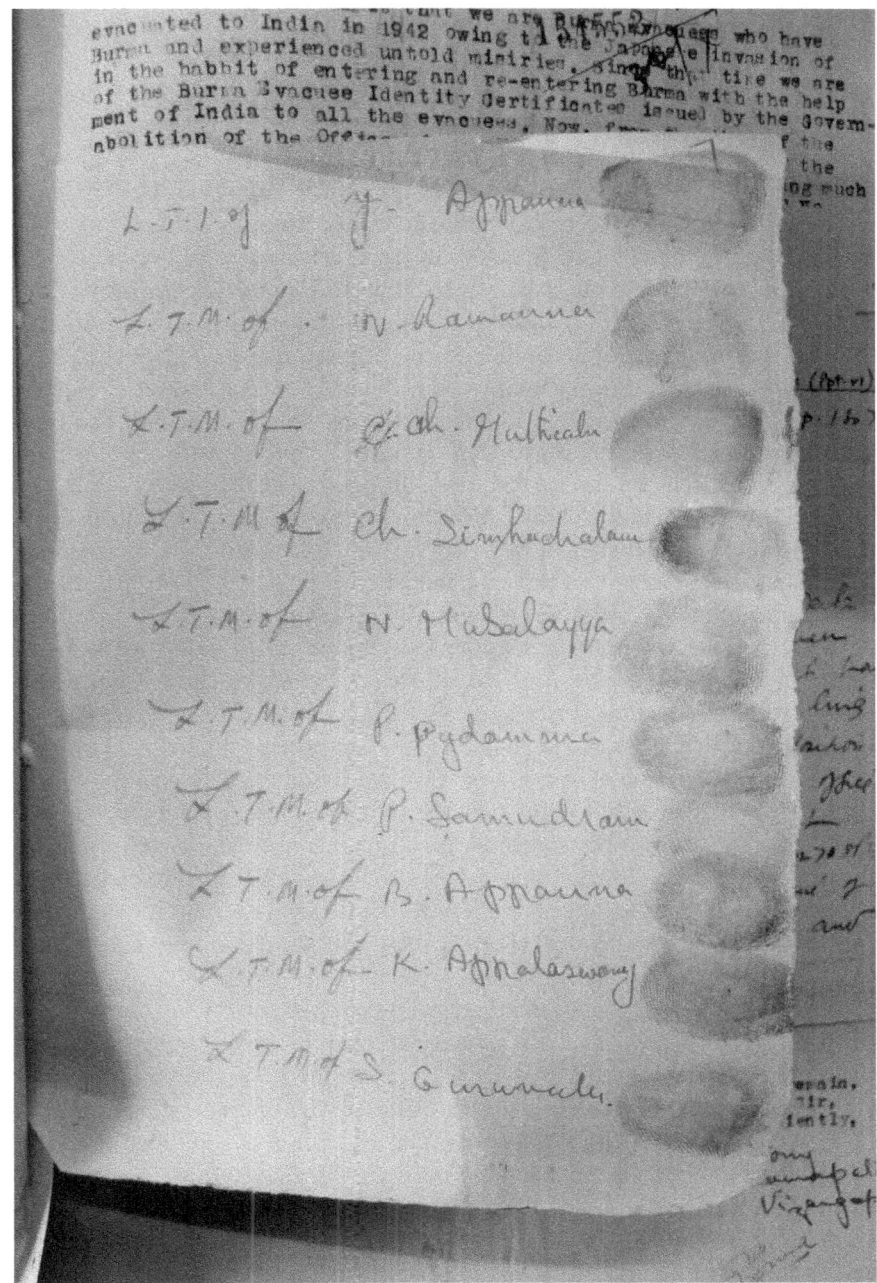

Figure 3.1. • Evacuee letters and petitions circa 1950, stored in the Andhra Pradesh State Archives and Research Institute in Hyderabad, India. © Emma C. Meyer

Postwar Arrangements

By October 1950, the Home Department of the Madras provincial government began receiving petitions and telegrams from groups of evacuees living in Visakhapatnam. The petitioners characterized themselves in different ways, including as "Burma Evacuees of Visakhapatnam District" and also as "poor people." They emphasized their long-standing connections to both India and Burma. In one letter, the "undersigned Burma Evacuees of Visakhapatnam District" wrote that they had been "in the habit of frequently visiting Burma from the last 30 to 40 years."[32] A separate letter, signed with the thumbprints and signatures of more than twenty individuals, claimed that its authors had "permanent residence" in Burma and owned properties and lands there as well. In "those olden days" before the war, the petitioners claimed that they had been forced to go to Burma due to crop failures, insufficient funds to support their families, and a lack of job opportunities in India.[33]

Their long association with Burma had been temporarily ended during the war, when the petitioners had fled "to India by the land route through hills and forests, [experiencing] horrible troubles ... [with] a heavy loss of money and other valuables." The "calamity" of the evacuation had led to "all of us [becoming] too poor to maintain our families in India. As we were entirely depending on the business which we used to do in Burma, our financial position has become worse since we could not get proper work to do in India. ...." With the war's end, however, the Burma evacuees explained that their situation was one of continuing movement and migration in the much-altered circumstances of the postwar era. After Burma's reoccupation by Allied forces, the petitioners wrote that they had resumed "going to Burma and we made several trips on the strength of the Burma Evacuee Identity Certificates issued by the Government of India." This travel was conducted "freely and easily from Visakhapatnam Port," which was "the convenient and nearest Port to all our villages."

By 1950, however, significant changes in transportation availability, access to bureaucratic offices, and new paperwork requirements again threatened these migrants' connections to Burma. Letters sent by evacuees to Indian provincial and national administrations were riddled with references to the closure of Visakhapatnam port for passenger traffic, the fall in the number of steamships traveling between India and Burma, the relocation of the Burmese Vice Consul's Office to Madras, and the closure of emigration offices at Visakhapatnam. Additionally, the planned phasing out of the Evacuee Identity Certificate, which was to go into effect by the end of 1950, was of specific interest to evacuees. The Evacuee Certificate was to be replaced with "passports issued by Indian Republic and entry Visas issued by Burmese Vice Consul at Madras." In addition, those intending to migrate would need a No Objection certificate obtained from the Protector of Emigrants whose office had been shifted from Visakhapatnam to Madras. Each of the letters concluded with the same three demands: reopen the Visakhapatnam Burmese Vice Consul Office, move the Protector of Emigrants office from Madras to Visakhapatnam (or prevent the Visakhapatnam office from closing), and "make arrangements to board the ship at Visakhapatnam harbour and order the shipping managements to send their ships to Visakhapatnam."

As their petitions made clear, however, Burma Indian evacuees' appeals to provincial and national administrations in India were not only about improving ease of access to travel facilities but also a matter of survival. Evacuees claimed that they could not remain in India due to poor economic conditions there. One letter attested, "We are starving here for food and raiment as the crops failed this year due to no rain in some parts and due to excess of water in other parts. We are weakened financially due to the failure of crops. ..." Another letter also pointed to crop failures, floods, and drought, saying that "at present days we with our families are actually starving in these Districts."

These harsh circumstances compounded the effects of the recent closures and the discontinuation of the Evacuee Identity Certificate. As one letter explained:

> We beg to state our difficulties ... increased when the new system of obtaining Indian National Passports has come into force. We are waiting since [so many] months to return to Burma. We have submitted our applications for passports nearly two months ago and we have not received anything from the authorities concerned.[34]

Traveling to port cities—whether nearby Visakhapatnam or the distant ports of Calcutta or Madras—to secure documentation and passage to Burma presented substantial difficulties for the petitioners. Evacuees living in Visakhapatnam and surrounding areas described Calcutta and Madras as big, unfamiliar cities. As one letter explained, "Calcutta Port is nearly 500 miles and Madras 500 miles. And also we do not know the language of those ports, i.e., Tamil, etc. We are all Telugu people." The trip there and back (and sometimes several trips, depending on the time taken to process paperwork, secure tickets, etc.) would cost money, as would finding accommodation during their sojourn. "If we go to Madras in these hard days," one letter concluded, the result would be "the greatest expenditures and have to be in hot sun without shelters."

The representations of Burma Indian evacuees shed light on a host of multiple, interwoven rights and privileges that evacuees sought to claim. Their customary mobility across the Bay of Bengal, for instance, could not be continued without access to bureaucratic offices, documentation, and convenient modes of transportation. In turn, mobility was not a goal in itself. Evacuee petitioners tied it to their economic strength, their ability to escape poverty or harsh circumstances, and their ability to survive in times of misfortune.

Burma Indian evacuees who came forward to local offices to sign their names or affix their thumbprints to letters and petitions, actions that took place years after their displacement from Burma, provide an example of the diverse arenas in which displaced people sought to influence decision-making about their treatment.

Conclusion: Evacuee Activism and Return at War's End

The end of the war brought few certainties for approximately half a million Burma evacuees who survived the desperate escape to India between 1941 and 1942. Both governments and nongovernmental committees debated seriously whether and how evacuees would be allowed to return to Burma, as did evacuees involved in local demonstrations. These debates and the historical circumstances and contexts in which they emerged reveal that responses to displacement in modern South Asia has regionally specific roots and cannot be understood by appealing only to the standards and practices of the post–World War II international refugee regime that developed in Europe.

Debates over evacuees' futures necessarily responded to and attempted to build upon existing colonial-era policies and procedures designed to regulate migration between India and Burma. One persistent question prefaced upon older policies was whether evacuees should be treated as part of the larger body of migrants from India or whether their wartime suffering and displacement warranted them extra rights and consideration. This question was especially asked about "unskilled" laboring evacuees, who had been banned from entering Burma by the 1941 Indo-Burma Immigration Agreement. At the heart of this debate was the broader issue of whether displaced people could be governed under general migration channels, or whether parallel systems should exist to regulate their mobility. The administrations of India and Burma innovatively agreed to allow evacuees to travel between the two colonies using their Evacuee Identity Certificates. This solution was highly local and temporary, but it proved to be a popular and durable system for at least some (but certainly not all) Burma Indian evacuees.

The accounts of evacuees (including Sanyassiah's observations), the debates of the emigration subcommittee (many of whom were Burma Indian evacuees), and the petitions and letters of evacuees in Visakhapatnam District highlight previously unexplored and undervalued archival sources. They are important because these historical accounts, fragments though they may be, demonstrate how actively engaged evacuees were in shaping policies related to their migration, documentation, and residence. In that way, evacuees resisted passive acceptance of migration policies and shaped the conversation around their proper treatment in the postwar era.

Emma Meyer completed her PhD in history from Emory University in 2020 with a thesis titled "Resettling Burma's Displaced: Labor, Rehabilitation, and Citizenship in Visakhapatnam, India, 1937–1979." Her research, which focuses on histories of forced migration between India and Burma (Myanmar) in the mid-twentieth century, traces the historical development of refuge-making in modern South Asia.

Notes

1. Although R. Sanyassiah does not give his full name in his letters that have been preserved in the Indian National Archives, it is likely that he was Reddy Sanyassiah, who is listed among the prominent Telugu-speaking residents of Burma. See Murty, *Burmaloo Telugu*.
2. National Archives of India [NAI], Ministry of External Affairs (SIM Branch), File No. 26–40/48-SIM(E).
3. Prakash et al., "Introduction," 2.
4. British Library [BL], Asian and African Studies [AAS], India Office Records [IOR], File No. IOR/V/15/232, no. 432.
5. Visakhapatnam was routinely spelled as "Vizagapatam" in English during the 1940s. To avoid confusion, I have used the newer spelling of "Visakhapatnam."
6. National Archives of India [NAI], Department of Indians Overseas, Evacuation Branch, File No. 115–6/43-O.S.
7. NAI, Ministry of External Affairs (SIM Branch), File No. 26–40/48-SIM(E).
8. Zamindar, *Long Partition*; Roy, *Partitioned Lives*.
9. Chatterji, "Citizenship," 1050–51.
10. Robinson, "Too Much Nationality," 344–45; Betts, "International Cooperation," 56–57.
11. Bhagavan, "Towards Universal," 123.
12. Oberoi, "South Asia," 37–41; Ho and Robinson, "Introduction," 263.
13. Satyanarayana, "Birds," 94, 99–100.
14. Pandian and Mariappan, *Ayya': Accounts*; Chakravarti, *Indian Minority*, xix.
15. Amrith, "South Indian Migration," 133.
16. Adas, *Burma Delta*, 208.
17. Amrith, *Crossing*, 184–85; Adas, *Burma Delta*, 204–8; Guyot-Réchard, "Tangled Lands," 4.
18. Amrith, *Crossing*, 191.
19. Amrith, *Crossing*, 216–17.
20. Leigh, *Evacuation of Civilians*, 1.
21. Amrith, *Crossing the Bay*, 204.
22. BL, AAS, IOR, File No. IOR/V/15/232, no. 432.
23. Meyer, *Resettling*, 228–29.
24. NAI, Commonwealth Relations Department, Overseas Section (II), File No. 50–2/44-O.S.
25. NAI, Commonwealth Relations Department, Overseas Section (II), File No. 50–2/44-O.S.
26. NAI, Commonwealth Relations Department, Overseas Section (II), File No. 50–2/44-O.S.

27. NAI, Commonwealth Relations Department, Overseas Section (II), File No. 50-2/44-O.S.
28. In May 1945, R. N. Banerjee (the Secretary to the Government of India, Department of Commonwealth Relations) and U Tin Tut (a Burmese barrister and ICS officer), held further talks. See BL, AAS, IOR, File No. L PJ 8 214.
29. NAI, Home Department, Jail Branch, File No. 227/45-Jail/AN.
30. Pandian and Mariappan, *Ayya's Accounts*, 63–65.
31. "Return of Burma," 10.
32. Andhra Pradesh State Archives and Research Institute [APSARI], Development Department, GO 4780, 23-11-1950.
33. Andhra Pradesh State Archives and Research Institute [APSARI], Development Department, GO 4780, 23-11-1950.
34. Andhra Pradesh State Archives and Research Institute [APSARI], Development Department, GO 4780, 23-11-1950.

References

Adas, Michael. *The Burma Delta: Economic Development and Social Change on an Asian Rice Frontier, 1852–1941*. Madison: University of Wisconsin Press, 2011.
Amrith, Sunil S. *Crossing the Bay of Bengal: The Furies of Nature and the Fortunes of Migrants*. Cambridge, MA: Harvard University Press, 2013.
———. "South Indian Migration, c. 1800–1950." In *Globalising Migration History: The Eurasian Experience*, edited by Leo Lucassen and Jan Lucassen, 122–48. Leiden: Brill, 2013.
Betts, Alexander. "International Cooperation in the Refugee Regime." In *Refugees in International Relations*, edited by Alexander Betts and Gil Loescher, 53–84. Oxford: Oxford University Press, 2011.
Bhagavan, Manu. "Towards Universal Relief and Rehabilitation: India, UNRRA, and the New Internationalism." In *Wartime Origins and the Future United Nations*, edited by Dan Plesch and Thomas G. Weiss, 121–36. New York: Routledge, 2015.
Chakravarti, Nalini Ranjan. *The Indian Minority in Burma: The Rise and Decline of an Immigrant Community*. London: Oxford University Press, 1971.
Chatterji, Joya. "South Asian Histories of Citizenship, 1946–1970." *Historical Journal* 55, no. 4 (2012): 1049–71. https://doi.org/10.1017/S0018246X12000428.
Guyot-Réchard, Bérénice. "Tangled Lands: Burma and India's Unfinished Separation, 1937–1948." *Journal of Asian Studies* 80, no. 2 (2021): 293–315.
Ho, Elaine Lynn-Ee, and Cabeiri deBergh Robinson. "Introduction: Forced Migration in/of Asia—Interfaces and Multiplicities." *Journal of Refugee Studies* 31, no. 3 (2018): 262–73.
Leigh, Michael D. *The Evacuation of Civilians from Burma: Analysing the 1942 Colonial Disaster*. London: Bloomsbury, 2015.
Meyer, Emma. "Resettling Burma's Displaced: Labor, Rehabilitation, and Citizenship in Visakhapatnam, India, 1937–1979." PhD diss., Emory University, 2020.
Murty, K. K. *Burmaloo Telugu vaani*. Hyderabad: International Telugu Institute, 1977.
Oberoi, Pia. "South Asia and the Creation of the International Refugee Regime." *Refuge: Canada's Journal on Refugees* 19, no. 5 (2001): 36–45.

Pandian, Anand, and M. P. Mariappan. *Ayya's Accounts: A Ledger of Hope in Modern India*. Bloomington: Indiana University Press, 2014.
Prakash, Gyan, Nikhil Menon, and Michael Laffan, eds. *The Postcolonial Moment in South and Southeast Asia*. New York: Bloomsbury Academic, 2018.
"Return of Burma Refugees: Plans to Repatriate Half a Million." ProQuest Historical Newspapers: *The Times of India*, 26 October 1945.
Robinson, Cabeiri deBergh. "Too Much Nationality: Kashmiri Refugees, the South Asian Refugee Regime, and a Refugee State, 1947–1974." *Journal of Refugee Studies* 25, no. 3 (2012): 344–65. https://doi.org/10.1093/jrs/fes030.
Roy, Haimanti. *Partitioned Lives: Migrants, Refugees, Citizens in India and Pakistan, 1947–1965*. New Delhi: Oxford University Press, 2012.
Satyanarayana, Adapa. "'Birds of Passage': Migration of South Indian Laborers to Southeast Asia." *Critical Asian Studies* 34, no. 1 (March 2002): 89–115. https://doi.org/10.1080/146727102760166617.
Zamindar, Vazira Fazila-Yacoobali. *The Long Partition and the Making of Modern South Asia: Refugees, Boundaries, Histories*. New York: Columbia University Press, 2007.

CHAPTER 4

Khao-I-Dang Refugee Camp
Local Hosts and Hauntings of the Third Indochina War in a Transit Zone

Khathaleeya Liamdee

This is a story of Khao-I-Dang Transit Center (KID) and other former refugee camps/camps along the Thai-Cambodian border for those who escaped the armed fights and political turmoil from their home countries to Thailand during the late Cold War era.[1] Many readers may have heard about the Cambodian genocide carried out by the Khmer Rouge while they were in power between 1975 and 1979. Instead of remembering mass killings in Cambodia as sui generis events, the story of border refugee camps highlights the continuation of the postcolonial regional conflicts and wars. Atrocities from the First Indochina War against the French colonization to the American War in Vietnam and the Cambodian genocide did not simply end when the brutal regime was toppled by Vietnamese military intervention in 1979.[2] Cambodia's ongoing transition to peace requires a deeper understanding of both postcolonial struggles and of Cambodia's relations to the neighboring countries. I asked people who witnessed or were involved in the camp operation to recount this story from the perspective of Thailand, Cambodia's neighboring country on the west and northwest, where Thailand's border with Cambodia turned into another battlefield during the Third Indochina War, which is also known as the Cambodian Civil War or the Cambodian-Vietnamese War. I take the accounts of former border camps as a point of departure to record not just terrified stories but also the everyday lived experience of the people who resided or worked in the confined spaces that were not necessarily recorded in the official documents.

With a handful of parties involved in the Cold War in Southeast Asia, the Third Indochina War reflected how bipolar politics between liberal-democracy and socialist-communist realms could not simply be explained in such complicated historical contexts of the region. With the shifts of armed conflict from the American war in Vietnam to Cambodia, the splits between the China and USSR alliance, and the divisions among the Communist Parties in mainland Southeast Asia, revisiting how the regional peace processes were negotiated through the operation of Khao-I-Dang and other border camps in Thailand can underline how the idea of humanitarianism landed and developed in Southeast Asia during the Cold War.

Most of the border camps lasted almost two decades, including the Khao-I-Dang (KID) camp, the primary site of analysis for this chapter. Though KID was designated to be a temporary transit center, it became a multidecade site due to the prolonged conflict, which was caused by the failure in peace negotiation among the Cambodian political parties and the international involvement of the USSR, China, and the United States.[3] Meanwhile Thailand, a country that itself never experienced colonization or modern warfare, became a site of temporary humanitarian shelters, a resettlement center for asylum seekers, and a pathway for military supplies and essential logistical materials from elsewhere to the anti-Vietnamese resistance troops in the mountains close to the border.[4] The humanitarian missions during the Third Indochina War delayed the process of reconciliation and peace settlement in Cambodia after the country was ruined by the Khmer Rouge genocide.

The stories told in this chapter are Thai local host narratives. The subjects' experiences shed light on how humanitarianism functioned in Thailand during the Third Indochina War. I had conversations with former camp staff members who were subcontracted employees in Khao-I-Dang and other camps from 1979 until the camp closed in 1993. They were willing to recall their memories about their work experiences in the camps, and I believe that these shared narratives can break the silenced and faded history of the Cold War in Southeast Asia and also help us understand both the presence and absence of it within historical memory and record. These personal narratives offer an alternative way to connect the origin of a war that caused mass displacement and resettlement with Thailand's struggles as a host country. These narratives further complicate this history as those who fled to Thailand were denied refugee status by their host country even as shelters were provided both publicly and clandestinely. The official narrative of the Cold War in Thailand rarely includes the voices of the nearby villagers or the local camp staff that operated as local hosts. Their self-censored, silenced, and untold stories haunt the conversations of these former camps. These firsthand accounts reflect how the violence of war was remembered at the camp sites and highlight how people may not wish or be able to talk about the remembered war directly.

Talking to these local hosts also allows me to portray how Thailand's policies on humanitarian intervention changed throughout the conflict, often resulting in confusion and muddled understandings of the country's humanitarian processes. Initially, Thailand was reluctant to receive the displaced persons. Border camp shelters were only allowed to be built as temporary structures since the Khmer Rouge seized the power in Phnom Penh and after the disagreement on the recognition of the Vietnamese-backed government at Phnom Penh in 1979. Later, instability within domestic politics of Thailand caused swings in refugee management that were undeniably tied to political interest within the region after the United States—Thailand's Cold War closest ally—had left Vietnam.[5] Since the US withdrawal, displaced persons could either reside with the guerrilla troops on the Cambodian side or walk across the border to Thailand and then reside in the border camps. This pattern of movements became common until the end of the conflict in the late 1990s.[6] Each camp location had different protocols for receiving the residents depending on the permission from the Thai authorities and Cambodian political affiliations, including the Khmer Rouge, the FUNCINPEC, and the KPNLF.[7] These three anti-Vietnamese political resistance groups even formed the Coalition Government of Democratic Kampuchea (CGDK) as Cambodia's government-in-exile in 1981 at the Thai border. Throughout these years, Thailand has always firmly stated that eventually every refugee must leave Thailand and either return to their home country or resettle in a third country. Around 235,000 Cambodians succeeded in resettling through KID, and the rest were sent back to Cambodia through the repatriation program in 1993.

The Evolution of Thailand as a Zone of Transit and Shelter

"Perhaps, it is because of our strategic location," my diplomat friend told me. At the heart of mainland Southeast Asia, Thailand, formerly known as Siam, has kept itself from being completely colonized or attacked by any colonizers, as has occurred in other Indochinese territories and Burma. Transforming from a traditional political entity reigned by Chakri Dynasty to become Siam, an early twentieth-century nation-state that grew from the monarchy's success in territorializing the lands through negotiation with the French and the British during the colonial era.[8] As a newly established nation-state, Thailand did not find border and immigration controls necessary until the arrival of emigrants from China and later from Indochinese countries fleeing the civil war.

Since humanitarian intervention was first introduced to Thailand during the Cold War, Khao-I-Dang became one of the best-known and largest border camps in Thailand, co-operated by the United Nations High Commissioner for Refugees (UNHCR) and the International Committee of the Red Cross

(ICRC) between 1979 and 1993. It was a special camp that functioned as a final relocation place for the Cambodian displaced persons who were qualified to receive a refugee status, but only if they successfully applied for the resettlement program. The Thai authorities created a few terms relating to the refugee issue that are not abided by the UNHCR, which led to the exception for those who had not yet received a refugee status to reside in United Nations Border Relief Operation (UNBRO)–supported camps.[9] By these means, they were able to relocate to any border camp, including secret paramilitary bases, except KID. Not only were a large amount of Cambodian displaced persons allowed to reside in the border camps, but the personnel of all Cambodian resistance factions were also secretly permitted to patrol and train with Thai soldiers along the border. The border control here was flexible, though the Thai government said otherwise to the public and international community. Undoubtedly, this act did not help resolve the conflict among Cambodian political factions. It was used as a way to balance power among internal factions, China, and the West and to protect the country's sovereignty from potential attack by Vietnam, a political rivalry from the past that was rising with communist ideology, which was considered a national threat at that time.[10]

Locating a Silenced yet Haunted Story of Khao-I-Dang

My first field trip to Khao-I-Dang was in 2018, twenty-five years after the camp was demolished. I visited the site with help from the caretaker who worked for Thailand's Royal Forestry Department (RFD). There are only a few drivable roads inside the conservation areas left over from when the camp was active. The caretaker told me that the RFD intentionally let the trees grow thicker to stop people from conducting wood-smuggling activities in this area. All the remaining roads are reserved only for staff transportation. There are also a few residential buildings for the RFD staff and soldiers who are currently assigned to look after and patrol the conservation project. Walking into the forest conservation area, now fully covered by trees, I found it difficult to imagine how the camp operated back then.

Topographically, Khao-I-Dang is located in Sakaeo Province, Eastern Thailand, where it sits on a lower plain and slightly farther from Sankamphaeng Range and Phnom Dangrek Range, a mountain range that is used for border delineation resulting from the 1904 and 1907 Franco-Thai treaties. Unlike the Phnom Dangrek region (Lower Northeastern Thailand), the estimated elevation of the Sakaeo area is lower, more akin to the Khmer Plain toward the central Mekong basin and the Angkor complex in the southeast and the foothills of the Kravanh Mountains in the south. With similar landforms, traveling routes across the Khmer Plain and to the Dangrek region during the precolonial and colonial eras had been popular and convenient either by foot or by vehicle until the Khmer Rouge seized power in 1975. The borders were then closed for safety reasons. If we start a journey to visit KID from Dan Klong Luk (Aranyaprathet)—Poi Pet, a Thai-Cambodian border pass—it is located thirty kilometers north of the border pass.

After the camp's demolition in 1993, this area was transformed to the forest conservation project named "Tabtim Siam 08." It is one of eight projects first established in December 1992 after Princess Chulabhorn—the youngest daughter of the late King Bhumibol—visited border camps Site K and Site E in Borai, Trat Province, next to the Pailin Province of Cambodia.[11] According to the UNHCR and former Khao-I-Dang staff as they explained it to me, there were seven *sangkat* (units) in KID consisting of traditional bamboo huts made with *ya kha* (thatch) and protective barbed-wire fence that were laid out in a parallel fashion. The camp logistics, facilities, and food and water supplies were provided by more than twenty international aid agencies. The humanitarian agencies assigned a number of NGOs to carry out the camp construction and maintenance. The refugees themselves were responsible for the construction of their own shelters.

The humanitarian support in the Khmer border camp system beyond Khao-I-Dang was limited because it oftentimes depended on negotiations between Thailand as a host country, the Cambodian resistance group leaders, and international humanitarian organizations. In other words, the UNBRO and Western countries withheld certain humanitarian actions to avoid political conflict with Thailand and the Cambodian resistance groups that controlled the camps. Despite international hesitance, most of the resistance leaders were allowed to receive medical treatment at the hospitals in Thailand, and many guerilla soldiers had regained their physical and financial strength while residing in the camps, where they received international humanitarian aid. The leaders of the CGDK were permitted to travel to Bangkok with the protection of the Thai army. These negotiations were one of the reasons the resistance coalition party was able to maintain its international recognition and hold onto its seat in the UN General Assembly until 1990.[12] Indeed, the amount of financial assistance through Thailand, China, and the United States was an essential factor in maintaining the encampment along the border throughout the civil war in Cambodia.

However, the ongoing political tension still caused frustration and ambiguity to the aid workers, both foreigners and Thai staff. A terrible example of this was the Preah Vihear incident, where a large group of Cambodians were ordered to walk back to Cambodia through the steep cliff mountain areas of the Phnom Dangrek range.[13] Many Cambodians were pushed over and killed by Thai soldiers in 1979, and the aid agents came to realize that humanitarian assistance and funds had been misused for the military activities of both

Thai armed forces and Cambodian resistance parties, specifically the Khmer Rouge. The ethical concerns among the aid workers were different than those among foreigners and the locals. On the one hand, the foreign staff began to question whether their involvement was helping or actually might be perpetuating the civil war. On the other hand, the local hosts, both camp staff and government officials, mostly avoided these topics or were reluctant to share, asking me not to mention the unpleasant parts in my writing.

Khao-I-Dang from the Perspective of the Local Hosts

A sign in front of a Spanish-style building indicates the Khao-I-Dang learning center. The learning center is on the left side when entering Tabtim Siam 08 forest conservation area. The exhibition inside the building displays texts and images documenting the life of Cambodian refugees in KID. There is a guestbook for visitors to sign and share their impression of or personal connection to KID. Entries range from former camp residents or their children who were born in the West to former soldiers and staff of KID. Skimming through the guestbook was emotional. KID holds so many memories that are impossible for someone who didn't share that experience to comprehend. Even though the situation was temporary, those experiences affect people for the rest of their lives.

The precise location of Khao-I-Dang is next to the office of the Sakaeo Wildfire Control Station, where first-time visitors like me could mistake this office as the location of KID. For those who wish to visit this place for the first time: the staff members of the wildfire station are still willing to guide visitors to the correct entrance. These staff members are deeply knowledgeable about KID as they have lived through and witnessed the camp era that lasted more than a decade. The camp's existence undoubtedly has had an impact on them. There are haunting stories told by the wildfire station staff about the history of their workplace, which used to be a ritual cemetery zone of KID. "That car sometimes moved by itself . . ." recalled one. Another described "skeletons of dead bodies covered by fabric sheets [that] could be found in the jungle and in pots that were thrown into the reservoir, alongside discarded medical equipment . . ."

These short stories sent chills down my spine. Even if the history of Khao-I-Dang and the border camps have been silenced by the locals themselves, their echoes continue to haunt the region through stories. The locals do not speak about these things overtly for several reasons, among them their refusal to partake in the story to take back individual agency, or as an act of social control to manipulate collective memories and national history. However, these ghost stories allow the willing to relive the history and speak when there is a chance to do so. This brought me to the question: What would be an appropriate and meaningful way to tackle the silence of the camp stories thirty years later and from the local host perspectives?

A few years after my first visit to Khao-I-Dang, I was introduced to Uncle Lek, a former KID staff member who had a special connection to KID. Uncle Lek worked for Christian Outreach (COR), a subcontracted nongovernmental organization for the UNHCR.[14] He was responsible for building and maintaining the systems of electricity and water lines for the whole camp since the beginning of the KID operation. With such a crucial task, he remembered this place well enough to be able to take the former refugees to the exact spot where they used to live in KID, even though the postcamp landscape had been replaced by the forest conservation project. Uncle Lek gave me this analogy: "Imagine your life being confined within limited space for more than a decade, like we have been locked up because of the COVID-19 pandemic but within only four square kilometers and with much more difficult conditions."

After the opening of the Khao-I-Dang learning center, former colleagues occasionally asked Uncle Lek to be the lead tour guide for the Cambodian returnees. These returnees had once lived in KID and had made their way to the West, and they now wished to see where they or their parents had lived in KID.

The experiences of the returning camp residents themselves are distinct from those of the local staff, villagers, and authorities. Uncle Lek told me that he once took care of a visitor who wished to find the location of the *sangkat* where they used to live in KID. He detailed that it was heartbreaking for him to witness as the visitor could only stand in front of the exhibition building and cry for two hours, never stepping inside the conservation areas. Throughout these times guiding visitors, he was able to take most of them to the spots they wished to see. I asked how he could remember a landscape that had gradually changed for decades. He told me that he could recall each section through the marked trees that had grown since the camp operation, as he had been one of the mapmakers for the camp's electricity plan. He was confident that there was no way he would get lost, even though the place is full of new trees that had been planted well after the establishment of Tabtim Siam 08. His experience was one of many stories that, to be understood, one needs to be aware of how each narrative is tied to unique and layered experiences and positions within the camp. What makes Uncle Lek's stories stand out from others was that he had opportunities to meet so many former refugees as they returned to the site. He was able to witness not only the refugees' lived experience during the camp's operation but also the wave of emotions that poured out during the returning visits and the impact of those memories. These witnessed emotions and experiences complicate, expand, and go beyond the words written in the guestbook at the learning center.

Some Inconvenient Truth from the Former Camp Staff

Another former member of the camp staff, Aunt Fang, displayed her thirty-year-old Khao-I-Dang photo albums to show me what she looked after in the camp (see figure 4.1).[15] Aunt Fang graduated with a vocational certificate degree from Surin Province and heard about a contract job in KID through a newspaper advertisement passed along from her aunt in Bangkok. She was qualified for the job as she was a Thai citizen who could speak Khmer, which the application requested. Many people from Surin and Buriram had taken advantage of their ethnic Khmer heritage to join the mission of the international nongovernmental organizations that were the subcontractors of the UNHCR and the UNBRO. She was recruited by CARE International, a non-governmental organization as kitchen staff. She told me that she had to learn how to drive a truck to distribute food supplies for the camp residents in each *sangkat* every day. The supplies consisted of steamed breads (one to two thousand pieces a day) and rice with pickles and other side dishes. These supplies made up three meals a day for those who could not cook for themselves and for those who worked in camp facilities such as the hospital, the mental health clinic, and the church—the last of which also had a children's learning center. Along

Figure 4.1. • Aunt Fang showing her Khao-I-Dang photo album, 2018.
© Khathaleeya Liamdee

with the daily kitchen routines that ensured the basic quality of food services, the photographs shared with me recorded leisure times and the ordinary life of Cambodian refugees in the camp. These photos showed events such as a Halloween party, a sports day, and a wedding ceremony.

Working life inside the camp gave Aunt Fang the opportunity to befriend Cambodians through the language study program. There Cambodians would take Thai- or English-language classes in preparation for the resettlement program while Aunt Fang would learn the Phnom Penh dialect from the Cambodian staff. From time to time, she was also assigned to visit other camps in case there were special requests from the UNBRO. These experiences helped her understand how different camps were organized and separated by political affiliations or resistance groups. Her work experience with Cambodians was full of complex issues and competition, as she said, "I somehow became a rude person because I had to shout and ask the camp residents to be in lines or to be on tracks as there were so many people. Waiting could frustrate their satisfaction; some of them were choosy and demanding."

In her final year at Khao-I-Dang (1993), she was asked to help with departing registration for those who were leaving for third countries or being sent back to Cambodia by buses controlled by the UNHCR, the ICRC, and the Royal Thai Army (RTA). Departure names had to match those given by residents when they first arrived and registered at the camp. She recalled the difficulty of this task: there was no way to ensure that the registered numbers would match with the actual ones as people often secretly left or entered the camp, eluding the guards and soldiers. However, in the end, no one was allowed to remain in Thailand. They were forced to leave to participate in the general election sponsored by the United Nations Transitional Authority in Cambodia (UNTAC) as agreed by all parties that signed the 1991 Paris Peace Accord—excepting the Khmer Rouge. That was how she looked back and reflected her decade of experience. Our conversation ended with her reflection:

> It was a feeling of excitement and anxiety rather than being scared. My *farang* (white) colleague once expressed their curiosity about why Thai staff were not scared as much as they were. It was actually scary, but my teenage self was not scared at all. Thinking about the dark scenery of the mountain near Khao-I-Dang at night when there were bombings. I had to hide myself and anxiously waited in silence or even had to relocate to other area by bus, it was surely not enjoyable but CARE and other organizations, they took care of the local staff very well.

For the local staff members, camp was a workplace, a place to earn money, and an opportunity to interact with foreigners in an international environment. This job came with much more flexibility compared to jobs with Thai government agencies or private companies. Their relationship to the Aranyaprathet area was slightly different from the camp neighboring villagers depending on where they came from. The work experience in Khao-I-Dang and other border camps had affected their lives afterward. Uncle Lek lived in Aranyaprathet for many years before moving back to Buriram for retirement while Aunt Fang returned to Surin Province and continued working as a cook at the Surin School for the Deaf.

I also got to talk to Uncle Rath, a man who used to work as a driver for the French mission during the last part of the war. He had a chance to travel to several camps, namely Site B, O'Trao, Site 8, and Khao-I-Dang.[16] His experience was not attached to any single camp. He managed to earn money not only from the foreign aid agency but also from the camp residents who asked him to run errands. One of these errands was developing camera film at the store in Muang Surin District. "Photographs were very important to people in the camp," he explained. "Photographs could help people find their lost family members."

Uncle Rath's experience during the war reflected his feeling toward the situation and his interaction with the Cambodian resistance groups. He stated that he felt more connected to and sympathetic toward the Khmer Rouge because they were more sincere and treated him like their comrade, unlike people in Site B (Surin Province). Site B housed mostly middle-class people who often interacted with Thai staff more like employees of the Westerners. In his opinion, there was a highly hierarchical relationship within Site B between staff and residents. At the same time, he witnessed how the Khmer Rouge remained financially strong. They did this through receiving secret aid from foreign states supplied to challenge Vietnamese influence over the government at Phnom Penh. Just as significantly, they conducted illicit business that enabled them to buy weapons and keep their troops along the border despite internal conflicts and weak control by Khmer Rouge leaders.

The Untold Story from the Neighbor of Khao-I-Dang

While the Cambodians fled to Thailand, the Thai villagers along the border were also impacted by the war. The fraught border situation came not solely from the influx of the Cambodians but also from the damage to the border communities caused by armed fights, bombs, and looting. Cross-border mobility and business were disrupted. The border villagers on the Thai side were already in a marginalized part of the country with a lack of access to financial support and infrastructure development. The fact that Thai locals were relegated to begging for food exchange or distribution from the border camps indicates that the Thai state did not provide for these citizens or their communities. Some regional authorities would even secretly establish political or economic deals with Cambodian resistance parties.

I was fortunate to meet with Yai Lah, an elder who has lived next to Khao-I-Dang and had a special connection with the Thai soldiers and the camp residents.[17] She provided insightful details of the dark side of the camp that I would never have been able to learn from the government authorities or foreign aid agencies. Yai Lah told me that there used to be only six households in the village, including hers. At nights, the villagers had to hide in the jungle from the frequent looters who came to rob their belongings. She and her husband hid money under the soil so that the thieves could not find it. Although Thai authorities tried to dissuade villagers from living close to the camp, the villagers depended on the money they made doing business with the camp. Yai Lah and her husband participated in these exchanges to survive the economically desperate conditions of the border region. Villagers would take requests from camp residents to get goods such as cigarettes and silk from Aranyaprathet or Bangkok, or exchange Thai baht for US dollars. Despite the high chance of being shot, whether intentionally or accidentally, Yai Lah risked her life many times to deliver goods to her clients in the camp. In secret she would pay bribes or squeeze through two- to three-layered barbed-wire fences. At some point during these exchanges, she believed that there might be spy targeting and following her during the daytime, only to attack at night because of her wealth from this gray business. Because of the danger, she was forced to send her kids away to another province, and she herself sometimes had to hide in the jungle or in the temple at night, where the monks would give her a temporary safe haven. She endured it all because it was the only way to reliably earn enough for almost a decade. After the camp closure, she struggled to find that amount of income anywhere else.

The story told by Yai Lah is rare, and its type is impossible to find in official documents. I learned this from other informants who mentioned the violence they witnessed but refused to share any details or asked me not to write about it. Yai Lah's story exposes another side that only the locals in these border communities could experience. As she lived at the edge of the camp, she learned where and how she could get into the camp and to what *sangkat*. Her intimate encounters and business with the residents allowed her to learn about the camp in detail, including a hospital (the only spot that Thais could access the camp to receive medical services), a hair salon, a kitchen, small shops, a Buddhist temple, a Christian church, a learning and training center, and places to access sex work services, all in Khao-I-Dang. She also remembered how each *sangkat* was operated and affiliated with different, often unfriendly political groups. Violence easily broke out in KID between Thai special forces and the Cambodian refugees, or simply armed Cambodians who used guns or poisons to resolve interpersonal conflicts.

Rewinding Ambiguous Voices: Pathway to Reconciliation

"This is not our history, why do you study about this?" one of the villagers who lived near Tabtim Siam 08 inquired of me when I asked them to talk about Khao-I-Dang. This sentence has stuck in my mind since then. Still, I believe that the above should not be the only way to represent how the KID camp stories have been silenced or became an unapproachable history to the public in Thailand. Various forms of silence operate within Thailand regarding its time as a refugee host country during wartime. Standard education avoids and neglects this particular event in Thailand's national history. However, the local hosts who lived nearby, who witnessed and experienced the violence of the war, as well as those who worked inside the camp themselves, express this history in other forms. It comes out in ghost stories, in intimate memories, and in photographs, but also in some of their refusal to reengage with the violence caused by the Thai State.

Understanding this paradox and ambiguity in Thailand's refugee and humanitarian history as told by the local hosts complicates traditional accounts that often obscure the human element of these conflicts and their consequences. These hidden stories regarding complicated and controversial humanitarian aid can provide further insight into why the Third Indochina War lasted for over twenty years. Cambodian refugee management from the host perspectives could be characterized as flexible and welcoming, but it simultaneously displayed a fear of communist expansion from Vietnam. These mixed impulses motivated policies that were designed to protect national sovereignty through a complicated process that turned the border zone into a mix of battlefields, guerilla strongholds, and humanitarian shelters all at the same time. The Thai-Cambodian border became the front line of the Cold War, a zone of transit, and the site of clandestine movements that contributed to the prolongation of Cambodian civil war and the continuity of political faction in Cambodia until the present. Lastly, I hope this chapter, and the stories contained within it, becomes a useful resource for political reconciliation within Cambodia and across the region.

Khathaleeya Liamdee a lecturer in the Department of Sociology and Anthropology, Faculty of Political Science, Chulalongkorn University. She holds a PhD in anthropology from the University of Washington. She completed her dissertation titled "On the Move across Phnom Dangrek: Mobilities and Silences in the Thai-Cambodian Borderland" in 2020. Her current research examines Thailand's pandemic preparedness and border surveillance in the time of COVID-19.

Notes

1. There were displaced persons from Cambodia, Laos, and Vietnam that escaped the wars to Thailand. This chapter discusses only the camps for the Cambodians during the Third Indochina War.
2. The Second Indochina War was also known as the Vietnam War (1955–75).
3. There is no evidence of direct involvement from either the USSR, China, or the United States; however, the ongoing demining projects in Cambodia and Thailand have found landmines produced in these countries. For example, models found in the Surin area include antitank mines (AT), unexploded explosive ordnance (UXO), and antipersonnel mines (AP). Sirisai, "Background of TDA."
4. Thun, "International Responses."
5. There was a brief moment of open-door policy welcoming all displaced persons (late 1979–early 1980) before it was disrupted by the regime change and evolved to the phase of humane deterrence (1980–89), when the heavy fighting occurred between the Vietnamese-backed troops and the anti-Vietnamese troops at the border.
6. The final phase lasted beyond the general election in 1993 as some resistance groups were dissolved or banned from the election. For example, the Khmer Rouge was able to maintain their armed troops along the Thai border until 1999. Rogge, *Return to Cambodia*; Muntarbhorn and Mantāphọn, *Status of Refugees in Asia*.
7. Full name of FUNCIPEC is in French: Front Ui National pour un Cambodge Indépendant, Neutre, Pacifique Et Coopératif, or the National United Front for an Independent, Neutral, Peaceful, and Cooperative Cambodia in English. It is a royalist political party of Cambodia founded in 1981 by King Norodom Sihanouk, while the KPNLF (Kampuchean People's National Liberation Front) is a right-wing and pro-Western political group in opposition to the Vietnamese-backed government in Phnom Penh, founded in 1979 by Son San.
8. Mead, *Rise and Decline of Thai Absolutism*.
9. The first term relating to refugee issues in Thailand is *"Phu Lee Phai,"* or "refugee," which referred only to the those who would be qualified for resettlement programs to third countries. The rest of the refugees were classified as *"Phu Oapphayop"* (displaced persons, or those "who escape from dangers due to an uprising, fighting, or war, and enter in breach of the Immigration Act") or *"Phu Lopnheekaomuang"* (illegal immigrants who have received a special allowance for a temporary stay in the provided shelters or border camps administered by the UNBRO). The UNBRO was a temporary humanitarian agency that provided services in the controversial and politicized border camps, including to the displaced persons under the Khmer Rouge and other anti-Vietnamese factions. Vickery, "Refugee Politics."
10. Vietnam had been a political rival to Siam (Thailand) since the precolonial era. Later, Thailand engaged with the idea of domino theory to portray communism as a dangerous ideology, necessitating the country's protection from Vietnam's influence, which had already succeeded in Laos and Cambodia. Terry, *Condemned to Repeat?*
11. *Tabtim* in Thai means "red sapphire," while *Pailin* means "blue sapphire." The Tabtim Siam project consists of Sites K and E (01); Site 8 (02); Site 2 (03); Site B (04); Site 8 (05); O'Trao (06); Huay Chan (07); and Khao-I-Dang (08), covered in Sakaeo, Trat, Surin, and Sisaket Provinces.
12. Amer, "United Nations and Kampuchea."

13. The documentary film *Ghost Mountain* (2020), produced by a son of the survivor from the killing fields, depicts the Preah Vihear Massacre as the second killing field, or "Dangrek Genocide." Around forty-three thousand Cambodian refugees who had recently arrived in Khao-I-Dang refugee camp were forced onto buses and driven fourteen hours east to the area near Preah Vihear. They were then forced down the Dangrek cliff, and over ten thousand lost their lives due to injury, starvation, malaria, and landmines. Those who refused to go down the cliffs were mercilessly shot by Thai soldiers. Deth, "Geopolitics of Cambodia"; Hinton, "Khmerness and the Thai 'Other.'"
14. Interviewed on 18 May 2022. Uncle Lek gave permission to use his actual nickname for his story.
15. Pseudonym, interviewed on 28 June 2018.
16. Pseudonym, interviewed on 2 June 2018.
17. Pseudonym, interviewed on 6 July 2018.

References

Amer, Ramses. "The United Nations and Kampuchea: The Issue of Representation and Its Implications." *Bulletin of Concerned Asian Scholars* 22, no. 3 (1 September 1990): 52–60. https://doi.org/10.1080/14672715.1990.10413112.

Deth, Sok Udom. "The Geopolitics of Cambodia During the Cold War Period." *Center for Southeast Asian Studies, University of Hawai'i at Manoa* (14 August 2009). http://hdl.handle.net/10125/10715.

Hinton, Alexander. "Khmerness and the Thai 'Other': Violence, Discourse and Symbolism in the 2003 Anti-Thai Riots in Cambodia." *Journal of Southeast Asian Studies* 37, no. 3 (2006): 445–68.

Lynch, Virginia, and James Taing, dirs. *Ghost Mountain*. Documentary, Short, 2020.

Mead, Kullada Kesboonchoo. *The Rise and Decline of Thai Absolutism*. London: Routledge, 2004. https://doi.org/10.4324/9780203644300.

Muntarbhorn, Vitit. *The Status of Refugees in Asia*. New York: Oxford University Press, 1992.

Rogge, John. *Return to Cambodia: The Significance and Implications of Past, Present, and Future Spontaneous Repatriations*. Dallas, TX: Intertect Institute, 1990.

Sirisai, Amornchai. "Background of TDA." *Thai Civilian Deminer Association* (blog), 18 June 2021. https://tda.or.th/background-of-tda/.

Terry, Fiona. *Condemned to Repeat? The Paradox of Humanitarian Action*. Illustrated edition. Ithaca, NY: Cornell University Press, 2002.

Thun, Theara. "International Responses to the Khmer Rouge's Diplomacy 1979–1991." Thesis, Chulalongkorn University, 2010. http://cuir.car.chula.ac.th/handle/123456789/32548.

Vickery, Michael. "Refugee Politics: The Khmer Camp System in Thailand." In *The Cambodian Agony*. 2nd ed. Routledge, 1990.

CHAPTER 5

A "Lucky Escape"
Ethnic Cleansing and What Happens When International Humanitarianism Fails

Kathie Friedman-Kasaba

It is ironic, on the one hand, that I, who cannot find my way out of a paper bag, should find myself a student of international migration. On the other hand, it is entirely logical because one of my chief questions concerns how migrating people avoid getting lost or stuck amid all the obstacles that mark their journey. Relatedly, I was very late arriving to Esad and Refika's apartment on the dark and rainy February night that I interviewed them because, in the pre-GPS era, I kept getting lost on the way.[1] Overwhelmed and, at one point, ready to give up, I phoned from my car to reschedule the interview.[2] Esad persuaded me to persevere, telling me that no matter how long it took, he would wait for me. He really wanted to tell me his story. It is a compelling story about how a refugee found his way to saving himself and his family from genocide in Bosnia by taking advantage of luck when the international humanitarian regime failed.

Until the moment of his lucky escape, Esad's place in deteriorating former Yugoslavia looked pretty grim: Slovenia, Croatia, and Macedonia had already proclaimed their independence by summer 1991 and had been internationally recognized. The former Yugoslav National Army (JNA) together with Serb paramilitaries had seized one-third of Croatia's territory, and both the Serb and Croatian presidents had designs on multiethnic Bosnia and Herzegovina (or Bosnia) to further their national territorial ambitions. In January 1992, the Bosnian Serb nationalist party proclaimed a sovereign "Republika Srpska" (Serb Republic or RS) with the intention of merging Bosnian "Serb Autonomous Regions"—which were ethnically mixed—and preventing Bosnia from becoming independent with its multiethnic territory intact.³ The writing was already on the wall when, in order to fulfill European Community conditions for recognizing Bosnia, the referendum on Bosnian independence was organized in March 1992. As the last, most multiethnic, and thus most contentious republic to declare its sovereignty, violence in Bosnia was predictable. Indeed, attacks on civilians and fighting over territory started in different parts of the country almost immediately. On 5 April 1992, only a few days before Esad escaped the massacre in Zvornik, peace activists called for an antiwar demonstration in Sarajevo, and more than one hundred thousand people of all ethnicities turned out. Bosnian Serb snipers fired on the crowd, killing six people.

On 6 April the United States and the European Community recognized Bosnia as an independent state, and on 22 May it was admitted into the United Nations. Thus, although Bosnia had achieved early international recognition at both the diplomatic and humanitarian levels, luck proved more valuable to individuals. Despite formal recognition, the vulnerability of Bosnian Muslim civilians especially in border towns and villages was seriously underestimated, if not entirely disregarded. Many individuals, like Esad, survived by virtue of transforming luck into opportunity. Through his own agency, efforts, ingenuity, skills, and determination—but especially in combination with his personal relationships—Esad escaped the carnage in Zvornik and brought his family to safety. Two additional stories of flight—that of Meliha, a teenage girl, and Mirza, a young army recruit—illustrate similar themes but also variations based on context and positionality. Common to all three stories, however, and to most stories of forced displacement since then, is how luck fills the gap when international humanitarian protection is absent by either default or design.

The siege of Sarajevo, the concentration camps of Prijedor, and the Srebrenica genocide have come to symbolize the war on civilians in Bosnia. But ethnic cleansing, or "the violent expulsion of certain populations in order to create ethnically homogeneous territories," exemplified the objectives, long-term consequences, and brutal practices of paramilitary and former Yugoslav National Army troops.⁴ Approximately 2.2 million Bosnians, or half of the prewar population, were expelled from their homes. Of these, 1.2 million settled in European or other countries, including more than 140,000 in the United States, and 1 million remained internally displaced in Bosnia.⁵ As the war's atrocities exploded onto the media and the magnitude of the refugees crossing European borders grew, the crisis became difficult for states to ignore. A Bosnian graduate student in Austria at the start of the ethnic cleansing campaign in early April 1992 told me how the streets in his Vienna neighborhood began to fill up with shell-shocked and dazed refugee families looking for help. From the open windows of his apartment one day, the wails of forsaken refugees drew his attention to the pavement below, and that was his first recognition of one of the consequences of ethnic cleansing.

By the end of July 1992, the UNHCR called an international meeting on humanitarian aid for the already hundreds of thousands of displaced victims of the war in the former Yugoslavia.[6] Ironically, the meeting signaled the beginning of the end of the golden age for Geneva Convention refugees. Forcibly displaced people were encouraged to stay in their countries of origin, and humanitarian aid was promised to be provided in the midst of conflict zones to selected internationally protected "safe havens" and "security corridors." The shameful failure of the "safe area" measure, cynically referred to as "the right to die in one's country" after the genocide in Srebrenica or as "the negation of the right to seek asylum" led to the focus on a new strategy of last resort for host countries bordering the former Yugoslavia.[7] Bypassing the Geneva Convention, the concept of temporary protection (TP) was born. If, in accordance with international law, a state could not *refoul*, or force refugees and asylum seekers to return to a region where they are likely to face persecution, the new UN-endorsed TP status made it legal to accept them for only a very limited time, with very few social rights (no family reunification, employment, education, travel documents, and identity cards in many cases), so as to preclude integration and then send them home as soon as possible. Until this point, the interpretation and implementation of the UN Refugee Convention in Europe comprised permanent residence and integration.[8] When the war ended with the Dayton Peace Accords in 1995 and the UNHCR officially lifted temporary protection in December 1996, many refugees could not return safely to their ethnically cleansed former places of residence. I return now to the story of Esad, Refika, and their family, ethnically cleansed from Zvornik at the start of the war, temporarily protected in Germany, and then interviewed by me after resettling as refugees in the United States. Seemingly a paradox, their story of luck occurs in tandem with the erosion of international humanitarian protection.

Esad and Refika's Lucky Escape

Esad, a Bosnian Muslim man, in his early sixties when I interviewed him, escaped the Zvornik massacre and subsequent ethnic cleansing campaign very early in the 1992–95 Bosnian war. Zvornik, a border town between Bosnia and Serbia on the Drina River, was the second major city in the war ethnically cleansed and seized by Serb forces. Before the war, the city was composed of 61 percent Bosnian Muslims and 29 percent Bosnian Serbs. By the end of June 1992, the city was nearly completely Bosnian Serb.[9] Today, it is part of the Serb Republic.

Luck, both good and bad, played an oversized role in Esad's memories of escaping the massacre when it began on 8 April 1992 and eventually finding safety outside of Bosnia. Working in the communications industry at the time, he attributed "luck" to his "knowing more than an average person in [my] city [about the coming violence] because [of] the pieces of information that came to [my] office" about the military buildup that had begun on both sides of the Drina around the time of the referendum for Bosnian independence in February or March. At the time of the massacre, he was lucky when a younger Bosnian Serb colleague yelled down at him from an office window to run away because paramilitary soldiers were looking for him. Esad had at that moment returned to his office building to warn the others, but his Serb colleague screamed: "Forget about us. Just get lost," meaning, "Do not let the Bosnian Serb paramilitary forces find you." It was common practice, according to many of my informants, for the Serb civilian population in many towns to be warned to leave before ethnic cleansing campaigns got started. Zvornik was no exception.[10] When the massacre was over, the Serb population returned. While some of my informants were helped by Bosnian Serb colleagues who warned them to leave before attacks, others were exploited or robbed by their Bosnian Serb neighbors who told them to run away but leave their house key and belongings for them.

Esad's luck continued after his colleague warned him away from the office. Eventually, he found his way home to his family in the city that evening, but not yet to safety.

> I also heard from other people that by night—when we were not supposed to leave our houses—that groups of people are coming and taking people out of the houses and that they were disappearing. Then I decided to try to leave by myself with my family, without anybody's help, though I knew that there were barricades and checkpoints every ten or twenty kilometers on the road.... It was very dangerous to drive on those roads because there were very many little villages and towns on the roads, and the *Chetniks* [Bosnian Serb paramilitary troops] literally—as we would say in our language—they were growing there like mushrooms after the rain. I was lucky in the whole situation. I remembered something that I had in the trunk of my car. Actually, I purchased a new car maybe a month before the war started—a pretty new car from a guy from Serbia with license plates from Serbia ... and I didn't return those plates, though I had the new ones. I already had the new ones on my car, so I decided to again put back the old license plates from Serbia. Then I put my wife and the kids in the car, and the license plates were really very helpful on all of the checkpoints.

When I asked Esad if the license plates for Serbia were sufficient to get him through Bosnian Serb paramilitary checkpoints, he told me the ingenious cover story he and Refika contrived. "I said that 'my wife is sick, she has hepatitis and I'm taking her to the hospital in Belgrade, because they were not able to help her in our little town,' so that they wouldn't be willing to open the car, ask us for our documents, and to check them hard, because, you know, the disease was contagious." I was "lucky," Esad concluded. Refika echoed his conclusion: "It was luck," she repeated.

Yet, as Esad continued with the story of his family's journey out of Bosnia, it became apparent to me that luck was a more complicated concept than I had initially assumed. He had help skirting around dangerous checkpoints on the road from an acquaintance, a Bosnian Muslim refugee who was already hiding at the home of a Bosnian Serb on the other side, in Serbia. When Esad phoned this "semi-friend," he provided detailed driving instructions. Esad's luck and safety thus far was based not only on his resourcefulness and ingenious storytelling but especially on his use of personal relationships—his Bosnian Serb colleague and then another Bosnian Muslim refugee.

From Serbia, Esad, Refika, and their two young children continued on to Germany. The kindness of German train attendants helped them enter the country. "We didn't have any visas for Germany. Germans let us through ... I believe they knew that we were refugees. The train attendants ... were waving us, and they said, 'We'll see each other soon. Good luck.'"

Though Esad had many experiences with luck, good and bad, during his journey to safety, the most revealing to me was the story about when he and his family found themselves living illegally in the Hamburg Botanical Gardens for more than a week. Pretending to be a tourist, Esad lit a cigarette and was approached by a German citizen for a match. "She noticed that my German is not that good, and she asked me where I was from. I told her who I was, and I told her that I'm nobody and nothing now.... She said, 'You know, I'm a member of a humanitarian organization that is helping Bosnian refugees. And recently I received a call from a guy who said that he might be willing to accept a family.'"

Esad's point in telling me this good luck story was not to make a statement about being rescued by a humanitarian organization. Quite the contrary. Esad used the chance encounter to make his own good luck. "Please give me his phone number," Esad told the German citizen in the park. "She said I'll give it to you tomorrow." Then Esad replied, "I can't wait until tomorrow. Give me the phone number now." When the German with space in his apartment told him on the phone, "It doesn't work that fast. I have to see who you are and then I will decide," Esad replied, "I'm waiting for you on the street, and I'm giving you half an hour. You can decide to help me or not." The man came right away and picked the whole family up and took them to the apartment. "We changed our luck," Esad declared. Esad, Refika, and their two children lived in Germany with a temporary visa for the next six years, until the end of the war in 1995.

But renewing temporary protection after one, three, or six months was "humiliating for us," Esad asserted. "We had to go on the street at 2 AM to stand in line and wait until 9 AM to hand over our applications for the visa.... I think that they were doing that intentionally, just to put pressure on us to find another solution and to leave Germany.... That was the worst thing that happened to me, I mean except for the war, that I had to wait so long in those lines [sometimes controlled by policemen with dogs] just to get one stamp in my passport." With the German government expelling Bosnians, even those who had been subject to ethnic cleansing in what had become the Serb Republic, Esad and his family were becoming desperate. At one point, Esad stated that they contemplated a collective suicide by burning themselves in the middle of Hamburg. Luckily, they heard one day from some other Bosnians that the Evangelical Church was preparing documents for refugees to apply for the United States. At the end of the interview at the American Consulate in Frankfurt, they were finally informed that they would eventually become citizens of the United States.

Refugee luck is activated by the agency of refugees. It involves tenaciously making use of the right people miraculously showing up at the right time in order to obtain help. Luck is important when international diplomacy fails and when there is no organized humanitarian protection system or when that system has been eroded, constrained, and limited by gaps. For Bosnian refugees and asylum seekers like Esad, the attribution of luck to their survival signifies their determination to use an unexpected, unplanned, or chance encounter with a stranger, colleague, distant acquaintance, fellow refugee, or old friend to meet their needs when international humanitarianism fails.

Esad and Refika's luck, as well as their sons', was contingent on their supportive relationship to each other. If Esad had been alone at the paramilitary checkpoint, and if Refika had not acted to protect him and their sons with her fake illness, it's unclear if any of them would have survived. At the same time, their luck derived in large part from Esad's professional status, the knowledge he derived from it and how he deployed it strategically along their journey to safety. In other words, Esad's luck was also a function of the agency his gender, family status, age, and class conferred upon him. But a Bosnian Muslim refugee need not have been a family man or a middle-aged professional to have a lucky escape.

The Story of Meliha's Tenacity

Meliha (who asked to be called "Micky") was a fifteen-year-old Bosnian Muslim girl from an affluent family who left her hometown in northern Bosnia alone shortly after the war started. I interviewed Micky in the United States when she was in her early twenties. Micky's luck was similarly mediated by her gender, age, and class—but these demographic variables intersected to make the circumstances of her lucky escape very different. Though she derived no less agency from her gender, age, and class, her relationships, experiences, and deployment of that agency diverged considerably from Esad. Clearly, her age and gender made her more vulnerable in wartime. Yet, Micky declared, "Destiny, I don't believe in it at all.... My grandmother would say, if it's destined for you, then it's going to happen. I think it was because I was an eccentric kid, I would say 'You and your destiny!' It's going to happen if I decide it will happen."

It could have been a typical argument between mother and teenage daughter over housecleaning that prompted Micky to leave home in Tešanj for the weekend and stay with her cousins in Doboj, which was part of the RS after 1995. However, the context for the row was Micky's frustration with the seemingly endless surge of recently displaced and hungry refugees her mother kept inviting to eat at their home. With international aid organizations not in evidence, it was up to Bosnians to help other Bosnians. The very weekend Micky arrived at her cousin's apartment, the city of Doboj was occupied by Serb paramilitary units and the Serb-dominated Yugoslav National Army.

> I go there for a weekend thinking nothing would happen. It was Friday night, and we were watching a movie, as we are sitting right now. And suddenly army trucks were coming in. A long line of them, never ending. Huge convoy of trucks. They parked and kept jumping out of the trucks.... They were calling on the speaker phone saying that the town is occupied, we are freed by the Yugoslav National Army and that we are going to be protected by them. It was so well organized. They knew exactly where they were going. They had lists of paper of each apartment building, the names of non-Serbs.... They asked who I was because I wasn't on their list.... They went, trust me, through every single apartment.... Making us wear white ribbon around the arm so we could be recognized.

Micky lived under Serb occupation with her cousins for roughly four months. Every night soldiers came "door to door to door, the doors that need to be visited—the non-Serbs." According to the UN, Serb authorities in Doboj municipality detained Muslim and Croat civilians in thirty-three detention centers under inhumane conditions, while Serb paramilitaries terrorized the population. Muslim and Croat monuments were deliberately damaged or destroyed through shelling or explosives. The takeover of Doboj and the threats and intimidation toward Bosnian Muslims prompted many thousands who were able to leave to go to the town of Tešanj.[11] While in 1991 Bosnian Muslims comprised 30 percent of the population, by 1997 they had been reduced to 0.6 percent, the result of murder and forced displacement.[12] When I asked Micky if the International Red Cross provided any assistance during this time, she responded scornfully: "Are you kidding me?! The Red Cross showed up a year and a half later, after the whole genocide was done in Bosnia, in Doboj."

Although Serb authorities severely restricted the mobility of non-Serbs, one day when the cousins ran out of food, Micky decided to go out to buy bread without the white ribbon on her arm. She was severely beaten and remembers waking up in a Serbian hospital. Luck entered in the form of a Bosnian Serb doctor who was an old friend of her father's. Immediately upon recognizing her, the doctor gave her a Serbian pseudonym and instructed her not to speak at all while she was in the hospital, no matter what, fearful that specific Bosnian language words and even minor pronunciation differences would give away her identity. He promised to get her out of occupied Doboj. And so, for months Micky held onto her silence. The doctor, "an educated man who grew up in Bosnia and had Muslim friends," had himself been beaten for "refusing to do certain things for the Yugoslav army." He was part of "a little group of Bosnian Serbs from Doboj who were organizing people to try to escape. He released me from the hospital to this Serbian guy who took me to this house." From there, Micky was able to get back to her mother in Tešanj.

As if this were not lucky enough, once back in Tešanj Micky's mother used the family's money to buy a seat for her daughter on one of the last UNHCR-arranged convoys leaving the city for refuge in Split, Croatia. The convoy "was only for pregnant women or women with small kids.... My mother bribed them." Micky's mother sewed DM into the jeans Micky wore for the trip.

> Depending on which border we would hit I would either be sitting or under the seat. At the checkpoint, the guys come on the bus and check who is on the bus. We were accompanied by UN soldiers. Except when we went on one Serbian border there was no UN and they forced us all out of the bus.... We were really scared and wondering if we were going to pass that border, but finally we passed. It was a long trip, over twenty hours from Tešanj to Split [with many detours].... The Serbs were bombing Karlovac, and we were driving through the whole thing. It was really scary. We survived amazingly.

How does luck operate in Micky's experience? Micky considers herself lucky in the same way many Bosnian refugees I've interviewed view luck. "I thank my God I was lucky and this [what I went through] is nothing. And to somebody here [in the United States] that seems abnormal to say, but I have gone through nothing compared to what some other people in Bosnia went through." Micky's survival in Doboj was a function of a chance encounter with a family friend in a hospital and his relationship to an informal local group rescuing Bosnian Muslims. No other organized international humanitarian organization appears in the story of Micky's journey until the UN convoy is ready to leave Tešanj for Croatia. And, as a fifteen-year-old girl, she accessed the convoy only through her mother, her family's wealth, and their connections. Like Esad and Refika, Micky's luck was dependent on her own inner resolve and active use of local relationships and family connections.

Mirza's Circuitous Journey

Unlike Esad, Refika, and Micky, Mirza's journey began in a predominantly Bosnian Muslim city, Visoko, that remained part of central Bosnia both during and after the war. But the fight to prevent ethnic cleansing was fierce, and when he was eighteen and ready to join the Bosnian army, Mirza was shot in the hip by snipers while crossing the street. "I received a note to go for recruitment, but I got shot. It was kind of lucky. If I had stayed, who knows what would have happened."

After surgery in a makeshift hospital, Mirza was discharged to his parents' home, close to the front lines. "Bombshells were falling everywhere. I thought I was going to die." At that point, early in 1995, his parents procured travel documents for Mirza to join his aunt in Croatia, and from there the plan was for him to travel through Hungary and onward to safety at his uncle's in Sweden. The problem was that "in Hungary, the Hungarian officials questioned me and saw I didn't have a visa to go to Europe, so they took me off the train and sent me back to Croatia and all the money I had was left on the train above my head. I didn't think about it because I was stressed."

Mirza found himself in Zagreb again, alone and limping. As luck would have it, a Bosnian Croat overheard him asking for help in the train station. He offered to give Mirza shelter. "He asked me where I was from ... and then he told me his name. I was kind of skeptical why he would help me—plus I'm Muslim. I was kind of scared. But I was tired, exhausted, and injured. I said okay. I'll be prepared. Whatever happens, happens. I just want to lay down and sleep. And when I woke up the next morning, he cooked me breakfast." Interestingly, the man's wife was Serb, and their son was in the Serbian army. Both had left him, and he was alone. Mirza stayed for three days, until the man told him about a refugee center for Bosnians on the island of Obonjan, off the coast of Croatia. He remained in the refugee camp for thirteen months, applying for refugee status first in Canada, then New Zealand, and then Australia. Finally, after a series of denials, Mirza was accepted as a refugee in the United States, his last choice country.

Mirza's story revisits and highlights important themes in a war refugee's path to safety. First, the need to actively improvise during a tortuous journey across war zones, checkpoints, and multiple border crossings. Second, the act of transforming relationships with family, colleagues, and even strangers into luck when humanitarian organizations were absent. Finally, the curious participation of other nationalities (even "enemy" nationalities) in providing protection or giving sanctuary along the journey. Though these themes were also present in the stories of Esad, Refika, and Meliha, their personal characteristics and contexts produced distinct experiences.

The Significance of Luck in a War Refugee's Journey to Safety

An account of people's lived experiences of escaping the violence of the war in Bosnia has much to contribute to the sparse literature on the refugee journey as a unit of study in itself because of its significance to the process of "becoming" and "being a refugee."[13] Among the universe of themes, I focus primarily on one—luck. For each case examined here, I ask about the international humanitarian context for the emergence of luck. When and why does luck intervene on the journey? What function does luck perform in a refugee's telling of their story of escape? What is the relationship of luck to agency? Is *luck* just another word for *fate*? What role does luck play in the random surreal chaos of war when customary expectations of others are suspended for who knows how long? Luck is a window into refugees' subjective understandings and explanations of how they experienced the process of forced migration as organized humanitarianism failed and "the architecture of protection" once provided by the international refugee regime shifted to an "architecture of repulsion."[14]

How did Bosnian refugees experience the post–Cold War shift in the international refugee regime to a strategy of containment in place during wartime? What were the implications for the forcibly displaced when the humanitarian relief operations of the United Nations Protection Force (UNPROFOR) in Bosnia concentrated on the strategy of sending convoys of food and medicines to "safe areas" like Srebrenica or reopening the Sarajevo airport for airlifted supplies rather than protecting or evacuating civilians under attack? Although, according to the UNHCR's chief of operations in Sarajevo during the war, UNPROFOR made attempts to transfer "vulnerable citizens across front-lines. ... UN Security Council resolutions relating to Bosnia failed to explicitly address the issue of civilian movements, focusing largely on calls for unimpeded access for the delivery of 'humanitarian supplies' and the creation of 'safe areas.'"[15] From Micky's perspective, ethnic cleansing in Doboj and genocide in Bosnia were completed before the International Red Cross showed up. An even more cynical view was expressed by Kada Hotic, one of the founders of the Mothers of Srebrenica organization for relatives of genocide victims, when I interviewed her at the NGO's Sarajevo headquarters in 2006: "We were deceived and betrayed by the international community and the UN who was there but did not do anything to help us," she declared. At various points in their forced displacement predicament, Bosnian refugees came to recognize that they had been abandoned and were alone. As agents of their own lives, it was up to them to figure out how to make their own luck and save themselves.

The notion of refugee agency is part of theory but remains relatively unexamined because refugee voices describing their everyday subjective responses to wartime displacement have been scarce. Because the individual refugee is virtually the only source of information about the actual experience of escaping to safety, the telling of the journey story exposes agency, even and especially if constrained by barriers. Refugee stories of flight cut through pernicious stereotypes of refugees as passive, dependent, and immobilized by trauma and suffering. However, when the story is told only from the point of view of the international refugee regime or international humanitarian organizations, the resourcefulness, motivation, and tenacity that is needed to escape and find safety remains invisible. Maneuvering through haphazard journeys, refugees like Esad, Refika, Micky, and Mirza exerted themselves as active agents by strategizing and making judgments and calculations about preserving their safety. In wartime, when little was under their control, luck appeared in the form of opportunities to take advantage of.

Lucky opportunities always appeared in the form of connections to other people. We could perhaps term this a form of refugee social capital. Luck was activated by Esad when he used information and resources provided by colleagues, friends, and strangers to bring his family to safety on the dangerous journey out of Zvornik to Germany. Micky was lucky when, because she had decided not to wear the white ribbon on her arm identifying her as Bosnian Muslim, she was brought to a Bosnian Serb hospital in Doboj. There, she determinedly complied with a Serbian doctor friend of her father's to keep her silence for months until she was healthy enough to be smuggled into a safer region. Finally, using her mother's wealth and connections, she hid in one of the few UN civilian convoys to cross active war zones and made it out of the country. After being shot, Mirza refused to stay in the country and attempted to use both close and distant family connections to leave. Unwilling to give up after losing his money and facing barriers of artillery and proper papers, he luckily found himself in the position to take advantage of a stranger's generosity until he could locate relatively more stable shelter. Bosnian refugees acted as agents in charge of their own safety as they made use of lucky connections during their complicated journeys across and out of war zones.

Refugee Voices and Refugee-Centered Humanitarianism

As the post–Cold War international humanitarian regime moves evermore in the direction of the containment or repulsion of refugees, particularly non-Western, Middle Eastern, or Muslim refugees, luck seems likely to assume an increasingly important role.

Analysis of the journeys in which refugees discuss their resourcefulness and lucky escapes can contribute to the emergence of paradigm-shifting representations of refugees and disrupt their stereotyped portrayals as helpless immobilized victims. Bosnian war refugees learned the hard way that they needed to rely on their own agency. When international humanitarian organizations did not show up as they had expected, they were driven to invent their own solutions. Importantly, because luck is activated by way of connections to others, the magnitude of strictly individual agency cannot be romanticized. Instead, the supportive role of family, friends, colleagues, neighbors, strangers, and even other "enemy" nationalities[16] stands out in refugee stories of their lucky journeys to safety. Moreover, depending on the degree of protractedness of the refugee situations, new or emerging humanitarian actors, such as other refugees, or local faith-based or diaspora organizations may step in to fill in the gaps in international assistance.

Most importantly, a focus on the lived experience of lucky escapes also helps to build a critique of humanitarianism during wartime. In an era of increasingly eroding humanitarian protection for refugees, the provision of safe corridors and temporary protection will not be enough to close the gap in protection that the violently displaced experience during the most perilous parts of their journeys to safety. In practice, they may actually introduce additional insecurity and precarity to refugees if they are offered instead of conflict prevention or peacekeeping and instead of ordinary Geneva Convention refugee status.

The refugee voices highlighted here contribute to what may be conceptualized as a refugee-centered humanitarianism, amplifying the strategies refugees employ to address their emergency needs and daily concerns while displaced. For Bosnian refugees in the 1990s, as well as for many other war refugees of the global South, the toolkit in a refugee-centered humanitarianism might include these tactics among others: the early prevention of moves toward ethnic cleansing in rhetoric and practice; provisions for safe legal travel across checkpoints and borders; encouragement and material support for refugee-centered networks throughout the journey; and access to UN Convention refugee rights and status for all forcibly displaced persons rather than mere temporary protection. A refugee-centered humanitarianism would go far in ensuring that refugees and asylum seekers will not need to assign their survival to a lucky escape.

Kathie Friedman-Kasaba is associate professor in the Jackson School of International Studies, University of Washington. She is the author of *Memories of Migration: Gender, Ethnicity, and Work in the Lives of Jewish and Italian Women* (SUNY Press, 1996) and coauthor of *Creating and Transforming Households: The Constraints of the World-Economy* (Cambridge University Press, 1992).

Notes

1. I am indebted to Denis Bašić for simultaneous interpretation from Bosnian to English during interviews, to Peter Lippman for arranging interviews in Sarajevo and translating, and to Sarah Dabagh, Sarah Goldberg, and Jeanine Schmitz for transcriptions. Most of all, I am grateful to the refugees who trusted me to honor their truths and relate their experiences. The names of all refugees used in this chapter have been changed to protect the identity of interview subjects.

2. Materials in this chapter are part of a book in progress, *The Afterlife of Ethnic Cleansing: How Refugees Redefine Citizenship and Belonging*. The study is based on nearly one hundred interviews with Bosnian refugees from the 1992–95 war and their U.S.-born adult descendants. Interview collection was covered by two IRB approvals: #22333 and #42934. The great majority of interviews were with Bosniak/Bosnian-Muslim or mixed-nationality Bosnian refugees (Muslim-Serb; Muslim-Croat; Croat-Serb), since these were the groups most likely to become forcibly displaced and admitted as refugees to the United States. Whenever informants wanted and for whatever reason, I employed the services of a Bosnian refugee who provided simultaneous translations back and forth between Bosnian and English. Interviews, which lasted between one to four hours each, primarily took place in the Pacific Northwest in informants' homes, coffeehouses, or my university office. The project has been funded in part by a UW Royalty Research grant and the UW Simpson Center.
3. Baker, *Yugoslav Wars*, 57.
4. Bougarel et al., *New Bosnian Mosaic*, 5.
5. Franz, *Uprooted*, 14; Mišković, "Home," 223.
6. Joly, "Temporary Protection," 48.
7. Joly, "Temporary Protection," 69.
8. Joly, "Temporary Protection," 54.
9. Tretter et al., "Ethnic Cleansing," 8.
10. Goetze, "Witness Says."
11. United Nations, *International Tribunal*.
12. International Criminal Tribunal for the Former Yugoslavia.
13. BenEzer and Zetter, "Searching," 299.
14. Fitzgerald, *Refuge*, 6.
15. Cutts, "Humanitarian Operation."
16. Broz, *Good People*.

References

Baker, Catherine. *The Yugoslav Wars of the 1990s*. New York: Palgrave Macmillan, 2015.

BenEzer, Gadi, and Roger Zetter. "Searching for Directions: Conceptual and Methodological Challenges in Researching Refugee Journeys." *Journal of Refugee Studies* 28, no. 3 (September 2015): 297–318. HeinOnline.

Bougarel, Xavier. "Introduction." In *The New Bosnian Mosaic*, edited by X. Bougarel, E. Helms, and G. Duijzings, 1–35. Burlington, VT: Ashgate, 2007.

Broz, Svetlana. *Good People in an Evil Time: Portraits of Complicity and Resistance in the Bosnian War*. New York: Other Press, 2004.

Cutts, Mark. "The Humanitarian Operation in Bosnia, 1992–95." New Issues in Refugee Research Series Working Paper No. 8, Policy Research Unit, UNHCR, Geneva, Switzerland, May 1999.

Fitzgerald, David. *Refuge beyond Reach*. New York: Oxford University Press, 2019.

Franz, Barbara. *Uprooted and Unwanted: Bosnian Refugees in Austria and the United States*. College Station: Texas A&M Press, 2005.

Goetze, Katharina. "Witness Says Serbs Knew Zvornik Attack Was Coming." ICTY Tribunal Update. Institute for War & Peace Reporting, 13 December 2008. https://

web.archive.org/web/20081213102134/http://www.iwpr.net/?p=tri&s=f&o=347820&apc_state=henptri.
International Criminal Tribunal for the Former Yugoslavia. "The Prosecutor V. Jovica Stanisic and Franko Simatovic." Case No. IT-03-69PT, 2007.
Joly, Danièle. "Temporary Protection and the Bosnian Crisis." In *Global Changes in Asylum Regimes*, edited by D. Joly, 48–78. New York: Palgrave Macmillan, 2002.
Mišković, Maja. "Of Home(s) and (Be)Longing: Bosnians in the United States." In *The Bosnian Diaspora: Integration in Transnational Communities*, edited by M. Valenta and S. Ramet, 223–40. Burlington, VT: Ashgate, 2011.
Tretter, Hannes, et al. *"Ethnic Cleansing Operations" in the Northeast-Bosnian City of Zvornik from April through June 1992*. Report of the Ludwig Boltzmann Institute of Human Rights. Vienna, Austria, 1994.
United Nations. *International Tribunal for the Prosecution of Persons Responsible for Serious Violations of International Humanitarian Law Committed in the Territory of the Former Yugoslavia since 1991. Prosecutor v. Momčilo Krajišnik*. Case: IT-00-39-T, 27 September 2006.

CHAPTER 6

Benevolent Arts
The Persistence of Mercy in Humanitarian Logics
Arzoo Osanloo

Tehran's vibrant theater culture does not shy away from exposing the pressing global issues of our time. One particularly compelling production, which ran through 20 March 2017 in the Iranian capital's grand City Theater, is *Manus*, a play about refugees awaiting processing to Australia. *Manus* is the eponymous name for the island province in Papua New Guinea where the Australian government leased land in 2001 to build a detention center as part of its "Pacific Solution," to contain asylum seekers off its shores.

Created and directed by Nazanin Sahamizadeh, *Manus* is "documentary theater" that presents verbatim the words of Iranian refugees, based on research and interviews she conducted over a two-year period.[1] This new genre of theater, itself a relatively new art form in Iran, is a cultural production in which activists, artists, and intellectuals employ dramatic theater art as a vehicle to motivate audiences toward feelings of empathy and compassion for the plight of others. This exhortation includes compassion toward distant others who inhabit differing milieus, whether they be race or ethnicity, religion, nationality, social class, or gender.[2] In this vein, *Manus* highlights the difficult experiences of refugees caged inside the island province's detention center. The refugees express their dreams and desires, even as they encounter an ever-diminishing welcome.[3]

While focusing on the plight of refugees incarcerated on Manus Island, Papua New Guinea, the play highlights the travails of asylum seekers, including those fleeing Iran. At the same time, it subtly holds a mirror up to Iran's treatment of Afghan refugees. *Manus*, the play, attends to Iran's unique position as major sender of and host to refugees. While appeals to compassion are important to motivate social actors, the ubiquity of appeals to benevolence are redolent of entreaties for sovereign mercy. These petitions to power entrench hierarchies and inequality while shifting demands from justice-based human rights—which are born of the inherent dignity of human beings—to pleas for charity, aid, and relief.

Manus, the Play

Manus opens to a sparse, black set evoking a blank screen.[4] The only lighting is a follow-on spotlight that shines on the actors as they speak their lines. The light is invocative of a lighthouse or fog light that illuminates a boatperson's plight. The refugees are clad in a muddy, eerily neutral shade of gray—pants, skirts, shirts, sweaters, shawls, and shoes. The only color is a shock of bright red, variously gleaming suitcases, or, at times, jerricans upon which the actors sit, stand, and speak (figure 6.1). Deep red and burnished, the suitcase-jerrican resonates with both the luster and profundity of their desires for future, the slippery unattainability of their dreams and ambitions, and finally, the banality of their acts and circumstances (see figure 6.1). If the suitcase contains their hopes and dreams, the robust liquid container, the jerrican, provides the awkward contradiction of the flotillas and sunken boats on which the refugees made their way to shore.

Each character is inspired by an actual person, a real refugee, whom Sahamizadeh interviewed, sometimes in person and other times through the WhatsApp messaging application. In correspondence with the refugees and through the use of messaging apps, Sahamizadeh was able to collect bits of data that allowed her to piece together their stories and narrate a thoughtful story arc for each. The play ultimately features eight of these asylum seekers, five men and three women.

The play progresses with lines unfurling as statements of truth, each refugee humanized through speech acts, declaring their truth, often in short staccato statements. One by one, the follow-on spotlight illuminates each of the eight individuals sitting atop a red suitcase-jerrican as they narrate their reality:

> My prison is the most beautiful prison in the world.
> It's like a swamp here, the more you struggle, the deeper you sink.
> You know that the largest smuggling in the world is that of human smuggling.
> Death brought me here; it ruined my life.
> The conditions here are great for going crazy.
> Our memories are injured. We have to think to remember.
> We are ruined; we came here to be ruined.
> They tortured us mentally; they cussed at us, they insulted us.
> The first thing the psychologists here ask you is, "Do you intend to kill yourself?"

Figure 6.1. • Poster advertising the play, *Manus*, 2017. Designed by Javad Ateshbari. Used with permission.

> I want to leave. Because of you, I want to leave.
> Escape—I have thought a lot about this.
> I have been in limbo for years.
> This is Manus, an island surrounded by an ocean and not connected to any place.
> This is Nauru, a small country in the middle of the water, in the hands of Australia.[5]

Later, the audience learns that the words were taken from the context of each individual's story. Yet, when taken together, these lines, this opening polylogue, represent a whole life experience of asylum seeking. Later, the words will be repeated in the context of each refugee's story.

Creator and director Sahamizadeh spent considerable time developing a methodology for researching the subject of the play. In interviews, she explains how she found her interlocutors, "through a reporter named Behrouz [Boochani]," and collected their stories, "in interviews on the phone" with "people at Camp Manus [and Nauru]." To develop the script, Sahamizadeh notes, "We tried to use people with different mindsets. There was this diversity in the interviews that we conducted with real asylum seekers."[6]

The resulting stories comprise the true-life accounts of these eight individuals. One common theme they invoke is the dehumanization wrought by law and its power to exclude. *Manus* invokes the dehumanization of refugees and asylum-seekers through juridical acts of placing prohibitions on a person's body and thus reducing a human being to the condition of naked life—a term for someone who lacks any legal status and thus recourse to state protections.[7]

> I arrived here three years ago.
> What's my crime?
> I'm seeking justice.
> I didn't pick my family.
> Why after three years am I still in this illegal prison?

This character picks up on the act of banishment and exposes the failure of human rights protections in a world organized by nation-states. Such protections can be enlisted only through the nation-state's acknowledgment of that human as worthy of relief—an act that requires a state's juridical recognition. Arendt's idea of humanity notes this crucial form of recognition and goes further to suggest that having voice within a community is what being fully human actually entails.[8] While the asylum seekers could not speak back to the Australian state or gain legal recognition, through *Manus*, Sahamizadeh not only allows the asylum seekers to speak but also intersperses their communication with actual films of Australian officials addressing the concerns of the state—security and border protection.

Just five minutes in, the Australian state's spokesperson affirmatively marks his unrecognition. A clip projected on the dark backdrop of the set finds the white male gaze of nonrecognition, stating, "I don't know anything about his personal circumstances." And yet, in affirmatively unknowing, he (en)titles the most famous refugee awaiting processing, Behrouz Boochani, who shed the light of notoriety on Australia's refugee policies and raised awareness of the inhumanity apparent at the Manus Island detention center. In *Manus*, Boochani, the character, has an opportunity to speak back to the official and inscribe his experience and his humanity into the record.[9]

> I am Behrouz Boochani. I was a journalist in Iran.
> I sold my clothes so I could buy a mobile and disseminate news of this place.
> Everybody knows me.
> I am a free human being; I can't tolerate modern-day slavery.
> I am Behrouz Boochani.
> I am still alive, and this man is a liar.

The blending of actual words with rapportage, Sahamizadeh explained, allowed for "an impact on audiences and helped to convey more sense of the subjects and details of the asylum debate, and [we] use them alternately in the structure of the show."[10]

Representations of asylum-seeking individuals and their diverse experiences also allow for explorations of different themes rooted in the encounter with waiting and the passage of time. The enduring quality of time passing that the play captures so well evokes the central contradiction embedded in protracted humanitarian emergencies. *Manus* shines a light on humans who are made to wait by the very hosts, states, and NGOs whose purported purpose and raison d'être are to attend to the urgency of humanitarian situations. Their enduring presence is not just a reminder but also a conveyor of the processes that stretch out time. These include a humanitarian time that extends liminality into a state of being and a form-of-life, a life that cannot be separated from its political, social, economic, and ethical surroundings and cannot, thus, be reduced to its bare essence without attention to the conditions that produce it.[11]

The play speaks to the unabated quandaries of asylum seeking. It collapses any distinction between the carceral waiting indicative of contemporary refugee processing and the punitive detention of criminal justice. The characters' verbatim language mixes seemingly disparate vocabularies, highlighting common human experiences, such as loneliness and losing track of time, while also underscoring the unique and contradictory atmosphere of being alone in densely crowded conditions. Sahamizadeh notes the layered and conflicting affects that refugees on *Manus* experienced in interviews she gave about the play: "Prison scares people out of loneliness more than anything. [T]his is the most amazing contradiction in a prisoner's life that is lost in time and seems to be in an eternal bond with thousands of faces, smiles, tears, and bitter dreams."[12]

Manus sheds light on the necessary acknowledgment of one's humanness by the state, a precondition to obtaining human rights, despite arguments that they are inherent. The sovereign gaze of the state upon its fortunate citizens reflects a privileged scope of protection from which some lives could be brought into and made to matter to donors, funders, relief workers, scholars, activists, and ultimately, perhaps, some state actors, even while others remain out of the realm of recognition. Sahamizadeh uses the set and stage to write these bodies back into the scenes, quite literally, by projecting scenes of the horrors of Manus onto the bodies of the actor–asylum seekers: "From the beginning, during the writing, I had this idea in my mind. In fact, this idea emphasized that the bodies of these people are used in the discussion of asylum. The conditions of asylum are such that people's bodies and souls are challenged to achieve their goal of staying in another country."[13]

The hostility with which many nation-states regard forced migrants suggests the need for a new politics of understanding the shifting worth of subaltern others. These include not just those who need support where they are, or those who have made it to our shores, but now those whom we, in the global North, have banned. Those who, as a result of their state of indeterminate expulsion, make up the constitutive others of ourselves, form a human border of otherness underscoring the resident population's us-ness. The play's final scene finds Boochani perched atop a pile of red suitcase-jerricans performing a soliloquy on righteous madness and might:

> There is a tree in the middle of this prison. I went up it. It's very hard to climb, but I am a kid from the village. I had prepared an announcement the night before. I went up the tree as an actor, a poet. Everyone came. I stayed up there for ten hours. I talked to them politically. I gave three lectures. I was a real anarchist and a crazy poet. They brought psychologists, police. I threatened to jump. I got rid of them all.
>
> I said, "You must apologize to me." There are many people who will die for their beliefs. They apologized. I said I wanted music. I wanted to listen to Mozart. They said, "No," and again I insisted.
>
> Be sure when a poet on a very faraway island goes up a tree in a prison and wants music as his first request, he has the power and he is crazy enough to jump. They found the music for me.
>
> [Mozart plays in the background].
> I felt I was on the theater stage.
> [Pauses arms outstretched, looks up].
> From here, I hear the punching of a crazy man on a decayed heavy bag. I see the coconut trees that look at the forgotten prisoners, like sad prostitutes. I see the lines to the toilet, the cold showers. I can even see the island of Nauru, the women who walk on the hot sand and the children whose only game is to make paper boats and to sink them in the rainwater beside their tents. I can see a mother who begs her fourteen-year-old child to open the stiches on his lips. I can see a child who has wanted to talk on the phone for three months, but she has lost her voice because she ate laundry detergent. In her mind, she calls out, "Mother, mother, mother." But she has no voice.
> [The stage goes dark].

Moments later, the theater is alight with a screen projecting a film of refugees' activities on Manus and Nauru, mostly children, playacting, variously, with black garbage bags. *Manus* ends with searing images of children playing with toy migrant boats in puddles of rainwater, simulating the drowning of refugees. And finally, the screen projects one final, scorching image—of Syrian child Aylan Kurdi, washed up dead on the shores of a Turkish beach.

Our mutual and contemporaneous recognition—both South and North—of our respective nation-states' complicity in creating unstable conditions that lead to the outpouring of migrants fails to fully capture the contemporary moment. Now, increasingly, sovereignty is measured by placing bans and barriers to entry on forced migrants, reducing the possibilities for relief. Such legal prohibitions highlight territoriality as a precondition for recognition, and thus, respect for human life. Physical boundaries work to refract and reflect back the worth of our own lives through the very suffering of others. That is, the willful misrecognition of the lesser worth of another human being produces the constitutive other who matters.

For this reason, one of the most compelling components of *Manus* is the live audience to which its message was directed. While popular on social media and performed in Australia and several European cities, *Manus*'s primary audience is Iranians living in Iran. Through the different stories, most days performed before a full house, the actors speak to the audience from a context in which Iran is the sending country, albeit one that also hosts almost a million refugees, one of the highest rates in the world.[14] The stories of starvation, violence, rape, and death—due to infection, murder, and suicide—in Australia's offshore detention centers highlight the failures of the international refugee system to recognize the humanity of people fleeing persecution.

Sahamizadeh notes the violence inherent in the global issue of forced migration. The play's posters and handbill contain trigger warnings, noting that it is inadvisable for those fourteen and under or pregnant to attend the showing. Yet, Sahamizadeh finds significance in the raw telling of these stories, saying, "I believe it is obligatory for adults to see these images because they get an understanding of the living conditions of asylum seekers in a foreign country."[15]

Still, *Manus*, as a play, communicates through multiple layers of meaning. The Iranian audience hears the words of their compatriots who fled Iran but could not gain access to the freedoms they envisaged. By portraying the Iranians as the ones in need of compassion, the production of the play inside Iran inverts the hierarchies of power and casts new light on whose lives matter. The play offers a perspective by Iranians, in this case a female director, on the lives of Iranian refugees abroad while also holding a mirror to the Iranians' treatment of refugees inside the country, mostly from Afghanistan.

Yet another picture is also elicited: it is not that of beleaguered Afghan refugees entering Iran or of persecuted Iranian minorities and intellectuals fleeing. Instead, the flight of the sovereign, Iran's dynastic leader Mohammad Reza Pahlavi, ousted in the 1979 revolution, emerges as the contrast to these examples and may very well be the refugee flight par excellence. He was the exception to the state of exception. His ouster and search for refuge made legible the nation-state system as it operates and belied his claims to divine ordination. His inability to find a country willing to give him asylum exemplified the red lines of interest that determine global relations of power. Only a few countries were willing to host him because of the threat he posed to their national security. Former US secretary of state Henry Kissinger, critical of US policies toward the shah after he was deposed, referred to him as the "flying Dutchman looking for a port of call."[16]

What Does "Documentary Theater" Document?

The spare set design of *Manus* highlights a contrast between the actors, muted in humble and frayed clothing in leaden shades of pewter, set against the brightly colored red suitcases-cum-jerricans. Actors sitting astride or standing on these props evoke the many layers of affect associated with international travel: adventure, intrigue, joy, and class privilege. Suitcases adorned with stickers from Australia and its premier airlines proffer alluring fantasies about the freedom entailed in travel. At the same time, the jerrican conjures a more complicated and darker affect found in unintended flight.

First used by Germans in World War II, the jerrican speaks to white or Western audiences—not, however, sparking the affective joys associated with vacation travel but rather the fearful flights of persecuted Europeans in the wake of the Nazi holocaust. But for the Iranian audiences, the jerrican might also serve as a vehicle to reflect on the exhaustion of Iranians caught up in their country's fortune—both good and bad—of being an oil-rich country and thus necessarily trapped in the geopolitics of resource and labor extraction.

In this way, Sahamizadeh uses a stage prop brilliantly, both to expose geopolitics and to hail the numerous vectors of complication that arise from the politics of oil (jerrican) and lead to the politics of fleeing (suitcase). In doing so, she recognizes a range of populations in the plight of those forced to flee their home countries and lays responsibility for that flight boldly at the feet of numerous centers of power—not just the nation-state but also the global economy, supply chains, and geopolitics. Thus, *Manus* is far from an indictment of an individual country or policy. It is a beholding of the conditions of possibility within our global political matrix, with the flight of forced migrants at its center. That is, through *Manus*, Sahamizadeh puts on stark display the logical disorders born of our modern condition and aims to reflect on them as part of a contemporary lifeworld:

> The issue of illegal immigration has always been [present] because there have always been first-world and third-world countries and there have been people who migrated for a better life. But the story is that, in the last few years, when there have been many wars, like in Syria, this problem has intensified. We must not turn our attention to the issue of human rights on Manus or in Australia only for as long as it is covered in the news. Since we did this show [2017], there hasn't been a month or a week when there was no Manus in the news. But we need to talk about it before it comes to this point and look at its different dimensions.[17]

Sahamizadeh employs *Manus* as a vehicle to explore a global condition, even as it is a local one for Iranians on both sides of the coin—as hosts to millions of Afghans and as refugees themselves, forced to flee Iran. Thus, inasmuch as the jerrican embodies this dual positionality of Iran and Iranians, another important message that *Manus* conveys is one about compassion for others; others who are also ourselves. The audiences of *Manus* embody both the hosts and those who flee. *Manus* unabashedly hails not just the liminality in states of flight but also the constancy of instability and rapidly changing conditions that can move one from host to asylum seeker, from jerrican to suitcase, with just a turn of the wrist. Its message, then, is to prod the audience to an uneasy appreciation of the coeval conditions of being in a state of recognition and personhood, and thus endowed with rights, versus one of abandonment and naked life, and thus in flight. In *Manus*, the director signals that these dualities and potentialities exist in every individual, that we all embody privilege and despair, constancy and flight, and of course, are bearers of rights and recipients of care. The call to compassion is not a plea to the blessed or privileged but rather a recognition of constitutive conditions created by our time—a time of care.

Epistolary Reception and Modes of Care

While Sahamizadeh focuses on exploring contemporary social problems, her works also take up concerns of a wider global audience. *Manus*, staged in international festivals, reveals how a performative exploration of a contemporary global social problem plays in some of the world's important host cities, such as Berlin. Sahamizadeh spoke of the play's reception in cities around the world: "Audiences abroad made a very good connection to the play because this is a dilemma that the whole world is familiar with right now and people everywhere are following the news about it. Foreign spectators have made a profound connection with [*Manus*] and welcome it at international festivals."[18]

Historian Lynn Hunt has noted that empathy for distant others is a modern sensibility that emerges in tandem with the rise of the epistolary novel in eighteenth-century Europe. Hunt argues that the epistolary form of the novel permits a "learning of empathy" because there is no singular authorial point of view but rather several, through the characters' letter writing. This lack of authorship made it possible for readers to identify with characters who were quite different from themselves. Hunt finds that the epistolary novel "could produce such striking psychological effects because its narrative form facilitated the development of 'character,' that is, a person with an inner self."[19] Here, Hunt moves beyond the claim that literature permits readers to imagine being in another's shoes and instead argues that this empathetic understanding is based in a cognitive brain function that has a lasting biological effect. While Hunt distinguishes the epistolary novel from other literary forms, including theater, I suggest that the documentary style of *Manus*, with its narrative storytelling, confessional quality, and multiple points of view, contains the very epistolary features that permit audiences to react just as Hunt describes.

Indeed, theater possesses unique world-building qualities. French actor Jean-Pierre Darroussin has notably found that no other art form allows for the intimate relationship between the actor and audience, which "necessarily listens, witnesses, and hears what the actors say. And that is [theater's] key and unique difference from cinema or other art."[20] For Darroussin, theater, at its very core, is an encounter to be inhabited:

> Theater is a lived experience and those moments on stage are shared in real time. Theater creates a special relationship with the public; it exists only by virtue of this bond. And it is what makes society possible. The audience comes, accepts to sit in silence for hours, to listen to others who will speak of their feelings, sentiments, suffering, joy, emotions, struggles, rage, and, what's more, they [the actors] speak for this audience. The connection between the actors and spectators is unique and essential in the relationship of understanding of society and creates the link between words, authors, and audience.
>
> The actors are able to captivate the gaze of the audience with a simple gesture, to evoke their emotions with a slight detail. It is in these small acts that communication happens and in which spectators reach an understanding, even pleasure, as it penetrates their brains, if not their very pores, so much so that they think about, talk about, and analyze it. After they return home, they will continue to think and feel those sentiments that passed through them by the vector of pleasure, through the spectacle of theater. And with the enjoyment of the play, they remain thinking, curious, and open.[21]

The form of theater that documents verbatim voices offers a similarly epistolary space of recognition in which audiences come to feel the experiences of others who are actual people, as one audience member reflected to me: "What was mesmerizing was hearing their stories, knowing that they were actual people who had really lived these experiences. They weren't just made up out of the imagination of the playwrights and director."[22]

Viewers also noted the ordinariness of both the refugees and their desires: "I was really moved by the simplicity of the stories. They were not seeking anything extraordinary, just a safe and stable life free from suffering, discrimination, and intolerance. They just wanted to live normal lives." Seeing such "ordinary people" brought the refugees and their experiences out from distant space and closer to the audience members, both materially and metaphysically: "While the play was about a faraway island and how badly the Australians treat refugees, it also reminded me of the Afghan refugees living in Iran and how hard we, Iranians, have made their lives. They are the hardest of workers but are poorly paid. They are not respected, and yet, they have nowhere to go."

Beyond the refugees' ordinariness, viewers I spoke with picked up on the precarities of contemporary life that render life insecure with little movement: "What struck me was that these were very ordinary people. They could be me. It made me realize that at any moment, my life could devolve into a situation in which I would need to seek protection. Then this play also shows the fragility of any security in life. It shows that states do not want to help create a safe place for people who are fleeing."

Finally, several poignant reflections questioned the foundational basis upon which refugee regimes offer asylum or hospitality. Reflecting on the comparison with Afghans in Iran, one viewer told me, "They need to seek our mercy. And this is foremost in our religion. But then, I also wonder, is mercy really what they need? We Iranians are known for our hospitality, but we aren't very welcoming to the Afghans." Another added, "I don't think that hospitality is how we should approach the refugee crisis. Instead, we need to make sure that they are treated with dignity, that their human rights are respected. I am not sure that any country in the world treats refugees in this manner."

Indeed, refugees are recipients of benevolence, not rights. This insistence on the lack of rights is an important thread to follow. At the superficial level, the use of artistic and cultural materials not only arouses popular awareness but also evokes praise for cultural values that include benevolence, compassion, and hospitality. These values also accord with the state's use of mercy and its self-identification as a benevolent sovereign.

Manus's Reverberating Message—A Time of Care

Manus's popularity around the world may well document the plight of so many forced to flee their homes due to myriad conditions that may make life unlivable. While there is no doubt that this issue resonates throughout the world, there is a deeper potentiality that *Manus* taps into. *Manus* explores the current era in which the conditions of possibility for how to respond to the refugee crisis arise and take shape, a time in which discourses and policies of states and humanitarian organizations are more wrapped up in care work than in rights talk.

Today, critiques of neoliberalism and corporate greed, global inequality, and extractive and racial capitalism, and how they contribute to the plight of refugees, abound. This plight has both global, that is geographical, resonance and, at the same time, a temporal quality. Never before has the modern world witnessed the flight of so many. Yet the broad appeal to care and the sustained support for global care networks, what Didier Fassin has called "humanitarian government," has also had another, deeper effect.[23] That is, the persistence of protracted refugee and forced migrant crises has broadened the discursive logic of care-based approaches to social problems and has eclipsed calls for rights-based remedies. Indeed, some two decades ago, human rights scholar Louis Henkin referred to the right to seek asylum as "only half a right."[24] Now that half a right appears as a right to seek only minimal provisions to stay barely alive, it is no wonder that some have announced the end of the time of human rights.[25] Others have noted the inadequacy of the current international protections for forced migrants and have called for more legal protections and remedies.[26] Some have noted that the solution cannot rely wholesale on law and legality but rather require a recognition of the political stakes and the organization of political solutions around them.[27] In many of these works, scholars have noted the quandary Arendt highlighted over seventy years ago: that rights are based in territorial (state) recognition, and without them, humans fleeing a territory but with no territory to accept them are left at the mercy of states or the charity of humanitarian organizations.[28] But this sort of aid has nothing to do with the notion of human rights as inherent.

Indeed, in these approaches, the goal is an expansion of the kinds of care that relief organizations deliver in urgent, emergency situations, simply to sustain life at a bare minimum. This is how humanitarian care has eclipsed rights. The emergency has expanded into the realm of everyday life. This is partly due to the protraction and multiplication of such emergencies, but also because of nation-states' increased resistance to affording rights, not only to asylum seekers but also to their own citizens. Care work is not an expanding field only in situations of forced migration. It has become the paradigmatic method for states to address broader social issues, both internal to the country and external. Healthcare, eldercare, poverty, homelessness, and education are fields saturated with care-based approaches to serving the needs of humanity, and they are not based on an individual's inherent rights but rather on the state's discretionary power to be benevolent and merciful.

At the same time, recourse to compassion and hospitality idealizes and entrenches a particular type of care as a gift of mercy and legitimizes benevolence, particularly from the state. Unlike human rights, which states actively resist, mercy is discretionary. The state's discretionary authority draws from and embeds inequality.

Questioning the Paradigm of Hospitality

For decades, scholars have explored hospitality as the logical locus for providing forced migrants with some modicum of safety, even if in highly regulated and dystopian conditions of camps and, increasingly, prisonlike detention centers. Few, however, question this approach, preferring, instead, to engage the universality of hospitality as the source for welcoming distant others. They find it embedded in its own undoing, an aporia, in which the will to provide safe haven is undone by the overstayed welcome.[29] Hospitality, as the paradigmatic logic for safety and security in an interconnected world, elides the globally unstable conditions that contribute to or produce such migrations in the first place. This logic serves to dehistoricize and depoliticize the refugee in order to create the conditions for humanitarian organizations to present their situations as opportunities for hospitality.[30] In such contexts, what is also laid bare is the logic of the state's interest that marks who obtains the sought-after relief to be resettled in the global North. This logic requires some "affective resonance" with asylum seekers, that is, an unspoken but shared sense of social connection, which induces a moral compulsion to act.[31] Those who do not move the sensibilities of the polity are subject to a different kind of humanitarian governance and remain in the global South, nonetheless.

Yet what *Manus* shows us is that states in the sought-after global North have designed policies and programs that make the journey to seek asylum, which is the only right refugees possess, rife with decrepitude and danger. These stark and violent conditions divulge a kind of necropolitics—an instrumentalization of human life and governing through its slow destruction—of the very lives they are supposed to be saving from persecution.[32] What is less visible in a play about a singular detention center is the lengths that countries in the global North go to work together to make such undesirable conditions of reception in the first place.[33] In such contexts, the terms *care* and *hospitality* are, at best, ill-advised and, at worst, opportunistic attempts at evading responsibility.

Appeals such as these, to benevolence, compassion, and hospitality, which arise in part from documentary theater, signal much more than their resurgence in Iran. Rather, they are in concert with a broader, globally enduring logic of mercy that is not unique to Islam or Iran. Rather, this logic of mercy is an outcome of contemporary humanitarianism which operates through neoliberal market logics that rely on and entrench inequality and have come to eclipse human rights. Not only do the laws governing the management of forced migrants depend on sovereign power but, I suggest, appeals to care have also overtaken rights-based demands in a world in which humanitarianism has become a normative mechanism of governance. Thus, *Manus*, the play, as social commentary, resonates because it speaks to the broader, more epic failure of a global system that continues to exploit lives for labor and also fails to protect the suffering of distant others because all protections still derive from the willingness of self-interested nation-states to be charitable and humane. And so, it is through this exploration of the ringing social commentary that is *Manus* that I suggest that humanitarian care captures the zeitgeist of our contemporary period.

Arzoo Osanloo is professor in the Department of Law, Societies, and Justice at the University of Washington. She is a legal anthropologist and has previously worked as an immigration and refugee attorney. She is the author of the award-winning *Forgiveness Work: Mercy, Law, and Victims' Rights in Iran*

(Princeton University Press, 2020), which examines Iran's criminal justice system through its emphasis on victims' rights, forgiveness, and mercy, and *The Politics of Women's Rights in Iran* (Princeton University Press, 2009), which analyzes the politicization of Iranian women's "rights talk." Her current project examines the impact of sanctions on Iranians.

Notes

1. Esmaeili, "Interview with Nazanin Sahamizadeh." Sahamizadeh conducted research and interviews, while two writers, Leila Hekmatnia and Keyvan Sarreshteh, wrote the play.
2. For a brief history of Iranian theater, see Sahamizadeh, "Introduction."
3. In April 2016, Papua New Guinea's Supreme Court found that the detention center on Manus Island violated the country's constitutional right guaranteeing personal liberty and issued a ruling to close the facility. After it closed, asylum seekers remained until 2021.
4. I viewed the play through a streaming link sent to me by the director.
5. All excerpts transcribed and translated by the author.
6. Esmaeili, "Interview with Nazanin Sahamizadeh."
7. Agamben, *Means without End*, 4.
8. Arendt, "Decline of the Nation-State," 296.
9. In 2018, Boochani published his own award-winning memoir tracking his years in Manus Island's detention center. He used WhatsApp to send snippets of his writing for collection and, later, publication. See Boochani, *No Friend but the Mountains*.
10. Esmaeili, "Interview with Nazanin Sahamizadeh."
11. Agamben, *Means without End*, 3.
12. Esmaeili, "Interview with Nazanin Sahamizadeh."
13. Esmaeili, "Interview with Nazanin Sahamizadeh."
14. UNHCR, *Mid-Year Trends Report*.
15. Esmaeili, "Interview with Nazanin Sahamizadeh."
16. Kissinger, "Kissinger on the Controversy."
17. "Nazanin Sahamizadeh: Why Don't They Support Documentary Theatre?"
18. "Nazanin Sahamizadeh: Why Don't They Support Documentary Theatre?"
19. Hunt, *Inventing Human Rights*, 43.
20. Laporte, *France Culture*, "Affaires culturelles."
21. Laporte, *France Culture*, "Affaires culturelles."
22. I interviewed eleven attendees and culled comments published in online sources, including, https://www.tiwall.com/p/manus (accessed and translated on 9 March 2022).
23. Fassin, *Humanitarian Reason*, 1
24. Henkin, "Refugees and Their Human Rights," 1079.
25. Hopgood, *Endtimes of Human Rights*, 12.
26. Benhabib, "End of the 1951 Refugee Convention," 96; Donkoh, "Half-Century of Refugee Protection," 267.
27. Behrman, "Legal Subjectivity and the Refugee," 21.
28. Arendt, "Decline of the Nation-State," 296.
29. Derrida, "On Cosmopolitanism," 17.

30. Malkki, "Speechless Emissaries," 389.
31. Ticktin, *Casualties of Care*, 13.
32. Mayblin, Wake, and Kazemi, "Necropolitics and Slow Violence," 110–11; Mbembe, "Necropolitics," 14.
33. Ghezelbash, *Refuge Lost*, 3.

References

Agamben, Giorgio. *Means without End: Notes on Politics*. Translated by Vincenzo Binetti and Cesare Casarino. Minneapolis: University of Minnesota Press, 2000.

Arendt, Hannah. "The Decline of the Nation-State and the End of the Rights of Man." In *The Origins of Totalitarianism*, 267–302. New York: Schocken Books, 1951.

Behrman, Simon. "Legal Subjectivity and the Refugee." *International Journal of Refugee Law* 26, no. 1 (2014): 1–21.

Benhabib, Seyla. "The End of the 1951 Refugee Convention? Dilemmas of Sovereignty, Territoriality, and Human Rights." *Jus Cogens* 2 (2020): 75–100.

Boochani, Behrouz. *No Friend but the Mountains: Writings from Manus Prison*. Translated by Omid Tofighian. Sydney: Picado, 2018.

Derrida, Jacques. "On Cosmopolitanism." In *On Cosmopolitanism and Forgiveness*, translated by Mark Dooley and Michael Hughes, 3–24. London: Routledge, 2001.

Donkoh, Bemma. "A Half-Century of International Refugee Protection: Who's Responsible, What's Ahead?" *Berkeley Journal of International Law* 18, no. 2 (2000): 260–67.

Esmaeili, Ahmad Mohammad. "Interview with Nazanin Sahamizadeh." *Iran Theater*, 21 February 2017. Retrieved 27 November 2022 from https://theater.ir/fa/91898.

Fassin, Didier. *Humanitarian Reason: A Moral History of the Present*. Berkeley: University of California Press, 2012.

Ghezelbash, Daniel. *Refuge Lost: Asylum Law in an Interdependent World*. Cambridge: Cambridge University Press, 2018.

Henkin, Louis. "Refugees and Their Human Rights." *Fordham International Law Journal* 18, no. 4 (1994): 1079–81.

Hopgood, Stephen. *The Endtimes of Human Rights*. Ithaca, NY: Cornell University Press, 2013.

Hunt, Lynn. *Inventing Human Rights: A History*. New York: W. W. Norton, 2007.

Kissinger, Henry. "Kissinger on the Controversy over the Shah," *Washington Post*, 29 November 1979.

Laporte, Arnaud. *France Culture*, "Affaires culturelles," 24 October 2022. Retrieved 7 November 2022 from https://www.radiofrance.fr/franceculture/podcasts/affaires-culturelles/jean-pierre-daroussin-est-l-invite-d-affaires-culturelles-6987013 (translated on 7 November 2022).

McNevin, Anne, and Antje Missbach. "Hospitality as a Horizon of Aspiration." *Journal of Refugee Studies* 31, no. 3 (2018): 292–313.

Malkki, Liisa. "Speechless Emissaries: Refugees, Humanitarianism, and Dehistoricization." *Cultural Anthropology* 11, no. 3 (1996): 377–404.

Mayblin, Lucy, Mustafa Wake, and Mohsen Kazemi. "Necropolitics and the Slow Violence of the Everyday: Asylum Seeker Welfare in the Postcolonial Present." *Sociology* 54, no. 1 (2020): 107–23.

Mbembe, Achille. "Necropolitics." *Public Culture* 15, no. 1 (2003): 11–40.

"Nazanin Sahamizadeh: Why Don't They Support Documentary Theatre? Because It Screams and Protests." *Sarpoosh*, 20 January 2018. Retrieved 3 March 2022 from https://www.sarpoosh.com/art-cinema/theater/theater961008146.html (translated on 3 March 2022).

Sahamizadeh, Nazanin. "Introduction." Translated by Hossein Nazari. In *New Iranian Plays*, edited by Aubrey Mellor and Cheryl Robson, 7–24. Twickenham: Aurora Metro Books, 2022.

Ticktin, Miriam. *Casualties of Care: Immigration and the Politics of Humanitarianism in France*. Berkeley: University of California Press, 2011.

UNHCR. *Mid-Year Trends Report*, 2021. Retrieved 3 December 2021 from https://www.unhcr.org/statistics/unhcrstats/618ae4694/mid-year-trends-2021.html (accessed December 3, 2021).

PART II

AID, INTIMACY, AND HUMANITARIAN PRAXIS

CHAPTER 7

Humanitarian Departures
Reflections of a Refugee Aid Worker
Ilana Feldman

"The local personnel are refugees who have been entrusted with the job of serving their refugees." So opened a reflection written in March 1950 by a Palestinian refugee working with the League of Red Cross Societies (LRCS) in Lebanon.[1] Another local aid worker, Lebanese in this case, thanked the LRCS for requesting these reflections as the organization prepared to wind down operations: "It is an excellent occasion for me to speak about my impressions during my work in the League of Red Cross Societies. Moreover, it is a very good idea to spread out all over the world, the distress of the Palestine Refugees, their kind of life and their hope." The fundamental hope of most displaced Palestinians, as they repeatedly insisted and observers regularly reported, was to return to their homes and lives in Palestine. This hope was not—has not—been fulfilled. And Palestinians have been refugees for more than seventy-five years.

For most of this time, the United Nations Relief and Works Agency for Palestine Refugees (UNRWA) has provided humanitarian assistance to this population. The very existence of this agency, launched in 1950, was prompted by the recognition that the Palestine refugee problem was not going to be resolved quickly. Prior to UNRWA's establishment, UN aid to refugees was delivered by international organizations (volunteer agencies in the parlance of the time): the American Friends Service Committee in Gaza, the International Committee of the Red Cross in the West Bank, and the LRCS in Jordan, Syria, and Lebanon. These organizations took on the task with the explicit understanding that their missions would be short term. Their replacement by UNRWA represented a kind of failure (a failure to end displacement), but it was not due to any failing in their work.

As part of their wrapping-up processes, each of these organizations took stock of their work, offering suggestions and advice to the incoming UNRWA and thinking about the consequences of their experiences for their future work. The reflections penned by LRCS staff were part of this wrapping-up process. They are now preserved in the archives of the International Federation of Red Cross and Red Crescent Societies (IFRC), as the LRCS has been known since 1991. This chapter opened with quotes from two testimonies. It takes as its central focus a third reflection, written by a Palestinian refugee who was also an aid worker. Habib Homsi was a staff member who served in the Beirut District Office. His reflection provides insight into issues that have been central to the aid dynamic in the Palestinian case, and which resonate far beyond it. These themes include the double position of being a refugee and a humanitarian provider; the multifaceted demands that refugees make of aid organizations, which then shape humanitarian missions; and the governance role of aid organizations.

Humanitarian assistance has changed significantly in the decades that followed. Aid has ebbed and flowed as Palestinians have been targets of repeated attacks and have experienced multiple waves of displacement. In 1950 all registered refugees received a rations allocation. Today almost none do. UNRWA's always limited resources are regularly reallocated across its multiple fields of operation, as civil war in Lebanon or Israeli attacks on Gaza dramatically increase needs in particular locales. Humanitarian work has also changed as the industry itself has transformed, with shifting ideas about best practices in aid delivery and support for vulnerable populations. Consistent across the decades is the fact of continuing displacement, failure to resolve the underlying reasons for this displacement, and the ongoing presence of UNRWA and other international organizations in Palestinian lives.

I encountered the reflections of soon-to-be-former LRCS workers when I conducted research in the IFRC archives for my book *Life Lived in Relief: Humanitarian Predicaments and Palestinian Refugee Politics*. This book, based on both archival and ethnographic research, traced the Palestinian refugee experience living with, and against, humanitarian assistance for (at the time of writing) seven decades. The IFRC archive is one of many repositories of records of Palestinian displacement and the long response to it that I visited in the course of my research.

These repositories contain the archives of multiple humanitarian organizations, such as those of UNRWA, the International Committee of the Red Cross, the American Friends Service Committee, and the World Council of Churches. They include Palestinian records housed in formal institutions, such as the long-standing Institute for Palestine Studies in Beirut and the new Palestinian Museum Digital Archive, based in Birzeit in the West Bank. These records include oral histories,[2] such as the Nakba Archives, created by Diana Allan and Mahmoud Zeidan and now maintained by the American University of Beirut.[3] Many Palestinian records of displacement are privately held, as people kept papers and objects from their lives before 1948, including, famously, keys to their lost and often destroyed homes.[4] Accounts of displacement and its aftermath can also be found in newspapers from around the region, in memoirs, and in various forms of literary production.

None of these repositories are innocent, of course. It has long been observed that state archives tend to erase certain narratives and produce (as well as reproduce) "hierarchies of credibility."[5] Archives of international bodies such as the United Nations and the ICRC may have slightly different security concerns, but they too seek to protect the reputation and operations of the organization through their archival practice. Counternarratives, which in the Palestinian case often focus on proving existence, the fact of Palestinian dispossession, and the continuing righteousness of their claims in the face of widespread denial, have their own silences and reproduce their own hierarchies.[6] That all accounts and all collections of documentary evidence are partial and interested does not mean, though, that they cannot tell stories beyond the frameworks that their institutional founders intended, nor that they are equivalent. Strategies of reading both "against"[7] and "along"[8] the grain can reveal other facets of these archives and their materials.

The LRCS testimonies I consider here are mini memoirs, but memoirs produced on request. They offer microhistories of world historical events. As such, they provide a window into both how people experienced displacement and its aftermath and the globally resonant impact of these events. For the LRCS, they provided an opportunity to gather lessons learned from this experience, to contribute to the evolution of best practices in aid delivery, and also to make a permanent record of a job well done. They likely served a similar purpose for their authors, and they were also a requirement of their jobs. At least some of these employees would have been looking ahead to the next job, perhaps with the successor organization. Writing a testimony offered an occasion to mark the relationships they had built with their colleagues and bosses, as well as to leave a record of their personal efforts and accomplishments in often difficult circumstances. Whatever motivation people brought to the task, these documents provide crucial details for understanding the nature of aid work and the dilemmas and pleasures that humanitarian personnel experienced in doing that work. From the perspective of many years, many decades hence, they showcase how early in the displacement and aid process certain long-term dynamics emerged and how lasting many of the concerns expressed by these first responders have proven to be. Even though the reflections were documents of professional evaluation, they are replete with emotion. They speak of hope, exhaustion, gratitude, misery, and relief. The passage of time lends a poignancy and an additional layer of tragedy to some of the feelings expressed, especially around the acute longing for home.

This chapter is structured as a back-and-forth between Habib Homsi's testimony and my reading of it. I include the reflection in its entirety.[9] Each segment is followed by commentary, not only on the testimony but also on the broader course of Palestinian refugee history. The document reveals challenges that humanitarians face wherever they work. In reflecting on the then-recent past, Homsi's account also projects the then–Palestinian future. This singular document, part of a collection of other similar reflections, produced at a particular, early moment in the long Palestinian story of displacement and humanitarian activity, sheds light on the lives of millions and on struggles across many decades.

Becoming Humanitarian

March 17th, 1950
From: H. G. Homsi
    Beirut District Office
    Beirut

In response to your letter of March 9th, 1950 I have pleasure in giving you hereunder a short expression of my impressions and experiences during my service in the League.

When the Palestine conflict was at its height I was one of those unfortunates who had to leave my home and country for lack of the means of defence and seek refuge in the Lebanon. From April 1948 onward we lived in the hopes of an early return. When time dragged on and the winter of 1948/49 approached it became apparent that the refugee problem was deteriorating badly and rapidly.

Hopes of returning home at an early date had vanished.

Before he was a humanitarian, Homsi was a refugee. He opens his reflections by recalling his displacement and that of his community. In describing these circumstances, he moves between the singular and plural: "*I* was one of those unfortunates who had to leave *my* home and country." "*We* lived in the hopes of an early return." The loss was personal and collective. The fundamental experience was shared, even as distinctions soon entered in. That Homsi became an aid worker was a key distinguishing feature of his own trajectory. And it was also not entirely remarkable.

The dual position of refugee and humanitarian, recipient and provider, was, and remains, a common one. Much of the scholarship on humanitarian actors focuses on foreign personnel, highlighting the tensions and frequent inequities across the transnational divide.[10] As significant as these dynamics are, it should also be remembered that large numbers of staff in any given humanitarian instance are local, many from the community receiving aid.[11] These local personnel, with their related tensions and inequities, are also a shaping force in the international humanitarian order. In the Palestinian case, 95 percent of the UNRWA's staff are Palestinian refugees themselves (a deliberate agency policy), and significant numbers of personnel of the many other organizations that have provided assistance to Palestinians over the decades are as well.[12] An accurate account of the humanitarian "scene"—in Palestine and elsewhere—needs not only to recognize this double category but also to, arguably, center it.

Working as a humanitarian provider changes a refugee's experience of displacement. The daily existence of a busy aid worker will not be defined by boredom, as is the case with so many refugees.[13] An employed refugee will face fewer acute material challenges than do the many so-called "idle" displaced. But being a humanitarian worker does not free refugees from the consequences of loss. Homsi's reflection makes that clear. From the vantage point of today, the recognition that "time [had already] dragged on" by early 1949 adds an additional dimension to the tragedy of the long Palestinian displacement. It serves as a reminder that people who left their homes as fighting advanced to their villages, after hearing about massacres in other towns, or were expelled by Zionist (later Israeli) forces never anticipated that this was an irrevocable move.[14]

They left, as Homsi says, because they lacked the means of defense, and they anticipated that when fighting stopped they would return. They have lived since then not only with their desire to return unfulfilled but also with the persisting sense that things have gone on too long. In pairing a statement about the receding hope for return with a comment about the acuteness of refugees' material needs, Homsi participates in a common rhetorical trope among Palestinian refugees. The archival record is filled with petitions and letters from refugees that do just that—insisting that both are urgent needs.[15] Ethnographic research among Palestinian communities reveals a similar insistence.[16]

Humanitarian Responsibilities

Means of shelter, clothing and nourishment for refugees were very scarce in cities and did not exist in places outside of cities.

It was at this critical moment that the League of Red Cross Societies came out here with a life-line. Every one focussed his hopes on the League to rescue the life and health of the refugees.

That was the primary feeling we had at the time. Later on the refugees began to hope for more and more out of the League. They began to come forward for help on various matters. They began to look at a District Supervisor as though he were a Palestinian Consul. The following is only a part of the functions performed by a District Supervisor, in addition to his League duties:

a) issue certificates of births, deaths and marriages to refugees for registration with Government,
b) issue certificates, proving identity of refugees to the Security Department for the issue of visas,
c) send out S.O.S. in search of stranded members of families all over the League area, as well as in Iraq, Palestine and Gaza.
d) settle family disputes between spouses and parents and children.
e) issue certificates for exemption of refugees from Municipal house taxes.
f) arrange for release on bail of refugees arrested by the Police on minor offences.

In brief the refugees looked to the League not for material and medical relief only, but also for social, cultural and civil services. Official departments were sick and tired with refugees and their problems and the unfortunates had forcibly to turn their face toward that human organization that was out here to serve them freely and indiscriminately, with no ulterior motives, political, racial, or religious.

Humanitarian agencies enter when neither national governments nor self-help efforts are able to meet people's needs. Or at least that is what is supposed to happen. In too many circumstances, in fact, no international response is forthcoming. This frequent neglect is one reason Doctors Without Borders regularly publishes lists of what it calls "forgotten emergencies." The Palestine problem, and the attendant Palestine refugee problem, is one of the world's longest unresolved conflicts and mass displacements, but it has rarely been forgotten. Rather than showcasing the problem of humanitarian absence, then, Palestine illuminates the limits of humanitarian presence. The United Nations, and the League of Nations prior to the UN's establishment, was directly involved in Palestine's fate. And when 750,000 Palestinians were made refugees after the UN supported the country's partition into two, the need to be involved in both aid and in seeking resolution was widely recognized. In one form or another, aid has continued for seven decades. Resolution has never been achieved.

Even with a quick recognition of international obligation to assist the displaced, such aid was not immediate. Homsi's reflection captures the precarity of early displacement. Before the establishment of camps and before the consolidation of aid efforts, people struggled to find food and shelter. This is not to say that there was no help before international organizations arrived. Local charities and individuals offered assistance. And refugees helped each other. But the need was greater than these efforts could support. When Homsi reflected on how Palestinians responded to the LRCS's arrival, his own shift from aid recipient to aid provider comes through. When he commented that "everyone focused his hopes on the League," he is part of that everyone. When he reflects that "later on the refugees began to hope for more" and describes what they expected from the district supervisor, he speaks from the position of the provider. The refugee aid worker does not simply make a passage from one position to another but experiences both, in different intensities at different moments.

The list of duties—as assigned by refugees, not necessarily by job description—brings attention to tensions between humanitarian providers and refugees around mandate/jurisdiction/limits of responsibility that are part of many aid circumstances, and that have been central concerns in the Palestinian instance.[17] Looking from the vantage point of today, with many decades of life-making in displacement, the expansive view that refugees take of the responsibility of agencies (notably UNRWA) that provide support for their communities is not surprising. Though the fact that it is not surprising does not make it any less a source of conflict. As Homsi's account underscores, it is not only with the passage of many years that people want more for their lives and ask more of their service providers. In this instance, they asked for documentation and intercession to help with various Lebanese government offices (police, tax, family registry), for cross-border support with family reunification, and for help in managing family dynamics. Although humanitarian agencies rarely fulfil all the demands that people have of them—especially demands for political representation—it is equally difficult for them to keep their missions as constrained as they initially envisioned.

A Tough Job

As the League commenced its operations, it began primarily with the feeding of refugees. It was a very tough job making a registration of the refugees to ascertain their correct number. As the relief programme became successful in the Lebanon, a movement of refugees from other countries commenced towards this country. Such refugees said they moved in here because they could get proper rations and medical treatment and camp accommodation. The repute of the Lebanon administration had already travelled far and wide and refugees elsewhere began to have an incentive to move towards what they believed to be the new land of "Milk and Honey," the Lebanon.

The rationing of refugees was followed by providing camp accommodations for the needy. Then there was the marked advance of the medical services, followed by the educational, vocational and cultural services of the Social Welfare Department. These successive improvements and expansions in the operations of the League have left their indelible mark of the refugees. Their condition of health has improved. The death rate in the Lebanon has decreased, while the birth rate has increased sharply.

Even apart from the expansion of work that results from refugee demands, humanitarian work frequently proceeds in stages—first handling the most acute needs (in this instance, food) and then moving to provide other vital goods (shelter, medical care). In reflecting on this process, Homsi refers briefly, and somewhat elliptically, to a central and long-enduring concern among humanitarian providers about getting refugee numbers right: "It was a very tough job making a registration of the refugees to ascertain their correct number." Getting and maintaining accurate population counts is viewed by humanitarians as crucial for this work. And given that the resources provided are never enough to sustain people, refugees have an interest in a maximal count. These basic features of aid delivery mean that this care enterprise has punitive and coercive components equally baked in.

Along with the more widely familiar process by which people seeking asylum are interrogated to ascertain if they do in fact have a "credible fear" of persecution and therefore qualify for asylum, aid providers who distribute food, medicine, and shelter to people experiencing disaster or displacement also have to make determinations about eligibility. In the Palestinian case, access to relief meant fitting into the emerging definition of a "Palestine refugee," later codified by UNRWA as "persons whose normal place of residence was Palestine during the period 1 June 1946 to 15 May 1948, and who lost both home and means of livelihood as a result of the 1948 conflict." Humanitarian providers have worried a great deal about fraud in the ration rolls. And as they took action against this perceived fraud, they often worried about the consequences to themselves and their own sense of ethics in having to put suspicion at the center of their relationships with people in need.

In some locales to which Palestinians fled, most especially the Gaza Strip, these determinations required distinguishing among people who all had demonstrable need, but only some of whom had "lost *both* home and means of livelihood." In a place like Lebanon, the concern was more about counting correctly and eliminating fraud in the numbers, such as through inflating births and not reporting deaths. As time went on, and as ration allotments came to be graduated depending on income levels, it also meant correctly capturing people's sources of financial support. What was a small point in Homsi's reflection came, over the years, to be a defining characteristic of the aid regime and of the relationship between refugees and humanitarian actors.

Another aspect of this passage that bears commenting on is Homsi's account of people moving to Lebanon as a result of the success of the LRCS efforts. He highlights this movement to underscore how well the LRCS accomplished its task. Repeated movement is also a general feature of displacement. People move again for a variety of reasons—following the pathways of family and friends, because an initial site of refuge has become inhospitable, because violence has also moved, because (as Homsi recounts) reports suggest that services are better in a different place. Refugee arrival, and departure, is never a singular event.[18]

Refugee Expectations

The refugees expect more out of the League. Not aware of the limited scope of operations of the League for relief only, they look upon it as part of U.N.O. They consider

U.N.O. is primarily responsible for their plight and they therefore want U.N.O. to put them back into their country and homes. Grateful as the refugees are for the relief they have been receiving they expect more help, mainly in the political sphere, for their resettlement on their holdings in Palestine.

This passage returns to the question of responsibility—both the adjudication of blame and the assertion of obligation to resolve displacement and dispossession. And it also raises the question of understanding—in this case the understanding, or lack thereof, on the part of refugees of the roles and responsibilities of humanitarians. With its direct role in the circumstances that led to both displacement and dispossession, Palestinian refugees have always viewed the UN as responsible for helping to redress their loss. And, as noted above, the UN has recognized some responsibility to address the different aspects of the Palestine problem. As the years have dragged on, refugees have developed a distinct set of expectations of UNRWA, the UN agency dedicated to supporting Palestinian refugees, in contrast with other international NGOs that have provided assistance at various times and in various places where refugees live. Before the establishment of UNRWA, the LRCS, ICRC, and AFSC were commissioned by the UN to deliver UN-funded aid, so refugees were correct in understanding them to be part of the UN response and therefore not entirely mistaken in making them an audience for demands for political resolution that were directed at the UN.

In pointing to "the limited scope" of the league's operations, Homsi underscores a position that humanitarian actors often insist upon—that their mandates are limited, that they are strictly nonpolitical in their actions, and that they do not have either governance or judicial authority. In saying that refugees were "not aware" of this scope, he identifies them as lacking in understanding, a fairly muted claim. Other humanitarian providers have expressed similar views in much stronger terms, arguing that it was fundamentally unfair of refugees to expect them to have any role in political resolution and sometimes accusing them of mendacity as much as ignorance in their political activities.[19] And refugees themselves, in the face of charges of either ignorance or manipulation, have often argued both that the boundaries between political and humanitarian activity (and responsibility) have never been as clear cut as agencies might like to claim and that, as the affected population, they should have some influence on the direction and scope of humanitarian activity.

Humanitarian Relations

Whenever possible, relief was served out speedily. In one case League trucks brought 18 families from Zerka to Beirut and were all huddled into a Mosque. It was on a Saturday at 1:30 P.M. when Mr. Brandt sent me a list of their names. That same afternoon they were registered, each of the families in detail, and on Monday noon they all got their full rations. There are not enough words to describe the effect of this service on that group of tired, hungry, and penniless human beings.

One cannot help but notice the humanity and great understanding of the Field Directors. It is thanks to these that full cooperation and common understanding continued to exist between the Field Directors and their operatives. Indeed this was true not only of the Field Directors but of all the Senior personnel of the League. This is the first impression I had when I first came in contact with the League. There was never an attempt to snob the refugees or the local staff. It was the true democratic spirit expounded in most tangible form. This has won our hearts, gratitude and high esteem for our senior officers.

In these paragraphs, Homsi brings attention to the positive impact of aid work on those in need, and he especially highlights the human connections that are central to the process. In describing positive outcomes, he emphasizes both efficiency and understanding in his description of LRCS operations. Efficient and effective aid delivery has long been viewed by humanitarians as an ethical imperative. The conflicts over counts and possible fraud have generally been seen by humanitarians as part of their effort to ensure ethical aid provision.[20] Since fraud control efforts created animosity and suspicion between providers and refugees, they also raise the question: How vital are good interpersonal relations and respect to an ethical aid mission? One critique of the humanitarian enterprise has been that providers tend to be imperious, assuming that they know better what people need than do recipients. Another critique is that humanitarian agencies operate with a color bar, with international staff more highly valued (and paid) than local staff.[21]

In the international humanitarian system, "localization" has received considerable attention in recent years. The IFRC identifies it as a key goal in its current operations, defining localization as "increasing international investment and respect for the role of local actors, with the goal of reducing costs and increasing the reach of humanitarian action" and also as a "way of re-thinking the humanitarian sector from the ground up—recognizing that the overwhelming majority of humanitarian assistance is already provided by local actors."[22] The current focus, and vocabulary, of localization is a product of the 2016 World Humanitarian Summit, a gathering of many of the world's largest humanitarian organizations. An outcome of the summit was "the Grand Bargain," a stated commitment by donors and organizations to "support local and national responders on the frontline, improve the use of cash and increase flexible funding."[23] The Grand Bargain is not the first attempt to change the dynamics of aid practice; the concept of "participatory development" has been around since the 1970s.

And even prior to the emergence of concerted efforts to change the humanitarian system, as Homsi's story underscores, local participation has always been a key part of aid delivery. This participation takes several forms. One is the importance of local hires for the delivery of aid, both from within beneficiary communities and including other locals. Another, often unsanctioned, form of local participation consists of diverse efforts by recipient populations to effect the form, direction, and style of humanitarian assistance provision. Recipients do not have the power of donors, but they too exert influence.

The voices of local personnel demanding change in humanitarian operations have grown increasingly loud in recent years.[24] But even as there is plenty of evidence of (international) humanitarian arrogance, it would be a mistake to attribute too much of the problem in humanitarianism to these interpersonal problems. Similarly, it would be a mistake to overinterpret the success of more positive relationships, such as those Homsi describes. Of course, it seems inarguably better for people to treat each other with respect, whatever position they occupy, but the biggest problems in humanitarian action are structural, not personal. These problems can frequently be summed up as the inadequacy of bringing humanitarian tools to respond to political problems.

Persistence

> Another impression is the harmony prevailing amongst the various members of the League. They come from all nationalities and various countries, of different languages and dialects. Yet they were all united under the Red Cross Flag. They were out here for service to their "fellow human beings." They acted in the Rotary Spirit of "Service above Self." This unselfish human motive of each and every one of them has helped create an atmosphere of service and thus join in the alleviation of the misery of the refugees.
>
> The League operations and activities have proved beyond any shadow of a doubt that when people of varied and different nationalities meet in a joint endeavour, with sincerity and eagerness, to serve and fulfil a mission, they will certainly succeed. The Palestine Refugee problem has proved more than an example of this. Let us hope that this operation will open wide the doors for international understanding, cooperation and brotherhood in all other spheres of life.
>
> Looking back over the last 15 months' service, I cannot but stand up and raise my hat in respect for you as head of this organisation and its main brain and for all the senior personnel of the League, for their large hearts, common understanding, sympathy and devotion, as well as for the valuable services rendered by the League to the refugees.

The reflection ends with an expression of appreciation for a series of humanitarian ideals: multinational cooperation for the good of humanity, the principle of service above self, the successful alleviation of suffering, and the potential for a broader and deeper project of "international understanding." Homsi affirms that the LRCS mission has exemplified these ideals. Whether he actually felt as positively about the experience as he stated in this reflection is impossible to know, but his evaluation is not out of step with the other reflections the LRCS gathered, whether penned by local or international personnel.

Humanitarianism has long been caught in the tension between an ethics of responsibility and an ethics of conviction.[25] Is it by outcome or intentions that the ethics of an operation can be judged? Is it the details of the work or the principles that undergird it that matter most? And how much do either of those matter if the entire approach to a problem is fundamentally flawed or limited?[26] The Palestinian experience with humanitarian aid, and the humanitarian encounter with the Palestine problem, shed light on global aid dynamics. These dynamics persisted far after the end of the LRCS mission.

This persistence is a reminder of a crucial part of this story: the conclusion of the LRCS mission (along with those of the ICRC and AFSC) in 1950 was just at the beginning of the long, and continuing, Palestinian story of displacement. As another local LRCS employee ended his reflection, "Thus the days go by while the refugee trods [sic] wearily on the tragic path, like a thirsty man who is following a mirage in the desert. There seems to be no end to more suffering and more misery. In the meantime, the nations of the world who could not avert this catastrophe are contributing generously to cover the cost of remedies. But there is no remedy, and there will be none, for 'be it ever so humble, there is no place like HOME.'"

Ilana Feldman is professor of anthropology, history, and international affairs at George Washington University. Her research focuses on the Palestinian experience, both inside and outside of historic Palestine, examining practices of government, humanitarianism, policing, displacement, and citizenship. She is the author of *Life Lived in Relief: Humanitarian Predicaments and Palestinian Refugee Politics* (University of California Press, 2018); *Police Encounters: Security and Surveillance in Gaza under Egyptian Rule* (Stanford University Press, 2015), and *Governing Gaza: Bureaucracy, Authority, and the Work of Rule, 1917–67* (Duke University Press, 2008), and is coeditor of *In the Name of Humanity: The Government of Threat and Care* (Duke University Press, 2010).

Notes

1. All the reflections discussed here are from the International Federation of Red Cross and Red Crescent Societies Archives, File A0403-2 19740, Personal Experiences.
2. Sayigh, "Nakba and Oral History."
3. https://www.nakba-archive.org/
4. Seikaly, "How I Met My Grandfather"; Saad, "Materializing Palestinian Memory."
5. Stoler, *Along the Archival Grain*; Trouillot, *Silencing the Past*; Dirks, *Autobiography of an Archive*.

6. Swedenburg, *Memories of Revolt*; Seikaly, "How I Met My Grandfather."
7. Said, *On Late Style*.
8. Stoler, *Along the Archival Grain*.
9. Homsi, "Personal Experiences, Beirut District Office, Beirut. March 17, 1950."
10. Beckett, "A Dog's Life"; Fassin, "Humanitarianism as a Politics of Life"; Hor, "Everyday Emotional Lives"; Carpi, "Epistemic Politics"; Benton, "African Expatriates and Race."
11. Sundberg, "National Staff"; Heathershaw, "Who Are the 'International Community'?"
12. Farah, "UNRWA through Employee Eyes"; Feldman, *Life Lived in Relief*.
13. Dunn, "Politics of Nothing."
14. Allan, *Voices of the Nakba*.
15. Irfan, "Petitioning for Palestine."
16. Feldman, "Reckoning with Time."
17. Husseini, "UNRWA and the Refugees."
18. Feldman, "Conflicted Presence."
19. Feldman, "Untimely Optimism."
20. Hyndman, *Managing Displacement*.
21. Redfield, "Unbearable Lightness of Expats."
22. Retrieved 25 February 2022 from https://www.ifrc.org/localization.
23. Retrieved 25 February 2022 from https://interagencystandingcommittee.org/system/files/grand_bargain_final_22_may_final-2.pdf.
24. Slim, "Localization Is Self-Determination."
25. Fassin and d'Halluin, "Truth from the Body."
26. Pallister-Wilkins, "Saving the Souls of White Folks."

References

Allan, Diana. *Voices of the Nakba: A Living History of Palestine*. London: Pluto Press, 2021.

Beckett, Greg. "A Dog's Life: Suffering Humanitarianism in Port-Au-Prince, Haiti." *American Anthropologist* 119, no. 1 (2017): 35–45.

Benton, Adia. "African Expatriates and Race in the Anthropology of Humanitarianism." *Critical African Studies* 8, no. 3 (2016): 266–77.

Carpi, Estella. "The Epistemic Politics of 'Northern-Led' Humanitarianism: The Case of Lebanon." *Area* (2021). Doi: 10.1111/AREA.12770.

Dirks, Nicholas. *Autobiography of an Archive: A Scholar's Passage to India*. New York: Columbia University Press, 2015.

Dunn, Elizabeth Cullen. "Humanitarianism, Displacement, and the Politics of Nothing in Postwar Georgia." *Slavic Review* 73, no. 2 (2014): 287–306.

Farah, Randa. "UNRWA: Through the Eyes of Its Refugee Employees in Jordan." *Refugee Survey Quarterly* 28, nos. 2–3 (2009): 389–411.

Fassin, Didier. "Humanitarianism as a Politics of Life." *Public Culture* 19, no. 3 (2007): 499–520.

Fassin, Didier, and Estelle d'Halluin. "The Truth from the Body: Medical Certificates as Ultimate Evidence for Asylum Seekers." *American Anthropologist* 107, no. 4 (2005): 597–608.

Feldman, Ilana. *Life Lived in Relief: Humanitarian Predicaments and Palestinian Refugee Politics*. Berkeley: University of California Press, 2018.

———. "Reckoning with Time: Vexed Temporalities in Human Rights and Humanitarianism." In *Humanitarianism and Human Rights: A World of Differences?* edited by Michael Barnett, 203–18. Cambridge: Cambridge University Press, 2020.

———. "Conflicted Presence: The Many Arrivals of Palestinians in Lebanon." *Migration Studies* 10, no. 2 (2022): 190–213.

———. "Untimely Optimism: International Attention, Palestinian Disappointment, and the Persistence of Commitment." *Anthropological Quarterly*. Forthcoming.

Heathershaw, John. "Who Are the 'International Community'? Development Professionals and Liminal Subjectivity." *Journal of Intervention and Statebuilding* 10, no. 1 (2016): 77–96.

Homsi, H. G. "Personal Experiences." Beirut District Office, Beirut. 17 March 1950. International Federation of Red Cross and Red Crescent Societies Archives, File A0403-2 19740.

Hor, Amoz. "The Everyday Emotional Lives of Aid Workers: How Humanitarian Anxiety Gets in the Way of Meaningful Local Participation." *International Theory* (2021): 1–30. Doi:10.1017/S1752971921000166.

Al Husseini, Jalal. "UNRWA and the Refugees: A Difficult but Lasting Marriage." *Journal of Palestine Studies* 40, no. 1 (2010): 6–26.

Hyndman, Jennifer. *Managing Displacement: Refugees and the Politics of Humanitarianism*. Minneapolis: University of Minnesota Press, 2000.

Irfan, Anne. "Petitioning for Palestine: Refugee Appeals to International Authorities." *Contemporary Levant* 5, no. 2 (2020): 79–96.

Pallister-Wilkins, Polly. "Saving the Souls of White Folk: Humanitarianism as White Supremacy." *Security Dialogue* 52, no. 1 (Suppl) (2021): 98–106.

Redfield, Peter. "The Unbearable Lightness of Ex-pats: Double Binds of Humanitarian Mobility." Cultural Anthropology 27, No. 2 (2012): 358–82.

Saad, Dima. "Materializing Palestinian Memory: Objects of Home and the Everyday Eternities of Exile." *Jerusalem Quarterly* 80 (2019): 57.

Said, Edward W. *On Late Style: Music and Literature against the Grain*. New York: Pantheon, 2006.

Sayigh, Rosemary. "The Nakba and Oral History." *Journal of Holy Land and Palestine Studies* 17, no. 2 (2018): 151–68.

Seikaly, Sherene. "How I Met My Great-Grandfather: Archives and the Writing of History." *Comparative Studies of South Asia, Africa and the Middle East* 38, no. 1 (2018): 6–20.

Slim, Hugo. "Localization Is Self-Determination." *Frontiers in Political Science* 3 (2021): 80.

Swedenburg, Ted. *Memories of Revolt: The 1936–1939 Rebellion and the Palestinian National Past*. Fayetteville: University of Arkansas Press, 2003.

Stoler, Ann Laura. *Along the Archival Grain*. Princeton, NJ: Princeton University Press, 2010.

Sundberg, Molly. "National Staff in Public Foreign Aid: Aid Localization in Practice." *Human Organization* 78, no. 3 (2019): 253–63.

Trouillot, Michel-Rolph. *Silencing the Past: Power and the Production of History*. Boston: Beacon Press, 2015.

CHAPTER 8

Quiet Aid

Barbara Schöfnagel's Private Humanitarianism in the Socialist Gray Area (and What Else the Global East Can Teach Us)

Cristian Capotescu

In March 1988, a letter from West Germany reached Barbara Schöfnagel's home in Vienna. The sender, a medical student from Munich, Siegfried Gassner, wrote with an ambitious proposition: responding to the severe material shortages that had been reported from Romania under its socialist leader Nicolae Ceaușescu, Gassner and two colleagues intended to charter a vehicle and deliver baby food and other scarce essentials of daily living to families across the Iron Curtain. Unfamiliar with facilitating such an unlikely aid campaign into the socialist bloc, Gassner contacted Schöfnagel, the foremost authority on delivering aid to Romania at the time. Gassner hoped to learn from Schöfnagel about Romanian border policies, lodging, gas supply, and local contacts—"to keep it simple, everything one would need to know to organize such a trip," as he put it.[1] Such inquiries were not uncommon in Schöfnagel's buzzing mailbox, where nearly daily correspondences arrived through her far-flung network of private donors, émigré associations, church groups, and volunteers in Eastern Europe. Schöfnagel was a self-described folklore dancer, mother of four, community organizer, and, after 1989, a Viennese politician and social attaché of the Austrian government to Bulgaria and Romania. In the 1980s she was also a pioneering "private humanitarian" in a field that bore unique challenges, dangers, and risks in one of the lesser-known parts of the humanitarian world.

When Gassner sought Schöfnagel's advice in spring 1988, organizing humanitarian assistance to one of the socialist bloc's most authoritarian states was no small feat. The defining question determining the success and failure of any such campaign: Could any aid be delivered to a repressive political regime such as Romania, and if so, how? Behind the Iron Curtain, distinct challenges confronted private humanitarians like Schöfnagel (and aspiring ones like Gassner) that were unlike what aid workers encountered in the southern hemisphere. In such crisis zones, civil wars, military conflicts, and natural disasters set off large-scale displacements and caused immense loss of human life and material devastation. However, such cataclysmic events led less often to permanent embargoes or the removal of humanitarian organizations by local governments. In contrast, socialist states like Ceaușescu's Romania prohibited aid organizations from entering their territory—not for months or years, but decades. Such entry bans became indefinite barriers depriving humanitarian organizations of an elemental foundation for their work: unfettered mobility across national borders and autonomy to operate independently from the state. What made conditions in the socialist bloc different from the global South was also the relative stability of statehood during states of emergency. Few countries in Eastern Europe after 1945 plunged into domestic disarray (except for Czechoslovakia in 1968) or slid to the brink of institutional collapse (before the tremors of 1989). Instead, Ceaușescu's Romania and other socialist regimes wielded the power of their brute security apparatuses, chief among them their fortified border regimes and secret police, to restrict passage into the country for undesired visitors. Representatives of humanitarian organizations who managed, against all odds, to slip through border controls had only cleared the first stage of their dangerous journeys. Behind the Iron Curtain, the threat of running afoul of a massive surveillance machinery capable of tracing and persecuting them internally was constantly looming over them. In short, in the socialist bloc, there was no escaping the state.

Private humanitarians like Schöfnagel adapted to these political conditions by disassociating themselves from the field of international humanitarianism. During her remarkable forty-eight-year career as a private humanitarian, Schöfnagel was not affiliated with a Western aid organization or trained in what increasingly became a professionalized humanitarian field. Avoiding the cachet of a professional humanitarian was, in fact, one of Schöfnagel's recipes for success. In this, her work also differed operationally from prominent aid organizations in the global North that focused on building capacity, scaling up assistance, and mobilizing government and public support to fund their campaigns. Schöfnagel developed instead a wide array of community-based strategies and informal repertoires to make aid runs across Romania's heavily surveilled borders. Significantly, her activities remained no secret to the socialist state. Schöfnagel's campaigns often occurred in plain sight with detailed knowledge of socialist officials and the secret police or *Securitate*. Schöfnagel's informal aid work thus offers insights into a peculiar form of informality that allowed her to evade capture by the Romanian authorities, not through techniques of deception and clandestine trafficking but through a practice of "graying." In Schöfnagel's aid giving, graying referred to the process of reworking a Western humanitarian format to the specific social norms governing socialism's societal structure, notably its "gray area." To ensure her assistance reached recipients across the Iron Curtain, the circumstances and organization of her aid work had to remain "quiet," as Schöfnagel put it.

Based on personal materials, memories, letters, and interviews with Schöfnagel, this chapter presents a rare view of an alternative humanitarianism in the socialist bloc. The discussion first elucidates what is meant by the socialist gray area and explains how Schöfnagel's practice of graying fit in. It then examines Schöfnagel's various tactics and assistance vehicles that combined cultural and material forms of care. Finally, the focus turns to Schöfnagel's campaigns under conditions of state surveillance and ends with the eventual collapse of her work shortly before the end of state socialism in the summer of 1989.

Above all, Schöfnagel's story demonstrates that "graying" was not a form of acquiescence to the restrictive policies of the Ceaușescu regime banning humanitarian organizations from operating in Romania. Graying her aid required Schöfnagel instead to preserve the appearance of compliance with socialism's social codes and render her campaigns legible to what state authorities deemed acceptable while pursuing her true agenda cautiously and deliberately. In this region of the world—the Second World as it was referred to until the end of the Cold War—where aid often occurred in such "quiet" ways, Schöfnagel's private humanitarianism transpired not as part of liberation struggles and postcolonial development as was common in the global South. It also did not occur within the framework of Western humanitarian organizations. Schöfnagel's was instead a humanitarianism sui generis at the margins of the international humanitarian regime. Her work straddled authoritarianism, Cold War geopolitics, and rusty Marxist welfare utopias in that liminal (yet vast) geographic region that, given its distinct characteristics, should be treated as a region in its own right, as the "Global East" of humanitarianism.[2]

Humanitarianism in the Gray Area

In the late 1980s, Gassner's exchange with Schöfnagel came on the heels of years of draconian austerity measures the Ceaușescu regime implemented to shore up the country's external loan repayments.[3] Trapped in an escalating debt spiral in the early 1980s, the Romanian state introduced bread rationing, sharply reducing the population's access to butter, corn, flour, milk, sugar, and a lengthy list of essential consumer goods. Likewise, electricity, warm water, and gas were shut off without warning, sometimes twice daily. Medical supplies became sparse, and millions of apartments remained dark and unheated in the winter. In the words of Romanian historian Vlad Georgescu, the dire conditions of life amounted to a "bizarre process of demodernization ... in a state that produced cars but banned driving, built housing developments but withheld heat and running water, announced that it had harvested the biggest grain crop in history but put its people on meager bread rations."[4]

Responding to Gassner's plan of delivering aid to Romania, Schöfnagel cautioned that border controls would thwart any attempt to transport aid into the country without careful preparation. Schöfnagel warned Gassner, "An aid trip is doomed to fail if it is recognized as such by border officials. It is possible that you will not be granted passage and will be banned from visiting in the future. I am familiar with such cases."[5] These obstacles notwithstanding, Schöfnagel offered some encouragement, adding that there existed viable methods of crossing borders. But, she insisted, Gassner had to follow the script that she would lay out for him. Schöfnagel instructed:

> If you want to help, you need to find the middle ground (that indefinite gray area in Romania) between the legal and illegal. You should travel as a "tourist." Should you carry a few extra items with you, such as foodstuffs, clothes, medicine, and travel literature, you can declare them for personal use. Of course, everything would have to be packed accordingly. You will be permitted to bring about 300 Deutsche Mark in gifts to Romania, but foodstuffs, medicine, and used clothes are prohibited from being given as gifts! Nobody will ask questions if you happen to "forget" some of your belongings in the country.[6]

Schöfnagel's reference to a gray area alluded to the sphere of informality in socialist societies, where citizens exchanged, traded, and obtained goods, favors, and services otherwise unavailable or hard to come by. The socialist gray area was not akin to a "black market" (in the Western sense), where citizens (or members of a mafia) would engage in smuggling and corrupt dealings to evade the law. Instead, it was part and parcel of the economic and social fabric of the system. Moreover, there was not just one gray-colored area but many areas in different shades of gray, stretching along and across society in varying tones and intensities. In a sense, everyone lived in the gray area, navigating it daily and in the full knowledge that the boundaries between "official" and "unofficial," "legal" and "illegal," were blurry and negotiable. Socialist state institutions, too, shaped and formed the gray area; they were built on a symbiotic web of informal exchanges and relationships that sustained state activity and economic life.[7]

Schöfnagel was cognizant that humanitarian campaigns had to adhere to the same logic of grayness. Western donors like Gassner, who wished to avoid running afoul of the state's prohibition of foreign aid, had to adopt the social codes of the border. Graying his activities meant for Gassner to employ a tactic of making himself legible to the state under a different visitor category ("travel as a tourist") and reappropriate a range of repertoires to make his activities less conspicuous ("pack accordingly and forget something when you leave"). However, successful passage across the border was only the first step. Inside Romania, Schöfnagel advised, Gassner had to heed additional precautions to ensure that his campaign would not "do more harm than good." Her supplementary instructions included:

> The gasoline supply is unpredictable.... As a foreigner, you can purchase gasoline vouchers at the hotel (in exchange for Deutsche Mark). Therefore, you will not have to wait for days in those long lines in front of gas stations. However, I always advise people to tank gas very frequently and never run the tank down to the last drop. Gasoline stations often do not work, sometimes, they are out of gasoline, and you might not find supplies in every city. As a foreigner, you will be required to buy hotel vouchers in the West and find lodging in state-run hotels. It is *PROHIBITED* to stay with friends or acquaintances! In Transylvania, Protestant pastors will serve as contact persons.... You may ask them to take your goods and distribute them. Given the difficulties of transporting large quantities of foodstuffs across the border, I recommend that you only bring items unavailable in Romania (baby food, baking powder, pepper, margarine, butter, etc.). Everything else (flour, sugar, coffee, cocoa, salami, cheese, canned sausage) can be currently purchased in the intershops for foreigners in exchange for valuta. Of course, all of this would have to be done quietly and without drawing attention.[8]

What Schöfnagel's lengthy list revealed was the extent to which private humanitarians maneuvered a landscape of contingencies and certainties. The former group of arrangements, such as gasoline supplies, were difficult to control, but the latter could be reasonably found (and leveraged) during an assistance trip with the help of trusted middlemen willing to distribute provisions (e.g., Protestant pastors). Interspersed throughout were fluid risk factors dependent on domestic supply chain conditions affecting the availability of foodstuffs and consumer items as well as shifting state regulations. Like Gassner, those aspiring to become private humanitarians had to acquire knowledge and expertise about navigating border passage and state laws under changing conditions. Graying one's work thus involved gaining deep familiarity with the prevailing social codes in Romania and learning how to tap local networks and middlemen. Graying also included knowledge of how to avoid drawing the attention of Romania's secret police, the *Securitate*, which employed one of the largest bodies of informants and spies in the socialist bloc. Schöfnagel's warning that Gassner could do "more harm than good" highlighted the possibility of drawing the *Securitate*'s attention, with the associated risks and dangers to one's safety and that of one's collaborators if identified as a "hostile element."

Armed with Schöfnagel's instructions, did Gassner succeed? In correspondence from 31 March 1988, Gassner agreed to reconnect with Schöfnagel once his plans matured to the point of readiness. After this last communication, Gassner's traces disappear in Schöfnagel's personal collection, leaving little indication of whether his operation was ultimately successful—or if it ever materialized. Despite its incompleteness, the Gassner-Schöfnagel exchange offers a glimpse into the cross-pollinating connections among private humanitarians. Experienced practitioners like Schöfnagel shared their lay expertise with novices like Gassner, and through such informal networks, a transnational landscape of loosely connected and decentralized private humanitarian campaigns spread in Cold War Europe. Importantly, this exchange also highlights how Schöfnagel's work hinged on her ability to gauge where the socialist gray area began—and where it ended. In regard to humanitarian assistance, this gray area had a threshold, a delimiting boundary within which it was possible to coordinate aid "quietly" and "from person to person," as Schöfnagel described it. Likewise, Schöfnagel's ability to move across the Iron Curtain depended on a range of tactics, such as Trojan horse maneuvers and a sprawling network of private donors that funded her aid campaigns over the years. For almost two decades, her aid activities operated in plain sight of the state yet below the official threshold of the socialist gray area that international organizations failed to clear as they continuously ran up against the Ceaușescu regime's prohibition of foreign aid.

Humanitarianism Disguised as Folklore and Cultural Tourism

How did the career of one of the Cold War's most remarkable private humanitarians begin? Barbara-Wiebke "Bärbel" Schöfnagel, was born to Walter and Luise-Margarete Mückstein in Vienna in 1948. After completing her school education, Schöfnagel joined her parents' family business and worked as a dental assistant from 1967 to 1973. In this period, Schöfnagel also married her husband Dieter, with whom she had four children. Alongside managing her growing family, Schöfnagel followed her vocational interests in accounting, dance instruction, and tourism, and she stoked a keen interest in the associational life of folklore and youth gymnastics groups in Vienna. In the summer of 1970, Schöfnagel was suddenly thrust into the humanitarian arena. During a massive flooding event in Romania, a third of the nation's territory was inundated by waves of excess water and deadly mud cascading from the Carpathian Mountains into the Romanian lowlands. Large-scale destruction followed, and hundreds of thousands of residents lost their homes in the floods. At the margins of a burgeoning international relief campaign, a wave of private solidarity initiatives appeared across Central Europe. In Austria and West Germany, private citizens supported the relief efforts through donations, care packages, and volunteer expeditions into the afflicted areas.[9] Schöfnagel joined in, inspired by her aunt's initiative to send packages from West Germany to Transylvania, a historical region in Central Romania. Like many other volunteers, Schöfnagel mobilized her local network of friends and acquaintances, and through a concerted effort, ten truckloads worth of clothes, foodstuffs, and household goods were collected for Transylvania. After the flood of 1970, Schöfnagel was spurred back into action on two more occasions. In 1975, a second flood hit Romania, and in 1977, a 7.2 magnitude earthquake struck the Romanian capital city of Bucharest, prompting Schöfnagel again to fundraise on behalf of the country's disaster victims.

In the late 1970s, Schöfnagel's work pivoted toward cultural tourism and assistance in Transylvania at the community level, which would later transform into her signature assistance campaign "Stille Hilfe nach Siebenbürgen" (quiet aid to Transylvania). Early activities were organized through the Volkstanzkreis Schönbrunn, a folklore ensemble for traditional Austrian music, dance, and singing. Formed in 1974 by the Schöfnagels to cultivate Austrian folklore at home and abroad, the Volkstanzkreis staged performances in Vienna, and soon, trips followed to the Eastern bloc countries of Czechoslovakia, Hungary, Poland, and Romania. In Transylvania, the Schöfnagels focused their efforts on introducing Austrian folklore to the community of Romania's German minority of Transylvanian Saxons.[10] This cultural exchange program occurred against the backdrop of deteriorating conditions for Romania's ethnic Germans (as well as the Hungarian and Jewish minorities) under the weight of the regime's Romanization efforts in the 1970s. Schöfnagel's visits thus coincided with an emergent wave of advocacy of Western émigré and refugee groups rallying around the threatened minority status of Romania's German community. Unlike many such groups, Schöfnagel's work did not pursue a revisionist or ethno-nationalist mission but sought to preserve Transylvanian heritage through material support and cultural exchange.

In 1978 and 1979, two visits with her Volkstanzkreis culminated in well-received performances in the Transylvanian city of Sibiu. Schöfnagel wrote of the first tour, "Our goal was to visit the country and understand the people and their problems. We organized a night of folklore (*Volkstumsabend*), where we performed folk songs, dances, and music. Through our dancing and singing, we forged a bond with the locals and began understanding the problems of the German population."[11] Above all, these personal encounters in Sibiu left a lasting impression on Schöfnagel. "I developed a deep fascination for the country and its traditional way of life, while the plight of its people touched me deeply," she recalled. "Since that time, it became impossible to tear myself away from this country."[12]

Upon her return from Sibiu in July 1978, Schöfnagel resolved to help the Transylvanian Saxons, many of whom, she worried, could not sustain their cultural heritage amid growing ethnic discrimination and economic hardship. As a result, Schöfnagel collected books and materials on German folklore as well as empty cassettes to record lectures on Austrian folklore dances for instructional use in Transylvania. To accomplish the twin task of cultural and material support, Schöfnagel organized a fundraiser among friends and members of her Volkstanzkreis. Donations received through this initiative included books, clothes, household goods, music tapes, and shoes, which Schöfnagel sold in a flea market in Vienna to support the campaign financially. She said, "With the money, we bought embroidery material, music sheets for brass bands, baby food, medicine, Kent cigarettes (for bribing), and everything difficult to get or unavailable."[13] In Schöfnagel's campaign, concerns over the cultural preservation of Germaneness (*Deutschtum*) in the East mingled with material provisioning to help sustain ethnic life in Transylvania. This dual effort was tailored to the needs of Romania's German minority, becoming the modus operandi of Schöfnagel's work henceforth.

Interfering in Romania's fraught minority politics was not without risks, and Schöfnagel recognized that the regime had little appetite to allow organized transfers of foreign aid in support of the ethnic Germans—or the population as a whole. In a communiqué to donors and supporters, Schöfnagel noted, "[The] Romanian state rejects any official/organized aid. The explanation is that everything is available in Romania, and no foreign aid is needed. Therefore, any support must give the impression that it is between private citizens in Austria on behalf of private citizens in Romania."[14] As a result, Schöfnagel's campaigns were tethered to person-to-person exchanges, and they had to be done "quietly." The implications of this form of gray-area maneuvering were clear, as Schöfnagel pointed out to her donors in Vienna: "My activities are not supported by an association or official organization, for I worry that should my work come to the attention of Romanian authorities, they will not permit this kind of aid."[15] Thus, Stille Hilfe was born. The general premise of Schöfnagel's "quiet" work in the socialist gray area—mobilize private donors in Austria and funnel aid through informal channels in Transylvania—went nearly unchanged for the remainder of the socialist period.

Schöfnagel's Stille Hilfe encompassed various forms of assistance, and over time, her campaigns adapted to evolving local needs. Against the backdrop of continued austerity measures that had battered the population since the early 1980s, her assistance turned to the most elementary needs of daily living. Schöfnagel explained, "At the beginning, our focus was more on cultural aid. Since 1981, food provisioning has moved to the center of our work because the country's economic supply chains have broken down. For instance, at the moment, milk, milk powder, or baby food for newborns are unavailable."[16] One of Schöfnagel's assistance vehicles consisted of gift packages that provisioned recipients directly with a wide assortment of essential goods. Schöfnagel also frequently mobilized her Austrian donor community to send packages to acquaintances, friends, and anonymous recipients in Transylvania. Over the years, her Viennese home served as a transit point from where volunteers helped send tens of thousands of aid packages to Romania. To disguise these exchanges, Schöfnagel developed the following tactics:

> I bought groceries with our family bus. In my living room, older women gathered and filled out the consignment notes in different fonts and for the different groups of recipients. The recipients were local persons of trust, and the senders were the respective donors [in Austria]. Younger volunteers packed the food parcels. Every package contained different packaging (for instance, we did not use the same kind of margarine). We used different package boxes, different colors for the wrapping paper, and different cords that we tied differently every time. This way, the parcels did not immediately stand out as "organized" packages. In the beginning, I brought about 10–12 parcels (always only 2 per district) to the post office every day to ensure they did not arrive at the same time.[17]

However, Schöfnagel was keenly aware that aid through packages alone would yield unsatisfactory results. High postal and customs fees, lengthy delivery times, loss, theft, and arbitrary handling by Romanian officials introduced many uncertainties. Thus, in the early 1980s, cultural tourism became Schöfnagel's primary vehicle for assistance. Educational travel excursions, or *Studienreisen*, brought groups of Austrian and West German tourists to select destinations in Transylvania several times per year. Schöfnagel's visits focused on historical sites where remnants of German culture were still visible and alive, as in the cities of Brașov, Mediaș, Sibiu, Sighișoara, and other destinations. There, members of Schöfnagel's travel groups discovered and experienced Transylvanian history, art, folklore, and cuisine in intimate new ways.[18] Alongside visits to picturesque Transylvanian towns, the contacts forged between Schöfnagel's Western travel groups and the local German community bore distinctly preservationist aspects. Through these encounters, friendly relationships were created, which transformed, in some cases, into enduring friendships that, over the years, became new conduits for person-to-person assistance across the Iron Curtain and served to maintain German cultural heritage, *Deutschtum*, in the East.[19]

In a period of restricted mobility and geopolitical division, Schöfnagel's *Studienreisen* (averaging seventeen tours annually between 1979 and 1989) offered a welcome opportunity for cultural contact, but they also served an alternate purpose. Notably, under the veneer of *Studienreisen*, a second layer of activities—a system of private assistance—lurked. Schöfnagel developed and refined her methods over the years, resulting in Trojan horse tactics that mingled her preservationist vision of cultural support for the Transylvanian Saxons with her strategic, if "quiet," campaigns of bringing assistance into the country. To ensure that aid provisions were moved across borders without state interference, Schöfnagel oversaw all aspects of border crossings, including "packing supplies the right way," as she put it. Schöfnagel explained the procedure:

> In my private home in Vienna, we stockpiled everything people in Romania needed, including clothing, household goods, foodstuffs, medicine, light bulbs, tools, baby supplies, and much more. In addition, I collected old suitcases, where I neatly packed these items as part of our "holiday luggage." Tour members were only allowed to bring one piece of luggage and one personal bag for clothes and travel items. Everything else was stowed away in clever ways in the bus. We were able to load up to 70 suitcases (clothing, hygiene items, light bulbs, matches, candles, Kent cigarettes, medication, a Bible, shoes, and much more) inside the bus. Under each seat, we placed a box with foodstuffs—supposedly for personal use. We filled the nets in front of each seat with books—supposedly our travel literature. Coats, jackets, and rain gear were piled up on the hat rack. The 1/2 liter tetra pack milk was not only suitable for personal consumption, but I also hid Lei [Romania's foreign currency] in these packets in a laborious process.[20]

Romanian state borders were infamous for coercive controls and invasive scrutiny of visitors. Travelers often found themselves at the mercy of state officials, making improper gestures, misspoken words, or unsanctioned behavior grounds for expulsion, entry bans, or worse. State officials were notorious for searching for illegal goods, including bibles, drugs, weapons, and political material. However, carrying large quantities of licit items into the country could cause problems as well, since state authorities also persecuted individuals engaged in illegal trading schemes. As a result, Schöfnagel had to keep excessive quantities of scarce goods to a minimum to mask the true extent of her aid provisions. "Packing correctly," thus, required that supplies be dispersed into equal amounts among Schöfnagel's tour members.

This tactic of diffusion notwithstanding, the passage at state borders remained difficult, and there Schöfnagel's Trojan horse had to do most of the work. As Schöfnagel frequently traveled to Romania, she began to adopt border tactics to build rapport with state officials. Before entering a border station with a tour bus, Schöfnagel would inform her travel group in detail about the border procedures. This occurred while the tour bus was still in Hungary. Once the tour had arrived at the Romanian border, Schöfnagel would instruct her travel group to put on a jovial and relaxed attitude, sing songs, and project cheerfulness. Schöfnagel also prepared small gift baskets for the commandants of border stations, insisting that her "small attentions" were not bribes and that they be given in "broad daylight" to ensure that all border personnel witnessed the procedure. Such ceremonious gift deliveries were part and parcel of a ritual dance between Schöfnagel and state officials, resembling, not incidentally, the decorum of diplomatic exchanges. Schöfnagel's border gifts were calculated gestures that established familiarity between her and border officials and honored the "good work relations" between both sides. Schöfnagel noted:

Border controls were lengthy, complicated, and could only be managed through the cooperation of all travelers.... We never bribed customs officials. I always prepared a little attention with "Greetings from Vienna" that included a lipstick, a large bar of chocolate, tropical fruits, female tights, and other assortments. At the end of the year, I sometimes delivered a gift basket with tropical fruits to the entire border station— as an attention from our tourist bureau for the good cooperation....[21]

Once the travel group had arrived at its destination in Transylvania, tour members were given the opportunity to meet with family and friends to exchange supplies. Those without personal contacts could leave consumer items behind or, as Schöfnagel put it, "forget" them with curators, pastors, and neighborhood elders who organized distribution in their communities. With the worsening supply situation in the late 1980s, Schöfnagel rounded out her assistance vehicles by purchasing large quantities of foodstuffs and consumer goods in Romania's "intershops" directly. Such consumer stores were common in the socialist bloc, offering the exceedingly few customers with access to foreign currency a wide assortment of scarce luxury goods. The ability to procure daily essentials locally (e.g., butter, cheese, flour, sugar, and coffee) became a cost-effective method for Schöfnagel to funnel aid to communities in need, but it also moved a significant part of her logistics directly under the nose of the Romanian authorities.

Below the Threshold:
Humanitarianism under Conditions of State Surveillance

As her tactics grew more and more brazen, Schöfnagel was surprisingly able to continue her assistance campaigns. In fact, the *Securitate* recruited numerous informants over the years to obtain intelligence about Schöfnagel's activities, beginning with her visit to Sibiu with her Volkstanzkreis as early as 1978. Alarmed by the unannounced arrival of the Volkstanzkreis, the *Securitate* dispatched an informant with the codename "Mihai Boboc" to collect information about Schöfnagel.[22] His investigations revealed that Schöfnagel's entourage planned to perform a folklore program in Sibiu and visit the city and its surroundings. "Boboc's" information gathering painted a granular picture of Schöfnagel's private meetings, personal conversations, group activities, and a car accident with a pedestrian in which Schöfnagel was involved. Although, for the first time, a connection was established between Schöfnagel and her aunt's aid campaigns during the floods of 1970 and 1975, there was little indication that the regime considered these activities undesirable.[23]

Subsequent visits to Transylvania provided further opportunity for the *Securitate* to assemble a detailed profile of Schöfnagel. Some *Securitate* sources described her as a "very punctual, strict, and disciplined" person who did "not tolerate discussions" in her travel group.[24] Other sources claimed that Schöfnagel was a "stingy woman" who seemed to engage in "cult-like" activities with her Austrian travel groups.[25] At the hotel "Bulevard" in Sibiu, where Schöfnagel regularly booked lodging, informant "Magda" gathered information for the *Securitate* for nearly seven years. About a visit at "Bulevard" in 1987, where Schöfnagel was accompanied by her husband Dieter, "Magda" communicated to Bucharest:

> Mr. Schöfnagel, a very quiet man, follows what he is asked to do regarding room selections. Because he works very well with the Romanian tour guide, the program follows Bucharest's suggestions. When Ms. Schöfnagel is in charge, things are different. She takes care of accommodations and meals, and she knows exactly what the group needs. She is a very authoritative woman with a strong personality, intelligent, and quick. When the reception assigns her a room, she will either not take it or take it and come back later to ask for a different room. She is very attentive and polite but remains distant. She does not cross boundaries and wastes no time in conversations with anyone.[26]

The suspicion in "Magda's" reports was not uncommon for informants and spies in the period. The institutional culture of the *Securitate* was driven by the directive to assess, anticipate, and uncover the "hidden agendas" and false identities of potential regime foes.[27] As a result, "Magda's" remarks about Schöfnagel were in line with the "truths" the *Securitate*'s surveillance apparatus was to unearth and indeed *produce*. In spite of her growing dossier, Schöfnagel's motivations remained elusive to the *Securitate*. Assessments of her persona shifted from observations alleging that Schöfnagel sought to forge connections to ethnic German intellectuals (most of whom were known regime critics) to favorable remarks about her cautious, law-abiding behavior that suggested she was careful to avoid conflicts with Romanian authorities.[28] The difficulty in pinning down what was behind Schöfnagel's continued interest in Transylvania eventually prompted the *Securitate* to extend its surveillance deeper into her private life. On several occasions, informant "Haralambie" reported visits of *Securitate* spies to Schöfnagel's home. In 1980, an informant observing Schöfnagel during a visit to Vienna noted Schöfnagel's disdain for domestic labor and the unorthodox gender regime in her family: "Although she is a housewife, her sense of running a household is very questionable. She said that she spent a lot of time building her new house. In the family, she makes the decisions. Her husband is very quiet."[29]

As part of the *Securitate*'s expanding surveillance of Schöfnagel, her assistance campaigns, too, moved increasingly into focus. During her visits in the early 1980s, informants observed that Schöfnagel donated clothes to the poor and brought foodstuffs into the country. Subsequent investigations revealed that she donated money to the elderly and compiled lists of people she promised to help.³⁰ Likewise, members of her travel groups were reported to the authorities for passing along packages with clothes, consumer items, and foodstuffs to acquaintances, relatives, and the needy.³¹ In 1981, informant "Claudia Ștefanescu" noted that she had participated in one of Schöfnagel's tour programs and helped distribute assistance to large families in the cities of Sibiu and Mediaș. The "Ștefanescu" report provided the *Securitate* with private addresses and names of recipients, offering the most detailed insight into Schöfnagel's Stille Hilfe in the early 1980s.³² In later years, informants confirmed that the main purpose of Schöfnagel's visits was to supply Protestant parishes with assistance for the needy. Yet, despite the mounting evidence about Schöfnagel's work, the regime did not intervene.

In a sudden change of events in June 1989, Schöfnagel's ability to keep her work "quiet" came to an end. During her summer tour to Transylvania, she was informed at the Romanian border that the state had declared her a persona non grata. What prompted the surprise indictment? The exact circumstances remain blurry, but to understand the change in state attitude, it is useful to recall the notion of threshold. Despite the often undefined and porous boundaries between legal and illegal in socialism's gray area, there existed a clear distinction between desired and undesired forms of foreign aid. While international organizations were prohibited from delivering assistance, the Romanian regime exempted small-scale assistance from person to person that remained free of Western government involvement. For nearly two decades, Schöfnagel followed these informal rules by "graying" her work. This threshold, however, was breached when the Austrian state extended its support to Schöfnagel in 1988. In light of dramatic economic hardship in Romania, the Transylvanian Saxon émigré association (*Landsmannschaft*) and members of the Freedom Party (FPÖ) successfully petitioned the government to match private donations supporting humanitarian initiatives for the German community. As a result, the working group of the *Landsmannschaft*, where Schöfnagel led and coordinated her campaigns to Transylvania, gained a new statute as a government-backed charitable organization, with Schöfnagel becoming its de facto director.³³

The success of this initiative was resounding. In a donor communiqué in July 1989, Schöfnagel announced that the infusion of government funding had significantly expanded her campaign's financial clout and allowed her to help more recipients in Transylvania than ever before, a matter that grew increasingly urgent in the terminal days of the Ceaușescu regime. This accomplishment notwithstanding, the travel ban against her in the summer of 1989 demonstrated that to assist communities in need, the appearance of compliance with the socialist state's restrictions against organized foreign aid still had to be maintained. For those with the requisite expertise of how to gray their activities, possibilities abounded to move assistance "quietly" across borders, as Schöfnagel's Stille Hilfe had for many years. For those who stepped outside the gray area by appearing to conspire with foreign governments, as Schöfnagel eventually did, the Iron Curtain came crashing down.

Epilogue

By dint of luck, Schöfnagel's travel ban ended with the regime's collapse only a few months later in December 1989. However, Schöfnagel's story and many other similar episodes of private humanitarianism in the socialist period were forgotten decades after the end of the Cold War. The reasons were manifold. New maps divided the post–Cold War world into "Global North" and "Global South," and with them, humanitarian practices in the Global East like Schöfnagel's, which had existed neither in the archetypical "Western" or "non-Western" contexts, disappeared from view. Ironically, despite its evident biases and flaws, the outdated earlier three-worlds model had recognized a degree of complexity that got lost after the end of the Cold War. Lost was the history of private humanitarians like Schöfnagel, who grayed their work to maneuver Cold War divisions and authoritarian state power in a region that belonged to neither North nor South. Lost also was that the socialist welfare utopia in some socialist states like Romania was an object of humanitarian intervention long before its collapse due to a relentless push for austerity. The main protagonists of these assistance networks were not Western governments and international relief agencies. They were instead ordinary people like Schöfnagel, who traversed the continent's geopolitical divides and moved aid across borders "quietly"—a difficult if not impossible task for humanitarian organizations after 1945. Finally, lost was a sense that under authoritarian rule keeping humanitarian campaigns informal was a necessary tactic for Schöfnagel and other private humanitarians, who leveraged their lay expertise to advance their work through culturally resonant forms of rapport building and an arsenal of evolving and layered assistance vehicles and Trojan horse tactics. By adopting a Western aid format to the social arrangements of the socialist bloc, Schöfnagel and many private humanitarians like her expanded the possibilities for transnational care in Cold War Eastern Europe.

What becomes evident from Schöfnagel's story is that reappraising humanitarianism beyond the West also requires thinking deeply about how much the standard North-South binary obscures our knowledge of humanitarian gray practices and the social worlds their practitioners inhabited that lay outside or in between these two spheres. In our current geopolitical moment with its resurgent authoritarian East, this consideration should prompt an ever more urgent search for new global maps where the staggering diversity of humanitarian practices is more fully recognized.

Cristian Capotescu is a postdoctoral scholar at Columbia University and associate director of the Trust Collaboratory, a newly launched interdisciplinary center studying the social dynamics of trust. Cristian holds a PhD in history (2020) from the University of Michigan, Ann Arbor. In 2020–21, he joined the University of Washington's Mellon Sawyer Seminar *Humanitarianisms: Migrations and Care through the Global South* as a postdoctoral scholar.

Notes

1. Barbara Schöfnagel's correspondence with Siegfried Gassner, 11 March 1988, in Barbara-Wiebke Schöfnagel, private material collection, Vienna (hereafter referenced as *SPMC*).
2. The term "Global East" is borrowed from Martin Müller in "In Search of the Global East," 734–55.
3. Capotescu, Sanchez-Sibony, and Teixeira, "Austerity without Neoliberals."
4. Georgescu, *Romanians*, 272.
5. Schöfnagel's correspondence with Gassner, *SPMC*.
6. Schöfnagel's correspondence with Gassner, *SPMC*.
7. See Kochanowski, *Jenseits der Planwirtschaft*.
8. Schöfnagel's correspondence with Gassner, *SPMC*.
9. Capotescu, "Migrants into Humanitarians," 293–312.
10. Romania's German community consisted of several ethnic subgroups, with the Saxons representing the largest among them; see Koranyi and Wittlinger, "From Diaspora to Diaspora," 96–115.
11. Letter Schöfnagel (Juli 1978), *SPMC*.
12. Schöfnagel, "1970–2000—30 jähre Hilfstätigkeit" (Mai 2000), *SPMC*.
13. Unpublished memoir, "Meine Hilfsmaßnahmen Richtung Rumänien/Siebenbürgen aus dem Gedächtnis von Barbara (Bärbel) Schöfnagel in Stichworten von 1970 bis 1990" (16 May 2016), *SPMC*.
14. Letter Schöfnagel to Reinhard Rosenbusch (3 September 1988), *SPMC*.
15. Letter Schöfnagel (Juli 1978), *SPMC*.
16. Letter Schöfnagel to Reinhard Rosenbusch.
17. Schöfnagel, "Meine Hilfemaßnahmen," *SPMC*.
18. Schöfnagel, "Siebenbürgenreise 910," *SPMC*.
19. See Koranyi and Wittlinger, "From Diaspora to Diaspora," 96–115.
20. Schöfnagel, "Meine Hilfsmaßnahmen," *SPMC*.
21. Interview with Barbara Schöfnagel, Vienna, 13 May 2017.
22. Securitate file on Schöfnagel (3 July 1978), *SPMC*.
23. Securitate file on Schöfnagel (4 July and 6 July 1978), *SPMC*.
24. Securitate file on Schöfnagel (25 April 1985), *SPMC*.
25. Securitate file on Schöfnagel (2 May 1988), *SPMC*.
26. Securitate file on Schöfnagel (27 September 1987), *SPMC*.
27. Verdery, *My Life as a Spy*.
28. Securitate file on Schöfnagel. Report filed by officers Balici and Smaranda (undated), *SPMC*.
29. Ibid. (6 November 1980), *SPMC*.

30. Ibid. (5 February 1988), *SPMC*.
31. Ibid. (2 October 1980), *SPMC*.
32. Ibid. (5 March 1981), *SPMC*.
33. Schöfnagel, materials Transylvanian Saxon Working Group (*Arbeitskreis*) from December 1988 and July 1989, *SPMC*.

References

Capotescu, Cristian. "Migrants into Humanitarians: Ethnic Solidarity and Private Aid-Giving during Romania's Historic Flood of 1970." *East European Politics and Societies* 35, no. 2 (May 2021): 293–312.
Capotescu, Cristian, Oscar Sanchez-Sibony, and Melissa Teixeira. "Austerity without Neoliberals: On the Sinuous History of a Powerful State Technology." *Capitalism: A Journal of History and Economics* 3, no. 2 (Summer 2022): 379–420.
Georgescu, Vlad. *The Romanians: A History*. Columbus: Ohio State University Press, 1984.
Kochanowski, Jerzy. *Jenseits der Planwirtschaft: Der Schwarzmarkt in Polen 1944–1989*. Göttingen: Wallstein, 2013.
Koranyi, James, and Ruth Wittlinger. "From Diaspora to Diaspora: The Case of Transylvanian Saxons in Romania and Germany." *Nationalism and Ethnic Politics* 17, no. 1 (2011): 96–115.
Müller, Martin. "In Search of the Global East: Thinking between North and South." *Geopolitics* 25, no. 3 (2020): 734–55.
Schöfnagel, Barbara-Wiebke. Private material collection, Vienna (referenced *SPMC*).
———. Interview, Vienna, 13 May 2017.
Verdery, Katherine. *My Life as a Spy. Investigations in a Secret Police File*. Durham, NC: Duke University Press, 2018.

CHAPTER 9

Yūsuf's Struggle

Negotiating Development and Charity in a Palestinian Refugee Camp

Gözde Burcu Ege

Yūsuf has lived almost all his life in al-Naṣr Palestinian refugee camp (the Victory camp) in Amman, Jordan. Like most of his friends, he received his education through a boys' school in the camp provided by the United Nations Relief and Works Agency (UNRWA), which has been the primary agency responding to the plight of Palestinian refugees since 1949.[1] At the age of twenty-four, Yūsuf and his friends founded a charity and development association, al-Ḥayāh (Life), which targets the children and youth of his camp.[2] This association, where he spends most of his time and energy, is the culmination of his and his friends' efforts to create a camp-based humanitarian project that prioritizes what they see as the real needs of the refugee children and youth.

Humanitarianism is often imagined from a global North perspective to be intrinsically good, politically neutral, and delivered by international organizations to respond to emergencies.[3] With humanitarian workers going to multiple missions around the world, this imaginary elicits the illusion of "a global moral community" based on a common humanity and does so despite deep inequalities among countries as well as among those who help and who receive this help.[4]

My friendship with Yūsuf and fieldwork with al-Ḥayāh volunteers revealed a different humanitarian imaginary. Yūsuf's volunteer work is directed toward his own refugee camp community and its generalized precarity, which he saw as extending into the future, making the streets unsafe, the youth hopeless and the camp inhabitants preoccupied with their survival. Yūsuf and his volunteer friends are themselves "children of the camps" and interact with the children and youth in the association with a sense of legitimacy and expertise. Their vision of what it means to do humanitarian work does not require the abstract distance of strangers or an apolitical idea of an imminent "emergency" that can be addressed with temporary relief aid.

Yūsuf's humanitarian imaginary, rooted in his work within his own community, cannot be understood through invocations of shared humanity between aid providers and recipients occupying separate social worlds. Yūsuf is not primarily motivated by religious conviction, though he is Muslim, or religious imaginaries that scholars have identified in other global South contexts.[5] Ultimately, rather than being bound by humanitarian conventions that came from the global North or the hegemonic approaches of Islamic charitable institutions with whom they often operate in proximity, Yūsuf's work springs from his individual experiences of growing up in a Palestinian refugee camp in Jordan and being accultured by a previous generation of Palestinian refugees in these camps. As a refugee-citizen in a Palestinian refugee camp in Jordan who is serving his own community by constantly navigating relationships, limitations, and future aspirations, the humanitarian imaginary that Yūsuf draws on emerges from practices of care that he learned growing up in the camp.

These practices of care are today known as ʿamal fityanī (boys' work) across Palestinian refugee camps in Jordan. Yūsuf and other Palestinian volunteers trace the beginning of ʿamal fityanī to a summer camp activity for orphan Palestinian children in the aftermath of the 1967 Arab-Israeli War. Described primarily as a form of developmental care by current volunteers, its origins remain contested and are attributed either to the Palestinian Liberation Organization or to a collaboration between the Young Men's Christian Association (YMCA) and the UNRWA. ʿAmal fityanī can be best understood as a repertoire, or a "whole set of means [a group] has for making claims of different kinds on different individuals or groups" because it provides a framework of engagement toward children in the refugee camps.[6] Repertoires both enable and constrain people's actions, providing them with familiar routines to use that can be altered from within.[7]

Yūsuf's story of how al-Ḥayāh was established demonstrates how "being of the camp" is an important aspect of his work, guiding his aspirations for the future of the camp residents and granting him access to ʿamal fityanī. He and his friends innovate this repertoire for their own purposes even while they are constrained by the political and social limitations governing their lives as simultaneous refugees of Palestine and citizens of Jordan. At the core of this humanitarian imaginary resides a commitment to remain in what Yūsuf calls "the thick of things," managing relations with his fellow camp residents. Navigating the precarity of camp life alongside them, Yūsuf aspires for what he perceives as development even though the reality on the ground pulls him toward providing forms of economic assistance, a dissonance that he tries to overcome by keeping aid discreet.

Entering the Camp, Meeting Yūsuf

I met Yūsuf in the early days of my fieldwork in al-Ḥayāh, an association established in 2015 in al-Naṣr camp. One of thirteen Palestinian refugee camps in Jordan, al-Naṣr camp in East Amman is officially named the Prince Hassan Neighborhood. It is administratively located in the Amman governorate and hosts over twenty thousand Palestinian refugees, most of whom were displaced in the aftermath of the 1967 Arab-Israeli War. Today, in addition to Palestinian refugees, this small camp, which the UNRWA considers unofficial, hosts Sri Lankan, Bangladeshi, and Egyptian migrant workers as well as Syrian refugees who took advantage of the affordable accommodation and public transportation facilities the camp provided.

If it wasn't for a young woman I met serendipitously in downtown Amman, al-Naṣr camp and al-Ḥayāh association might not have appeared on my radar. A young Palestinian woman working in an international NGO as a nutrition specialist in al-Za'atarī with Syrian refugees, Nisreen took immediate interest in my research and arranged for me to visit al-Ḥayāh, where her sister Zaynab was volunteering.[8] There I met a network of young Palestinian volunteers across the refugee camps of Jordan, including Yūsuf.

When I started visiting al-Ḥayāh in late 2017, the association had about sixty volunteers, young men and women ranging from the ages of fifteen to thirty, working with around three hundred boys and girls from within and around al-Naṣr camp. Despite knowing Yūsuf since the early days of my fieldwork, it took us almost five months to establish rapport. One probable reason for this was the gender-segregated socializing norms of the camp that prevailed in milder forms inside the association: young men and women who otherwise may not even greet one another in the street would converse with one another and collaborate in activities directed toward the children.

In the initial five months, I mostly shadowed Zaynab, a student at the University of Jordan and one of a relatively small number of female volunteers in al-Ḥayāh, while at the same time teaching Turkish to a group of teenagers. If it weren't for one unforgivingly cold Friday in February, I might never have become friends with Yūsuf. That day, volunteers moved the sports sessions, generally undertaken in the garden of the UNRWA boys' school, indoors, and since the association's rooms didn't allow space for team sports, Yūsuf decided to teach table tennis. Zaynab, the guide for a group of fourteen-year-old girls, didn't know how to play table tennis, and Yūsuf was reluctant to guide these teenage girls the way he had with the boys: by holding their hands and showing them how to throw the ball. Moreover, most of the boys already knew how to play, which made the girls a bit upset. I volunteered and told Yūsuf that I could help teach the girls. During the session, I also played against Yūsuf, and to boost the girls' morale, I made a real effort to score against him.

It was my small spontaneous victory that gave me some street credit in Yūsuf's eyes; he lovingly called me *dawaween*, a term that people usually associate with troublemakers and that, I was later to learn, meant something somewhat different for Yūsuf. He thanked me and told me that he was surprised by my skills since the girls in the camp generally didn't play table tennis.

In the aftermath of this episode, we started to converse more often. In time, the topics we covered extended from political situations in Jordan, Türkiye, the United States, and Palestine to the daily events in the association, the gossip of the camp, our families and friendships, and our aspirations and disappointments in life. In the meantime, our social interactions exceeded the boundaries of the association to my house in Jabal al-Hussein, cafés in downtown Amman where we played cards and smoked *'argile* (hookah), and Yūsuf's old car. This car was at times a free space for our socialization in upscale neighborhoods like al-Webdeih in which we listened to music late at night, and at other times it was Yūsuf's vehicle for a series of consecutive sales jobs that necessitated driving to different parts of Amman to sell different products at different times: chocolates and chips for corner stores in popular neighborhoods, and during the COVID-19 pandemic, masks to various stores in East Amman.

Being of the Camp: The Camp as an Environment That Governs

Yūsuf's grandparents, displaced from a village in Hebron, came to Jordan after the 1967 Arab-Israeli War and started living in the al-Naṣr refugee camp. His nuclear family is one that chose to stay in the camp despite eventually having the economic means to leave it. In fact, after his grandparents died, his family was the last among his relatives to remain in the camp. For Yūsuf, the refugee camp's meaning was never limited to political significance as a metaphor for Palestinian refugees' right of return: it was a place where his people had lived for generations and established intimacies stemming from their common experience tied to this place. The children's handprints on the walls of al-Ḥayāh and the accompanying writing that reads "I am the camp" should be understood as a reflection of their insistence on keeping their project integrated to their community (see figure 9.1).

Yūsuf appreciated his father for choosing to stay in the camp despite having a generally conflictual relationship with him. He often criticized those who

Figure 9.1. • A wall on the rooftop of al-Ḥayāh association (translation: I am the camp), Amman, 2018. © Gözde Burcu Ege.

left the camp as soon as they improved their economic situation, calling their escape an act of selfishness. Although his two uncles and their families no longer lived in the camp, they were still closely connected to its socioeconomic life. One of his uncles, a man described by Yūsuf and others as a charitable, religious, and respectable person, still has a small grocery store in the building adjoining al-Ḥayāh. The other used to be a volunteer in the management of the camp's long-standing Youth Club.[9]

Coming from an extended family where men were socially and economically invested in the camp, one may think that it was no wonder that Yūsuf became a volunteer in the Youth Club and, later, founded an association with his friends. However, Yūsuf's trajectory is more complicated than continuing a family legacy of social work. In fact, both he and others told me repeatedly that growing up, his reputation in the camp was that of a troublemaker who constantly stirred things up, was routinely involved in physical fights, and often ended up in the police station. Yūsuf would sometimes narrate these fights in a humorous fashion, not refraining from sharing the details of occasions when he emerged victorious and others when he got beaten up. It was clear from his description that he saw these confrontations not as a testament to youthful machismo but rather as minor components of a broader struggle for the moral and physical well-being of the camp.

As our friendship developed, Yūsuf started to tell me about the difficult circumstances that led him to become the kind of person people called a troublemaker. When he was in eighth grade, his father went bankrupt after his clothing store was robbed, and he went to South Africa to work with a tradesman from the same village in Palestine as his grandfather for four years. Yūsuf told me that this was the first turning point in his life, since he felt the responsibility for providing for his family as the oldest son among two sisters and a younger brother:

> That period probably was the period of my life that affected me the most. We didn't have money. In the seventh grade, I used to steal my father's car. As a small child, and I was very short, I would put a pillow on the seat and drive the car. Then, suddenly, we lost everything. And there was also a lot of debt. And because I was the oldest in the house, it was very difficult for me. I was very fat in the seventh grade, now look at the pictures from the eighth grade, I became like a skeleton. I worked a lot. Also, we weren't sure about my dad's situation, South Africa was very dangerous. Every day, we would receive a phone call: your dad is dead.

According to Yūsuf, it was primarily this necessity of providing for his family that put him in environments where he had to learn how to act tough. Starting with seventh grade, he worked a variety of jobs: in the camp's bazaar, in the small coffee shops in and around the camp, and in construction work. His behavior must have troubled his family; one of his uncles allegedly called Firas, a Youth Club volunteer six years Yūsuf's senior, and asked him to lure Yūsuf into becoming a volunteer there with the hopes that he would calm down and "stay out of fights a little bit."

Yūsuf told me that he immediately liked volunteering since he felt like he could change the things he didn't like about life in the camp by working on the upcoming generation. From the time he started working in the streets, he told me, he kept diaries of camp life: which family was from where in Palestine, who married whom, who organized large iftars during Ramadan, which youth initiative did what, who joined protests, and who worked in whose parliamentary election campaigns, among other things:

> Even when I was a child, Burcu.... You know the drug dealers would use the *bastaat* [street vendor stands] in the bazaar of the camp to sell drugs at night. Someone would stick the money on a stand, and the other would come and put the drugs. I used to scream from the top of my lungs: police, police. Of course, there were no police around, I used to do it to frighten them. I was just a child, and I was trying to stop the drug trade in my own way.

His volunteering did keep him out of fights "a little bit," because he found a new place where he could invest his energy.

As a young man with a lot of male relatives and who didn't refrain from trouble, he still believed in the necessity of being involved in fights. Whenever he talked about a fight in the camp, he would add, "The environment governs your life, you can only escape but so much." Now, however, as a twenty-seven-year-old man who has founded an association with his friends, he told me that he only fought "smart and strategically."

Establishing al-Ḥayāh

If Yūsuf's father's four years of absence was one turning point, his meeting Faruq in the university was another. He and Faruq met through Firas when Yūsuf called Firas to borrow money to buy a required textbook for class. Firas directed him to Faruq, and the two soon became inseparable. Despite never having lived in a Palestinian refugee camp, Faruq also came from a refugee household where the Palestinian cause was important, and he was also a volunteer of *'amal fityanī* in another refugee camp, Muḥaṭṭah. In the third year of college, when Yūsuf dropped out because of financial difficulties, he took Faruq to the Youth Club to work with him.

In 2015, Yūsuf and Faruq decided to leave the Youth Club and open their own association in al-Naṣr camp with five other friends. In doing that, they relied on the repertoire of *'amal fityanī*. They replicated *'amal fityanī*'s designation of volunteers as guides, supervisors, and helpers as well as the titles of the children as boys and flowers (girls) instead of referring to them with a title that would denote beneficiaries. They also took the ritualistic aspects of the Friday programs and started and ended their programs with children and volunteers establishing a circle and chanting words about Palestine, the camp, and the right of return. Moreover, just as I had seen in visits to the Ḥusayn, Muḥaṭṭah, Baqāʾ, and Weḥdāt camps, supervisors shared the knowledge and social, cultural, and artistic skills they had acquired from their volunteer leaders, and guides were advised to pay attention to children's problems at school, home, and in the street and come up with solutions.

While relying on this repertoire, Yūsuf and his friends also wanted to innovate by putting additional emphasis on sociocultural education while inculcating values of community service and refraining from charity as much as possible. Yūsuf and Faruq told me that it was because of their desire for innovation and the opposition they faced in the Youth Club that they ended up leaving the Youth Club and opening their own association. When Faruq started volunteering in the boys' committee of the Youth Club with Yūsuf, the committee was very weak, and there were only four other volunteers. Yūsuf was particularly upset about the way the new management approached the children:

> They were just petting the heads of the children, expressing pity because the child is an orphan or poor, and feeding him a sandwich and making him play some football. Then, go home! Nothing else. How does this benefit the child? Nobody is dying of hunger! It only makes him feel bad! We wanted to do additional programs with the children, not only on Friday. We wanted to innovate the program, we wanted children to learn things, to develop themselves. We became forty volunteers and started to push for these things, and the problems started.

Identifying as a son of the camp himself, Yūsuf often voiced his desire that children not be tied to the institution through economic aid. He didn't want them to feel like they were objects of pity. He wanted the Youth Club to become a place where children and volunteers spent time whenever they wanted. Through his volunteer work, Yūsuf wanted to contribute to the creation of a specific kind of Palestinian refugee generation: a generation that knows their historical and cultural Palestinian roots as well as their rights as refugees; that is equipped to overcome their socioeconomic marginalization in Jordan but does so without severing their ties and disinvesting their energies from the camp community.

After much conflict, Yūsuf and his friends understood that they were going to be booted from the Youth Club and decided to open their own association. Upon receiving approval from the Ministry of Social Development, they transformed Yūsuf's family building into the space for their association and, according to them, established the first association run solely by youth in any Palestinian refugee camp in Jordan. The youthfulness of al-Ḥayāh must have been so unusual for the networks of Palestinian camp volunteers that some compared it to the youth's role in the Egyptian revolution, as other youth groups allegedly started to open their associations in different refugee camps after al-Ḥayāh.

In addition to this renewed emphasis on sociocultural development, they also tried to create their own institutional ethos in which the youth in management would remain active volunteers on the ground instead of only fulfilling administrative roles or fundraising. Yūsuf told me that they hope to prevent both a stark generational difference between volunteers and children and a management that is unaware of the needs of both. This commitment is reflected in their critiques of the INGOs that worked in the kingdom as well. In fact, many of them considered INGOs' ethics as being insufficiently humanitarian. For them, INGOs implemented short-term projects when funding was available, depended on salaried labor and the knowledge of so-called experts who generally had no idea of the realities of their recipients' lives, and undertook projects aiming to inculcate individualist notions of development rather than a community spirit.

Incessant critique of the INGOs, however, didn't mean that they refrained from consulting their friends who were working in the thriving INGO sector of Jordan. Yūsuf told me:

> We noticed that we gave the child something cultural, but there is something bad psychologically or socially. He starts to understand culture, music, Palestine, plays chess, his schoolwork becomes better.... But the psychosocial problems remain, like he or she keeps beating other children, or remains scared and silent. We decided to stop and ask people. If you want to make a revolution, you should look at other revolutions in the world, but also you can't just imitate them, right? We talked to our professors in the university. Also, Waseem was working at CARE International with Syrian refugees, we talked to him. But we didn't work in the same way; we understood the idea and adapted it to our own program. For example, they had an activity for the little boys and girls, something like "healing through singing," we immediately understood that this won't work in the camp because the boys already see themselves as men. However, you can use theater for social development here, too. It makes sense. Or you can't treat a volunteer like a paid employee; a volunteer is here because he or she wants to give from his heart, not because he will be compensated, so you can't just give orders to him or her and say: This is your job, but you should let them be creative. You should create an attractive atmosphere so that volunteers and children want to keep coming.

Yūsuf describes a desire to learn new approaches while pointing out the new atmosphere in which some of the *'amal fityanī* volunteers, like his friend Waseem, found a space for themselves in the newly boosted INGO sector in Jordan following the Syrian refugee crisis. Yūsuf and his friends selectively adopted these new approaches to their program and still relied on their sense of expertise coming from "being of the camp."

Being in the Thick of Things

For Yūsuf, being a good volunteer in the camp means being a *dawaween*; an endearment he called me when I beat him at table tennis, said something witty in a conversation, or did something he thought was clever while teaching Turkish to children. According to him, *dawaween* doesn't simply mean a troublemaker: it comes from the word *diwan* in Arabic, the place where people with influence host their guests. Thus, he argued, being a *dawaween* means being experienced in different *diwan*s, learning their rules, making these rules work for your own goals, and even changing the rules once you get the opportunity. To be able to do this means to be and remain in "the thick of things."

Yūsuf is indeed in the thick of things. He is a refugee from Palestine, a citizen of Jordan, and a resident of the camp. He is a young man making his way through life with sporadic jobs, helping his family economically while at the same time investing most of his energy in an association for the upcoming generation of camp refugees. Moreover, he is a person who would pay attention to the gossip in the camp, pick the brains of the other volunteers, join every wedding and funeral in the camp, make sure to keep good relations with the UNRWA school where most of the children were getting their education, and coordinate children's participation in intercamp events. One day, he could be sweeping the floors of the association or fixing the bathroom, the next day he could be wearing a suit and talking with a member of parliament who joined an iftar event the association organized. He is also a curious person who closely follows the activities of other associations, the Youth Club of the camp, the Muslim Brotherhood charities, international and royal NGOs to learn from them or simply to know who their competitors were.[10] Inside the association, he usually teaches sports-related subjects, but his main role is to create and perpetuate relationships inside and outside the camp.

Being in the thick of things also requires him to tailor the way he interacts with different people. For example, Yūsuf told me that there is a need to prevent people who are known to be drug dealers from approaching the boys, and that the only language these people understand is fear. To show that he isn't afraid to flex his muscles, he would instigate at least one big fight every year with some of these men in the middle of the camp. When I was still in Jordan, someone stole the market stand that always stood in front of the association. Volunteer boys used to populate this stand to sell various products whenever they needed to raise money for their families. The next day, the stand was in its place, and Yūsuf told us he recovered it by dragging down the person who stole it and taking it by force. The fight wasn't so much to recover the stand, he told me, but to show others that they shouldn't mess with the association. *Tamtheel* (performance) was his answer to why these fights were needed: "If someone is a thug you can't reason with them."

In dealing with other people, Yūsuf used to tell me, there is a need to engage in other tactics. One day, after almost a year of my fieldwork, a volunteer told us in a meeting that he had invited a certain sheikh, Hussein, to volunteer as a Quran teacher in the association, an informal announcement that made some volunteers present giggle. Since I knew that the association didn't have such a program, I asked Yūsuf whether they wanted to develop a religion program, a question he ridiculed. "No," he said with a huge laugh, "Even if we wanted, we wouldn't do it with this guy! He just pretends to know Islam, but the only thing he does is to spread slander about the association because there are girls and boys in the same space." Apparently, Yūsuf was behind the idea of inviting him to stop him from slandering the association, and they did it with the full knowledge that this man would never give "a day of his life" to benefit others.

Finally, as a Palestinian refugee-citizen who had a project, he had to interact with the Jordanian state in particular ways. For example, he told me that when the Jordanian intelligence agents called him in the first year of the association and asked him why so many young people had joined, he reverently replied that they were implementing the kingdom's vision: empowering the youth of Jordan. He would even begrudgingly accept the fancy dinner invitations of parliamentary candidates who would only talk about Palestine and Palestinian refugee camps right before the elections because he had to sustain these relationships to keep the association open.

The Father of Salt: Aspiring for Development

Before the Ramadan of 2018, Yūsuf confided his frustration about donor interest in organizing iftars for the children, and I asked him the reasons behind his frustration. In his famously mischievous manner, he recounted his oft-repeated phrase, "Nobody is dying of hunger in the camp." Then, he told me the story of the nickname he received when he was still a volunteer in the Youth Club. Yūsuf and his friends wanted Ramadan to be an opportunity for camp children to engage in activities they couldn't find in the camp and socially develop themselves, such as playing in an amusement park, spending time in nature, or watching a theater play. But the Youth Club used to accept any iftar invitation, regardless of what kind of meals it entailed or the activities before or after the breaking of fast. Yūsuf was young and didn't have decision-making power, but he would still carry salt and pepper in his pockets to give the donors the message that "feeding people" is not enough, and that's why they called him "the father of salt" (*Abū al-milḥ*). It turns out, in this Ramadan too, most donor interest focused on providing meals without any planned activities for children to attend before or after breaking their fasts.

Yūsuf's insistence on engaging in what he perceives as development provides a powerful critique to the political necessity that surrounds humanitarian projects whose main goal often centers around saving lives.[11] This prioritization of development took its place in other conversations and practices of the association as well. For example, every Friday, the association provides a simple breakfast for the children and volunteers. Taking pictures during this time is forbidden for all, and others warn new volunteers beforehand. In one of the training sessions, Yūsuf's friend Mahmoud warned the new volunteers in the following way:

> Some of the children may not have food at home, your job is to understand this and come to the management. We deal with it without making the child feel it. Don't talk about this among one another. Also, never take pictures while children are eating. Even in Ramadan iftars. The child shouldn't feel like the association is feeding him, he should come if he is happy here, if he feels that the association benefits him with its programs.

This warning revealed that the precarious realities of camp life cannot always easily be contained. Conversations that implied precarity became particularly prominent in the context of Ramadan, since the heightened activities of giving created expectations for different stakeholders: children wanted to go to as many iftar events as possible, and families, who were normally only in contact with the association to talk about their children, kept inquiring about donation boxes. Apart from the Islamic holidays, Yūsuf and his friends mainly focused on the sociocultural activities they prepared for children.

Despite his insistence on development and refraining from charity, Yūsuf and his colleagues did engage in discrete practices of economic aid. If I hadn't been friends with some of my young interlocutors like Yūsuf and families in the camp, I would have remained unaware of the economic aid and emotional support the association silently provided to the families of Palestinian and Syrian children. For example, when one of the boys was shocked by an exposed electrical wire in 2016, it was Yūsuf and his friends who brought him to the hospital and covered the hospital bills. On other occasions, while accompanying Yūsuf as he sold chips to small stores around Amman, I witnessed him bringing along some of the younger volunteers whose parents were struggling economically so that they could make some money that day.

In November 2019, when the association posted on Facebook about the passing of a ten-year-old boy in Dara'a, Syria, for instance, I understood how intimately connected this child's life had been to that of Yūsuf. That day, Yūsuf came to my house in a horrible mood. He told me how much he and his friends had insisted that the family not return to Syria. He mourned for the fact that this small child had lost his father to the war, temporarily ended up in a place like al-Naṣr camp, and lost his life upon returning to Syria by stepping on a landmine while playing with his friends. Yūsuf had named him Baibars, because like the historical Baibars, one of his eyes had a cataract, and he didn't want the boy to see this as a defect but as something he shared with a great historical figure. The boy also had problems with his heart, and the association had funded a heart operation for him. The day before the family returned to Syria, Yūsuf prepared a birthday party for his sister, whom some of the youth in the association had rescued when their first house in the camp caught fire.

By the end of 2019, Yūsuf came to me with what he perceived as a very tragic realization: that many families were having difficulties putting food on their table. Moved and frustrated by the severity of the situation, he told me they may need to accept any iftar offer for the upcoming Ramadan. "Every year the situation gets worse," he said sadly. The COVID-19 pandemic made life even more severe in the camp, and many young people who used to find sporadic employment became indefinitely unemployed, including Yūsuf, who, at the beginning of the pandemic, worked to distribute hygienic masks to small shops. When Ramadan arrived, the volunteers organized a large iftar event via Zoom, with volunteers carrying food from the association to the houses of the families.

Reconciling the Need for Aid with Aspirations for Long-Term Development

Yūsuf's work critiques humanitarian imaginaries governed by the logic of emergency and centered around saving lives. Instead, he engages in the daily, intimate, and long-term forms of care that refugees provide to their communities at the margins of the international humanitarian regime, revealing the shortcomings of imaginaries that create apolitical, short-term, and top-down responses to refugee needs and aspirations. Moreover, he reminds us of the importance of knowledge grounded in experience. He remains in the thick of things and continues to navigate relationships, limitations, and future aspirations instead of holding onto fixed moral principles that prioritize outside expertise, humanitarian conventions, or religious convictions.

As a long-term refugee from Palestine, a citizen of Jordan, a resident of a camp, and a young man, Yūsuf cares for refugees by drawing on a repertoire of caregiving practices that were created by previous generations of refugees and working within a humanitarian imaginary that is intimately connected to his own life in the camp. His approach demands more than temporary relief. Yūsuf makes it possible to envision a generation who knows their historical and cultural Palestinian roots as well as their rights as refugees, a generation empowered and equipped to overcome socioeconomic marginalization in Jordan, a generation that can do so without severing their ties and disinvesting their energies from their fellow camp residents.

For a young man like Yūsuf who tries to prioritize these long-term goals for his community, the precarity of camp life too often hinders these aspirations. Despite these frustrations, Yūsuf's daily efforts to reconcile the realities on the ground with his aspirations are ongoing, and he remains committed to caring for his fellow camp residents. When the association's face-to-face activities were suspended in accordance with COVID measures, Yūsuf opened a small store in the camp where he sold snacks that children enjoy. Today, some of the younger male volunteers still work there from time to time to support their families. During the peak of the COVID-19 crisis, the store became a place where he could stay in touch with the children of the camp. In this way, Yūsuf perseveres in modeling the possibility of preserving the ties he has shown to be so valuable and investing his energy in the camp community.

Gözde Burcu Ege was a predoctoral fellow of Mellon Sawyer Seminar, Humanitarianisms during 2020–21. Her dissertation, "From Crises to Ordinary Precarity: Palestinian Youth as New Practitioners of Humanitarian Governance in Amman, Jordan," is based on two and a half years of ethnographic research conducted in Amman, Jordan.

Notes

1. It had two mandates: first, in collaboration with host governments, to provide direct relief and works programs, and, second, "to consult with interested Near Eastern governments concerning measures to be taken in preparation for the cessation of international assistance for relief and works project." See Bocco, "UNRWA and the Palestinian Refugees," 231.
2. The names of the people and al-Ḥayāh association have been changed for confidentiality reasons.
3. For a critique of humanitarianism's equation with moral goodness, see Fassin, *Humanitarian Reason*, 244; for a case study on Doctors without Borders and the power dynamics among its international and local volunteers, see Redfield, "Unbearable Lightness of Ex-pats," 366; for an analysis on the relationship between emergency imaginary and humanitarian intervention, see Calhoun, "World of Emergencies," 373.
4. Malkki, "Zealous Humanism and Its Limits," 189; Fassin, *Humanitarian Reason*, 252.
5. In the context of Egypt, see Atia, *Building a House in Heaven*, 80; Mittermeier, "Revolutions Don't Stop Charity," 25.
6. Tilly, *Contentious French*, 4.
7. Tilly, *Contentious French*, 6.
8. For more information on al-Zaʿateri camp, see https://www.unhcr.org/jo/refugee-camps.
9. Established by the UNRWA in the 1950s, by 1970s voluntary community members with UNRWA supervision were running these Youth Clubs. In Jordan, by 1986, the Jor-

danian state took over the supervision of the Youth Clubs. See al-Husseini, "UNRWA and the Refugees," 11.
10. During the martial law that started with a staged coup attempt against King Hussein in 1956 and lasted until the regime-led liberalization in 1989, Islamic social providers, particularly the Muslim Brotherhood under the Islamic Center Charity Society, organized most extensive services. See Brumfield, "Governing Charitably." Starting in the 1970s, funds and foundations established by the members of the royal family became the main institutions to facilitate the entrance of foreign aid to Jordan. See Sato, "Islamic Charity and Royal NGOs in Jordan," 6.
11. Trapp, "You-Will-Kill-Me Beans," 413.

References

Al Husseini, Jalal. "UNRWA and the Refugees: A Difficult but Lasting Marriage." *Journal of Palestine Studies* 40, no. 1 (2010): 6–26. doi:10.1525/jps.2010.XL.1.006.

Atia, Mona. *Building a House in Heaven: Pious Neoliberalism and Islamic Charity in Egypt*. Minneapolis: University of Minnesota Press, 2013.

Bocco, R. "UNRWA and the Palestinian Refugees: A History within History." *Refugee Survey Quarterly* 28, nos. 2–3 (2009): 229–52. doi:10.1093/rsq/hdq001.

Brumfield, Nicholas J. "Governing Charitably: The State, Civil Society, and Welfare in Jordan." ProQuest Dissertations Publishing, 2017.

Calhoun, Craig. "A World of Emergencies: Fear, Intervention, and the Limits of Cosmopolitan Order." *Canadian Review of Sociology* 41, no. 4 (2004): 373–95. doi:10.1111/j.1755-618X.2004.tb00783.x.

Fassin, Didier. "Conclusion: Critique of Humanitarian Reason." In *Humanitarian Reason: A Moral History of the Present*, 243–257. 1st ed. Berkeley: University of California Press, 2012. doi:10.1525/j.ctt1pptmk.

Malkki, Liisa H. "A Zealous Humanism and Its Limits: Sacrifice and the Hazards of Neutrality." In *The Need to Help*, 165–98. Durham, NC: Duke University Press, 2020. doi:10.1515/9780822375364-003.

Mittermaier, Amira. "Revolutions Don't Stop Charity." In *Giving to God: Islamic Charity in Revolutionary Times*, 21–49. Oakland: University of California Press, 2009.

Redfield, Peter. "The Unbearable Lightness of Ex-pats: Double Binds of Humanitarian Mobility." *Cultural Anthropology* 27, no. 2 (2012): 358–82. doi:10.1111/j.1548–1360.2012.01147.x.

Sato, Marie. "Islamic Charity and Royal NGOs in Jordan: The Role of Monarchial Institutions in Its Balancing Act." *Asia-Japan Research Academic Bulletin* 1, no 31 (2020): 1–12. doi:10.34389/asiajapanbulletin.31.

Tilly, Charles. *The Contentious French: Charles Tilly*. Cambridge, MA: Belknap Press of Harvard University Press, 1986.

Trapp, Micah M. "You-Will-Kill-Me Beans: Taste and the Politics of Necessity in Humanitarian Aid." *Cultural Anthropology* 31, no. 3 (2016): 412–37. doi:10.14506/ca31.3.08.

CHAPTER 10

"They Are *Muhajir*, We Are *Ansar*"
Godforsakenness at the Myanmar-Bangladesh Border

Tanzeen Rashed Doha

There are two open tabs on my computer screen and a notebook at my desk. The first tab has a digital image of a Rohingya imam leading prayers in Balukhali, Cox's Bazar, at the site of a *masjid* (mosque) under construction. The second tab takes me to a Hadith website that cites the Prophet's dreams about Medina as the destination the of the first *hijra* (migration).[1] The notebook at my desk has texts related to recent conversations with Bangladeshi Islamists about their work with the Rohingya. The texts take multiple forms: long sentences, short remarks, crossed-out thoughts, question marks, exclamation marks, interpretive comments next to ethnographic statements, and blank spaces.

The imam, the mosque's religious leader, in the image is leading obligatory prayers under the open sky. The mosque under construction is a simple rectangular space at this point. There are bamboo sticks piled in front of the imam that will be used in the future to build the mosque. In the background, in the hills, are small temporary homes. The black-and-white image is gloomy. The deathworld the image fails to capture exceeds its representation, but the image as a tiny, shattered piece, like a shard of broken glass, interrupts the secular flow of digital reproduction.

The Hadith website, citing the Prophet's loving wife Aisha, reports that he dreamed of Medina before the *hijra*. Medina, in the Prophet's dream, is "a land of date palm trees, between two lava fields, the two stony tracts."[2] It is a place of tranquility, a place where soft mannered believers hospitable to the Prophet and his companions greet them. Boys and girls see the Prophet and exclaim in joy, "This is the Messenger of Allah (peace and blessings be upon him), he has come."³

The field notes are stories of devastation, what is referred to in Islamic discourses as a *"fasad"*—not just political violence but a disequilibrium of global scale caused by Man's desire for sovereignty and audacity to rebel against a divine order. The interlocutors in these notes experience abandonment—a feeling of being left alone by communities, neighbors, states, and the world as such. God himself appears quiet. Did God forsake them? It is precisely in moments of absolute loss that a believer depends on the Unseen (*ghayb*)—on what cannot be perceived by the senses but under whose gaze death finds an ideal home in those who submit, and life finds tribulation in those who persist.

How are trials and tribulations in the deathworld of the present read from within the classical texts of Islam's discursive tradition? How do the ulama, like the imam in the image, in their conviction find nearness to Allah in the aftermath of forced migration of the Muslim community? My notes do not tell me if the imam had dreams of hospitality across the border, but I do know that the Prophet's dreams in reports from his wife tell of the possibility of a true welcome after migration.

The Prophet's dreams show us that hospitality receives its form when those who have migrated (*muhajirin*) arrive.⁴ When strangers and guests arrive, it is as if angels have arrived; a divine light illuminates a dark world. Their hosts and helpers (*ansar*) now have the opportunity to please Allah. Contrary to secular humanitarian charity in which the volunteer helps the dispossessed refugee, there are no victims or volunteers in these interactions between the Rohingya and the Bangladeshi Islamists. The suffering travelers as the companions of the leaders of the first Muslim migration (the *sabireen*) remain steadfast. They find brotherhood in calamity. In the certainty of death, they emulate the Prophet. It is as if life is breathed into them in the dreamscape of the Prophet. It is as if they are his companions, his brothers.⁵

• • •

Jahan dedicated his time in three different locations in the Rohingya camps in Cox's Bazar: Palongkhali, Balukhali, and Kutupalong. Jahan volunteered from his religious school (madrassa) and joined others in Islamist efforts to help the Rohingya during two different waves of migration. First, in 2016, he and other madrassa clerics and students provided materials, money, and food in small packets. The camps were not yet ready, so they could only help the Rohingya while they were still on the move without a clear idea of an actual place of refuge. Jahan walked alongside the Rohingya in their journey. What does it mean to walk alongside fellow believers who are distressed and in despair? What does it mean to walk without a clear destination? What does it mean to engage in service (*khidmat*) while being on the move?⁶

Jahan spoke very little in those encounters. During the 2016 migration, words were mostly used for the sake of collective recitations (*dhikr*), to ask Allah for forgiveness, for mercy, for help. Jahan listened more and made himself available and adequate to history. Even though the local dialect is similar to the Rohingya language, there was a language barrier. This barrier was also an opening for a world of the quiet, a meditative silence, in which believers grasp the place of divinity within calamity, within catastrophe. This mode of quietude is not about divine vindication. Jahan is not wondering why a perfect God allows for suffering. His quietude is literal. Jahan does not initiate active conversations with the other, nor does he ask himself questions or inquire Allah for answers in desperation. The moving non-enunciative space is a place where utterances and speech acts become impossible. This inability to find words creates the conditions for a leap of faith, a reliance on God (*tawakkul*), generating a meditative space of stillness. The recitations—praising the Unseen—signal full submission. They squeeze out speech and construct a singular world of Allah's ninety-nine names. They prepare a ground in a groundless world—a temporary refuge, a transient condition in which human contingencies are subsumed under a divine order of divine names—only to be groundless again.

Jahan's approach reminded me of a specific Prophetic story in the Hadith. In Sahih Muslim, Anas reports that a woman suffering and experiencing grief said:

> "Allah's Messenger, I want something from you." The Prophet (peace be upon him) responded: "Mother of so and so, see on which side of the road you would like (to stand and talk) so that I may do the needful for you." He stood aside with her on the roadside until she got what she needed.

Some have translated the last part "until she got what she needed" more specifically as "until she was able to say what she wanted to her heart's content."[7] The Prophet did not initiate a conversation but rather allowed for the fellow believer in distress to speak as much as she needed. When the Prophet asks, "On which side of the road you would like (to stand and talk)?" he not only gives permission to the woman to share her thoughts, but he also orients himself and the woman in relation to the road on which they were both standing. This positioning and orienting prepares a particular kind of space that is generative for theological counsel. In 2016, when Jahan walks alongside the Rohingya, their bodies in motion—in remembrance of God position themselves in relation to one another within a War on Terror at the outskirts of nation-states—transgress secular spatiality and allow for a sense of belonging without having to dwell in a home.

In a more recent conversation, I asked Jahan about the 2016 migration and the construction of the space of non-enunciation and the meditative mood of the encounter:

In 2016 when the Rohingya Muslims crossed the border and arrived in Cox's Bazar, escaping Burmese state violence, you had mentioned that the Islamists from your madrassa and other areas had to organize very quickly. But it seems the lack of preparation in terms of organizing materials and resources allowed for a different approach in the way you accepted them and tended to their needs. You spoke little in those interactions. The description of it seems to have this mood of stillness. Of course, it was a time of calamity, but behind it or beneath it there was a kind of quietness.

Jahan responded:

The migration was unexpected. The government at the time did not officially state they would allow the Rohingya to come in. The Rohingya traveled into Cox's Bazar regardless, and we felt obligated to be there, to do whatever we could. We were not prepared. We tried to provide them with some essentials, but our lack of preparation meant that we received them, welcomed them, but did not have enough materials for them. We did not speak much. Their condition made us silent. We wondered why Allah allowed such devastation and despair.

The Rohingya and the Deobandi students worked at the margins and in-between spaces of nation-states. It was unclear if the Rohingya would settle somewhere on the Bangladeshi side or if they would return to Myanmar. Precarious either way, such mobility of the Rohingya destabilizes a predetermined secular space—signaling a kind of geographical indeterminacy and volatility. The movements in the border region, immediately outside of the killing fields of the Burmese state and barely within Bangladesh, do not necessarily signify an outside-of-nation-state cartography as much as it denotes the manner in which the War on Terror constricts and puts pressure on movements while simultaneously tracing and following along the pathways created by enemy combatants. This demonstrates not just how the war is global but also how capacious it remains in its own transgressive powers. Put differently, while there are moments of interruption of secular geography by the movements of the Rohingya in their dynamic with the Deobandi Islamists, it is the war itself that transgresses secular boundaries even as it engages in a secularizing war against Islam—the attempt to de-essentialize its orthodox structure. The War on Terror creates statelessness, which exceeds the notion of migration because for believers (*mu'min*), such a condition demands a rigorous exploration of concepts like *hijrat* (migration) and *jihad* (struggle) in the classical tradition of Islam to make them historically adequate in the present.

As the Rohingya as the *muhajir* (refugee-migrants) and the Bangladeshi Islamists as the *ansar* (helpers), contests secular cartography to construct an experiential space as the body of the *umma* (Muslim community) in the border region, I am reminded of Maurice Merleau-Ponty's observation that "the body inhabits space (and time, for that matter) … in motion because movement is not content with passively undergoing space and time, it actively assumes them, it takes them up in their original signification that is effaced in the banality of established situations." Jahan explains the instability of not having established camps and the temporariness of space:

> We did not know where they would go. We were unsure. Are they arriving here and disappearing within the country? Or, are they returning to Burma after a few days of respite? We wanted to be there in the immediate context when they arrived. That was important to us. To be present.

It is in this context without "the banality of established situations" that the Rohingya find themselves finding new space in their movement as the body of a damaged *umma* (Muslim community). But there is a difference between individual body spatiality that acts and a collective mass moving as a body—a broken-off piece of the *umma*—in a situation of permanent war that has to act. To act and to have to act are not the same phenomenon. The Rohingya create space as subjects of the Burmese War on Terror, as a mass in which they are not the representation of a sum total of individuals but are an abstract mass who are persecuted within the historicity of the War on Terror. This mass, the disfigured part of the *umma*, immanently violates secular historicity as it inhabits space in motion. For the Rohingya "the banality of established situations" is also an experience of constant (re)adjustment to new techniques of war. Even though they are accustomed to an established structure of war, they encounter unexpected shifts and deviations. The "established situation" of war is antifoundational, has self-movement within it, and is without a predictable pattern in the way it surveils, targets, tortures, and disciplines the Rohingya. Because of this inherent heterogeneity, the War on Terror forces the Rohingya to adjust to varying speeds and intensities of motion. Even as they are creating a new space in the camps, the Rohingya Muslims are subjects of suspicion, always at risk of being without a ground. In other words, a brutal banality—and a banal brutality—is present whether there are "established situations" or not. They are on the move, as *muhajirin*; as framed by the War on Terror, they are also stateless strangers, and terror suspects.

I pressed Jahan to tell me more about the condition of silence and sense of curiosity and their relation after hearing the following two sentences in his articulations: First, that "their condition made us silent at first"; and second that "we wondered why Allah allowed such devastation and despair." Is silence a necessary condition as one wonders about why God allows what he allows? This was not a demanding gesture toward God but rather a political-mystical exploration of godforsakenness: a journey into absence in the most elemental sense. Jahan clarifies:

> We are not like the seculars. We do not doubt God. We want to have a sense of our condition. God is intervening through absence. What exactly is this intervention? We

want to feel this intervention in our heart [*hridoy*], we want to grasp it on the inside [*bhitor theke bujhte chai*].

God forsakes us in order to not forsake us. This awareness of a condition among the Islamists—of a particular kind of godforsakenness in which God abandons because He remains—works in direct opposition to atheist existentialism. Jean-Paul Sartre, as an atheist existentialist, emphasized that existence precedes essence, which makes God unnecessary, and therefore, subjects can be free.[8] In Jahan's statements, however, there is less of a focus on the sequence of existence and essence; instead, through feeling and sensing, he arrives at an instinctual antihistorical question mark. A believer like Jahan interrogates how God intervenes through absence and calls into question the secularizing strategies of the War on Terror.

Jahan explains to me that, while the actual interaction with the Rohingya in 2016 involved silence and minimal speech, during nighttime the Deobandi Islamists engaged in spirited analytical conversations on the possible causes and conditions of this divine catastrophe. A sermon (*khutba*) given by leading twentieth-century Islamic scholar Syed Abul Hasan Ali Nadwi in the early 1960s at Rangoon's Surti Jamah Masjid soon became the basis of these conversations. The text of the speech (in the original Urdu as well as Bengali translations) began to circulate widely in various madrassa networks. The core message from the sermon is clear in the following excerpt:

> Everything in this *duniya* [world] is *dhongshoshil* [destructible]. Property, respect, everything will end one day. What will remain eternally is only Allah's name, active work [*mehanat*] in Allah's path, and active work and sacrifice [*qurbani*] for Allah's din.... If you take time outside of your business and work to propagate and establish Islam, then Allah Ta' Ala will gift you with power in this country and paradise in the next life. But if you do not do so, then remember, you will not be able to even stay in this country. Not as a political figure, I am saying this through the light given to me by Allah as a believer [*mu'min*]—it will become impossible for you to stay in this country if you do not try with all your spirit to propagate and spread the true religion [*din*].[9]

Jahan and his Islamist companions, in their own analysis, not only agreed with Syed Nadwi's emphasis on Islamization at the base of society through moral reform (*da'wa*), they observed that the problem was exasperated by the failures of struggle (*jihad*) against the Burmese state. Jahan explained:

> We were listening to Shaykh Nadwi's *khutba* over and over again during this time. He predicted the crisis [*shongkot*] faced by the Rohingya in Myanmar many years ago. But I also spoke to other *ulama* [religious scholars] during this time who had participated in struggle [*jihad*] against the Burmese state. They told me that many of the traveling *mujahideen* [Islamic fighters] from Bangladesh were detained by the Burmese security because corrupt elements in the Rohingya had collaborated

with Burmese intelligence. Some of our *ulama* blame the failures of the *jihad* on this moral corruption. Shaykh Nadwi was right, the society at large needed *da'wa* [moral self-reform], but under the new circumstances there was no alternative to armed *jihad*. And, a real breakthrough would be possible if the Rohingya with the help of other Muslims had an ongoing successful *jihad* without any moral deviance.

In a different context, in Kashmir, anthropologist Cabeiri Robinson shows how processes and transformations in the real, social world produce *jihad* in the concrete sense. She calls this "the social production of *jihad*."[10] Jahan's emphasis reverses Robinson's point. *Jihad* becomes an objectively necessary ethical instrument for the construction of new social relations, resulting in the jihadi production of the social. In other words, Rohingya militancy as *jihad* aims to displace the given order for a new social. Jahan's emphasis on the simultaneity of *da'wa* and *jihad* is not rooted in secular agency and freedom; it emerges from an antihistorical aspiration to exceed the immanence of history and disarticulates and reconfigures freedom itself. In other words, *jihad* in this specific discourse is the name of a dynamic transgression of the present.

In the autumn of 2017, when the camps were established, Jahan and other Islamic workers not only carried and distributed food and donated money and other essentials, they also built twelve mosques and installed thirteen tube-well water pumps and some toilets. Jahan says, "Our main objective this time was to build *masajid* and to organize money to pay salaries for permanent imams and teachers." At the time, Jahan did not realize that there would soon be government intervention. The months September through November now felt distant. Those three months allowed for unrestricted opportunities to engage in Islamic activity. By wintertime, the regime restricted their efforts, only allowing licensed NGOs to work in the camps. The government gave orders to destroy many of the mosques. While they gave practical justifications—such as avoiding having too many mosques in the same few blocks—there is suspicion among the *ulama* that this was a strategic security measure of de-Islamization of the camps by the regime. Jahan confirms:

> In the last four years, there has been a decrease in Islamic activity for the Rohingya. In the past, Islamists used to visit the camps to teach the Qur'an and Hadith to give them relief ['*shantona*], but that is not possible anymore. Now, most of the work is done by government-supported NGOs.

While Jahan did not directly condemn the NGOs, he appeared to have a sense of their limitations in the Islamic context. He stated that the NGOs would not know how to help the Rohingya with their own self-preservation because they would look at them simply as "refugees."

To an anthropologist well aware of critiques of liberal-secular humanitarianism, this was an ideal point in our conversation where I felt compelled to press

Jahan to explain more and to give an example of how the Rohingya were more than refugees. Jahan, instead of deconstructing the Western basis of humanitarianism, utilized Islamic vocabulary and concepts to make his point. "As the Rohingya were forced to migrate, making a *hijrat*, to Bangladesh there were many mid-level and senior *ulama* among them who had classical knowledge. This knowledge could have been used for their own welfare, to help them stand up with dignity again," he said. I asked him if he had the opportunity to meet with the Rohingya *ulama*. Jahan replied:

> At our madrasa, I read a book on Arabic linguistics [*bhashatotto*]. The book was written in Urdu. The author was a Rohingya *alem* [a religious scholar]. Our madrassa historically had a connection with the training of the Rohingya in classical Islamic education. When we went to the camps, we heard that a renowned *alem* was among the refugees. I asked for his name, and they said: Maulana Azam. I realized then that he is the author of the linguistics book I studied in my Daurae-hadith program. I met him at the camp. We spoke in Arabic.

I asked, "Why did you speak in Arabic? You lived in Chittagong for so long. The local dialect is similar to the Rohingya language, right? You could have also spoken to him in Urdu. Why Arabic?" Jahan paused, and then tried to explain:

> There are several dialects in Chittagong depending on specific regions, and I could not catch the Rohingya dialect that well. I don't know why we did not speak in Urdu though. We spoke in Arabic. It happened spontaneously.

The first encounter between Jahan and Maulana Azam is not ideal.[11] The student does not meet the author at a seminar or conference. As a true student (*talib-ul-ilm*), he is active in the world; he translates the verses of the Qur'an into his concrete life; his heart (*qalb*) is affected by the stories of Rohingya suffering initiates a step toward humility—a need to receive himself as an ordinary believer in a divine order who has to find himself, realizing that he can grasp himself precisely when the world that makes him disintegrates. It is in these moments of divine tribulation, as he witnesses history in fragments, that he encounters the Real through hospitality. Maulana Azam arrives within the appearance of accidents of death and destitution. He arrives within those three to four months before government restrictions when the community (*ummah*) takes care of itself. He arrives after making *hijrat*, after migrating. The student (*talib-ul-ilm*) receives him, listens to him, pays attention to him, inquires about his well-being and about the condition of his soul. Jahan does not know yet that the maulana is the author. Someone in the camp mentions the senior *alem*'s name: Maulana Azam! Jahan remembers. Jahan becomes curious. He is concerned in an affectionate way. He wants to make sure the maulana is unharmed. He is also anxious. The maulana's book taught him Arabic linguistics, opened up a new language with a grammar to decipher an entirely new world. That author whose book he read in the early years of the *Daurae Hadith* program is present in front of him, in flesh but with a broken heart across from the killing fields of the Burmese state.[12]

Jahan's body stiffens. He is anxious. It is a strange circumstance for a first meeting with an *alem*-author who was formative in his Islamic learning. But there is a second kind of anxiety that is much more elemental and fundamental. This other anxiety initiates a feeling of groundlessness. In the border regions, cartographies reveal themselves as apparitions, and states appear to lose stability. The student and the maulana find themselves elsewhere as if in another geography. This elsewhere has a regionality outside of known regions. Even though they encounter each other in a secular geography, there is a disruption of "the obviousness" of a secular spatiality—in which the condition of "not being at home" is not essentially about the absence of community, or exclusion from a citizen-state, or the overall failure to find sovereignty but rather reveals itself to be a primordial condition. Absence and exclusion in the given order, however, in the immediate and concrete deathworld, work as the entry point for a speculation on absolute absence, resulting in a foundational anxiety.

As words are uttered and language mediates speech, both the student and the maulana refuse their mother tongue. Jahan speaks in broken Arabic, and the maulana responds in perfect Qur'anic Arabic. When I asked Jahan why he spoke in Arabic, he did not have a precise answer. He paused. The pause before speech, before language, is the distance between the two forms of anxiety—the nervousness with which Jahan made sense of the fact that the author he read had participated in the migration and arrived and the more fundamental anxiety that shakes the very ground of the world Jahan inhabits. There are moments of silence within and in between anxiety, and a lack of destination even as words are uttered in speech acts.

Even though his reasoning appeared pragmatic at first, Jahan's utterances and sentences within the problem of language have within them the same kind of groundlessness. The space, the camps, and that specific region is both a place and a nonplace. It is home, it is not home. It is home precisely because it is not home. It is an attempt to move away from ruin, from gunfire. And in language as well, in Jahan and the maulana's refusal of regional languages in favor of Qur'anic Arabic, there is the momentary possibility of the emergence of an elsewhere in which there is a dwelling without permanence.

Jahan's encounter with Maulana Azam is not primarily between a reader and an author. It is not just a meeting between a maulana (graduate religious scholar) and a *talib-ul-ilm* (student of knowledge). Even though they meet each other unexpectedly in the midst of devastation, it is not an encounter between a refugee and a humanitarian worker. The essence of their first meeting is not the tragedy of a humanitarian catastrophe. What the given circumstances make clear is that there is in fact a divine responsibility—a kind of caring-for that obligates Jahan toward Maulana Azam. This exists long before their first actual encounter in the refugee camps, before the first time reading his book on Arabic language theory in the madrassa, and even before his first imagination of what it might mean to meet him one day—whether in dreams or as they have met in the border regions between Rakhine and Cox's Bazar in the corridor of the War on Terror.

Jahan began a conversation with Maulana Azam about the condition of the Rohingya in Myanmar. The scholar's response shifted from the personal (biographical) to the political past as he shared his political-theological observations. Jahan explains:

> Maulana Azam shared his personal memory of Chittagong. He studied in Chittagong. He inquired about one of his *alem* friends from the past. I asked him about the Rohingya situation, and asked what he thought was the root cause of this massive catastrophe [*boro shongkot*]. Maulana Azam recited the famous Qur'anic verse from Surah Ra'd: "Indeed, Allah would never change a people's state of favor until they change their own state of faith. And if it is Allah's Will to torment a people, it can never be averted, nor can they find a protector other than Him." I asked him how this verse [*ayat*] applies to his community. The maulana explained: "Our problem is that we keep thinking about OIC [Organization of Islamic Cooperation] funds and how they will help us. This kind of thinking is inside our people. The Burmese authorities commanded us to leave. And, now we are here. There is no thinking of resistance [*protibader kono chinta nai*]. Since the eighties, the Rohingya have assured themselves by thinking that if anything happens, we will move to Bangladesh. People from the Rohingya nation are spread out in different parts of the world. They left their home and their heritage.

A second scholar, Maulana Abdullah—who wrote in Urdu and Arabic about the Prophet's family and heritage—standing next to Maulana Azam, chimed in and provided nuance to the conversation:

> Yes, it is true that the resistance has been unsuccessful, but you have to remember that the Rohingya are not targets only because they are Muslim. There are other Muslims in Rangoon. The Myanmar society is fine with them. Those Muslims are established there. They have recognition and are respected. The Rohingya are looked at as a different '*jaat*' [nation or race], as poor, and as later immigrants to Burma and are treated as foreigners. Some of the non-Rohingya Muslims in Rangoon also hate us.

Maulana Abdullah's valuable insights add the question of subalternity to Maulana Azam's Qur'anic assessments and ethico-political frustration.[13]

The two insights enhance each other because the concern over the status of faith among the Rohingya becomes less of a moral concern when their subaltern condition is identified. While Mahmood Mamdani's contextualization of the production of "good Muslims" and "bad Muslims" in the political-historical post-911 world is relevant here, the question of the Rohingya exceeds the occupation of "the bad Muslim's" positionality. The Rohingya are enemy combatants as "bad Muslims" within the contingencies of the War on Terror, of course, but they are also what *the political* cannot register as subjects, and in this sense, they challenge Western assumptions about humanitarianism and secular aid. They arrive, they remain silent, they disappear. Or, they arrive, they find a temporary home in divine language, and they haunt the secular present as they disappear again.

• • •

The abstract question of human nature is not at the surface of interactions between the Rohingya and the Islamists at the border region. But "what is it that makes us who we are?" remains as a curiosity, a question mark, an object of inquisitiveness that emerges in the midst of devastation. Islamic classifications and categories initiating practices of silence, speech, and analysis explode binaries of essence/existence, determination/free will, and despair/agency. In the immanent place of wretchedness, where one feels damned, godforsakenness is the condition of possibility of what flickers.

God—the Merciful—remains on his throne.

By tracing the pause between speech and language, the stillness of believers in states of despair, the immanent unfolding of a momentary space outside and in between given cartographies of nation-states, this ethnographic meditation has dwelled on the fundamental anxiety beneath movements that trouble the narrative arc of secular historicism.[14] The conversations between Jahan and the Rohingya *ulama* reflect a fragment of a global Deobandi discursive tradition. By rehistoricizing classical Islamic stories of helpers (*ansar*) and migrant-refugees (*muhajir*), from the Prophet's Medina to the present, such a discourse calls into question the assumptive logics of secular humanitarianism and displaces categories of humanitarian "volunteers" and "refugees." The chapter discovers varied observations in the encounters between Rohingya guardians, transmitters, and interpreters of religious knowledge (*ulama*) and Deobdandi practitioners—on moral self-criticism, political-theological critiques of the modern War on Terror states, and the possibility of antisecular geographies—that find a coherence in a contemporary Islamism. The chapter works itself out in movement within echoes of collective recitations in praise of God (*dhikr*) as it confronts displacement and calamity, withdraws from this-worldly resolution, and refrains from articulating a politically stable rhetoric in the present as divine texts and prophetic dreams in the classical tradition haunt the future of extinguished time.

Jahan's affirmation—"They [the Rohingya] are *muhajir*, we are *ansar*"—as he speculates on the condition of godforsakenness with extraordinary poise, can be (mis)read as a yearning to break history open in the present or as fetishized nostalgia for an ideal self-valorized community, but such statements in their sentiment explore in a state of perplexity what it means to obey the impossible in the utter absence of origins and grounds.

Tanzeen Rashed Doha is visiting assistant professor of anthropology at the University of Pittsburgh and previously served as a global racial justice postdoctoral fellow at Cornell University. Doha is the founder and general editor of the journal-magazine *Milestones: Commentary on the Islamic World*. He is also the founder and host of *Everything Is Fire: A Podcast on Crisis, Catastrophe, and Tribulation*.

Notes

1. "Migration" or "emigration" in Arabic (in South Asia pronounced *hijrat*). While practicing Muslims may think of migration in ideal terms, where the Prophet and his companions arrive at Medina and find refuge and a true welcome, in sites of contemporary warfare, migration is a devastating experience. Having said that, in traditions of twentieth-century Islamism, *hijra* is often conceptualized in ethico-political and pragmatic terms, with emphasis on the Meccan period when the Prophet and the earliest believers were persecuted for promoting God's revelations (Qur'an).
2. Al-Bukhari narrated on the authority of Aisha that the Prophet (peace and blessings be upon him) said to the Muslims, "I have been shown the land to which you will immigrate: it has palm trees between two lava fields, two stony tracts." *Ṣaḥīḥ al-Bukhārī*, no. 3905.
3. Narrated by al-Bara bin Azib (*Ṣaḥīḥ al-Bukhārī*, no. 3925).
4. In the classical sense, the *muhajirin* were the first migrants of Islamic history, the early converts to Islam who migrated with the Prophet. But in a general sense, the *muhajirin* as a concept has been applied to various Islamic histories of migration.
5. Anas ibn Malik reported, "The Messenger of Allah, peace and blessings be upon him, said, 'I wish I could meet my brothers.' The Prophet's companions said, 'Are we not your brothers?' The Prophet said, 'You are my companions, but my brothers are those who have faith in me although they never saw me.'" *Musnad Aḥmad*, no. 12169.
6. About *khidma* (service), Amira Mittermaier writes, "God, moreover, is continuously *made* present through rituals, such as prayer, sacrifice, and almsgiving, and through the very phrase *li-llah* and the way that it relentlessly orients charitable gifts away from the human recipients." Mittermaier, *Giving to God*, 7. In the context of the Rohingya/Islamist encounter, however, there is a larger emphasis on God as absent author; godforsakenness is a meditation on this condition of absence (which is different from nonexistence) during times of divine tribulation.
7. Thanks to Arif Rabbani, who clarified that the first translation for *ḥattā faraghat min ḥājatihā* ("until she got what she needed") is literal, and the second translation ("until she was able to express herself to her heart's content") is more interpretative within the context of the ḥadīth.

8. See Sartre, *Existentialism Is a Humanism*. In *On Suicide Bombing*, Talal Asad shows how suicide bombing through acts of extreme/absolute freedom disarticulates the genealogy and binary of freedom itself, creating horror in liberal moderns.
9. Nadvi, "1961 Burma Me Maula Ali Miya Nadvi ka Historical Bayan." The original is in Urdu, and the translation here is mine from a portion of the speech that was translated into Bengali and circulated in an Islamic text message group.
10. Robinson, *Body of Victim*.
11. *Maulana* is a title that denotes a Muslim religious leader, in particular a graduate of a religious institutions
12. This is a six-year intensive program on Islamic jurisprudence focusing on the foundational texts of Islam, the Qur'an, and the Hadith.
13. Gayatri Spivak in "Can the Subaltern Speak?" emphasizes the subaltern produced by the difference between being stateless and being a migrant. To be stateless is to not be registered in the civil society, where even if the Rohingya are to speak, the civil society cannot hear them. This world was created in those months in 2016 and 2017 where, within a specific discursive tradition of Islam in the border regions, encounters of silence and language were mediated.
14. Here I am engaging Koselleck's *Critique and Crisis* and Iqbal's "Reprising Islamic Political Theology" though my focus in this chapter—whether discussing the physical movement of the Rohingya and the Bangladeshi Islamists or the fundamental anxiety experienced by Jahan as he encounters a Rohingya *alim*—is less about the (in)validity of analytic categories like "crisis," "critique," or "historicism" than about the pauses, withdrawals, ruptures, and gaps within the dynamic of modern history's formation of itself as the secular. Islam is the most prominent name signifying such a phenomenon.

References

Asad, Talal. *On Suicide Bombing*. New York: Columbia University Press, 2007.
Iqbal, Basit Kareem. "Reprising Islamic Political Theology: Genre and the Time of Tribulation." *Political Theology* 23, no. 6 (August 18, 2022): 525–42. https://doi.org/10.1080/1462317X.2022.2092680.
Koselleck, Reinhart. *Critique and Crisis: Enlightenment and the Pathogenesis of Modern Society*. Cambridge, MA: MIT Press, 2000.
Mittermaier, Amira. *Giving to God: Islamic Charity in Revolutionary Times*. 1st ed. Oakland: University of California Press, 2019.
Nadvi, Maula Ali Miya. "1961 Burma Me Maula Ali Miya Nadvi ka Historical Bayan." YouTube, 7 September 2017. https://www.youtube.com/watch?v=c73XxpAgFsM.
Robinson, Cabeiri deBergh. *Body of Victim, Body of Warrior: Refugee Families and the Making of Kashmiri Jihadists*. Oakland: University of California Press, 2013.
Sartre, Jean-Paul, Arlette Elkaïm-Sartre, and Annie Cohen-Solal. *Existentialism Is a Humanism*. Translated by Carol Macomber. Annotated ed. New Haven, CT: Yale University Press, 2007.
Spivak, Gayatri Chakravorty. "Can the Subaltern Speak?" *Die Philosophin* 14, no. 27 (1988): 42–58. https://doi.org/10.5840/philosophin200314275.

CHAPTER 11

"We're All Humanitarians"
International Humanitarian Organizations, Islamist Service Societies, and the Practice of "Humanitariyan Jihad" *in Kashmir*

Cabeiri deBergh Robinson

An earthquake changed the landscape of northeast Pakistan in October 2005. It had its epicenter near Muzaffarabad, the capital of Azad Jammu and Kashmir (AJK), which is a part of the disputed territory of Jammu and Kashmir that is administered by Pakistan and claimed by India. Schools, hospitals, government buildings, and houses collapsed, and in mountainous areas, entire villages were buried in landslides. The earthquake killed over 80,000 people, injured approximately 120,000 people, and rendered 3 million people unsheltered as the winter season of the lower Himalayas approached.

This natural disaster brought numerous international agencies, state institutions, and national and transnational voluntary organizations together in a vast humanitarian relief project. Among the voluntary workers who contributed to the relief and rehabilitation efforts in the first days and months after the earthquake were members of militant organizations. Since 1986, AJK had been the center of organizing, recruitment, and training for both nationalist and Islamist militant organizations fighting against the Indian state on the Indian-administered side of the Line of Control (LoC) in an active armed conflict that began in 1989 and continues into the present. After the earthquake, Kashmiri members of these jihadi militant groups declared a temporary stop to their armed activities on the Indian side of the LoC in order to engage in the labor of relief and social welfare work—what they called *"humanitariyan jihad."*

These jihadis worked alongside delegates of international humanitarian organizations and global Islamic charities, medical personnel of several national militaries, soldiers and officers of the Pakistan Army and security services, and members of Pakistani domestic and transnational civil society groups, all of whom came to AJK to provide emergency relief during the first phase of the crisis. Their relief projects were supported by Islamic charities that competed with international aid agencies for philanthropic donations from Muslim communities around the world. Over the years, many of these workers, without renouncing the possibility of return to militant politics, continued to work as social welfare volunteers and eventually secured employment in local development NGOs.

As the focus shifted from rescue and relief to long-term reconstruction and rehabilitation, it became clear that the earthquake had transformed the social, economic, and political landscapes of AJK as well as the physical landscape. For the international community, an area that had long been a site of global humanitarian refusal became an acceptable terrain of humanitarian engagement because the disaster was "natural." For Pakistani civic voluntary organizations, four years into the War on Terror, AJK became a territory of compassion, a place in which Pakistani society's capacity for self-organization and self-care could be mobilized against the images of Pakistan as a place of perpetual crisis and institutionalized disorder, on the one hand, and as the object of militarized humanitarian interventions, on the other. For the demobilized members of active Islamic militant organizations, it became a domain of sacrifice, in which relief and aid work replaced armed jihad as a framework for protecting a vulnerable Muslim population. Eventually, AJK became a domain of welfare governance, in which social welfare became articulated as a form of state security provision that would continue to compete for funds and recognition with the border and national security concerns.

Fault Lines

The earthquake occurred in the morning on 8 October 2005. Schools, government buildings, houses, and other structures collapsed. Entire villages slid down mountainsides, and three of the refugee camps on the outskirts of Muzaffarabad disappeared into the Neelum River. Children and young people were already in school, and many were trapped in their school buildings and colleges and beneath the concrete slabs and iron bars that were the construction norm for modern buildings in the region. The two vehicle crossing points from Pakistan into Azad Jammu and Kashmir were both blocked with damage to their bridges, the roads leading to populated areas unpassable. Towns in the Khyber Pakhtunkhwa along the routes to the AJK crossing points were also severely impacted. Neither the AJK civilian government, which had lost core infrastructure, nor the Pakistan Army launched emergency response in AJK for days after the earthquake.

Instead, members of the Kashmiri militant groups operating in the region mounted the first coordinated response. They immediately declared a halt to all armed struggle activities and set to work in rescue and relief efforts. Demobilized members of jihadist organizations stepped into the task of caring for the injured, the displaced, and the dead. Others brought tools for extraction and worked alongside civilians who were desperately digging to reach survivors trapped under collapsed structures. These militant groups put their satellite communications technology to use locating people trapped in the mountains and carried the injured out of isolated villages on their backs. They carried mobile X-rays, centrifuges, and emergency supplies from storehouses located in Pakistan on their backs and pack mules when the roads were blocked. They set up all-weather tents and established secure and hygienic camps for those who had lost shelter. These tented relief camps were so well guarded that men felt comfortable leaving women and young children there—an essential contribution in the first days because these civilians joined in efforts to rescue their neighbors. They also established the first working field hospital with surgical capacity (including mobile X-ray and microbial analysis machines) and obstetric services (see figure 11.1). It was operating just thirty-six hours after the earthquake.

Figure 11.1. • Women's health unit of the Jamaat-ul-Dawa Mobile Medical Camp, Muzaffarabad, AJK. November 2005. © Cabeiri deBergh Robinson.

In comparison, the Turkish military had an operational field hospital running in Muzaffarabad five days later, the United States eight days later. Five weeks after the earthquake, when I was escorted on an official visit to a Pakistan military field hospital on the Line of Control (LoC) near the Chakoti border, the Pakistan Army's model civilian field hospital consisted of a tent, three chairs, and a table with a display of bandages, analgesics, and antimalarials (see figure 11.2). Even the United Nations High Commission for Refugees (UNHCR), which normally maintains large stores of tents and other supplies in Pakistan for its Afghan refugee operations, was unable to meet the needs quickly, as they had depleted their regional supplies during the relief work that followed the Indian Ocean Tsunami earlier in the year.

A commonly told tale in those first months went like this: Pakistani army troops, redeployed from the Punjab, showed up in AJK and then marched to the border to protect it from military adventurism by Indian troops. Or, troops arrived at a collapsed school with weapons but no heavy equipment suitable for extracting survivors from beneath the slabs of fallen concrete. A trope of complaints was, "The army showed up with bayonets, not shovels, and tanks, not bulldozers." (Many in AJK attributed this to Pakistan's interest in "Kashmir, not Kashmiris," but the same complaint was made in Islamabad where two

Figure 11.2. • Model military-civilian field hospital, Chakoti, AJK. November 2005. © Cabeiri deBergh Robinson

of the luxury apartment towers in the Margala complex had collapsed; the first military responders had arrived armed but not prepared for the task at hand.)

Days later, military relief missions deployed by Türkiye, China, Cuba, and the United States and formal humanitarian organizations, such as the UNHCR, International Committee of the Red Cross (ICRC), Mercy Corps, and Save the Children, arrived in AJK. By the time that delegates of the formal international humanitarian organizations established an operational presence on the ground in AJK, they found themselves working side by side with international volunteers who had arrived with extraction and mountain-climbing equipment, with soldiers from many national armies—including two Cuban army doctors who had, lacking their own transport, hitched a ride to Muzaffarabad in an American Black Hawk helicopter—and with militants from several groups on international designated terrorist organization lists.

In the early days and weeks after the earthquake, the militants and jihadis were widely regarded by Azad Kashmiri citizens to be the most responsive and effective relief and aid workers. Jihadi organizations had stores of such equipment already stashed in various locations around Pakistan, and their organizational structure was inherently adaptable. The demobilized members of jihadi groups were able to quickly organize themselves into informal brigades and then easily morph and re-form as new tasks demanded. They settled, if temporarily, into organized service committees (*khidmat-e-khalq*) with assigned tasks. Because these *khidmat-e-khalq* were organized around tasks or areas of expertise, they were eclectic in regard to their composition by nominal membership in jihadi organizations. These committees turned to well-established charitable foundations associated with either religious groups or with political parties to fund and support the committees' work longer term. They received support from multiple charities, which later became competitors with international aid agencies for philanthropic donations from Muslim communities around the world at a time when those agencies were facing lower-than-needed contributions and were worried about the problem of donor fatigue.[1] They also worked closely with Pakistani civic groups and domestic NGOs as receivers and distributors of donated goods that came from all over Pakistan.

Once the roads were open, social activists, political parties, and student volunteers organized charity drives that brought in donations from across Pakistan and mobilized diaspora communities to support small-scale relief initiatives. Professional humanitarian workers with strict hierarchical ideas of relief dispersal found it difficult to work with these various voluntary groups because Pakistani relief activists preferred to personally deliver goods and funds. Members of the *khidmat-e-khalq* were also willing to work alongside student volunteers who set up schooling within the camps for children—so that even within entirely jihadi-run relief camps, children were receiving tuition for the state educational curriculum.

Even several months into the six-month relief phase, the hospitals and camps set up in the days after the earthquake remained a vital resource for impacted residents of AJK. These relief hospitals and sites provided free medical care, whereas established hospitals in Pakistan required payment. Until the AJK government hospitals were able to resume some operations, many residents of Muzaffarabad used these emergency field hospitals.

Many locales and those affected were ambivalent about accessing the military hospitals set up by foreign states like the United States. Suspicion existed on all sides; once members of international relief delegations realized that a substantial contingent of the relief workers whom they had been working alongside were members of jihadist groups, they began separating their projects. International organizations either saw collaboration with these groups as a threat to their humanitarian principles or felt a renewed concern for the security of ground personnel because these potential allies were listed on state terrorist watchlists. At the same time, local residents suspected that they would not be treated well at American-run hospitals. Locals worried about exposure to products, including medicines, that contained *haram* (unclean and forbidden) ingredients. They also voiced concern that Americans were not able to distinguish between militant and nonmilitant Muslims and that civilians seeking medical treatment might be subject to investigation. But when Americans were able to earn the trust of locals, they were compared positively to the service groups formed by jihadi relief workers. One young man described a turning point after which locals in Muzaffarabad changed their opinion of the American field hospital:

> Our neighbor became very ill and had to go there. On the examining table, she began to vomit. The [male] doctor cleaned up the mess. He didn't pass that work to someone else, and he was very respectful to her and gave good treatment, even though she had dirtied him with vomit—he was just like the *khalq*, they don't think they are too good to take care of anyone. Afterward, her daughter-in-law cooked some food and brought it to the hospital in thanks. An officer came out and said, "You can't eat that, it might be poisoned." But the doctor took the food, and later we heard that the staff had been seen eating it. Then we know it would be alright to get care at that hospital.

If members of international humanitarian organizations and national militaries deployed on a humanitarian mission were unsure about continuing to work alongside irregular fighters, not all militants felt so worried. In the words of one young man who had recently set aside his automatic rifle in favor of a clipboard and ration book, and who was assigned by the head of a tented relief camp to give me a tour of the camp:

> There is no reason that we should not work alongside these foreigners. This is service. Christian, Muslim, Pakistani, American. We are all humanitarians. The meaning of the Kashmir Jihad is to defend the oppressed people of Kashmir. Now there is no need to cross this LoC, this is *"humanitariyan jihad"* ... we are all humanitarians.

The understandings of what it means to care for, and to be cared for, that emerged out of these practices in a moment of crisis show that for both the jihadis who claimed the title of "humanitarian" for their work, and for the victims of the disaster, care was not an experience that could be disentangled from the reestablishment of social and political relationships.

"We're All Humanitarians"

Disasters in their full sociopolitical manifestation are never just "natural"; they develop within a context of human social response and political management, and humanitarian responses to suffering cannot escape the historical conditions within which human suffering occurs.[2] The "emergencies" that develop around them (such as displacement and dispossession, food insecurity, and unequal healthcare delivery) develop from structural inequalities that predate the crisis that creates the emergency.[3]

The 2005 Kashmir earthquake was a measured 7.6 on the Richter scale and was categorized as category 8 (severe) on the seismic magnitude scale. The epicenter of the earthquake was in northeast Pakistan at the border between Kyhber Phaktunkwa (known as Pakistan's North-West Frontier Province until 2010) and the semiautonomous State of Azad Jammu and Kashmir (AJK). Pakistan and India had gone to war over Kashmir three times (1947–48, 1964, and 1971), and they fought an undeclared war in the Kargil region of Kashmir in 1999. Their armies also engage regularly along the militarized Line of Control (LoC) that divides the Pakistan-administered regions from those administered by India. These confrontations between two nuclear-armed states made the LoC one of the world's most volatile borderlands. In addition, there has been an armed liberation struggle carried out on the Indian side of the LoC that began in 1989 and continues in the present. Azad Kashmir, as AJK is known in local parlance, has served as an organizing ground for the armed wings of political parties as well as for jihadi organizations.

"Azad Kashmir" literally means "Free" Kashmir" or "Liberated" Kashmir. Since 1989, Kashmiri militant groups have been engaged in an armed struggle to institute a reunited and fully liberated political vision of the currently disputed territory. The members of jihadi organizations who stepped forward as active relief workers in the initial phase of postdisaster response in Azad Kashmir had a long association with what they refer to as the "Kashmir Jihad." From 1989 to 1993, antistate violence in Indian Jammu and Kashmir State was organized by transnational Kashmiri militant organizations with clear hierarchical command structures that paralleled allied political parties. By the mid-1990s, a number of organizations with no direct links to political parties other than jihad had become prominent in the struggle. These were the jihadi organizations (*jihādī tanzīms*). For some, the *jihād-e-kashmīr* (Kashmir Jihad) was part of a network of global struggles of Muslim peoples against the oppression of non-Islamic states. For others, the Kashmir Jihad was a defensive war against the oppression of Kashmiri Muslims specifically. These groups united in 1996 under the umbrella organization Muttahida Jihad Mahaz (United Jihad Front), also known as the United Jihad Council (UJC). In 1999, the UJC launched the Kargil offensive, and in the summer of 2000, the largest UJC organization declared a short-lived unilateral ceasefire.[4] Thus, by the early 2000s, *jihādī tanzīms* had become prominent enough to challenge the political parties that had first directed the armed insurgency. They recruited members and conducted fundraising campaigns transnationally using the hybrid notion of Kashmir Jihad as a struggle to protect Kashmiris against human rights violence by the (Indian) state.[5]

Before 2005, Kashmiri politicians, human rights activists, and refugee advocates had lobbied the international community for decades to turn its attention to the human impact of the Kashmir dispute. However, international humanitarian organizations (with the exception of Islamic Relief, which did have an active presence) had avoided becoming directly involved because they considered the forced displacement in the region to be a political issue and within the competencies of local government. Their refusal also avoided the question of whether the LoC should be treated as an international border and, therefore, whether people displaced across were merely "internally displaced."

However, four years into the War on Terror, the international community saw offering aid to earthquake-affected people in Kashmir as an opportunity to demonstrate its concern for Muslim victims. Delegates from several different international humanitarian organizations told me that it was important that their organizations provide relief to Muslims in Pakistan because the dynamics of the War on Terror politicized the humanitarian work they did in places such as Afghanistan and Iran. They expressed a personal belief that they were doing "real humanitarian work"; they also said that their organizations felt that their presence would build trust in those organizations with Muslim communities around the world.

(Islamic) Charity, (Islamist) Service Committees, and Islamic Humanitarianism

Many scholars and policy experts see "Islamic charities" as propaganda, a cover for transferring funds to terrorist organizations, and therefore approach Islamic philanthropy as a problem.[6] Even with this distrust, they acknowledge that Islamic charities and organized charitable work have become so extensive and impactful that it is imperative to work with them.[7] To deal with this, several

INGOs (such as the ICRC)—who see the values of Islamic charity and Western humanitarianism as fundamentally in competition with each other—have legal specialists on staff whose job it is to explain how humanitarian ideals can be expressed in Islamicate terminology, all to make it possible for humanitarian organizations to work with Islamic NGOs.[8]

Euro-normative humanitarian traditions have long sought to separate humanitarianism—as a practice of care for others based in unmotivated practice of alleviating human suffering—from the realm of the political.[9] These Euro-normative traditions require continuous ideational labor—mental gymnastics one might say—to stabilize the idea that humanitarianism is an inherently apolitical project despite its manifest political effects. Yet it is also well recognized that humanitarian organizations advance the ability of combatants to wage warfare, contribute to actually governing spaces or peoples who receive nominally temporary aid for long periods of time, and also use humanitarian institutions and infrastructure to develop social or political systems as matter of policy.[10] Against these ideals, much writing on the connection between humanitarianism and modern Muslim societies has argued that the highly regulated religio-political practices of compulsory charitable giving (*zakat*) and holding of religious endowments for community benefit stand in opposition to the values represented by international humanitarian norms.[11]

This characterization, however, has hampered the understanding of practices and theories of caring in Muslim societies. On the one hand, it prioritizes aspects of the Islamic tradition that are tied to textually legitimized and authorized ideals, entirely missing the reasoning behind these practices, which emphasize justice, compassion, and equity, not equality;[12] this ethical reasoning has been the defining feature of modernist Islamic political intellectual movements. On the other, the characterization that Islam's core tenants are incongruent with care and service fails to evaluate the practices and social effects of actual welfare work. A focus on practice and the labor of care work reveals the important connections between charitable funds and service committees, which are common institutional structures and mechanisms in Muslim societies.[13] As the humanitarian mandate has expanded and transformed globally, NGOs and faith-based organizations of various religious and political affiliations increasingly gain social authority and political legitimacy through work and service provision once reserved exclusively for the state and the international community.[14]

Understanding Islamic humanitarianism requires examining how people articulate Islamic values as a source of intellectual knowledge that underwrites logics of care as well as a force of faith. Members of jihadi and Islamist militant organizations whom I met in the earthquake relief operations described their involvement in the relief work as a part of their greater struggle (*jihād*) to serve and defend—a project they called *"humanitariyan jihad."*[15] This articulation did not originate with the leaders of these organizations but with the demobilized jihadis, many of them of Jammu and Kashmir origin, who declared a temporary stop to their armed activities in order to engage in the labor of relief work. In the first weeks, they operated through fluid work groups they referred to as self-organized groups, which did the work of *khidmat* (voluntary service). Within six weeks, the composition of these service committees no longer reflected the pre-October 2005 militant affiliations of the members. Individual workers had moved at will between different service committees, and established charitable trusts began to provide funds to support this voluntary labor.

The service groups were organized around categories of relief-associated labor. For example, some groups did sanitation work across multiple camps, others assisted in running field hospitals, others provided security in tented camps. The jihadis adopted an institutional structure for their humanitarian jihad based in Islamist party organizing practices, but which exhibited on the ground the fluidity of membership and disinterest in adherence to party ideology. Islamist political parties, those that seek to reform society by transforming the practices of the state, have a strong history of commitment to social welfare provision. Indeed, the paradigmatic structure of Islamist parties involves the formation of three wings—political, social welfare, and defense (military wing or allied militant group).[16] The structural mirroring with communist revolutionary groups is not accidental: Maulana Maudoodi, the founder of South Asia's first Islamist political party the Jamaat-e-Islami, was greatly influenced by Leninist thinking. The social welfare wings of such parties have long provided services to communities that have been ignored by the state.[17]

Over a decade later, many residents of Muzaffarabad who lived through the earthquake still recall those first days afterward. They remember who first responded to the crisis—self-named jihadis brought the first help they received, excavating survivors and delivering food and water to people unable to make their way through the rubble of the urban *mohallahs* (neighborhoods with structured social and political hierarchies). These groups also stayed in those neighborhoods and villages to bury the dead. As one man I've known for many years said to me, declaring his shame and his gratitude:

> [My children's mother] was carrying my three children, my brother and uncle and I carried father and grandfather out on a *charpai* [a cord bed]. In the end, I looked at the dead and then I walked over their bodies. When we came back, in each of those spots where there had been a body there was a flag with a number, and a notation of the burial ground where each of those bodies had been properly buried. I failed my neighbors, but in the end, the jihadis kept a list of the person's age and what they were wearing, and every family could find their loved ones in the ground where they had been laid to rest, and the funeral prayers said in their name.

What these jihadis did was deathwork, a form of care that extends alleviation of suffering to the dead, a group often excluded form Euro-Christian humanitarianism that is focused on the preservation of life and rarely on the healing that can come from caring for the dead.

Members of the jihadi organizations also referenced a political thinking that demonstrated a broad concept of security—although they were founded as vehicles for militant struggle, they also had a concept of logistical security that paralleled a human security framework. As the resident surgeon of the Jamaat-ul-Dawa relief camp and field hospital complex said to me:

> We know if there is some invasion or disaster, the common people suffer most, so we have to plan and be prepared for their safety. Our closest storehouse was in Balakot, but that was destroyed, so we had the supplies brought from Peshawar and Lahore.

He himself had been working in a free medical clinic in Lahore run by the Jamaat-ul-Dawa until they asked him to oversee the field hospital in Muzaffarabad. Members of militant groups like the Lashkar-e-Tayiba were able not only to tap into material resources and vast funding networks but also to connect with highly specialized expertise and established welfare activities that were already undertaken by the charitable trusts in other parts of Pakistan.

These groups also demonstrated their willingness to work with other aid groups that had no connection to Islamist parties or Islamic charitable trusts. Domestic Pakistani and transnational Kashmiri NGOs mobilized professional expertise—engineers, doctors, mountain climbers—to do volunteer work in Azad Kashmir. Then as international organizations began to get involved, the regional Pakistani and Kashmiri engineers, doctors, and other volunteers found that the demobilized members of the *khalq* were more willing to integrate them into their practices than the international organizations. Many of these expert volunteers became a vital resource to the AJK government in the reconstruction phase, but in the initial relief phase, the flexible structure of the Islamic groups allowed them to incorporate volunteers regardless of ideological affiliation.

Humanitariyan Jihad as Postdisaster Reconstruction Welfare Activism

Although members of jihadi organizations, Islamist nongovernmental organizations (NGOs), government militaries, and international humanitarian organizations worked together throughout the relief phase, there was increasing pressure to isolate the jihadis from the international effort. This was both because international humanitarian organizations were uncomfortable with the perceived politicization of their work and because Pakistani civil society groups—and the English press—were increasingly critical of international resources going to places other than secular civil society groups. After the initial emergency phase of rescue and relief and during the designated postdisaster reconstruction and rehabilitation phase—which began in 2006 and nominally ended in March 2014—international organizations began to pressure the Pakistani government to separate the jihadi volunteers from the international humanitarian project.

Reconstruction projects funded an array of economic, social development, and scientific initiatives and supported an emergent private sector. The UN emerged as the coordinator of a five-year Rehabilitation and Reconstruction Project (originally scheduled to conclude in 2011, it was extended to conclude in 2014) called "Build Back Better" that represented a form of development humanitarianism. It conceived of humanitarian work as a long-term process to rebuild sustainable civil infrastructure and build local capacity and expertise, but it distrusted government officials and institutions as corrupt and preferred to foster private initiatives and support private contractors. Historical restrictions on property ownership and employment created opportunities for AJK residents and documented state refugees to provide contract labor for international agencies and establish new local businesses, because Pakistani-owned firms did not have a foothold in the state. The presence of the UN and international nongovernmental organization (INGO) projects and foreigners, in a region that had been closely surveilled and though which financial regulation had been under tight Pakistani government control, allowed the establishment of new flows of capital that were not controlled by the government as a form of patronage. The rise of international access to AJK after the earthquake, new opportunities for private sector employment, and employment with international organizations laid the groundwork for a new and vocal public critique of Pakistani intervention in AJK political life.[18]

Postdisaster reconstruction funds were jointly administered by the United Nations and the Government of Pakistan through a new agency, the Earthquake Reconstruction and Rehabilitation Agency (ERRA), and a parallel government finance account. The ERRA distributed funds to the AJK State Earthquake Reconstruction and Rehabilitation Agencies (SERRA) of AJK and Khyber Phakhtunkhwa. The AJK SERRA also coordinated development programs run by IGOs and INGOs. The ERRA became a site through which the international community moved its substantial aid and reconstruction funds and established principles of transparency in funding and expenditure. In practice, this transparency was accessible for institutional funders, but local communities and the AJK government officials were kept from viewing the total picture regarding how money was spent. They questioned, for example, why funds were spent importing raw materials from Türkiye for the rebuilt campus of the University of Azad Kashmir, or why a team of Turkish engineers, all collecting overseas deployment and hazard pay, were running the project when Kashmiri engineers were unemployed. This financial aid system inculcated a notion that the local government was inherently corrupt and failed to recognize local expertise in professional fields (such as engineering, law, medicine, and education). At the same time, it protected a space for the emergence of Kashmiri civil society groups, religious and secular. For the first time in Azad Kashmir's postcolonial history, this civil society could withstand the political suspicion of the state security agencies and command resources independent of the Pakistani state and national elites.

The UN-led recovery and reconstruction project also sought to insulate itself from all forms of interaction with the Islamic charities, jihadi volunteers, or Islamic service societies that had been first on the ground during the rescue and relief efforts in those first six months after the earthquake. This separation took institutional form in the establishment of a new department within the AJK government in 2006: the Azad Kashmir Camp Management Organization. The AJK Camp Management Organization was established as the site through which humanitarian workers on the ground could appear to be accountable to local populations and civil society initiatives while also isolating themselves from the religious organizations that had spearheaded first responses during the relief phase.

Within the camps, though, former members of the *khalqs* continued to work with department employees and through them with the international organizations. The AJK government still used former *khalq* members to help daily operations and supply chain networks. These members had proven themselves effective camp managers when running their own camps, and the Camp Management Organization now relied on their experience and the trust that they had built with local communities. Over the years, several of these former *khalq* members were hired by international organizations to staff local offices, and several have moved on to international deployments. These workers did not renounce jihad, but over time their *humanitariyan jihad* began to refer to a struggle to establish norms of welfare provision within the AJK state, growing to become a term used to describe an array of ideas that range from civil volunteerism to political struggle for expanded rights within the domestic state structure.

Once the Camp Management Organization took over the refugee camps, former *khalq* members who did not work with the AJK government began to move to other projects funded by other charities—projects such as establishing free, well-staffed schools and health clinics in outlying areas and the development of very small-scale hydroelectric power projects to bring power to isolated mountain communities. In the short term, the projects and practices of the members' service committees were brought into closer alignment with the priorities of the charities. A year after the earthquake, activists no longer identified themselves by the militant organization to which they previously belonged. Members of the service societies and Islamic charities took up central roles in supporting the initiatives of local civic groups; they maintained a self-identification simply as jihadis without affiliation to a particular militant organization.

Thus, these demobilized militants, without renouncing violence or the legitimacy of the use of violence to achieve political ends, had effectively severed their connection with jihadi organizations. They still claimed engagement with a jihad for Kashmiris—now *"humanitariyan jihad"*—which was now reconceived as potentially permanent social welfare work and advocacy.

This rethinking of how best to serve Kashmir, what it means to struggle for justice, was part of a broader shift within AJK political thinking. Members of jihadi organizations contributed to this shift through their relief and social welfare work within the earthquake relief service committees. As one young man, who had started working for an international humanitarian organization as a translator after the earthquake and who is now a country director for another in Islamabad, said:

> I am Kashmiri and will always struggle for freedom [*azaadi*]. But our leaders hurt our people by making all development contingent on first getting full independence. What about women's healthcare? The end of child labor? Provision of education in the rural areas? Why should Kashmiri people be kept backward as well as be occupied?

Or, as an older man, a resident of a conservative area in one of the harder hit districts in the lower mountains told me:

> Pakistan always wanted Kashmir, but it never cared about Kashmiris. Then, this earthquake happened, and Pakistanis sent us their daughters [as volunteer doctors and nurses and aid workers]. We didn't send out our own daughters, but Pakistanis sent us their daughters. Now I think that Pakistanis have real love for Kashmiris. Now I allow my daughter to work outside of the house in service. It worries me, to have her work out of the house, but this is my sacrifice ... that I had to allow the daughter of my house to leave the house to serve her Kashmiri sisters and brothers.

Cabeiri deBergh Robinson is associate professor of international studies and South Asian studies at the University of Washington. She is a sociocultural anthropologist and previously worked with the International Committee of the Red Cross. She is the author of the award-winning book *Body of Victim, Body of Warrior: Refugee Families and the Making of Kashmiri Jihadists* (2013).

Notes

1. Pappas and Hicks, "Coordinating Disaster Relief"; Rehman and Kalra, "Transnationalism from Below."
2. Hannigan, *Disasters without Borders*; Bornstein and Redfield, *Forces of Compassion*.
3. Calhoun, "World of Emergencies."

4. Robinson, *Body of Victim, Body of Warrior*, 193–94, 270n27
5. This connection between rights and jihad was a cultural formation forged by the Kashmiri refugee community in AJK and Pakistan during the 1990s. See Robinson, *Body of Victim*, 171–200.
6. Burr and Collins, *Alms for Jihad*. See Benthall, "Overreaction against Islamic Charities," for a critique of this perspective.
7. van Bruinessen, "Development and Islamic Charities."
8. Hyder, "Humanitarianism and the Muslim World."
9. Fassin, *Humanitarian Reason*.
10. Bornstein and Redfield, *Forces of Compassion*; Feldman and Ticktin, *In the Name of Humanity*.
11. Bellion-Jourdan, "Islamic Relief Organizations"; Cockayne, "Islam and International Humanitarian Law"; Krafess, "Influence of the Muslim Religion"; Ghandour, "Humanitarianism, Islam and the West."
12. Osanloo, "Measure of Mercy."
13. Benthall and Bellion-Jourdan, *Charitable Crescent*; Minn, "Toward an Anthropology of Humanitarianism."
14. Duffield, "Complex Emergencies"; Chandler, "Road to Military Humanitarianism"; Hall and Biersteker, *Emergence of Private Authority*; Pandya, "Private Authority and Disaster Relief."
15. Bamforth and Qureshi, "Political Complexities"; Qureshi, "Earthquake Jihad"; Robinson, *Body of Victim*, 237–42.
16. Wittes, "Islamist Parties."
17. Roy, *Hamas and Civil Society in Gaza*; Nasr, "Pakistan after Islamization."
18. Robinson, "Dangerous Allure."

References

Bamforth, Thomas, and Jawad Hussain Qureshi. "Political Complexities of Humanitarian Intervention in the Pakistan Earthquake." *Journal of Humanitarian Assistance* (6 August 2007). Retrieved 12 December 2023 from https://reliefweb.int/report/world/political-complexities-humanitarian-intervention-pakistan-earthquake.
Bellion-Jourdan, Jérôme. "Islamic Relief Organizations: Between 'Islamism' and 'Humanitarianism.'" *ISIM Newsletter* 5 (July 2000): 15.
Benthall, Jonathan. "The Overreaction against Islamic Charities." *ISIM Review* 20 (Autumn 2007): 6–7.
Benthall, Jonathan, and Jerome Bellion-Jourdan. *The Charitable Crescent: The Politics of Aid in the Muslim World*. London I. B. Tauris, 2003.
Bornstein, Erica, and Peter Redfield, eds. *Forces of Compassion: Humanitarianism between Ethics and Politics*. Santa Fe: School for Advanced Research Press, 2011.
Burr, Millard, and Robert O. Collins. *Alms for Jihad: Charity and Terrorism in the Islamic World*. Cambridge; New York: Cambridge University Press, 2006.
Chandler, David. "The Road to Military Humanitarianism: How the Human Rights NGOs Shaped a New Humanitarian Agenda." *Human Rights Quarterly* 23, no. 3 (2001): 678–700.
Cockayne, James. "Islam and International Humanitarian Law: From a Clash to a Conversation between Civilizations." *International Review of the Red Cross* 84, no. 847 (2002): 597–626.

Duffield, Mark. "Complex Emergencies and the Crisis of Developmentalism." *IDS Bulletin* 25, no. 4 (1994): 2.
Fassin, Didier. *Humanitarian Reason: A Moral History of the Present Times*. Berkeley: University of California Press, 2012.
Feldman, Ilana, and Miriam Iris Ticktin, eds. *In the Name of Humanity: The Government of Threat and Care*. Durham, NC: Duke University Press, 2010.
Hall, Rodney Bruce, and Thomas J. Biersteker, eds. *The Emergence of Private Authority in the International System*. Cambridge: Cambridge University Press, 2002.
Hannigan, John A. *Disasters without Borders: The International Politics of Natural Disasters*. Cambridge: Polity Press, 2012.
Hyder, Masood. "Humanitarianism and the Muslim World." *Journal of Humanitarian Assistance* (22 August 2007). Retrieved 12 December 2022 from https://reliefweb.int/report/world/humanitarianism-and-muslim-world.
Krafess, Jamal. "The Influence of the Muslim Religion in Humanitarian Aid." *International Review of the Red Cross* 87, no. 858 (2005): 327–42.
Minn, Pierre. "Toward an Anthropology of Humanitarianism." *Journal of Humanitarian Assistance* (6 August 2007). Retrieved 12 December 2022 from https://reliefweb.int/report/world/toward-anthropology-humanitarianism.
Nasr, Sayyed Vali Reza. "Pakistan after Islamization: Mainstream and Militant Islamism in a Changing State." In *Asian Islam in the 21st Century*, edited by John L. Esposito, John Obert Voll, and Bakar Osman, 30–48. New York: Oxford University Press, 2008.
Osanloo, Arzoo. "The Measure of Mercy: Islamic Justice, Sovereign Power, and Human Rights in Iran." *Cultural Anthropology* 21, no. 4 (2006): 570–602.
Pandya, Chhandasi. "Private Authority and Disaster Relief: The Cases of Post-tsunami Aceh and Nias." *Critical Asian Studies* 38, no. 2 (2006): 298–308.
Pappas, Gregory, and Esther K. Hicks. "Coordinating Disaster Relief after the South Asia Earthquake." *Society* (July/August 2006): 42–50.
Qureshi, Jawad Hussain. "Earthquake Jihad: The Role of Jihadis and Islamist Groups after the 2005 Earthquake." *Humanitarian Practice Network* 34, no. 3 (2006). Retrieved 14 December 2022 from https://odihpn.org/publication/earthquake-jihad-the-role-of-jihadis-and-islamist-groups-after-the-2005-earthquake/.
Rehman, Shams, and Virinder S. Kalra. "Transnationalism from Below: Initial Responses by British Kashmiris to the South Asia Earthquake of 2005." *Contemporary South Asia* 15, no. 3 (2006): 309–23.
Robinson, Cabeiri deBergh. *Body of Victim, Body of Warrior: Refugee Families and the Making of Kashmiri Jihadists*. Berkeley: University of California Press, 2013.
———. "The Dangerous Allure of Tourism Promotion as a Post-conflict Policy in Disputed Azad Jammu and Kashmir." In *Cultural Anthropology Online, Fieldsights* 24 March 2014. https://culanth.org/fieldsights/the-dangerous-allure-of-tourism-promotion-as-a-postconflict-policy-in-disputed-azad-jammu-and-kashmir.
Roy, Sara. *Hamas and Civil Society in Gaza: Engaging the Islamist Social Sector*. Princeton, NJ: Princeton University Press, 2011.
van Bruinessen, Martin. "Development and Islamic Charities." *ISIM Review* 20 (Autumn 2007): 5.
Wittes, Tamara Cofman. "Islamist Parties: Three Kinds of Movements." *Journal of Democracy* 19, no. 3 (2008): 7–12.

PART III

REPAIR IN A WORLD OF CARE

CHAPTER 12

Red Coat, Denim Shirt
Conceptualizing Displacement across Generations

Rawan Arar

I knew my family had been displaced before I learned the word *refugee*. I remember sitting with my teta, my grandmother, in a glass-enclosed patio in Amman that opened onto their modest but vibrant garden where she grew figs, apricots, and cherries. That small patio doubled as Teta's bedroom after climbing the stairs became too burdensome on her knees. The patio was big enough to fit a wardrobe cabinet, a slender couch that transformed nightly into a bed, and a prayer rug that Teta unfurled five times each day. Two of my aunts slept upstairs in adjoining rooms. We moved in with them in 1993, when my mom was conducting her doctoral research in Al Baqa'a, a Palestinian refugee camp established in 1968.[1] My aunts graciously offered us their second bedroom. I was eight, my brother Yousef was six, and the youngest, Amr, was an infant. The qualities that made our family peculiar in Dallas morphed into the mundane characteristics that we had in common with the neighbors in Amman—we spoke the same language at home, practiced the same religion, and ate the same breakfast foods. That year was one of the most formative, and joyous, times in my life. I connected with members of my family for the first time, my Arabic skills grew stronger, and I enjoyed showing off the Quranic suras I memorized as part of my third-grade education. What I remember with unexpected clarity are the hours that Teta and I spent together after school before the working adults headed home for the day. She told me stories about my dad, who had stayed behind in Texas, and about their lives before in Bal'a, our small Palestinian village on the outskirts of Tulkarem.

The first lessons in displacement and dispossession that I can remember took place on that patio with my grandmother. Decades later, I would follow in my mother's footsteps by pursuing an academic career to examine refugee issues in Jordan and around the world. This chapter is about being a refugee scholar and the daughter of refugees—and how these distinct forms of knowing have collided in unexpected ways to yield insights that are not centered in academic scholarship. Authors divulge their positionality to reveal how personal characteristics—such as their race, class, gender, nationality, and more—influence access to the field, data collection, and analysis. Some authors may highlight their position as "insiders," sharing important qualities with the communities they seek to study, while others may identify as "outsiders," a position that can also yield research advantages associated with the author's perceived naïveté.[2] In Jordan, I am both an insider and an outsider. I am a Palestinian woman, whose family settled in Jordan after 1967. I study contemporary displacements in the same country where my family secured refuge. Some members of my family are currently registered with UNRWA, the UN agency charged with the humanitarian response to Palestinian displacement. Unlike most people in Jor-

Figure 12.1. • The author as a child, sitting on a swing with her father and grandmother (teta), in the patio space that would years later be transformed into Teta's bedroom. The photo is from author's family collection, taken in Amman, Jordan, around 1987. © Rawan Arar

dan, I have dual citizenship, Jordanian and US-American. I speak Arabic and English and can enter "international" spaces dominated by Western migrants/expatriates, some of whom are humanitarian aid workers that I met through my fieldwork. In some sense, I am (and am not) native, foreign, a refugee, and a care provider—I explore these labels, and their limitations, throughout this chapter. Reflexivity allows me to include my family's refugeehood—*"the experience of becoming and being a refugee"*—in the larger study of refugee reception in Jordan and throughout the region.[3]

Labels and Their Limits

The question "Who is a refugee?" has fueled decades of debate and scholarly inquiry because the word *refugee* has legal and social implications that are often in tension. Individuals who are legally recognized as refugees, most notably those who meet the definition described in the 1951 Refugee Convention, can secure entry across borders that are restricted to other migrants. In this way, states have turned *refugee* into a privileged legal category that applies to a delimited group of people. Some scholars and advocates want to expand the refugee definition so that more people can be afforded the opportunity to secure sanctuary in another country. Others warn that revising the legal definition may lead to new restrictions for individuals who would have otherwise qualified for refugee protections.

The notion that being a refugee is a privileged status is counterintuitive. How can experiencing the trauma of forcible displacement because of violence or persecution, leaving behind family, friends, and one's way of life, and the routine indignities of being a newcomer in a foreign land be a privilege? These debates often do not give the same level of consideration to how a person identifies—how individuals, groups, and communities relate to the refugee label. Some people eschew the label of refugee, especially when the designation has been racialized and associated with need or poverty. The receiving context can shape the stigma around the refugee label, which can in turn affect refugees' self-identities.[4] As sociologist Katherine Jensen finds, "Rather than a universal given, the meaning of refugee status depends on the rights, supports, and precarity it entails."[5] Some may proudly relate to the refugee label as a reflection of their community's shared struggle with less regard to the receiving context. Such is the case for many Palestinians around the world whose relationship to the refugee label is a reflection of the "ongoing Nakba," a term that evokes the 1948 displacement of approximately 750,000 Palestinians and the unceasing consequences of exile and occupation, as well as the obstructed right of return. Examining Palestinian displacement across generations requires that one gives primacy to personal identifications with the refugee label, even when refugeehood is not reflected in legal categorization. Blurring the boundaries of these categories, however, starkly contrasts with operational definitions that humanitarian organizations, lawyers, and policymakers require to achieve their goals. While engaging with these important limitations, this chapter invites the reader to consider personal and familial refugee experiences and the ways that they are used to create meaning and shape connections across refugee groups.

To consider how diverse experiences of refugeehood converge, both among members of the same refugee group and across groups, one must weave together various bodies of knowledge and consider the constraints under which they are forged. An important part of this tapestry is humanitarian-produced knowledge. Snapshots of global displacement require that humanitarian and state agencies label and count refugees.[6] Each year, the UNHCR, the UN's primary refugee agency, releases a report that includes the total number of UN-recognized refugees—27.1 million in 2021.[7] These counts serve political and practical purposes.[8] Refugee advocates and immigration restrictionists alike depend on headcounts to monitor the movement of people, to provide resources and support through aid, and to wield political power in negotiation tactics among states.[9] For the sake of practice, these types of knowledge production serve their purpose by delimiting who counts as a refugee. By creating bounded groups to achieve practice-oriented goals, this approach in turn deprioritizes how individuals understand their lived experiences. In 2021, there were 5.8 million Palestinian refugees registered with UNRWA, which operates in Jordan, Lebanon, Syria, Gaza, and the West Bank. A 2020 demographic study estimated that there are 13 million Palestinians worldwide.[10] Millions of Palestinians within the diaspora are not registered with the UN, but many identify with the refugee label.

Snapshots of displacement camouflage the passage of time. Noting the number of people displaced today does not recognize how long they have been in exile, how many times they have fled or migrated, and how they and others within their networks have been shaped by refugeehood. The terminology that is often used to describe multiple years of displacement is "protracted refugee situation," an operational definition that applies to a population of at least twenty-five thousand or more people from the same nationality who have been in exile for five or more years.[11] There is no standard terminology used to address the experiences of a population that remains in exile for generations. Nor is there an easily recognizable way to reference the experiences of prolonged exodus, which for Palestinians has occurred without the option for return. Some UN-recognized Palestinian refugees can demonstrate that their displacement has spanned more than seventy years, but others who are not recognized by the refugee label must bring their memories and personal stories of exile to bear witness against antagonistic actors who are invested in undermining Palestinian refugee narratives.

Binary language permeates the study of refugee displacement—a person is often characterized as either a refugee or not. While the divide among refugees and migrants has received the greatest amount of attention, other binaries are commonplace, including refugee/host, refugee/humanitarian, or refugee/citizen.[12] Yet, as Ilana Feldman and Gözde Burcu Ege argue in this collection, the line between hosts and refugees, or humanitarian workers and refugees, does not always mark difference.[13] Refugees can host other refugees, a phenomenon that Fiddian-Qasmiyeh has captured with the term *refugee-hosts*.[14] Dichotomies further deemphasize Palestinian refugeehood when individuals have acquired other statuses. Citizenship, or legal incorporation more broadly, is conceptualized as the end of refugeehood. The UNHCR's *Global Trends* report, for example, uses naturalization as the ultimate marker of incorporation, ushering an individual from a position of precarity to inclusion in the polity. Yet, even while citizenship can provide unparalleled protections in some countries, safety in the present does not negate the past. After more than half a century of exile, many Palestinians around the world have acquired legal status, but they continue to experience refugeehood.

Not all citizenships around the world are equal, and not all citizens within a country are treated equally. Palestinians with citizenship in one country may have greater rights than those in other countries. Most notably, Palestinians with Israeli citizenship experience systematic discrimination despite their legal status. Palestinian citizens in Israel face different forms of oppression related to the identification that they carry, which can determine where they are permitted to live, if they can travel, and who they marry. When scholars reimagine legal status at a familial level or consider the relationship of people to their broader ethnic networks, it becomes apparent that citizenship protections are limited when they are not extended to loved ones.[15] Moving from the individual to the community level of analysis—especially when co-ethnics are subjected to persecution—can provide important insights into how people identify with the refugee label. Operational labels may inaccurately represent people's lived experiences, and when adopted by scholars, these boundaries place limitations on methodological scope conditions and the theoretical breadth of our findings.

Baba's Red Coat

Arabic is my mother tongue; it was my first language. Yet, like Darwin's finches that grew into their own specimens through seclusion, I learned Arabic in a foreign space, following the instruction of my parents and their Arab American friends in San Antonio, Texas. My language was molded by unique connotations of kitchen Arabic. My mother's terms of endearment for my dad, for example, *falahi* and *barreed*, translate literally to mean "peasant farmer" and "person who gets cold easily." Yet, from my standpoint, these words were often paired with loving gestures. When she teased that Baba was *barreed*, she usually did something to protect him from the cold, such as excusing him from a night out or handing him a jacket. And so, I grew up associating the term for "gets cold easily" with some affection.

My language skills were stress tested when I moved to Jordan on my own for the first time. According to my university, I was an MA student conducting research abroad. But "abroad" could not have been closer to home. It seemed like everyone I was related to stopped by with food. My uncle would routinely drop off enormous quantities of produce from their bountiful farm on the outskirts of the city: a carton of figs or a bushel of pomegranates. That year was 2009. In addition to the approximately two million Palestinians who were registered with UNRWA, Jordan also hosted Iraqi refugees who fled after the 2003 US-led invasion. At the time, the estimated number of Iraqi refugees in Jordan was between 450,000 and 800,000, but these numbers were contested.[16] The UNHCR claimed that only 65,000 Iraqi refugees were receiving assistance by the end of 2008.[17] Despite contradictions in the actual number of newly arrived refugees, their presence was felt by Jordan's residents who observed changes in their society.

There was an effort to approach Iraqi displacement through the lens of the Palestinian response. But unlike Palestinians who settled in camps, Iraqi refugees lived in urban areas. This difference meant that the humanitarian response needed to be reimagined.[18] The first wave of displaced Iraqis included people who were able to bring their savings with them into exile. Observations fueled rumors, and the impression that Iraqi refugees were driving up housing and rent prices spread with unencumbered abandon. I witnessed the opposite. I was conducting interviews and volunteering with a small aid organization in an impoverished part of Amman. We went door-to-door to learn about, and document, Iraqis' needs, which often demanded far more than the small grants the organization could offer to cover groceries and rent in extreme situations. Urban living led to isolation for many Iraqis, which further contributed to the invisibility of poorer refugees. Individuals also took steps to isolate themselves—to practice "strategic anonymity" by withholding their personal information and avoiding relationships with others.[19] Iraqis who fled because of sectarian persecution were often targeted by name. The sectarian catalyst for their displacement also enhanced their fear of *refoulement*, being forcibly sent back to Iraq when it was unsafe for them to return.

As the winter months approached, I participated in a clothing drive to collect coats for Iraqi refugees. Jordanian winters are cold. The stone buildings offer little insulation, and the Texan in me was surprised to learn firsthand that homes can be colder inside than the weather outside. Heating costs were also exorbitant, so families often went without. I called my father to talk through the mundane logistics of the clothing drive. Where would we store the coats? How would we clean them? Could Baba think of anyone who may want to donate? The perception that "all Iraqis were rich" was a real obstacle to the work we were trying to do. "Why don't you focus on helping the Palestinians, instead?" I heard often enough that it became a predictable question.

Our conversation undulated between existential reflections on deservingness and the practical challenges of providing care. Then, Baba shared a story with me that I had never heard before, possibly because the topic had never been broached. He casually mentioned that, as a child, the only coat he ever owned was given to him by UNRWA. Baba described a red women's trench coat with a fur trim collar. Baba—the *barreed*, as my mom nicknamed him—wore this coat day and night, and even slept in it. He doesn't remember exactly how many years he wore the coat, maybe three or four years, long enough for him to grow into it, and then later out of it.

The conversation shifted. Instead of considering the logistics of aid, or in action-oriented terms, solving the problem of being cold, I was confronted with humanistic aspects of being a receiver. How did it feel to be known as the boy in the red coat? Did Baba feel uncomfortable wearing a woman's coat as a young man in his small village? These questions had nothing to do with the physicality of warmth but were instead social questions about his experiences. I also began to wonder about the woman who kept my father warm for years. Could she have imagined her red coat in the hands of a young boy in a small village in the West Bank? I was thankful that my father had this coat, but I would never want him to assume the burden of a debt. And why should he? Warmth is every person's right, I thought to myself.

Baba recalled that receiving secondhand clothing from UNRWA caused tension in their family. My grandfather was resistant to receiving handouts but acquiesced after Teta insisted. Baba, being one of ten kids, recalls how the clothing bundles were allocated based on the size of the family. The donations were not available in Bal'a, so someone needed to go to the neighboring village of Anabta once per month to bring home the lump of clothes. Baba remembers how his elder brother found it demeaning to show the rations card and accept a random pile of secondhand clothes for the family. He protested being the one to make the trip, but also yielded upon Teta's insistence. I only knew my uncle as a quiet and gentle person, so I was struck, and admittedly amused, by the image of him as a twentysomething begrudgingly running errands for the family.

Baba has shared countless anecdotes about Bal'a with me, from descriptions of their routine lives, including the crops they grew, to details about how Teta prepared her children to flee after receiving word that everyone in their village would be evicted. What strikes me about the red coat story is not only the surprising connection that a material object can manifest but also how

Baba only felt compelled to share this story when the circumstances of my life stirred a memory in him. While this experience is unique to my family's refugee story, familial connections to refugeehood among people in Jordan are common. Many of the young Jordanians I met on the front lines of the humanitarian response to Syrian displacement have similar stories about their parents and grandparents that shape how they understand contemporary displacement. Shared experiences of refugeehood can impact how newcomers relate to members of the receiving community. These connections influence how people build trust and make meaning in their lives. The global humanitarian infrastructure and corresponding policy data overlooks such blurred boundaries between refugees and aid providers—or more aptly put, among groups of people with refugee experiences who have different needs, opportunities, and legal statuses. This anecdote invites us to contemplate assumptions we may carry about being a "giver" and a "receiver." Such labels may only pivot a narrow few degrees away from the more common labels of "aid worker" and "refugee," but there are important insights that such a reframing invites us to reconsider. These include a move away from essentialized notions of people identified primarily by their need.

Mama's Denim Shirt

Ramadan is a holy month when Muslims fast from food and drink during the day. Sunset is like an alarm clock, and the *adan* (call to prayer) brings everyone to the dinner table. I was invited to have dinner at my uncle's house, which was across the street from where we lived with Teta as children. Undoubtedly, it is rude to keep hungry and thirsty people waiting to break their fast after they have abstained from food and drink since sunrise. I headed straight to dinner without stopping by my apartment to wash up after a long day spent in Za'atari camp conducting interviews as part of my doctoral fieldwork. Za'atari was the first major UN-run camp established for Syrian refugees. At peak density in 2013, Za'atari hosted nearly 144,000 refugees, but by that time in 2016, approximately 80,000 Syrians lived in the camp—a population size that would remain steady in the years to come.[20] By 2022, more than 670,000 Syrians would be registered with the UNHCR in Jordan, while governmental estimates have consistently been much higher.

I arrived at dinner unkempt but on time. It was a hot day. Sweat made the sand stick to my skin, and the wind had tangled my hair. I always wore something conservative with long sleeves and a loose fit when visiting camps, which was a lesson I learned from my teenage years spent being reprimanded by my mom for my clothing choices during our summer trips to Amman. On this day, I wore an oversize, faded, lightweight, denim button-down with blue, green, and purple stitching across the back and over the front pocket (see figure 12.2). I joined in as my aunts were setting the table. The first thing my aunt exclaimed when she saw me was, "You are wearing your mom's shirt!" I was astounded that she remembered. Mama had passed away three years earlier after a short and brutal battle with cancer—"the other war," as one Syrian woman generously put it, in acknowledgment of the enormous grief that comes with losing a parent. I inherited her wardrobe and found renewed style in garments I would have overlooked in the past. Wearing Mama's clothes made me feel closer to her, and I did so often.

"I recognize the embroidery on the shirt," my aunt said. Palestinian embroidery, *tatreez*, is unique and easily identifiable. Traditional dresses are embroidered with geometric floral patterns. *Tatreez* is often done with red thread on black fabric, but there are many variations that include a narrow array of colors. Pastel *tatreez* on a denim button-down was distinctive and unconventional, but the Palestinianness of the pattern was unmistakable. "Palestinian refugees she worked with in Al Baqa'a camp stitched it for her as a thank you," my

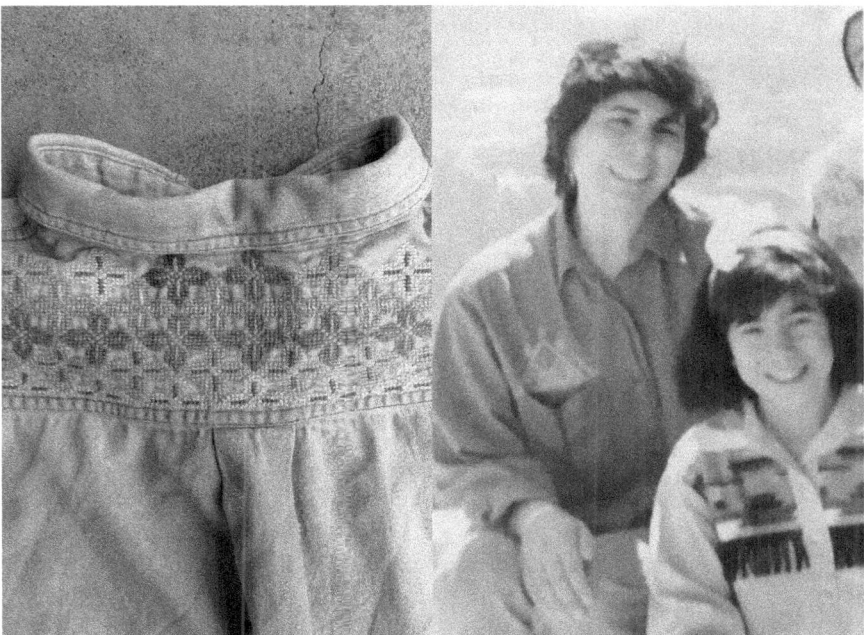

Figure 12.2. • Mama's denim shirt. The left panel is a closeup of the back of the shirt, which was embroidered for Mama by Palestinians she worked with in Al Baqa'a camp between 1993 and 1994. The right panel shows the author (age nine) posing with her mother, who is wearing the denim button-down shirt. Both photos are from the author's family collection. © Rawan Arar

aunt remembered, recalling the year Mama conducted her doctoral fieldwork. Mama researched the prevalence of diarrheal illnesses among Palestinian refugee children. After she died, I found stacks of photographs among her papers, still packaged in the Fujifilm envelopes with their negatives. Among the photos of bare living spaces, alleyways that demonstrated close quarters, containers of still water, and white brick homes broken to rubble, there were numerous photos of kids posing, playing, and laughing. Mama became a medical anthropologist, and she often told me how, in another life, she would have loved to work with UNICEF, the United Nations International Children's Emergency Fund.

This was the first time I learned about who stitched the button-down or that the shirt was a gift to my mother. There I was, twenty-three years later, my mother's grown daughter, wearing her same shirt, working as an ethnographer like she did, conducting interviews in a refugee camp in the same country. Many of the Palestinians Mama worked with were likely still living in Al Baqa'a, just as my family stayed in the same neighborhood. The similarities were striking. They broached questions about overlapping refugee populations and the limits of solution-oriented approaches to refugee displacement—especially in the case of generations-long exile. Humanitarian or policy-centric knowledge production separates hosts from refugees in order to delimit the beneficiaries of their projects. Yet this approach neglects the ways that refugee newcomers join diverse populations with their own relationships to forced displacement in Jordan.

Examining similarities across refugee populations can also lead scholars to consider important differences that are neglected in solution-oriented narratives about refugee displacement and reception. Jordan has hosted many groups, differentiated not only by their nationality or ethnicity but also by their year of displacement, the impetus for their fleeing, their unique needs and legal statuses, their political struggles and the challenges their communities face, and their differentiated treatment and access to resources and rights. Refugees' experiences in Jordan are affected by refugee policies in the region and around the world, including the fluctuation of international support, financial commitments to refugee aid, and geopolitical interests tied to their home countries. Critically examining these axes of difference while also holding space to note important similarities complicates solution-oriented knowledge production, which tends to examine refugee groups in isolation from one another.

This serendipitous connection draws attention to how coincidences of layered displacements are interwoven throughout the Jordanian landscape. I returned to my fieldwork in the days after our Ramadan dinner. At this time, I was partnering with an international NGO and shadowing Jordanian aid workers who spent their days in Za'atari and Azraq camps. I told the denim shirt story on one of our long drives from headquarters in Amman to the camps. Unbeknownst to me, one of the Jordanian-Palestinian aid workers passed the story along to a Syrian woman in Za'atari, who was also struck by the coincidence. She offered to continue the tradition by adding her own stitching to Mama's shirt.

Reflections on Refugeehood

Individuals who are recognized as refugees are only a subset of people who understand their personal and communal struggle as characterized by displacement and dispossession. Refugee displacement is often conceptualized as a linear progression, beginning with fleeing across a state border and moving toward refugees' local incorporation in the communities that receive them. Citizenship is used as a marker of full incorporation—the end of the linear story when refugees can depend on a state to have their needs met through their legal status. While linear narratives adequately reflect many people's lived experiences, they can simultaneously bracket the ways that refugeehood influences a person's life course, how they make meaning in the world, and how they connect with others. Pivoting away from prioritizing operational knowledge to an examination of people's lived experiences requires a different scope of analysis, one that includes folks with various legal statuses and possibly different kinds of needs than those who have been categorized or legally recognized as refugees.

The anecdotes above stand in stark juxtaposition to linear refugee stories. They provide insight into how refugeehood can be remembered and reintegrated into the present. Multiple timelines of refugeehood emerge in Jordan. The stories about Baba's red coat and Mama's denim shirt reveal some ways that refugee populations overlap and connect, and how refugee identities can be (or become) co-constructed when Palestinian experiences are woven together with Iraqi and Syrian experiences. Because remembering can be an iterative and shared process, memories take on new meanings when they are recalled and experienced with others, which in turn can shape how the children of refugees also make meaning. Instead of linearity, time can fold onto itself, and new beginnings emerge in the present. Shifting from the individual's experience to a community-level analysis, refugeehood can push scholars to think about precarity that threatens a group even while citizenship can provide protection for select members of the group.

To take a more comprehensive approach to the examination of refugeehood, it is useful to parse the competing operational interests that influence the limitations embedded in humanitarian-informed characterizations of refugees. More holistic examinations of refugeehood are abandoned for straightforward assessments that capture ongoing emergencies that are palpable to specified audiences, such as potential donors. The contemporary focus on Syrian refugees in Jordan, for example, overshadowed the experiences of other refugee groups in the country, even while the majority of Syrians lived below the national poverty line and many of their basic needs remained unmet. Globally, Syrians fell out of the international spotlight with the mass displacement of other groups, notably the more than seven million Ukrainians who fled in 2022. Mainstream refugee stories do not simply mirror an objective reality but reflect the interests of knowledge producers. Ukrainian displacement was not only about refugees' needs but also about the geopolitical and economic interests of powerful states. When we focus only on the most recently displaced group(s) and speak primarily about their most basic needs for food and shelter, many important topics remain underexamined. Recognizing the politics that are embedded in ostensibly neutral knowledge production is an important step to putting refugee status, as a legal or humanitarian designation, in conversation with refugeehood, as a reflection of an individual or group's lived experience.

Humanitarian organizations are not only charged with supporting refugees' needs, but they must also raise the funds that will make that effort possible. Herein lies a built-in disconnect when refugee beneficiaries—as opposed to people who identify with refugee issues—are the individuals whose experiences we are most likely to learn about through humanitarian reports, media accounts, and scholarly research. Representations of refugees, and of the work that humanitarian organizations have been able to achieve, are used to incentivize donors to contribute to humanitarian causes. Refugee issues are often described through frames of urgency that are tied to how contemporary humanitarian aid operates, specifically the cycles of pledging, monitoring, reporting, and grant writing. Urgency frames often focus on the most recently displaced, giving primacy to people who are actively fleeing across borders, which consequently marginalizes groups that have been displaced for decades and the ways that refugee populations overlap.

Collapsing differences among UN-recognized refugees and people who identify with the label can become problematic when lived experiences are overlooked for the sake of generalizable claims. While there is overlap between these two groups, they can also have distinct needs and experiences, especially in cases where individuals who identify with the refugee label also carry citizenship. The challenge for the scholar, then, is not only to recognize the role that refugeehood plays in an individual's or community's worldmaking but also to simultaneously consider how privilege influences life chances. An acknowledgment of refugeehood is not an argument for expanding the 1951 Refugee Convention definition but instead is a gesture of recognition to a population who may be excluded in mainstream accounts that adopt legal categories to draw conclusions about how refugees experience displacement and reception. Similarities across refugee groups broach unarticulated questions lodged below the surface in contemporary solutions-oriented conversations.

Rawan Arar is assistant professor in the Department of Law, Societies, and Justice at the University of Washington. As a scholar of refugee displacement, she studies how refugees' lives and life chances are inextricably tied to national and global policies, which create or impede access to basic needs and mobility. She is coauthor with David Scott FitzGerald of *The Refugee System: A Sociological Approach* (Polity Press, 2023).

Notes

I am grateful for the support of our Humanitarianisms working group and our conveners, Arzoo Osanloo and Cabeiri Robinson, who have also organized and edited this book. I thank David Scott FitzGerald, Chris Gratien, Rana B. Khoury, Lama Mourad, Lauren Olsen, and Gershon Shafir for reading earlier drafts of this chapter and offering thoughtful feedback. I would like to recognize Caroline B. Brettell, who was Mama's mentor and who advocated for her throughout the years of her graduate education. A very special thank-you to my parents and my family.

1. Arar, "Cultural Responses to Water Shortage."
2. Abu-Lughod, *Veiled Sentiments*.
3. Arar and FitzGerald, *Refugee System*, 6.
4. Ludwig, "Wiping the Refugee Dust."
5. Jensen, "Meanings of Refugee Status," 11.
6. Zetter, "Labelling Refugees."
7. UNHCR, "Global Trends Forced Displacement in 2021."
8. Crisp, "Who Has Counted the Refugees?"; Crisp, "Who Is Counting the Refugees?"
9. Arar, "New Grand Compromise."
10. Abuamer, "Palestinians Worldwide."
11. Frost, "Advancing Refugee and Citizenship Studies."
12. Hamlin, *Crossing*; Fiddian-Qasmiyeh, "Shifting the Gaze."
13. Ege, "Yūsuf's Struggle"; Feldman, "Humanitarian Departures."
14. Fiddian-Qasmiyeh, "Shifting the Gaze."
15. López, *Unauthorized Love*.
16. UNHCR, "Refugee Data Finder"; Fagan, "Iraqi Refugees."
17. USCRI, "World Refugee Survey 2009."
18. Crisp et al., "Surviving in the City."
19. Arar, "How Political Migrant Networks Differ."
20. Fakih and Ibrahim, "Impact of Syrian Refugees."

References

Abuamer, Majd. "Palestinians Worldwide: A Demographic Study." Review of *Al-Filasṭīniyūn fī al-ʿĀlam: Dirāsa Dīmughrāfīyya*, by Youssef Courbage and Hala Nofal. *Almuntaqa Arab Center for Research and Policy Studies* 4, no. 2 (2021): 108–14.

Abu-Lughod, Lila. *Veiled Sentiments: Honor and Poetry in a Bedouin Society*. Oakland: University of California Press. 1986.

Arar, Nedal. "Cultural Responses to Water Shortage among Palestinians in Jordan: The Water Crisis and Its Impact on Child Health." *Human Organization* 57, no. 3 (1998): 284–91.
Arar, Rawan. "How Political Migrant Networks Differ from Those of Economic Migrants: 'Strategic Anonymity' among Iraqi Refugees in Jordan." *Journal of Ethnic and Migration Studies* 42, no. 3 (2016): 519–35.
———. "The New Grand Compromise: How Syrian Refugees Changed the Stakes in the Global Refugee Assistance Regime." *Journal of Middle East Law and Governance* 9, no. 3 (2017): 298–312.
Arar, Rawan, and David FitzGerald. *The Refugee System: A Sociological Approach*. Cambridge: Polity Press, 2023.
Crisp, Jeff. "'Who Has Counted the Refugees?' UNHCR and the Politics of Numbers." UNHCR New Issues in Refugee Research Working Paper No. 12, 1999.
———. "Who Is Counting the Refugees? Displacement Data, Its Limitations, and Potential for Misuse." *Refugee History*, 4 August 2022, http://refugeehistory.org/blog/2022/8/4/who-is-counting-refugees-displacement-data-its-limitations-and-potential-for-misuse.
Crisp, Jeff, Jane Janz, José Riera, and Shahira Samy. "Surviving in the City: A Review of UNHCR's Operation for Iraqi Refugees in Urban Areas of Jordan, Lebanon, and Syria." UNHCR Policy Development and Evaluation Service, 2009.
Ege, Gözde Burcu. "Yūsuf's Struggle: Negotiating Development and Charity in a Palestinian Refugee Camp." In *Care in a Time of Humanitarianism: Stories of Refuge, Aid, and Repair in the Global South*, edited by Arzoo Osanloo and Cabeiri Robinson, 161–75. New York: Berghahn Books, 2024.
Fakih, Ali, and May Ibrahim. "The Impact of Syrian Refugees on the Labor Market in Neighboring Countries: Empirical Evidence from Jordan." *Defence and Peace Economics* 27, no. 1 (2016): 64–86.
Fagen, Patricia Weiss. "Iraqi Refugees: Seeking Stability in Syria and Jordan." *Institute for the Study of International Migration* and *Center for International Regional Studies* (2009), https://papers.ssrn.com/sol3/papers.cfm?abstract_id=2825853.
Feldman, Ilana. "Humanitarian Departures: Reflections of a Refugee Aid Worker," In *Care in a Time of Humanitarianism; Stories of Refuge, Aid, and Repair in the Global South*, edited by Arzoo Osanloo and Cabeiri Robinson, 131–44. New York: Berghahn Books, 2024.
Fiddian-Qasmiyeh, E. "Shifting the Gaze: Palestinian and Syrian Refugees Sharing and Contesting Space in Lebanon." In *Refuge in a Moving World: Refugee and Migrant Journeys across Disciplines*, edited by Elena Fiddian-Qasmiyeh, 402–14. London: UCL Press, 2020.
Frost, Lillian. "Advancing Refugee and Citizenship Studies through Research on 'Protracted' Refugees." *Newsletter of the Middle East and North Africa Politics Section of APSA* 5, no. 2 (2022): 31–38.
Hamlin, Rebecca. *Crossing: How We Label and React to People on the Move*. Stanford, CA: Stanford University Press, 2021.
Jensen, Katherine. "The Meanings of Refugee Status." *Contexts* 20, no. 1 (2021): 10–15.
López, Jane Lilly. *Unauthorized Love: Mixed Citizenship Couples Negotiating Intimacy, Immigration, and the State*. Stanford, CA: Stanford University Press, 2022.
Ludwig, Bernadette. "'Wiping the Refugee Dust from My Feet': Advantages and Burdens of Refugee Status and the Refugee Label." *International Migration* 54, no. 1 (2016): 5–18.
UNHCR. n.d. "Refugee Data Finder." Retrieved 22 November 2022 from https://www.unhcr.org/refugee-statistics/download/?url=2z1B08.

———. "Global Trends Forced Displacement in 2021." Retrieved 22 November 2022 from https://www.unhcr.org/62a9d1494/global-trends-report-2021.

United States Committee for Refugees and Immigrants (USCRI). "World Refugee Survey 2009—Jordan." 17 June 2009, https://www.refworld.org/docid/4a40d2aac.html.

Zetter, Roger. "Labelling Refugees: Forming and Transforming a Bureaucratic Identity." *Journal of Refugee Studies* 4, no. 1 (1991): 39–62.

CHAPTER 13

The Barrette
Unlikely Humanitarian Images and Practices of Repair

Jenna Grant

"That Barrette, It Is from China"

Syna held up a printout of a black-and-white photograph for us in the audience to see. The photograph depicted a girl who looked around twelve years old, though she may have been younger, it was hard to tell (see figure 13.1). In the photograph, the girl is concentrating on a dynamo suspended just below eye level by two wooden blocks. A voltmeter sits in the foreground on her worktable, and she is holding one of the test leads to a contact. She seems to be checking the voltage of the dynamo, from which wires crane out like unruly twigs from a nest. To her left, another girl is similarly attentive to her task. Behind them are three rows of worktables, students all engaging in similar "practical work," all wearing black long-sleeved shirts. Large windows backlight the scene, emphasizing the contrast between fuzzy elements of the photograph and those that can be seen in more detail—the girl's upper body and the cables of the leads. There is a silver barrette in the girl's dark hair, which is bobbed in the style compulsory at the time for women and girls. The barrette holds her hair in a gentle curve along her forehead and right temple. It anchors an imaginary line to her eyes, the test lead, and her graceful fingers. The barrette gleams, draws our gaze to it. It is a point of uncanny clarity in the photograph.

"That barrette, it is from China." Syna, a filmmaker, and her partner Pheaktra, an archivist, were calling attention to clues in the images, clues to the presence of foreign things and foreign people in a supposedly isolated Democratic Kampuchea. They, along with others in the workshop, had spent time studying

Figure 13.1. • Elizabeth Becker, *Untitled*, Phnom Penh, 1978. Courtesy of University of Washington Libraries Special Collections, Elizabeth Becker Cambodia and Khmer Rouge Collection.[1]

images and texts from an archival collection and were now presenting their responses to the group. This was just one example of how mundane clues such as the barrette prompted discussion about everyday life during the Khmer Rouge period, bringing complexity to a grave, terrible history most often told through sensational narratives of governments, fragmented memories of survivors, and numbing details of academic monographs in languages other than Khmer.[2]

The photograph of the girl with the barrette, along with the hundreds or so others in the Elizabeth Becker Cambodia and Khmer Rouge Collection (1970–88), are unlikely humanitarian images.[3] Humanitarian images are part of the broader genre "humanitarian communication," which Chouliaraki and Vestergaard define as "public practices of meaning making that represent human suffering as a cause of collective emotion and action."[4] For Chouliaraki and Vestergaard, humanitarian communication makes claims on us because of a universal conception of the human, in which humanity is "a shared condition of existential openness to violence—corporeal, social or psychological." It is the notion of humanity as "a shared condition of existential openness to violence" that explains the ubiquity of vulnerable bodies in humanitarian images.[5] The photographs in the Becker collection do not depict graphic violence, mass death, or obvious vulnerability or suffering. They seem to depict everyday life. Yet, these images depict what we now know to have been a humanitarian crisis—the Khmer Rouge genocide. These are images of performances of everyday life. Images of everyday dying.

The photographs in the collection are not traditional documentary or journalistic images, either. Though taken by US journalist Elizabeth Becker on a 1978 reporting trip, the unfreedom of the people in the photographs belies any sense of the images as objective documents. The photographs could only be made by someone working with the state's permission, within the state's tightly controlled view. Indeed, Becker called her trip "an incubated tour of the revolution" because of how her environment and activities were so tightly controlled by the government.[6] Becker was looking for evidence of human rights abuses. The Khmer Rouge, on the other hand, was looking to preserve its power, which required hiding its crimes and portraying itself to outside observers as the righteous sovereign. These images are thus products, indeed, ongoing sites, of struggle. An archive of difficult, quiet, disconcerting events. Fragments of a narrative that is not singular or resolved.

Yet, Becker's photographs capture so much. They contain details that cannot be controlled, even by the most authoritarian of governments. They are open to questioning, perhaps more so than images of patent suffering that show clearly that something bad has happened, or is happening, and thus something needs to be done, urgently. The very qualities that make Becker's photographs unlikely or inadequate humanitarian images—their seeming mundane-ness and normalcy, their quiet—are those that make them open to public and personal practices of repair. In other words, unlikely humanitarian images, like this of the girl with the barrette, are indeed sites for "collective emotion and action" but not by North Atlantic publics on behalf of distant others, the conventional schema in humanitarianism.[7] Rather, these images are sites for collective emotion and action by people living with the ongoing effects of humanitarian crises.

Imagining the photograph as a site for collective action is possible when we hold together multiple, different temporalities of the image. This archive of difficult, quiet, disconcerting images is not frozen in 1978. It is also an archive of other and yet-to-be-known events: workshops, funded by a Whiting Foundation Public Engagement Seed Grant, in 2019 and 2020; writing about it in 2022; events to come following publication on a website. Extending Ariella Azoulay's conception of the photograph as event,[8] I describe conditions of production of Becker's images alongside practices of relating to these images. If we consider the photograph as event-full, that it exists in multiple temporalities, we can see how critical understanding and questioning of unlikely humanitarian images are practices of repair that are part of the image, not other to it.

In this chapter, I present what is known about the context of the photograph of the girl with the barrette, including when it was taken, by whom, and for what purpose. I then discuss the activities of Archive Actions, a project of artists, community organizers, archivists, and university students that explores ways to "activate" the Becker archive. Archive Actions prioritizes the questions, critiques, and creative strategies of Cambodians and Cambodian Americans, with the intention that these communities be at the forefront of reparative work. It also insists that the caretakers of the image—librarians, archivists, scholars, and students at the university—are care-full about the ethics of access, digitization, and display. More than forty years later, collective emotion and action *can* emerge through conversations among artists, students, scholars, and archivists in Phnom Penh and Seattle. Their questions about history, subjectivity, and silence suggest that unlikely humanitarian images have an important role to play in practices of collective care and repair.

The "Incubated Tour of the Revolution"

There are some things we know about the image of the girl with the barrette because the photographer told us. US journalist Elizabeth Becker took this picture at the Institute for Scientific Training and Information in Phnom Penh in December 1978 during a two-week reporting trip to Democratic Kampuchea. Becker could not speak to the girl with the barrette. She did not learn her name, nor the names of any of the other children/students/laborers repairing broken mechanical parts in other departments. According to Thiounn Mumm, head of the committee of the institute, these students were "the young vanguard," chosen from the common people to participate in a "totally new experiment in technological education." Thiounn explained the experiment thusly:

- six months of training in basic science and calculation;
- six months of practice in cooperatives;
- six months of work in a factory;
- eighteen months of theory, including history, geography, and math;
- twelve months of work in a factory as technicians;
- eighteen months of further study.[9]

The proposed course of study and practice was longer than the duration of Democratic Kampuchea. Though the Khmer Rouge controlled different parts of the country in the 1970s, 1980s, and 1990s, their rule over the nation, which they renamed Democratic Kampuchea, lasted from when they took Phnom Penh on 17 April 1975 to when they were ousted from the capital on 7 January 1979—three years, eight months, and twenty days.

Elizabeth Becker was one of only two representatives from mainstream "Western" media to report from Democratic Kampuchea. From 9 December to 23 December 1978, Becker, working for the *Washington Post*, Richard Dudman, a senior reporter for the *St. Louis Post-Dispatch*, and Malcolm Caldwell, a scholar at the School of Oriental and African Studies (SOAS) University of London, were invited to witness and report on the human rights situation and the impending war with Vietnam. The government of Democratic Kampuchea hastily arranged this "incubated tour of the revolution" to counter reports from refugees who had escaped Cambodia of atrocities that included starvation, hard labor, violence both routine and impossible to predict, rape, denial of medical care, forced marriage, forced movement, and separation from family. The Khmer Rouge also hoped to convince the world that Democratic Kampuchea was the victim of unprovoked, imperialist aggression from Vietnam and that war was imminent. Indeed, two days after Becker left Cambodia, the People's Army of Vietnam and the Kampuchean United Front for National Salvation (dissident Cambodian communists and former Khmer Rouge who escaped purges in the Eastern Zone) invaded the country. They achieved their goal to overthrow the Pol Pot–Ieng Sary clique within two weeks.[10]

The trip began in Phnom Penh, where Becker had lived and worked for two years in the early 1970s reporting on the civil war. Returning to a Phnom Penh emptied of children, animals, monks, markets—of most people, including people she knew—prompted Becker to call it "a tropical twilight zone."[11] The tours of factories, refineries, the port at Kompong Som, even the temples at Angkor Wat could not tell her definitively what was going on. Workers did not appear to be suffering. In more than a few of her photographs, people are smiling. Of course, it is hard to know what their smiles are showing and what they are hiding.

I first saw the image of the girl with the barrette on a computer screen in the Libraries of the University of Washington (UW), where I am employed as associate professor in the Department of Anthropology. The archive includes personal notes, negatives, scanned photographs, and interviews from the 1978 trip, as well as political speeches, cultural propaganda, and United Nations reports in English, Khmer, and French dating from 1970 to 1988. Becker is from Seattle and an alumna of UW. For these reasons, and because the university has an established Southeast Asia collection and a dedicated librarian, she donated her materials to UW.

I was surprised to learn of this archive. Becker is a prominent figure in Cambodia studies (*When the War Was Over* was the first book I read about Cambodia). How could I not have heard of this archive? Part of the significance of this collection is the fact that there are so few documentary materials from Democratic Kampuchea. Our histories are based on memories of survivors and of cadres; forensic research in prisons and graves; official histories of governments long gone; diplomatic communications wrapped in various levels of secrecy.[12] In fact, I was not aware that there were any images of Democratic Kampuchea taken by people who were not Khmer Rouge. Let me emphasize this: visual histories of the Khmer Rouge are based on propaganda and documentary images taken by agents of a regime that perpetrated genocide.[13]

Becker's images do not solve this problem. Her "incubated tour" was highly controlled. She saw what she was allowed to see, from the "practical study" in the Institute for Scientific Training to the oil refinery, women threshing rice on the highway, and the traditional medicines factory. Yet, images capture more than what is intended to be included or left out. Becker's images are constrained by the Khmer Rouge, but not utterly controlled or authored by them. Might the images have counterhistories to offer?

History Is a Circle and a Spiral

Syna and Pheaktra, the filmmaker and archivist who singled out the barrette, were part of an Archive Actions workshop in Phnom Penh (2019). The primary intention of that and a subsequent Archive Actions workshop in Seattle (2020) was to explore methods of opening the Becker collection to Cambodians and Cambodian Americans so that they may learn from, challenge, and expand public histories of this period, of the Cold War, and of refugee experience in the United States. A secondary goal was to create networks for future work with the archive. The workshops introduced the Becker archive to artists, archivists, students, and community organizers in Phnom Penh and Seattle; explored what they want to know (or not know) about Cambodian and Cambodian American history; and gained insight on modes of research and representation that matter to different publics. In Seattle, the Archive Actions project involved Ammara Touch, a UW undergraduate researcher and community activist, and two graduate students, Sambath Eat, an artist and MA student in Southeast Asia studies, and Felicia Rova-Chamroeun, an MA student in museology.[14]

The Phnom Penh workshop, organized with Sopheap Chea, director of the Bophana Audiovisual Resource Center, took advantage of artists from around Cambodia being in town for the 2019 Arts 4 Peace Festival and Photo Phnom Penh.[15] Two archivists and twelve artists of different disciplines joined the workshop: painters, photographers, filmmakers, a dancer, and a writer. In Seattle, Ammara and I worked with Bunthay Cheam, a community organizer with the Khmer Anti-Deportation Advocacy Group,[16] to bring together eleven participants: community organizers, educators, artists, and students, and a Special Collections librarian who had to be present as we were handling materials. In what follows, I describe some of the conversations about history and repair prompted by these images and other materials in the Becker archive.

In Phnom Penh, one group asked about visual clues to the staging of the photographs, which led to a larger discussion of the kind of staging the Khmer Rouge thought important to do. They noted that the child laborers wear items from China—for example, the barrette. We discussed the presence of foreign, mostly Chinese, technical consultants in Democratic Kampuchea. This indication of Chinese support, if not collaboration, with the Khmer Rouge was notable to Cambodian participants in the workshop because Chinese imperial projects in contemporary Cambodia are expansive and controversial. Another group was drawn to an image of a street in a provincial town, a street without people, without chickens, with no signs of human or animal life. "It is like a puzzle," Roth said, "to try to piece together these different materials." People wondered about one of the Khmer Rouge staff that handled the visitors, Thoiunn Prasith, who is a main character in Becker's notes. Who was this man? Is he still alive? What was his job like, leading foreigners on "tours" of Democratic Kampuchea? In her notes, Becker expresses a fondness for one of her guides, Suon. What was this strange relationship between Becker and Suon like? How did it affect her photography?

Another group came away with the impression of history as a circle; rather, a spiral. A story of different and repeating departures: Lon Nol (leader of the Khmer Republic, the prior government) from Cambodia to exile in Hawaii; people from the cities to the countryside; the Khmer Rouge from Cambodia to Thailand. Becker herself, always with departure on the horizon. There is a sense of performance, Kong said; the route is planned and the scenes inside and outside are staged. "The performance is near the end, but the journey is not done." Some talked about the nature of the "mistake" in their materials. Many of Becker's photos are from the inside of a car. Some are oddly framed, including much of the car window and ceiling (for example, see figure 13.2). Is she trying to tell us something about a controlled view, or simply revealing the limits of her ability to freely observe and photograph everyday life and conditions?

Indeed, participants in Phnom Penh and Seattle debated the truths of images and texts in the archive. One photograph sparked a heated discussion about the unevenness of experience, and the role of luck and privilege in dictating life under the Khmer Rouge. The photo in question is a black-and-white scene of a relatively well-dressed older couple standing in front of a comfortable, traditional stilt home (see figure 13.3). "The location is Takeo," said Pheaktra, the archivist. "The village was a model village." There, people had enough to eat. They had decent clothes and housing. This "Potemkin Village" was an agricultural cooperative that actually functioned. People grew food and appeared self-sufficient. Pheaktra's knowledge was unique, formed through profession (he is an archivist working at Bophana and familiar with the image) and through kinship (his relatives lived in this village). Comparatively speaking, his relatives did not suffer greatly during Democratic Kampuchea, and it was some time before they learned that their experience was unique. People in the room were surprised that these villages existed, that there was anyone who had a reasonably good life under the Khmer Rouge. Some expressed anger. Why Pheaktra's relatives? What was their connection, how did they have this privilege? Or was their situation nothing to do with their positionality, just merely luck?

Figure 13.2. • Elizabeth Becker, *Untitled*, 1978. Courtesy of University of Washington Libraries Special Collections, Elizabeth Becker Cambodia and Khmer Rouge Collection.[17]

Figure 13.3. • Elizabeth Becker, *Untitled*, Takeo, 1978. Courtesy of University of Washington Libraries Special Collections, Elizabeth Becker Cambodia and Khmer Rouge Collection.[18]

A Seattle participant was struck by the ways that different regimes represented gender. Specifically, in magazines and booklets printed for foreign audiences, both Democratic Kampuchea and the People's Republic of Kampuchea depict women as having a full role in society. But we know different. "How to peel away the falsity of these representations," Darozyl asked, "as well as representations of Vietnam and Cambodia in eternal conflict? How can we do reconciliation between Cambodian and Vietnamese refugees in the US, undoing the indoctrination of victimhood and blame?"

Several people in the Seattle workshop noted the psychological perversion of various symbols, such as Angkor Wat on the Khmer flag, and the krama, a traditional, checkered scarf.[19] During the Khmer Rouge, the soldiers' uniforms included the red and white krama. The manipulation of potent symbols of Khmer identity creates a contradiction for many, especially diasporic individuals in the United States who seek to revive and reconnect with their roots in the form of artifacts like the krama, but who also must come to terms with its undertones of violence because of its association with a genocidal regime.

Analyzing these pieces of history raised conversation about the ways Cambodian Americans experience contradictions in their attempts to navigate Khmer identity and culture. Keo reflected on the time he created a flyer for a Khmer community event and received criticism from elders for his use of dark colors. He realized that their criticism "came from a place of unhealed trauma, because the dark colors reminded them of the Khmer Rouge. It's hard when they don't talk because you don't know," he said. In her notes from the workshop, Ammara wrote, "As Cambodian Americans work towards healing and building a collective Khmer identity, they must address the generational gap."

In the basement of UW Libraries, workshop participants criticized the ways knowledge about Cambodia and the Khmer Rouge period has been created and passed down. Bunthay commented on how colonialism has made many feel that "in order to learn about ourselves, we need to go to white institutions, which teach our histories through a Western academic lens." This lens claims legitimacy on all "facts" presented, and that "our parents' stories are not true or have less value." Bunthay articulates how repair work with the archive will require practices of unlearning and practices of honoring memory. Ammara stressed that stories have many sides to them and are granted power by whomever is able to perpetuate and speak them. At the same time, Sameth insisted, "it is a fine line we walk in seeking these memories. Often stories are the only thing that survivors can own and keep for themselves coming out of such violence, and that also must be respected." To disregard the desire for silence and to probe for information can be a form of extraction that continues to dehumanize the individual.

Participants in Archive Actions workshops studied Becker's photographs and documents and shared our puzzlement, responses, and ideas for future repair work. Their concerns echo those of scholars and artists who work with colonial images and images from the Warsaw ghetto. They prompt debate about issues such as: What historical truths do photographs show? To what extent are photographs determined by state control, and what might evade control? Whose experiences are privileged in the display of photographs of colonial life, war atrocities, or humanitarian crises? Do these photographs contribute to reparative research and practice, or does their circulation further traumatize survivors and descendants?[20]

Toward a Kind of Undercommons

Archive Actions brought the Becker collection to new publics in Cambodia and the United States. The project also connected UW students to artists and community organizers in Seattle, resulting in new collaborations on art, research, and activist initiatives in the Cambodian American community and with the university.[21] Our work came to a screeching halt in 2020 due to the global COVID-19 pandemic and uprisings around racism and police violence, from which we have yet to recover. The pandemic forced closure of the Bophana Center for months, seriously threatening its future, and UW Libraries Special Collections reopened for visits by appointment. Workshop participants in Seattle are dedicating their labor and energy to COVID-19 relief efforts in the Cambodian community and to antiracist activism.

In the coming years, we are aim to develop a website for the Becker Archive, which will require us to take up many of the difficult questions raised in the workshops and by critical digital humanities scholars. These are some of our premises:

- looking at these images should not be easy or passive;
- these images require contextualization;
- there needs to be a structural mechanism through which Cambodians and Cambodian Americans can guide the display or nondisplay of specific images;
- there needs to be a structural mechanism through which Cambodians and Cambodian Americans can shape the metadata that constrain how an image is categorized, thus how it can be searched for, and how it may be found.

These are some of our questions:

- How do we account for the fact that people did not provide consent to be photographed?

- How do we contextualize the violations that people in these images experienced? What is the minimum people should know to engage with the digital archive in a manner that respects the dignity of subjects?
- Should there be different levels of access to digital materials for different groups of people? Or should it be "open" to all with an internet connection?

Throughout the building and maintenance of this site, we must be intentional about the process of digitization and making images available online. In other words, creating a website for an online archive is not a simple question of translating materials from one medium to another and just letting them be. Important theoretical and practical questions must be wrestled with along the way, and not just by the leads on the project but by all involved. This requires valuing the intellectual and emotional labor of web designers, research assistants, and workshop participants through compensation, attribution, and recognition. We also value in similar ways the labor of those who will maintain the digital and physical archives.

One of our central concerns is the form that "context" should take. Knowing that the manner in which people display interest or formulate questions has a social history, what context is needed?[22] Should levels of historical, cultural, and political detail be nested, with points deemed crucial on display and points worth knowing available by clicking through? Art historian Temi Odumosu has posed the question thusly: "I am wondering if there is a way to develop an ethics of care for digitization that is able to signal to different kinds of users or audiences where and how sensitivity is required, not as an optional stance but as a prerequisite for the digital encounter."[23]

We also need to think carefully about the issue of property. Digitization and circulation of images on the internet can evade control. As anthropologist Emma Kowal writes, "The world of open access proliferates the decisions that need to be made.... Everywhere we are struggling with when to share and when to withhold. Perhaps the critical point is not whether something is open or closed, but who has the control to make this decision."[24] In this case, control is a positive value that protects vulnerable images from circulating without context and from misuse. Becker's images of people living under the Khmer Rouge should not contribute to stereotypical depictions of Cambodian people and the Cambodian nation as abject, failed, terrorized.

We want a website that structures how publics engage with the online archive and is also malleable in response to publics and events. What forms of knowledge can a platform incorporate, indeed, learn from? For example, if metadata could be altered by users of a public digital archive, might they become both an alternative catalogue clear to users and, borrowing from Odumosu, "a quiet undercommons reconfiguring the digital thoroughfares (associations, keywords, hyperlinks) that bring a public in encounters with challenging histories"?[25] Certainly a digital archive offers possibilities for public engagement; can it also hold tension? In Odumosu's terms, can a digital archive be a repository of the challenges images provoke?

Perhaps the broader stance toward images we must advocate is that there is more than one temporality for images. Media studies scholar and curator Ariella Azoulay has called this the "event" of photography, stressing that photographs are something that happens and something that continues to happen.[26] It can be challenging to conceive of historical humanitarian images in this way. To some audiences, the temporality of the girl with barrette or the couple standing in front of their home seems radically "other" in terms of time, place, and conditions. Thus, one strategy will be to curate a digital archive as an event-full space, a space for the documentation, discussion, contestation, and re-inscription of events. This places the common understanding of a photograph as a product of the stable and singular view of X (photographer, the state, the army, science) as *one among other* possible understandings of what a photograph is. In other words, the image of the girl with the barrette is one of many that came out of an encounter: between Becker, the girl, the camera, the students, the Khmer Rouge leaders. It was possible because a US reporter was a desirable witness, desirable even to an anti-imperialist communist regime that murdered people for alleged connections to the United States, one that gained moral strength as a result of US carpet bombing, chemical warfare, and regime change. Syna and Pheaktra's discussion of the photograph of the girl with the barrette is yet another temporality for this image. Their questions—and similar questions from students, archivists, activists, and artists—shift understandings of this history and this archive.

Now You Are a Part of It

I conclude with Odumosu's question, a difficult but fair question, a reparative question posed by an unlikely humanitarian image such as the girl with the barrette: "'Look, here is my story. I've experienced pain, and now you are a part of it; tell me what you intend to do with me?'"[27]

To use images in repair work, we must address each facet of this question. Repair work must tell a story about the contexts of images. These stories may change as people engage with the archive and new facts emerge. Repair work must acknowledge pain. The pain of subjects in the images, the pain of those who experienced or whose loved ones experienced this humanitarian crisis. Repair work insists that the viewer of a photograph becomes involved in the events of the photograph: "Now you are a part of it." Ethical involvement means questioning the event of the photograph when it was produced, and subsequent events such as curation, digitization, study, and display. Unlikely humanitarian images provoke questions about facts: about everyday life in extreme times and about spirals and connections over different time periods. Not just that there was suffering, for example, but that suffering was uneven, whether random or by design. Unlikely humanitarian images demand that we create spaces of dignity for subjects and for viewers with direct relation to subjects. They also require digital spaces that are open to and may be altered by descendants. Unlikely humanitarian images demand a considered response to the question: "Tell me what you intend to do with me?"

Jenna Grant is associate professor of cultural anthropology working in the fields of medical anthropology and medical humanities, feminist science and technology studies, visual anthropology, and Southeast Asia studies. Her book, *Fixing the Image: Ultrasound and the Visuality of Care in Phnom Penh* (University of Washington Press, 2022), is an ethnographic and historical analysis of medical imaging in Cambodia's capital.

Notes

1. Accession number 6036-001, box 1, folder 12.
2. On fragmented and episodic memory, see Kwan, "Time-Image Episodes"; Um, *Land of Shadows*.
3. Elizabeth Becker Cambodia and Khmer Rouge Collection, 1970–1988, 6036 (Accession No. 6036-001), box 352900, University of Washington Libraries Special Collections, Seattle, WA, https://archiveswest.orbiscascade.org/ark:/80444/xv40194. These materials are also available at the Bophana Audiovisual Resource Center: Collection of Elizabeth Becker, 1970–1988, EBK (Archive reference code), Bophana Audiovisual Resource Center, Phnom Penh, Cambodia, https://bophana.org/wp-content/uploads/2020/11/45.-Elizabeth-Becker.pdf.
4. Humanitarian communication includes newspaper articles, UN speeches, social media posts, and films that render "vulnerable others into language or image with a view to inviting audiences to act upon their vulnerability—to help alleviate their suffering or protect them from harm." Chouliaraki and Vestergaard, "Humanitarian Communication," 1.
5. Chouliaraki and Vestergaard, "Humanitarian Communication," 2.
6. Becker, *When the War Was Over*, 398.
7. Indeed, in 1978 and 1979, Becker's and refugees' claims about the regime's crimes were brushed aside. Throughout the 1980s, China, the United States, other capitalist powers, and the UN recognized the exiled Khmer Rouge as the legitimate government of Cambodia rather than the People's Republic of Kampuchea, the government that ousted the Khmer Rouge and was struggling to rebuild the country.
8. Azoulay, "What Is a Photograph?"
9. Becker describes her visit to the Institute for Scientific Training and Information in *When the War Was Over*, 406–8.

10. Becker, *When the War Was Over*, 398.
11. Becker, *When the War Was Over*, 402.
12. See Khatharya Um, *Land of Shadows*, for original research and a comprehensive analysis of published work on the genocide. See also the online archives of the Documentation Center of Cambodia (DC-Cam), the Yale Cambodian Genocide Program, and the Extraordinary Chambers in the Courts of Cambodia (ECCC).
13. See Rithy Panh's experimental essay film *The Missing Picture* on the problem of working with propaganda images, and creative strategies for both incorporating and critiquing these images.
14. Sambath Eat scanned many documents of the Becker archive, for which I am grateful. Eat's MA thesis, "Paste-Up Modernity," develops the concept of the "paste-up" to understand the incorporation of heterogenous Khmer and foreign images in postcolonial media. For her MA project, "Decolonizing the Narrative," Rova-Chamroeun's decolonial approach to oral history practice involved reworking the seemingly mundane consent form to reflect community ownership, conducting oral histories with Cambodian American community members of different ages, and working with the Highline Heritage Museum on an exhibition and permanent website: https://highlinemuseum.org/cambodian-oral-history/.
15. See https://photography-now.com/exhibition/142576 and https://arts4peace.cambodianlivingarts.org/kh/.
16. See https://www.khaagwa.org/.
17. Accession number 6036-001, box 1, folder 12.
18. Accession number 6036-001, box 1, folder 12.
19. See "Of Krama and Khmer Identity," in Ly, *Traces of Trauma*, for analysis of the krama in contemporary Cambodian art.
20. On colonial and postcolonial images, see Campt, *Listening to Images*, and Odumosu, "What Lies Unspoken." On film of the Warsaw ghetto see Hersonski, *Film Unfinished*, and Melamed, "Film Unraveled."
21. For example, Keo Sanh, one of the Seattle workshop participants, will be a resident in the Artist's Studio of the UW Burke Museum. Sanh, artist and founder of the renowned Eazy Duz It lowrider car club, will work on art for a car in the museum's parking lot, engaging the public in his process and discussing Cambodian iconography in his practice.
22. Redfield, in Kowal et al., "Open Question."
23. Odumosu, "Crying Child," S298.
24. Kowal, in Kowal et al., "Open Question."
25. Odumosu, "Crying Child," S299.
26. Azoulay, "What Is a Photograph?"
27. Odumosu, "Crying Child," S299.

References

Azoulay, Ariella. "What Is a Photograph? What Is Photography?" *Philosophy of Photography* 1, no. 1 (2010): 9–13.

Becker, Elizabeth. *When the War Was Over: Cambodia and the Khmer Rouge Revolution*. New York: Public Affairs, 1998.

Campt, Tina. *Listening to Images*. Durham, NC: Duke University Press, 2017.

Chouliaraki, Lilie, and Anne Vestergaard. "Introduction: Humanitarian Communication in the 21st Century." In *Routledge Handbook of Humanitarian Communication*, 1–22. Abingdon: Routledge, 2022. https://doi.org/10.4324/9781315363493.
Eat, Sambath. "Paste-Up Modernity: Visual Depiction of Modern Cambodia in the 1960s Magazine *Kambuja Review*." MA thesis, Southeast Asia Studies, Henry M. Jackson School of International Studies, University of Washington, 2021.
Hersonski, Yael. *A Film Unfinished*. Color and black-and-white, 91 minutes. New York: Oscilloscope Pictures, 2010.
Kowal, Emma, Todd Meyers, Eugene Raikhel, Peter Redfield, Sharon Abramowitz, Barbara Andersen, Eileen Moyer, Emily Yates-Doerr, and Jenna Grant. "The Open Question." *Medicine Anthropology Theory* 2, no. 1 (2015): 75–94.
Kwan, Yvonne Y. "Time-Image Episodes and the Construction of Transgenerational Trauma Narratives." *Journal of Asian American Studies* 23, no. 1 (2020): 29–59.
Ly, Boreth. *Traces of Trauma: Cambodian Visual Culture and National Identity in the Aftermath of Genocide*. Honolulu: University of Hawaii Press, 2020.
Melamed, Laliv. "A Film Unraveled: An Interview with Yael Hersonski." *International Journal of Politics, Culture, and Society* 26, no. 1 (2013): 9–19.
Odumosu, Temi. "What Lies Unspoken: A Remedy for Colonial Silence(s) in Denmark." *Third Text* 33, nos. 4–5 (2019): 615–29.
———. "The Crying Child: On Colonial Archives, Digitization, and Ethics of Care in the Cultural Commons." *Current Anthropology* 61, no. 22 (2020): S289–S302.
Panh, Rithy. *The Missing Picture*. Color, 92 minutes. Catherine Dussart Productions/Arte France/Bophana Production. Strand Releasing, 2014.
Rova-Chamroeun, Felicia. "Decolonizing the Narrative: Preserving Oral History in a Diasporic Community." MA thesis, Museology Program, University of Washington, 2020.
Um, Khatharya. *From the Land of Shadows: War, Revolution, and the Making of the Cambodian Diaspora*. New York: NYU Press, 2015.

CHAPTER 14

Memoir and a Sinking Ship
Reconstituting Humanity through Refugee Narratives
Megan Butler

What is it about Behrouz Boochani's memoir *No Friend but the Mountains* that makes it different from other accounts of refugee experiences? This is the question I asked myself before I started reading because it had been recommended so emphatically by colleagues who share my interest in memoirs of refugee experiences. In the book, Boochani describes his flight from Iran in 2013, his attempts to reach Australia by boat, and the six long years he spent in an offshore detention facility trying to claim asylum. The journey he described was familiar to me; harrowing sea crossings, intermittent humanitarian intervention, political machinations, and extended periods of waiting in dismal conditions form the skeleton of many refugee accounts, both fiction and nonfiction, from the last two decades. But I had an unsettled feeling after I finished reading. As with most memoirs, *No Friend but the Mountains* transcribes a life lived, or a part of a life lived, from the author's personal experience, so I had opened this book with the expectation that Boochani was the subject. Yet, I closed the book wondering who the subject of this book really was and what type of witnessing was being represented. Was it even a memoir at all?

While Boochani was existing in the barest conditions in a prison-like refugee camp on Manus Island, an island off the coast of Papua New Guinea, he used Facebook and WhatsApp messaging on a series of hidden phones to tap out thousands of texts. With the help of refugee advocates and translators, the texts were forwarded to Omid Tofighian, an Iranian-Australian translator in Sydney. Boochani texted in both prose and poetry when he could. Together, they decided that Tofighian would edit the texts into a narrative for publication, a process that would be convoluted at best while Boochani was held in a place where communication could be suspended by Australian authorities at any time and a phone was a rare commodity. *No Friend but the Mountains* was the outcome, and just seven months after its publication in 2018, it won both the Victorian Prize for Literature and the Victorian Premier's Prize for Non-Fiction, Australia's highest awards *for an Australian writer*. At the 2019 award ceremony in Melbourne—that Boochani could not attend because he could not leave Manus Island after six years of detention—the nominating committee called him a great Australian writer, although he had never been in the country and was barred from entry.

Receiving the awards was extraordinary, a dream come true for a writer's first book. The dream, however, was marred by Boochani's persistent detention and the contradictions riddling his predicament. He was receiving honorary citizenship from the same country refusing him entry. This odd and frustrating situation brought me back to my question of representation. Why this unusual move by Australia's literary community? Was it an act of resistance or atonement, or a mix of both? Boochani described being co-opted as an Australian writer and winning the awards as "a paradoxical feeling."[1] He was considered an honorary citizen by the awards committee and denied legal citizenship at the same time, and even though the consideration was symbolic, the denial definitely was not. His mixed feelings were understandable: Which Australians were offering political belonging and saw him—a Kurdish-Iranian journalist wanting to write free from persecution—as a like-minded member of their community? And which Australians were denying citizenship to him or anyone attempting to enter their country except by narrow legal channels? And what would it mean to belong to a place that worked so ferociously to keep you out?

Tofighian, Boochani's translator and editor, states that Boochani's intention was always "to hold a mirror up to the [Australian] system, dismantle it, and produce a historical record to honour those who [had] been killed and everyone who is still suffering."[2] This intent made readers witness to multiple actors and a brutal system, and muddied the question of representation that is usually so clear in memoir. Yes, aspects of memoir are here, since the genre can be narrowly defined as narrative of the author's personal memories, but *No Friend but the Mountains* is also the mirror the author intended because it is a narrative of the lived experience of national migration policies. Why is the distinction important? In four hundred pages, Boochani seems to say, come along, let me show you what it means to be adrift, to escape one punitive, corrupt regime (Iran) only to wind up in the "care" of another seeking to "protect" its sovereignty and citizenry (Australia). For those reading more broadly, he speaks to the citizens of countries whose systems of border management and refugee care compound suffering by shifting responsibility for both to countries in the global South. His story forces readers—me included—to reckon with ideas of citizenship and global responsibility and to understand what it means to seek refuge. In a common imagination of the refugee experience, the process is linear: it begins with hardship or war and ends with a happy relocation elsewhere. Boochani's experience disrupts this. His journey was meandering and indeterminate, and the refuge he received was often just as violent, dehumanizing, and degrading as the conditions he fled.

Imagining the Refugee

Until *No Friend But the Mountains* was published, most Australians knew little of the detention centers. Post–World War II immigration policies were liberal in Australia, and the country had a relatively open door until the early 1990s, when waves of Asian immigrants prompted the creation of the One Nation Party, a right-wing populist movement opposed to multiculturalism and Indigenous rights. The complaints of that fringe party seeped into the mainstream, and offshore detention centers were reopened during the 2010s as part of Australia's "Pacific Solution," a program to manage growing immigration numbers. Journalists were repeatedly denied access to the centers, and a grim law was passed in 2014 allowing convictions of up to two years in prison for "any doctors or social workers who bore public witness to children beaten or sexually abused [or] to acts of rape or cruelty."[3] Medical workers allowed into the prisons were barred from telling of the cruelty of the Australian jailers, the rank living conditions, the two young prisoners who set themselves on fire, or the young girl who sewed her lips together to protest her detention. In the book's introduction, Australian novelist Richard Flanagan tried to describe what was so disturbing about Boochani's experience. Australians, he wrote, "pride [themselves] on decency, kindness, generosity, and a fair go. None of these qualities were evident in Boochani's account of hunger, squalor, beatings, suicide and murder."[4]

No Friend but the Mountains reflected back to Australians a national reality at odds with individual understandings, or "imaginaries," that is, the ideas individuals have about their society that combine how things usually go with how they think things should go.[5] The Australian divide over Boochani, revealed by the literary community's decision to claim him as a member in opposition to the government's decision to brand him an unwelcome refugee, showed how far apart these imaginaries can be. *No Friend but the Mountains* showed a side of Australia that challenged the decency, kindness, and generosity Flanagan wrote about. It also deflated imaginaries about humanitarianism and the types of people seeking refuge, two aspects of crises often marshaled when political imaginaries impact national policy. Proffered as a solution for what was described as "invading hordes,"[6] the detention camp became a political and humanitarian problem in both Australia and Papua New Guinea in part because Boochani's book offered a counternarrative that estranged readers from their imaginaries.

All this was done not as a work of grand theory long considered but as one man's account cobbled together from texts that often leave traditional prose for a particular type of poetry called a Persian *ghazal*. Boochani wrote with *ghazals* to communicate in a different register, veering from the ordinary to understand the extraordinary in a way that defied simple assumptions about the place of refugees within the national and international community. In this mode, his writing radiates a connection between form and meaning and offers a powerful indictment of how systems operate at the level of the individual, where people and imaginaries meet. The *ghazals* are woven throughout to make some sense of his parallel traumas—they appear when his experience is more than he can bear or when he has moments of solitude that allow for expansive thinking. Originally an ancient Arabic expression of loss and the pain of separation from place or love, the *ghazal* was embraced by Persian poets nearly a thousand years ago and adapted to encompass love, loss, melancholy, and existential questions. The Persian form of layered couplets has been absorbed by poets all over the world and adapted through translations. Today, critics describe the *ghazal* as akin to looking in a broken mirror, with "each couplet like one of the shards of glass," reflecting a different perspective, and disrupting unities of voice and narrative.[7] From this point of view, the *ghazal* is a symbolic addition to *No Friend but the Mountains*, perhaps the final state of the mirror Boochani intended with the book, and a clue for me about why I found the narrative disturbing. All those shards prompt something more than bearing witness to a story well told, they also reflect readers into the narrative as part of the story and make the question of representation thick with additional questions.

Confronting the Political Imaginary

I can't believe what is happening to me /
All that hardship /
All that wandering from place to place /
All that starvation I had to endure /
All of it . . . /
So that I could arrive on Australian soil /
I cannot believe I am now being exiled to Manus /
A tiny island out in the middle of the ocean.[8]

Boochani wrote this *ghazal* after he and the other migrants he traveled with were rescued from the sea, their boat broken to pieces by the waves. An Indonesian fishing boat pulled them out of the water, then a British cargo ship sheltered them until an Australian warship took them onboard. They thought their journey was over, that safe in the custody of the Australian navy they could make their claims for asylum. From the top deck of the ship in a sentence that reads like a sigh of relief, Boochani wrote, "Whatever has passed, we have reached Australia. Life has shed its love on us."[9] But that love was short-lived when they were taken not to Australia but to Christmas Island, a speck of land in the Indian Ocean seven hours by air to the closest spot on the Australian mainland. There they were informed that they would be held indefinitely on Manus Island, a small island off the northern coast of Papua New Guinea that had been used as an offshore detention center since 2001. The migrants did not know they had arrived at a moment of intense political backlash against migrants arriving by sea to Australia, but they did know that if they were not on Australian soil, they could not make a claim for asylum; this was a crushing blow, only partially revealed by the anguish in Boochani's *ghazal* above.

At that same time in 2013, a conservative Coalition party aiming to take control of the Australian government introduced a "Stop the Boats" campaign as part of their plan called Operation Sovereign Borders. For many years, illegal entry to Australia by boat was negligible, and the term used was "irregular Maritime arrivals." In 2008, 161 people were intercepted; by 2013, that number had risen to 13,108, and the description shifted to "*illegal* Maritime arrivals."[10] If elected, the Coalition promised a zero-tolerance approach to illegal entry by boat. Election rhetoric raised the issue to crisis proportions, a situation worthy of exerting the nation's sovereignty, or the state's right to do whatever it deemed necessary to protect and maintain its borders. When the Coalition was elected, they put Operation Sovereign Borders into effect with forced offshore processing, stricter barriers to citizenship, and harsher penalties for illegal entry. In a message to smugglers and asylum seekers, Prime Minister Kevin Rudd warned, "If you are going to put someone onto a boat to come to Australia, we, the Australian government, are not going to allow you to settle in Australia. Everything else is secondary to that. That is the absolute core message."[11] Asylum seekers were characterized as dangerous invaders and drains on state resources, and advertisements like the one below, authorized and circulated by the government, used harsh language to keep them away (see figure 14.1).

The disbelief in Boochani's ghazal when he wrote, "I can't believe this is happening to me ... I cannot believe I am now being exiled to Manus," is visceral, as if an opportunity was all but plucked from his hands. Even though I was reading a book filled with words he had typed into a cell phone, I imagined them on a tear-soaked page. I thought of what these lines—neatly ordered and uniformly punctuated—said without saying, and in that empty space I read rage and indignation made all the more acute because he was powerless and impotent, a man with no control over his future and no future to control. Over the course of his six years in detention, the Australian government offered

Figure 14.1. • An advertisement to "Stop the Boats," part of the Australian Customs and Border Protection Service's 2013 Operation Sovereign Borders campaign. Wikipedia Commons, public domain (Creative Commons Attribution-Share Alike 3.0 Unported License).

Boochani two choices: return to Iran, or remain detained on Manus. Returning Boochani to Iran—a process called "refoulement," in which refugees or asylum seekers are involuntarily relocated to countries where they might be in danger—was a death sentence. Since Australia is a signatory to the 1951 United Nations Convention Relating to the Status of Refugees, the government's attempt at refoulement violated the convention and an essential principle of international human rights law. By keeping him off Australian soil, he could not apply for asylum, although years into his time on Manus he was informed that he could apply to become a citizen of Papua New Guinea. This provided another paradox.

The Papus, the natives of Papua New Guinea, were also his jailers because the detention center provided much-needed jobs to the poverty-ridden country. Although the Papus were not as vicious as the Australian guards, they nonetheless collaborated as willing partners in an inhumane carceral system that was eventually declared unconstitutional by the Supreme Court of Papua New Guinea in 2016.[12] Boochani's book revealed his dismal choices, and Australians, newly cognizant of the effects their government's practice of "refugee offshoring" and the conditions at the detention centers, recognized themselves as complicit in schemes intended to break the will and spirit of the detainees. Writing in the foreword, Richard Flanagan compared the treatment of Australians in Japanese POW camps during World War II to the treatment of the migrants in detention camps and asked, "What has become of us when it is we who now commit such crimes?"[13] I hear an echo of Boochani's *ghazal* in Flanagan's question, as if he is also saying, *I can't believe this is happening to us, who have we become?* This shift transforms the memoir into a reflection of the national imaginary that illuminates not shared ideals and moral values but shared offenses. The imaginary is gone, too, replaced by the effects of concrete policy and named people, living and dead.

Questioning Humanitarian Care

A war waged with numbers /
A numbers war /
The frisking hands of the Papus /
The imposing stares of the Australian officers /
The prisoners trapped in a tunnel of tension /
A huge feature of everyday life for the prisoners /
Day to day . . . /
A monstrous part of life /
This is what life has become, after all . . . /
This is one model constructed for human life /
Killing time by leveraging the queue as a technology /

Killing time through manipulating and exploiting the body /
The body left vulnerable /
The body an object to be searched /
Examined by the hands of others /
The body susceptible to the gaze of others /
A program for pissing all over life.[14]

This *ghazal* from deep in the memoir, written as Boochani's detention stretched past its fourth year, tried to make sense of the system in the detention center, which he knew was a fool's pursuit. The carceral system was designed to make sure no daily patterns were regularized and no routines were continual, keeping the detainees in an endless state of confusion. The offshore detention centers of Operation Sovereign Borders were meant to be punitive and degrading, a "program for pissing all over life," as Boochani wrote, although the detainees were never charged with or convicted of any crime. Queueing for food and toilets took an entire day. He wrote that "young men [stood] in the sun for hours, queueing for dirty, poor-quality food. The meat [was] like pieces of car tyre. Jaws struggle[d] to chew the badly cooked meat."[15] Sunburns from the queues, damaged teeth from the meat, communicable disease, malnourishment, and bites from pests in the jungle created healthcare needs that either went untreated or, if the injured detainee was allowed to visit the clinic, subjected him to levels of degradation that included, among other things, twelve body searches a day. When Boochani had a toothache, he refused to visit the clinic, called IHMS, because of the humiliation that accompanied a visit and the indifference of the staff. Instead, he allowed the Papus to insert "a red-hot wire right into the hole of [his] bastard of a tooth," knowing that if "he had confronted the IHMS system [his] soul would have been engulfed in thousands of IHMS letters, reports, and forms ... and then annihilated."[16] The prisoners admitted to the clinic soon found that they filled in forms and waited in lines for days to be placed on Schedule A, B, or C, depending on which doctor would visit when. The doctors, Boochani explained, were "perceived as messiahs, saviours, but none ever set foot on the island or in the prison. They are scheduled to come next month. But they never arrive."[17]

Boochani describes the waiting—for food, for doctors, for immigration lawyers, for news that his incarceration might end—as "a mechanism of torture used in the dungeon of time," and this, too, differentiates his account.[18] The refugees arrived on Manus shaken from their journey; when they finally left, they were scarred mentally and physically, and twelve were dead. As of this writing in mid-2022, 112 refugees remain on Nauru Island at a cost to Australian taxpayers of $220 million every six months.[19] New Zealand has agreed to offer those remaining a path to citizenship over the next three years, but by 2025, many will have been in the "dungeon of time" for more than twelve years.[20]

This kind of waiting does not fit into what is typically considered humanitarian aid because its cure is political, not material. It cannot be fixed by a doctor or with more food or with a safe place; this kind of waiting in detention or in a refugee camp is "ordinary, chronic, and cruddy," as opposed to situations that are "catastrophic, crisis-laden, and sublime."[21] Boochani details the care received in both types of situations—from the chronic and cruddy in the detention center described above to the catastrophic and sublime in his rescue at sea that follows—and each time it is inadequate.

After a terrifying night in the waves, Boochani and his fellow migrants were rescued by an Indonesian fishing vessel working in the same waters. The Indonesian sailors hauled the migrants aboard, and when the sun rose, the migrants realized they were in the shadow of an enormous British cargo ship stacked with containers that reached "the ceiling of the sky."[22] Blond-haired British sailors peered at the migrants from above then showered them with fresh water to remove the salt and sea from their tired bodies. Moments later the sailors lowered a small platform from their ship with packets of biscuits, cigarettes, and bottles of water. "The whole encounter with the British ship," Boochani wrote, "[was] characterized by extraordinary kindness," although the packet of biscuits was the only thing Boochani would eat for the next four days.[23]

Despite the size and stores of the British ship, the migrants remained on the Indonesian vessel without food for four more days because the Indonesian sailors had no food to share. Dazed with hunger, Boochani threatened other passengers to give him something to eat but soon recognized his folly: "Just imagine my behaviour, imagine my gestures, imagine me making that pronouncement. Imagine me, whose ribs are protruding from his body. Imagine me, a man whose ribs are so visible you could count them. Imagine me in this state, trying to assert myself in this way. What a ridiculous scene."[24] He was powerless and without the physical strength to demand a thing even as he was tethered to a boat that towered with commodities. When he thought he might die from hunger, Boochani found one greasy peanut behind the boat's engines that sustained him for the rest of the trip. Instead of lowering more food, the British sailors leaned over their decks to snap pictures with their cell phones, and in this moment, Boochani's mirror reflects the Western helper in a disconcerting way. The reader's gaze moves from the starving migrant to the copiously provisioned photographers to witness the disparities of aid. With extraordinary kindness, aid provides temporary but inadequate relief.

Boochani's description of his bare existence on the boat and in the camp disrupted humanitarian imaginaries, which at least presume a level of adequate care where it can be given, especially by wealthy nations whose national constitutions support basic human rights. While declarations of human rights grant dignity to the stateless and least fortunate in society regardless of circumstance, in practice, they are inextricably bound to political shifts. Under the present configuration of sovereign powers with the capacity to withhold or deny rights, citizens with rights are fated to observe "minimalist biopolitics," which are defined as the temporary administration of survival within wider circumstances that do not favor it.[25] In the detention center on Manus Island, in circumstances that correspond to the "ordinary, chronic, and cruddy," the prisoners were methodically demeaned. They were given just enough food to induce constant hunger but not starvation; they were supplied with latrines, but no tools to clean them, so they moved among foot-deep filth and stench; they were given beds and shelter, but in enclosures that broiled under the jungle sun making sleep a nightly leaching of sweat onto perpetually sodden mattresses. The aid Boochani received—from his rescue at sea to the day the detention center was officially closed in 2019—maintained minimal physical existence but destroyed the dignity or recognition afforded human beings in international treaties and humanitarian imaginaries. Although his story reveals different things to different readers, his discussions about humanitarian care implicate Western readers in the inadequacies of aid and make visible the systems at work that render the poor and disenfranchised powerless and dependent.

Rethinking the Emergency Imaginary

This whole mess /
In the darkness of midnight /
Looks like death /
Smells like death /
Embodies death /
The cries /
The screams /
The swearing /
The knocking about /
The sounds of the small children /
The heart-wrenching and painful sounds of the little children /
These sounds transform the chaotic boat into hell.[26]

In this *ghazal*, Boochani painted a sensory picture of the dark hours of terror in the Banda Sea. Waves crashed down on the boat, there was no light, there was nothing to do but hold tight to something bolted down and try to gauge the impact of the next wave. I have read scenes like this in other books, so I thought I had a good idea of what was happening and how it might feel, but the intensity of this *ghazal*—and many others within Boochani's telling of the night—make me question how much I can understand this type of desperation. What can I know if the person who had the experience has to break form to approximate it? This *ghazal* signals a pause in the bearable, a time when he could only choke on what was happening. For those escaping from somewhere hoping to reach somewhere better, this terror is an acceptable risk. The children's screams haunted Boochani that night and long after; his description of them haunts me, too, because it disrupts my emergency imaginary.

The emergency imaginary is curated by media outlets that carefully reproduce a few images from the thousands available to them to present the idea of emergency viewers and readers already know.[27] We are consistently presented with images that suggest "what men should be shown doing and women and children should be shown experiencing—we are accustomed to the look of violence, suffering, and need."[28] We are also accustomed to the look of aid. Western media, NGOs, and governmental aid organizations present images that show their capacity to alleviate suffering. The situation is usually narrated by someone else, an observer half a world away, or someone at the scene with the luxury to retreat. It is also narrated as an immediate need with a material solution, not a constellation of problems and crises often brought on by the inaction of the same governments coming to the rescue. Those in need are almost always rendered as voiceless, suffering masses or women and children. To combat the erasure of those in need, Boochani universalized the names he assigned his fellow travelers. He called them The Blue Eyed Boy, The Toothless Fool, The Penguin, The Guy With A Ponytail, and The Robust Muscular Guy, among others. Each is named with a capital-T "The," rendering them both singular and universal, and each is instrumental for the other's survival.

In his writing and his naming, Boochani presented an emergency that was not sated by Western aid. Aid, when delivered, was always the barest of offerings to maintain life at its most minimal. It was not enough when the British sailors offered biscuits, nor when the migrants were finally rescued by the Australian navy. The migrants were not being cared for; they were being managed. The real care given was between those sharing hardship, as it often is during emergencies. During Boochani's night of terror in the waves, the water pump died on the smuggler's boat while many of the passengers sprawled across the decks, sleeping out their exhaustion. "The water pump is a corpse," he observed, "as unmoving as the bodies all over the deck."[29] As sea water flooded the engine room, he formed a bailing chain with The Blue Eyed Boy and the captain's assistant—two buckets at a time to empty a room waist deep with water and leaking gasoline. The Robust Muscular Guy and The Guy With A Ponytail stepped in to help when the first team—malnourished and weak even before the need for exertion—began to flag. Boochani revealed that as kind as Western aid could be, it was a small part of what sustained his humanity during his emergency and its long, cruddy aftermath. The aid he received, whether by choice or by necessity, represents much of the aid given in emergency situations—small bursts of sustenance that have little effect on the larger problems that cause prolonged precarity. The nourishment he needed to maintain his humanity came from his fellow travelers and prisoners, whom he presented with multivalent personalities. Some were sympathetic, some brave, and some gentle, but others were not. Some were nasty, rough, or selfish, and Boochani's narrative challenged the idea that one needs to be "good" in order to be deserving, and that all aid is good, despite how it is packaged in photos or documentaries. In contrast to the emergency imaginary Western viewers are accustomed to, Boochani presented a form of care not usually recognized. He individualized this care with naming and so conveyed the realized capacity of *this* Robust Muscular Guy and *every* robust muscular guy who steps in where others or where nature create suffering.

This distinction purposefully differentiated voices normally marginalized in states of emergency. Boochani and Tofighian recognized their book as an explicit way to make claims on identity when other forces, such as the Papua New Guinean offshore camps supported by the Australian government, aimed to erase it. Tofighian was deeply engaged with Boochani's effort to name people, events, and systems at play within the detention center to make sure they were not swept away as distant situations happening to some distant other. He wrote that for Boochani, naming was "a way to affirm his personhood and establish a sense of authority; naming [was also] a way of reclaiming authority from the prison, disempowering the system and redirecting sovereignty back to the land."[30] Naming impacts the reader, too, so stories blurred by crowds or large numbers are refined and sharpened around a single individual in which readers might recognize themselves, or those they know. By awarding him with their highest honors, the Australian literary community recognized Boochani not as a migrant or a refugee or a prisoner but as a named and worthy individual in much the same way he recognized his fellow prisoners. In addition, the book created a wider circle of belonging of those who consumed his experience as observers yet recognized themselves as helping with aid that did not satisfy actual need.

Then What Makes This Book So Different?

Boochani is not the first writer to weave poetry into his prose, and a sweaty, stinking, insect-infested prison does not lend itself to the form as we generally conceive of it, but the long history of the *ghazal* distinguishes its inclusion here. As a collection of broken shards, the *ghazals* elevate *No Friend but the Mountains* beyond memoir to a reflection of views often left unconsidered or unobserved, like the images of the British sailors snapping pictures of the migrants instead of feeding them, or the Australian jailers responding to prisoners with force and obfuscation, or the Papu helpers reaping economic gain from unethical behavior, or other prisoners slowly descending into mental anguish and physical decay. These images shift the focus from the author's experience by showing the multiple consequences of Australia's offshore processing scheme, disrupting any single imaginary and complicating unity, a move that makes defining the "good guys" and the "bad guys" nearly impossible. The Australians, the Papus, and the British used the refugees to satisfy political or economic interests, which left Boochani and others like him on a prolonged odyssey of suffering and denial reflected in the book's style and title. That the Kurds have "no friends but the mountains" is a saying in their folklore born out in regions where they are fighting to establish a united Kurdistan and in the hostile environments they encounter even when they leave.[31] These interwoven realities reflected in Boochani's writing implicate the Western reader in disturbing, uncomfortable ways and speak to a readership beyond the confines of Western logics.

After what Boochani revealed, Aboriginal leaders rejected the authority of Australia's government to deny entry to anyone at any point along their national border. In protest, they sailed a flotilla to Manus Island in 2019 to distribute Aboriginal First Nations passports to the refugees.[32] Much like the gesture of citizenship Australia's literary community made with their awards, the actions of the Aboriginal leaders exposed the way politics played refugees as pawns in intersecting power struggles. All at once, the refugees on Manus Island were foils for the political might of Australia's conservative government, bodies co-opted in protest by the literary community, symbols of resistance for Aboriginal leaders, and examples of the limits of political systems. Yet even as their standing as a group was essential within these dynamics, the majority of them could only observe and be acted upon—individual refugees have few ways to make claims on their own behalf. Left in this impotent position, Boochani adapted in the only way he could: he wrote. His clandestine texts made readers witness to state practices that not only violated Australian and Papua New Guinean law but undermined international law.

Within his retelling, Boochani also showed how wealthy countries have shifted their humanitarian responsibilities to countries in the global South lacking the same standards for care that would be necessary if refugees were housed on their soil. This practice presumes the only ones who suffer are the displaced, but, in reality, host countries in the global South bearing the burdens of refugee resettlement are stretched beyond what they can accommodate and compromised by their willing participation. Citizens in wealthy nations, cognizant of the effects their country's harmful policies create, can respond with destabilizing resistance, and refugees, the people at the heart of migration issues, are exploited as expendable political or economic tools. In short, none of the participants is unharmed, especially the refugee who is dehumanized and suspended between death and life at its most minimal. Boochani's memoir made these overlapping intersections of politics and human rights visible and forced questions about borders as political containers in the imaginations of like-minded communities. For countries like Australia and the United States, historically populated by immigrants fleeing war, oppression, and lack of opportunity, *No Friend but the Mountains* prompts the questions: Why are open borders now closed, as if the process of becoming a nation is complete? And why are those seeking entry like Boochani judged so differently from those already inside, as if citizenship also conveys moral worth?

The imaginaries for both countries favor strong individuals willing to strike out despite hardship, to work hard and direct their destiny for the better, and to be optimistic in the face of adversity. Throughout Boochani's memoir, he described migrants and refugees with these characteristics in abundance, yet each day of waiting in political purgatory chipped them away so that the carceral system purporting to preserve a national imaginary was simultaneously eroding it. Boochani recognized this, and so did the Australian awards committee, which gave his powerful book an equally powerful afterlife. Because I've read so many refugee accounts, I spent much of this one looking for similarities to the others, but that unsettled feeling I had when I finished revealed a distinct difference. Was I also a character here? A Western reader reflected in the shards of Boochani's experience? As I see it, yes, I was—I am—and I suspect the Australians who reacted to the book, both the Aboriginals offering passports and the literary community offering awards, saw themselves as characters, too. The questions of representation that nagged at me throughout my many readings of *No Friend but the Mountains* were answered in its prose and *ghazals*. Boochani's testimony disrupted unities of voice and narrative by reflecting characters intricately bound to his story and peripherally complicit in its causes and effects.

Megan Butler is a PhD candidate in English at the University of Washington. Her interdisciplinary work bridges English, global mental health, and medical humanities. She worked in the publishing industry for twenty years before directing three local nonprofits for women and children living below the poverty line. Her dissertation, *Writing the Refugee: Labeling, Literature, and the Shifting Imaginary of a Field*, focuses on the changes in literature by and about refugees published over the last twenty years.

Notes

1. Wahlquist, "Behrouz Boochani."
2. Boochani, *No Friend but the Mountains*, 397.
3. Boochani, *No Friend but the Mountains*, xii.
4. Boochani, *No Friend but the Mountains*, xiii.

5. Taylor, *Modern Social Imaginaries*, 24.
6. Ford, "Guarding Our Borders."
7. Hall, "Like Looking in a Broken Mirror."
8. Boochani, *No Friend but the Mountains*, 88.
9. Boochani, *No Friend but the Mountains*, 77.
10. Phillips et al., "Boat Arrivals" (emphasis mine).
11. Yaxley, "Kevin Rudd."
12. Boochani's *No Friend but the Mountains* addresses the distinctions between the Australian and Papu guards throughout. More information about the relationship between PNG citizens and the camps can be found in the documentaries *One Way to Manus* and *Manus: Remember One Thing, We Are Human Beings*.
13. Boochani, *No Friend but the Mountains*, xiii.
14. Boochani, *No Friend but the Mountains*, 307.
15. Boochani, *No Friend but the Mountains*, 190.
16. Boochani, *No Friend but the Mountains*, 308.
17. Boochani, *No Friend but the Mountains*, 312.
18. Boochani, *No Friend but the Mountains*, 62.
19. Frost, "In Reversal."
20. Boochani, *No Friend but the Mountains*, 62.
21. Povinelli, *Economies of Abandonment*, 132.
22. Boochani, *No Friend but the Mountains*, 46.
23. Boochani, *No Friend but the Mountains*, 46.
24. Boochani, *No Friend but the Mountains*, 51.
25. Redfield, "Doctors, Borders," 344.
26. Boochani, *No Friend but the Mountains*, 26.
27. Calhoun, "Idea of Emergency," 33.
28. Calhoun, "Idea of Emergency," 33.
29. Boochani, *No Friend but the Mountains*, 22.
30. Boochani, *No Friend but the Mountains*, 374.
31. Açiksöz, *Sacrificial Limbs*, 17.
32. McNevin, "Refugees."

References

Açiksöz, Salih Can. *Sacrificial Limbs: Masculinity, Disability, and Political Violence in Turkey*. Oakland: University of California Press, 2019.

Boochani, Behrouz. *No Friend but the Mountains: Writings from Manus Prison*. Translated by Omid Tofighian. Toronto: House of Anansi Press, 2019.

Calhoun, Craig. "The Idea of Emergency: Humanitarian Action and Global (Dis)Order." In *Contemporary States of Emergency: The Politics of Military and Humanitarian Interventions*, edited by Didier Fassin and Mariella Pandolfi, 29–58. New York: Zone Books, 2010.

Ford, Clementine. "Guarding Our Borders from the Invading Hordes." *ABC News*, 25 July 2013. Retrieved 7 October 2021 from https://www.abc.net.au/news/2013-07-26/ford-guarding-our-borders-from-the-invading-hordes/4845426?utm_campaign=abc_news_web&utm_content=link&utm_medium=content_shared&utm_source=abc_news_web.

Frost, Natasha. "In Reversal, Australia Agrees to Send Offshore Refugees to New Zealand." *New York Times*, 24 March 2022. Retrieved 24 March 2022 from https://www.nytimes.com/2022/03/24/world/australia/new-zealand-offshore-refugees.html.

Hall, Michael. "Like Looking in a Broken Mirror." *The Bazaar of the Bizarre*, 27 June 2021. Retrieved 12 April 2022 from https://medium.com/the-bazaar-of-the-bizarre/like-looking-in-a-broken-mirror-a52f4cb69aa9.

McNevin, Anne. "Refugees and First Nations Sovereignty." Mellon Sawyer Seminar Speaker Series on "Humanitarianisms: Migrations & Care through the Global South." University of Washington, 16 October 2020. Retrieved 19 July 2022 from https://www.youtube.com/watch?v=QjrqfKLGIBE.

Phillips, Janet, and Harriet Spinks. "Boat Arrivals in Australia since 1976." Parliamentary Library Research Paper, 23 July 2013. Retrieved 22 November 2021 from https://www.aph.gov.au/about_parliament/parliamentary_departments/parliamentary_library/pubs/rp/rp1314/boatarrivals.

Povinelli, Elizabeth. *Economies of Abandonment*. Durham, NC: Duke University Press, 2011.

Redfield, Peter. "Doctors, Borders, and Life in Crisis." *Cultural Anthropology* 20, no. 3 (2005): 328–61.

"Stop the Boats–Operation Sovereign Borders." Australian Government, Australian Customs and Border Protection Service, 13 September 2013. Retrieved 12 October 2021 from https://commons.wikimedia.org/wiki/File:Stop_the_boats_-_Operation_Sovereign_Borders.jpg.

Taylor, Charles. *Modern Social Imaginaries*. Durham, NC: Duke University Press, 2004.

Wahlquist, Calla. "Behrouz Boochani: Detained Asylum Seeker Wins Australia's Richest Literary Prize." *The Guardian*, 31 January 2019. Retrieved 22 November 2021 from https://www.theguardian.com/world/2019/jan/31/behrouz-boochani-asylum-seeker-manus-island-detained-wins-victorian-literary-prize-australias-richest.

Yaxley, Louise. "Kevin Rudd Contradicts His 2013 Pledge to Ban Asylum Seekers as Part of a Papua New Guinea Deal." *ABC News*, 19 July 2017. Retrieved 22 November 2021 from https://www.abc.net.au/news/2017-07-20/kevin-rudd-png-asylum-seekers/8726470.

CHAPTER 15

The Gift of Food
An Islamic Ethics of Care
Amira Mittermaier

Giving a man a fish has a bad reputation. A common view holds that we're better off teaching men how to fish.[1] Despite and against this developmentalist consensus, food continues to be distributed around the globe day in and day out. Free meals change hands at soup kitchens, at places of worship, among neighbors, and at urban community fridges. In what follows, I tell the story of a particular space of food distribution, one grounded in an Islamic ethics of care. This space is called a *khidma*, which literally means "service" in Arabic. At first sight it seems straightforward: food is served to people. But the term *khidma* also contains another dimension. A spiritual economy runs alongside the visible, social, material exchange. The *khidma* is not only about one person giving, another person receiving, and a meal changing hands. It is also and centrally about God. By examining how the idea of "serving God" orients and shapes the gifting of food at the *khidma*, I show how an Islamic ethics of care disrupts a secular humanitarian logic.

The particular *khidma* I want to tell you about is located in Cairo, and more particularly in the buzzing downtown neighborhood of Sayyida Zaynab. Some middle- and upper-class Egyptians avoid this part of the city because they find it too crowded and unruly. Others seek it out specifically to visit Sayyida Zaynab after whom the neighborhood is named. At the heart of the neighborhood is the mosque in which Sayyida Zaynab, the Prophet Muhammad's granddaughter, is allegedly buried (see figure 15.1).[2] The mosque is a site of visitation and intense prayer, with hundreds of people imploring Sayyida Zaynab every day for intercession with God. The space is heavy with affect: worry, grat-

Figure 15.1. • Sayyida Zaynab mosque in Cairo, 2020. © Amira Mittermaier

itude, and hope. The mosque is also a site of distribution. Inside and outside its walls, pious givers distribute food and drink; some hand out sandwiches, others pour water into cups for those on their way to visit Sayyida Zaynab. One man feeds the feral cats around the mosque every day. The giving around the mosque is constant, and it is both spiritual and material. One of the most committed givers at the Sayyida Zaynab mosque was Shaykh Salah, who used to serve free meals twice a day to whomever extended their hand. This was his *khidma*, his act of serving.[3]

Shaykh Salah's daily giving at the mosque occurred in the midst of a city marked by extreme social inequality and filled with humanitarian actors. Besides the Egyptian Medical Syndicate, Médecins du Monde, the Red Crescent, the UNFPA, and UNICEF, there are countless Egyptian NGOs, including many Muslim and Christian organizations.[4] One of the most active and visible humanitarian actors in Egypt used to be the Muslim Brotherhood, the Islamist oppositional movement that was banned in Egypt in the wake of the 2013 military coup. The Muslim Brotherhood's humanitarian orientation was both inspired by the actions of Christian missionaries in Egypt and based on Islamic traditions that foreground the rights of the poor.[5] Like many other Islamist organizations, the Muslim Brotherhood used to run free or low-cost clinics and provided aid to low-income Egyptians across the country. In 1992, after an earthquake in Cairo killed over 550 people and injured nearly 10,000, it took the government over a week to provide relief. In contrast, within hours of the event, the Muslim Brotherhood and other Islamic organizations had come to help.⁶

The Red Crescent and Muslim Brotherhood are obvious players to be included on a map of humanitarian actors in Egypt. But there are also others who give, often day by day, but whose forms of care fit less easily into a frame of humanitarianism, among them Shaykh Salah and his *khidma*. *Khidmas* are more closely connected to Sufi traditions than to Islamist politics. A quiet space of giving, the *khidma* is situated outside of the logic, infrastructure, and rhetoric of humanitarianism. And it is from this location—from the margins of humanitarianism—that I want to reflect on possibilities of care that continue to exist in the time of humanitarianism but that are not exclusively centered on the "human." Shaykh Salah's *khidma* is an evocative site from which to think about, beyond, and against the ethos of humanitarianism. The *khidma* pushes back against habituated assumptions about what good, effective, sustainable, or truly compassionate care should look like. In particular, it lays bare the anthropocentric logic (and limits) of humanitarian reason. It allows us ask: When the human is the only actor we see, what do we overlook? What other forms of care might exist in the world? Which ideas of justice are at play in such spaces of care? Sticking closely to the *khidma*, this chapter offers insight into a religiously grounded form of care that is centrally oriented around God.

Shaykh Salah was ostensibly serving Cairo's poor. At the same time, he was serving God. Hidden from public view, he was deeply immersed in a practice of care without fitting the profile of a humanitarian actor. He did not run, or work for, an organization. He was not registered with the Egyptian Ministry of Social Solidarity or international funding agencies. He did not respond to crises and catastrophes. His work did not ride on compassion. And while he met people's needs, those who received help from him were neither members of particular groups (such as "migrants and refugees") nor representatives of "humanity" at large. They were simply people who showed up when he served food. He responded to need in the here and now, not to suffering in an abstract sense. His giving was quiet, and it was directed by and at God. God-centeredness, however, does not erase the human. Shaykh Salah was a deeply human actor, attending every single day to the needs of other humans, all the while refraining from sacralising the human.

The Visible/Invisible Nexus

A former army employee, Shaykh Salah was retired by the time I met him in 2011. A couple of years later he became a widower. He lived in Helwan at the outskirts of the city and at the end of the metro line. Taking the metro every morning (and learning much about people's needs and Egypt's current issues from the metro ride, as he told me), Shaykh Salah would arrive in the Sayyida Zaynab neighborhood and head toward the small apartment that he rented in a back alley adjacent to the Sayyida Zaynab mosque (the rent was paid by a donor). Then he would go to the market behind the mosque to buy ingredients (with money donated to him), or to the bakery to pick up stacks of discounted flatbread (*'aysh baladi*). After praying at the mosque, he would return to the apartment to begin his daily work of cooking—usually lentils or pasta.

Twice a day Shaykh Salah or his assistant Hassan would use a wheelbarrow to take the big, heavy pots over to the mosque where people were waiting for their daily share. Shaykh Salah would scoop the food onto metal plates and hand them to those lining up.

A homeless man in a wheelchair extends his hand. "Where were you yesterday?" Shaykh Salah asks him.

The next plate goes to a woman from the countryside who is visiting the Sayyida Zaynab mosque. "Eat this! It's a gift (*nafaha*) from Sayyida Zaynab!"

Receiving a plate, one man says, "May God increase [your ability to give]" (*rabbinā yazīdak yā ḥāgg*).

The next two plates go to homeless teenage boys. Shaykh Salah knows them well. "How are you today?" he asks with a smile.

He sees me: "Welcome *yā duktūra*, come help me!"

This is not the time for asking questions or for observing. Shaykh Salah hands me a scoop so I can help serve the food. This is a gift too: not the gift of food but the gift of being able to give food. Drawing me into the circulation, Shaykh Salah turns me into yet another medium of giving, helping to channel divine provisions to those who are hungry. These times at the mosque—the moments of distribution—are my most vivid memories of Shaykh Salah: I see him beaming with joy, giving with joy.

No matter what time of year, day of the week, or time of day, whenever I was in Cairo, I could head over to the Sayyida Zaynab mosque and find Shaykh Salah either at the mosque handing out food or in the small apartment cooking, washing dishes, or taking a break. The breaks were spent drinking tea and reading, usually a book associated with the Sufi tradition. Shaykh Salah's *khidma* became my default field site: whenever others canceled appointments or did not show up, I could visit the *khidma*. Shaykh Salah was always there. He gave and cared and cooked every single day—not only when he felt like it or during heightened moments of crisis.

While giving for spiritual reasons, Shaykh Salah was not naïve about the world or blind to structural inequalities. He was down to earth, had strong political views, and believed that, to overcome poverty, we need government intervention and to "teach the poor" to become more responsible. In theory, he thought that teaching a man how to fish is better than giving him a fish. But despite his occasionally judgmental tone and his developmentalist views, in practice he gave every single day. For him, serving food was a spiritual practice, directed *by* God, and ultimately directed *at* God as well. Shaykh Salah dedicated himself to giving not primarily to address human suffering but because he felt called upon by God to give and because he understood food to be a divine right. On the surface, Shaykh Salah seemed to be serving people: the homeless, street children, people from the countryside who had come to Cairo to pay a visit to Sayyida Zaynab, street vendors, the young policemen from the police station at the Sayyida Zaynab Square in search of a free lunch. And yet, if we situate his logic of giving at the interface of the visible and invisible (as he himself would), then he was not only serving people. He was serving God as well as Sayyida Zaynab.

Sayyida Zaynab, one of the daughters of Ali, the fourth caliph (and first Shia imam), and of Fatima, daughter of the Prophet Muhammad, died in 682 CE. But more than thirteen hundred years later, she was present as ever for Shaykh Salah, and she is present to those who visit her to ask for her intercession with God. As other members of *ahl al-bayt* (literally, the "people of the house"), those who were close to the Prophet Muhammad, Sayyida Zaynab partakes in a world of justice and care that exceeds a this-worldly frame. Members of *ahl al-bayt* are called upon to intercede with God when people face adversities, including when they feel let down by worldly authorities.[7] Hundreds of people come to the Sayyida Zaynab mosque every day to call for her intercession or to thank her. Having suffered much during her lifetime, she is said to be particularly receptive to women's afflictions.[8] Shaykh Salah's *khidma* was closely tied to her mosque and to Sayyida Zaynab's guidance. He followed a divine directive that was mediated by Sayyida Zaynab. She appointed him, put him to work, and made sure donors were directed his way so that he could continue his work of giving.

A widower, Shaykh Salah was actively pursued by two women who wanted to marry him. Even though he was not opposed to the prospect, the marriages did not occur because the women literally could never reach him. One would try to visit him, driving in from the countryside, and every time her car would break down. The other, who lived in Saudi Arabia, died suddenly—before she could convince Shaykh Salah to marry her and relocate. Shaykh Salah attested that a second marriage was not meant to be; "I belong to Sayyida Zaynab," he told me.

Rethinking the "Human" in Humanitarianism

Shaykh Salah was oriented toward God, the Prophet Muhammad, and the Prophet's saintly descendants (*ahl al-bayt*), first and foremost among them

Sayyida Zaynab. As he often reminded me in our conversations, the most important dimension of his giving could not be observed. But while embedded in an invisible, spiritual economy, and ultimately directed by God, Shaykh Salah was not oblivious to people and their suffering. One day when I visited him, he was noticeably tired. I asked if he wasn't feeling well. He told me he was suffering from high blood pressure and, to treat it, had drunk lots of hibiscus tea (*karkadeeh*) the previous night, which in turn kept him up all night as he had to use the washroom every hour.

Why was his blood pressure so high? I asked.

Because of his work: he carries the "worries of people and of the country." He feels with the poor, he told me.

Shaykh Salah's daily giving unfolded in a context of extreme social inequality—a context with which he was intimately familiar through his metro rides and through his daily contact with the vendors, homeless, and downtrodden around the mosque. When I first met him, in the immediate aftermath of the 2011 revolution, this same context had driven hundreds of thousands of people into the streets to call for "social justice" and, literally, for "bread."[9] While the Egyptian state had been offering some social welfare programs, many low-income Egyptians felt let down by the state. Much day-to-day support in Egypt came (and continues to come) through informal channels, NGOs, neighborhood networks, mosques and churches, and spaces such as Shaykh Salah's *khidma*. The kind of giving enacted by people like Shaykh Salah—daily, no conditions attached, and not directly affected by what is happening in the political sphere—allows those struggling in Egypt to get by, or at least not to go hungry.

Shaykh Salah started his *khidma* during the era of President Mubarak (1981–2011) and continued giving throughout most of the Egyptian uprising (2011)—except for a couple of days when the streets felt unsafe, and he stayed home. He gave under Muslim Brotherhood president Mohamed Morsi (2012–13) and continued giving under President Abdel Fattah el-Sisi (2014–present). He had opinions about these political shifts, but they did not affect his work. Ultimately, the world of politics receded into the background when Shaykh Salah did what he felt called upon to do: cook and distribute meals. The *khidma* functioned outside of the realm of politics. It was not driven by political interests, and it did not ride on political convictions. It enacted a giving that comes from God and is directed by Sayyida Zaynab. The way Shaykh Salah described it, the entire area around the Sayyida Zaynab mosque exceeds the realm of worldly politics—or more specifically, the last time we spoke, it was "outside of [President] Sisi's rule" (*khārig 'an hukm al-Sīsī*). In this sphere, Sayyida Zaynab rules.

Because of its seemingly apolitical orientation to an Elsewhere, the *khidma* was not subject to the kind of skepticism with which the charitable work of the Muslim Brotherhood was met over the years. Critics of the Islamist organization, already before the 2011 uprising and before the 2012 elections, worried about it expanding its network and political reach via its charitable activities: charity as a tool for buying votes. Such skepticism could less easily attach itself to Shaykh Salah's *khidma*, which was not pursuing political or personal gains, at least not in this world. The *khidma* was unaffected by changes in the political landscape, and it did not enact a politics of "humanity." As such, Shaykh Salah also never became caught up in weighing the suffering of humans or trying to determine deservedness. He gave to whomever showed up, unlike many Islamic charitable organizations in Egypt (and elsewhere) that extensively debate questions of deservedness. NGOs ask: Can Muslim *zakāt* (alms) funds be spent on non-Muslims in need? Does channeling funds to Somalians, Palestinians, or Syrian refugees make sense when there are citizens of one's own country suffering? Should we first help those close by? How do we prioritize among all those in need? Unfazed by such questions, Shaykh Salah trusted that those who showed up at the *khidma* were guests that had been sent by God. He did not pursue grand this-worldly goals such as eradicating suffering or putting an end to poverty. He simply gave.

Unlike the Muslim Brotherhood, which faced mass arrests, exile, and organizational breakdown after the military coup in 2013, Shaykh Salah continued giving. He fell under the radar of the state because he did not trade in the realm of politics. The only times when government interventions affected him was when the mosque's hours were shortened and when, during the COVID-19 pandemic, "gatherings" (*tagammuʿāt*) were forbidden around the Sayyida Zaynab mosque. Shaykh Salah responded to the latter crisis by handing out food in small plastic bags so people could eat elsewhere.

Throughout, the *khidma* fed people. And yet, in Shaykh Salah's own understanding, the *khidma* was just as much about a divine imperative as it was about human need. God-orientedness does not cancel out human-orientedness but leads to a different ethics, one that decenters the human. What we witness at the *khidma* is not *human*itarianism, but a God-centered ethics of care: Shaykh Salah gives to God, and God gives through him. Foregrounding the God-centered logic of the *khidma* helps undo the fetish of the human that organizes humanitarian reason. Simultaneously, it helps undo the focus on crises that lies at the heart of humanitarianism. Shaykh Salah gave day after day—quietly, repeatedly, persistently. He was not responding to worldly events; he was responding to God.

Submitting to God does not mean being passive. In Shaykh Salah's case, it meant acting consciously and intentionally. It meant hard work. He got up early every day, took the metro, and spent his days cooking, distributing meals, and doing dishes. The extensive labor behind his giving distinguishes it from less embodied forms of charity, such as transferring money via a mouse click to a *zakāt* fund. Shaykh Salah often emphasized that actions matter. He noted that on Judgment Day, it will not be about what you believe or know but about what you *did* in the world. That is also the reason why contributing one's labor—actively assisting Shaykh Salah—is better than just giving him money. In his words, "If someone comes and gives me money, that's good. If he brings me food, better. If he helps me cook, better. If he helps distribute, better. If he washes the dishes, even better!" Shaykh Salah implied that people's actions have consequences in the afterlife and in this world. God punishes and rewards long before Judgment Day.

One day, while taking a brief break from cooking, Shaykh Salah, an avid reader, read to me a hadith (prophetic saying) from a classic on Islamic ethics, al-Sha'arani's *al-Minan al-Kubra*, which he was studying at the time. The hadith had been preoccupying him. It says that people get the ruler they deserve. He explained:

> If people are bad, they get a bad ruler. During [president] Hosni Mubarak's time, people were selfish and had bad morals. The rich kept everything for themselves. It's okay to feed yourself and to have a home, but you shouldn't hoard money while there are poor people. . . . So God sent Mubarak. And it's like that around the world. There are signs of *Yawm al-Qiyāma*, Judgment Day. The coronavirus too. We're not in charge. We're being watched closely.

Once again, Shaykh Salah was not oblivious to politics, and he had his own take on what occurred in the political sphere. In his reading, President Hosni Mubarak, who was forced out of office during the Egyptian uprising in 2011, had been sent by God as a form of divine punishment in response to the Egyptians' bad morals and selfishness. In bringing the hadith to bear on worldly events (presidents and pandemics), Shaykh Salah emphasizes human agency and at once effaces it. If we make bad choices and act irresponsibly, we will be punished. Our actions have consequences. At the same time, we're not in charge. Shaykh Salah was not alone in reading the COVID-19 pandemic as a divine warning.[10] To me, his account was another reminder of how, in his view, human actions matter a great deal and are subject to divine reward or punishment. How we act matters even though we are never fully in control. Shaykh Salah lived this paradox to the fullest, giving every single day without taking credit for his giving. While looking to God, he cared deeply and acted accordingly.

Humanitarianism and Its Discontents

How might we place Shaykh Salah's *khidma* in conversation with humanitarianism? What kind of critique of humanitarianism emerges from this space?

Originally a theological term that emphasized Christ's human nature, *humanitarianism* since the 1830s has come to refer to the belief that a person's highest duty is to advance the welfare of humankind. Didier Fassin identifies "humanitarian reason" as a key ethos of our time and describes it as a set of moral sentiments organized around the suffering of others and the desire to remedy it.[11] Characteristically, humanitarianism focuses on crises—earthquakes and other catastrophes—but it is also at work in the bureaucratic dispensing of welfare directed at immigrants, refugees, the homeless, the unemployed, or the poor. At the heart of humanitarian reason is the human. In Arabic, humanitarianism is most commonly translated as *insāniyya*, a term that can also mean "humanity" and "humanism." Again, the *insān*, or humankind, takes center stage.

Critics have highlighted limits and blind spots of humanitarian reason. Didier Fassin notes that humanitarianism rides on the mobilization of empathy rather than the recognition of rights; it can erase or efface questions of justice.[12] Others point out that, while in theory humanitarianism has a global reach, it works through exclusions: not all suffering moves us; not all lives count equally.[13] Compassion is tricky, fragile, and selective. At the same time, the invocation of humanitarianism (particularly its global appeal, tied to the logic that we are all united by our shared humanity) can become the ground for military action. Talal Asad highlights the violence built into humanitarian logic.[14] Medieval theologians invested the crusades with *caritas* (love, benevolence, charity), and we find a continuation of this uneasy link in manifestations of "post-Christian military humanitarianism." Asad stresses that this is not a perversion of genuine humanitarianism but another articulation of its impulses. We might also think here of US forces marching into Afghanistan in 2001 under the banner of "saving Muslim women."[15]

Humanitarianism is by no means limited to players from the so-called global North or the "West." Humanitarianism, and with it "globalizing rescue industries," are also at home in the global South.[16] They can build on, and merge with, other histories of charity, including Islamic ones. Scholars have described non-Christian and nonsecular genealogies and trajectories of humanitarianism, including through nuanced accounts of Muslim humanitarianisms.[17] Others have written about a neoliberalization of Muslim forms of care, or about how *zakāt* (almsgiving) has been turned into a development tool.[18] These works remind us that Islam is not a sealed-off, static tradition, and that it is certainly not by definition antihumanitarian.

What attracted my ethnographic and analytical attention during my fieldwork, however, was a different form of giving—the kind that we find at the *khidma*. This kind of giving is not neoliberal, is not about helping the poor help themselves, or about development. But neither is it about compassion or a humanitarian impulse. It is a form of giving that involves God as an active player. Through Shaykh Salah's embodied practice, we can see what forms of care become possible when giving is not organized around the logic of the "human" and "humanity."

Shaykh Salah gave every day. He did not give to a particular group of people, and he never questioned whether those receiving his meals were deserving. He also did not care about being seen as good or charitable—about performing a certain kind of goodness. In fact, in the divine logic he embodied, your left hand is not supposed to know what your right hand is giving, and you are not supposed to worry about, or cater to, potential donors who might support your charitable work, including, in his case, those who pay the rent for the apartment in which he cooks, and those who pay for the ingredients.

From within a material and worldly frame we could ask questions about the *khidma*'s sustainability, and we could trace the ways in which Shaykh Salah's spiritual work effectively relied on other people's monetary contributions. To him, however, the donations were part of the spiritual economy he inhabited. He relied on donations to keep the *khidma* running, but the spiritual logic of the *khidma* circumvents, and pushes back against, the elevation of human donors. As Shaykh Salah often explained to me, you are supposed to trust that God will send people your way—both donors and those who receive your gifts. That is also why you should always keep everything in circulation. There is no need to store food or keep backup meals in the fridge. Trusting that God will provide is what keeps the *khidma* running.

Humanitarianism's concern for sustainability, or for ultimately bridging relief to development, falls to the wayside within a logic of giving that seeks to submit to God and trusts in God's provisions. Conversely, while money is needed to keep the *khidma* running, all material and monetary exchanges in such a space are already subsumed within a spiritual economy.

(Beyond) the End

By emphasizing the God-centered-ness of the *khidma*, I do not mean to suggest that God and human are radically opposed. Shaykh Salah was God-oriented and embodied a godly ethics, but he was also deeply human. He cared about those to whom he gave, and he had a frail body that suffered from high blood pressure and that was eventually killed by a virus. Shaykh Salah died on 18 January 2021, having contracted COVID-19—likely while distributing food at the mosque.[19] About a year earlier, the last time I saw him, he told me that it makes no difference to him whether he is "above or below the ground" since he was waiting to meet "our lord" (*rabbinā*).

Whether his *khidma* could be labeled humanitarian was not a question that preoccupied Shaykh Salah. It is a question that I brought to (or imposed onto) his space of giving—inspired by the larger project of rethinking humanitarianism(s) represented by this volume and the workshop that preceded it. Ultimately, this is not a matter of "yes" or "no," but it is a question that can invite us to rethink our categories. Looking closely at different forms of care, aid, and welfare can destabilize the lines commonly drawn between charity, development, and humanitarianism.[20] As Erica Bornstein notes, most scholars of humanitarianism would say that sponsoring the education of an orphan or giving to beggars is different from international humanitarian aid, but in her reading, these forms can be linked through the concept of the gift.[21] Destabilizing conceptual lines is important because it disrupts certainties about which forms of care are needed in the world today, including the common claim that we should shift from "charity" to "development"—the idea that teaching people to fish is better than giving them fish—or the idea that humanitarianism, with its orientation toward the abstract category of "humanity," is better than forms of aid that prioritize those close by.

One option for engaging critically with "humanitarianism" is to loosen our terms and to bring unlikely spaces like the *khidma* into a broadened frame. Another option is to let such spaces push back against the very logic of humanitarianism. I lean toward the latter option. In my view, Shaykh Salah's form of care cannot neatly be subsumed under even a widened framework of humanitarianism. Shaykh Salah was not a believer in "humanity" but a believer in God. His logic of serving (*khidma*) partakes in the same pious grammar that includes the logic of submission (*islām*) and worship (*'ibāda*), etymologically related to the term *slave* or *servant* (*'abd*). Shaykh Salah's giving was joyful and heartfelt, but it never relied on compassion. Just as important, the *khidma* did not displace justice. It was squarely about rights—not legal rights but Quranic ones, and more specifically *haqq al-faqīr* (literally, the right of the poor), the idea that the poor are entitled to a share of the wealth of those who are better off. Shaykh Salah believed that we all owe to God (all wealth comes from, and belongs to, God) and that we owe to the poor. He would often say, "I don't do this for divine rewards [*hasanāt*]; I do it because I owe to God, and I owe to the people." By giving to the poor, you make up for personal shortcomings, for having treated others unfairly, even unintentionally.

It is easy to poke holes in any form of care. From a critical point of view, Shaykh Salah's *khidma* is shortsighted. The food he provides is a mere drop in the ocean. Handing out meals perpetuates dependencies. While such criticism is within easy reach, I suggest pausing the critical impulse, at least temporarily, and asking what we might be able to learn from practices of care that unfold outside of the humanitarian matrix. My point is not to romanticize a religious logic of giving but to invite us to consider how such other forms of care disrupt the very logic of humanitarianism.

I deem this an important exercise because humanitarianism comes with its own blind spots. Not only can it privilege some humans in need over others (let alone humans over other beings); it can itself function as a ground for inclusion or exclusion in the category of humanity. Frequently, when I present on Muslim forms of care that I encountered during my fieldwork in Egypt, audiences deem them too selfish (instrumentalizing the poor to collect points for a place in paradise), or shortsighted (a "drop in the ocean"), or lacking compassion (giving because of a divine imperative, not because one truly cares). It is easy to dismiss other forms of care as uncaring or careless. By taking us into the logic of the *khidma*, I hope to have suggested a different reading. The *khidma* does not ride on human compassion, and it does not primarily respond to human suffering. But instead of reading it as lacking, we can consider how its form of care destabilizes the "human" in humanitarianism and points to other forms of care, including ones that are directed from and toward an Elsewhere. The *khidma* disconnects care from crises and catastrophes, and it disrupts the dichotomy of empathy/justice.[22]

Ultimately, the *khidma* is not about overcoming poverty. It is about divinely mediated circulation. While providing food to those who are hungry, the *khidma* decenters the human. The human is not the object of its intervention, and human sentiment or reason do not provide the ground for its form of care. In a world saturated with humanitarian reason, the *khidma* reminds us that other forms and spaces of care persist. Today Shaykh Salah's legacy is carried on by Hassan. A humble man and proud father of two toddler girls, Hassan used to assist Shaykh Salah, and he quietly took over the *khidma* after his death. The giving continues. After all, the *khidma* was never about Shaykh Salah as a person. It is about divine provisions and about Sayyida Zaynab making sure those around her mosque are fed.

Amira Mittermaier is professor of religious studies and anthropology at the University of Toronto. She is the author of the award-winning *Dreams That Matter: Egyptian Landscapes of the Imagination* (University of California Press, 2010), and of *Giving to God: Islamic Charity in Revolutionary Times* (University of California Press, 2019). Seeking to map out Egypt's post-2011 Islamic landscapes, she is currently working on a project titled "An Ethnography of God." This project also asks about the methodological, conceptual, and political stakes of making space for God in anthropology and ethnography.

Notes

1. Offering a critique of what he calls "the world's most widely circulated development cliché," James Ferguson reminds us that getting everyone to fish might not be the best way forward. It assumes that there are endless jobs for fishermen and endless amounts of fish in the world's oceans. It addresses only men and assumes that all these men are able-bodied. By tracing the effects of basic-income programs, Ferguson asks us to think away from the productionist paradigm. Ferguson, *Giving a Man a Fish*.

2. Others insist that Sayyida Zaynab is in fact buried in a suburb of Damascus, Syria. Regardless of whether the shrine in Cairo houses Sayyida Zaynab's body, the mosque is a buzzing site of visitation.
3. In this chapter I revisit my longstanding fieldwork with Shaykh Salah between 2011 and 2020, also drawing on additional visits and conversations I have had with him since completing my book on charity. Mittermaier, *Giving to God*.
4. In Egypt, humanitarian actors have included those dedicated to a colonial "civilizing mission," and others who have sought to use humanitarianism as a tool of decolonization. Möller, "Questioning the Civilizing Mission"; Framke and Möller, "From Local Philanthropy."
5. Baron, *Orphan Scandal*; Qutb, *Social Justice in Islam*.
6. Sullivan, *Private Voluntary Organizations*, xiii; Benthall, "Charitable Activities," 2–7.
7. Adly, "Saint, the Sheikh, and the Adulteress"; Reeves, "Power, Resistance."
8. Abu Zahra, *Pure and the Powerful*.
9. "Bread, freedom, social justice" was a key slogan during the Egyptian 2011 uprising.
10. Embaby and Mittermaier, "God in Times of Uncertainty."
11. Fassin, *Humanitarian Reason*.
12. Fassin, *Humanitarian Reason*.
13. Butler, *Precarious Life*; Butler, *Frames of War*.
14. Asad, "Reflections on Violence."
15. Abu-Lughod, "Do Muslim Women Really Need Saving?"
16. Amar, ed., *Global South to the Rescue*.
17. Benthall, *Islamic Charities*; Iqbal, "Theorizing Humanitarianism"; Mostowlansky, "Humanitarian Affect."
18. Atia, *Building a House*; Taylor, "Reflections on a Theory."
19. A neighbor of the *khidma* reported to me that, in fact, none of the people around the Sayyida Zaynab mosque contracted COVID-19 since they were protected by Sayyida Zaynab, and that Shaykh Salah must have contracted the virus from neighbors at his apartment in Helwan.
20. Mostowlansky, "Humanitarian Affect."
21. Bornstein, *Disquieting Gifts*.
22. Fassin, *Humantiarian Reason*.

References

Abu-Lughod, Lila. "Do Muslim Women Really Need Saving? Anthropological Reflections on Cultural Relativism and its Others." *American Anthropologist* 104, no. 3 (2002): 783–90.

Abu Zahra, Nadia. *The Pure and the Powerful: Studies in Contemporary Muslim Society*. Reading: Ithaca Press, 1997.

Adly, Eman. "The Saint, the Sheikh, and the Adulteress: Letters from the Heart Addressed to Imam el-Shafi'i in Cairo." In *Narratives of Truth in Islamic Law*, edited by Baudouin Dupret et al., 123–39. London: I. B. Tauris, 2008.

Amar, Paul, ed. *Global South to the Rescue: Emerging Humanitarian Superpowers and Globalizing Rescue Industries*. London: Routledge, 2013.

Asad, Talal. "Reflections on Violence, Law, and Humanitarianism." *Critical Inquiry* 41, no. 2 (2015): 390–427.

Atia, Mona. *Building a House in Heaven: Pious Neoliberalism and Islamic Charity in Egypt.* Minneapolis: University of Minnesota Press, 2013.

Baron, Beth. *The Orphan Scandal: Christian Missionaries and the Rise of the Muslim Brotherhood.* Stanford, CA: Stanford University Press, 2014.

Benthall, Jonathan. *Islamic Charities and Islamic Humanism in Troubled Times.* Manchester: Manchester University Press, 2016.

———. "Charitable Activities of the Muslim Brotherhood." *Journal of Muslim Philanthropy and Civil Society* 2, no. 2 (2018).

Bornstein, Erica. *Disquieting Gifts: Humanitarianism in New Delhi.* Stanford, CA: Stanford University Press, 2012.

Butler, Judith. *Precarious Life: The Powers of Mourning and Violence.* London: Verso, 2004.

———. *Frames of War: When Is Life Grievable?* London: Verso, 2010.

Embaby, Khadija Mohamed, and Amira Mittermaier. "God in Times of Uncertainty." *Religious Matters in an Entangled World* (blog), 21 April 2021, https://religiousmatters.nl/god-in-times-of-uncertainty.

Ener, Mine. *Managing Egypt's Poor and the Politics of Benevolence, 1800–1952.* Princeton, NJ: Princeton University Press, 2003.

Fassin, Didier. *Humanitarian Reason: A Moral History of the Present.* Berkeley: University of California Press, 2012.

Ferguson, James. *Give a Man a Fish: Reflections on a New Politics of Distribution.* Durham, NC: Duke University Press, 2015.

Framke, Maria, and Esther Möller. "From Local Philanthropy to Political Humanitarianism: South Asian and Egyptian Humanitarian Aid during the Period of Decolonisation." ZMO Working Paper, no. 22, 2019.

Iqbal, Basit. "Theorizing Humanitarianism for an Islamic Counterpublic." Allegra Lab, July 2019, https://allegralaboratory.net/theorizing-humanitarianism-for-an-islamic-counterpublic-muhum/

Mittermaier, Amira. *Giving to God: Islamic Charity in Revolutionary Times.* Berkeley: University of California Press, 2019.

Möller, Esther. "Questioning the Civilizing Mission: Humanitarianism and the Arab World in the 20th Century." In *Civilizing Missions in the Twentieth Century*, edited by Boris Barth and Rolf Hobson, 124–41. Leiden: Brill, 2020.

Mostowlansky, Till. "Humanitarian Affect: Islam, Aid and Emotional Impulse in Northern Pakistan." *History and Anthropology* 31, no. 2 (2020): 236–56.

Qutb, Sayyid. *Social Justice in Islam.* Oneonta, NY: Islamic Publications International, 1999.

Reeves, Edward. "Power, Resistance, and the Cult of Muslim Saints in a Northern Egyptian Town." *American Ethnologist* 22, no. 2 (1995): 306–23.

Sullivan, Denis Joseph. *Private Voluntary Organizations in Egypt: Islamic Development, Private Initiative, and State Control.* Gainesville: University Press of Florida, 1994.

Taylor, Chris. "Reflections on a Theory of Zakat." Allegra Lab, July 2019, https://allegralaboratory.net/reflections-on-a-theory-of-zakat-muhum/

CHAPTER 16

Mothering the Dead
Care beyond Life in Kurdistan
Mediha Sorma

Taybet Inan, mother of eleven, was killed on 19 December 2015 by the Turkish army during the curfew enforced by the state of emergency regime. Her body was left on the street to rot while her family watched for seven days (see figure 16.1). The image is a reiteration of her death from the short movie *7 days, 7 nights* by Ali Bozan. I am not sharing this image to provoke an emotional response. It is not here for the shock value. The point I am trying to make with this image is that it has no shock value. I still remember quite vividly how, when I saw the movie, I thought that she blended so smoothly with the debris of war. She was part of the debris of war. Her blood looks as black as the burn marks on the wall, on her right, probably the wreckage of a house. I was shaken to my core by my reception of the image, how I thought Mother Taybet did not stand out in this picture. She did not seem out of place. She seemed to fit. Then I pondered my reception. What had shaped my mental imagery so that I saw Mother Taybet as part of the debris? Was it merely oversaturation of Kurdish death? Was it simply desensitization? What was it that made a Kurdish body so intimately attached to death? And lastly, how do you care for a racialized body as a racialized body when you both are marked with death since birth?

The suffering and death of Kurdish people are presented as a normal part of their existence in contemporary Türkiye. Kurdish people are further seen as a distinct racial community, and their racialized bodies are excluded from the national and international humanitarian care frameworks. Under a never-ending state of emergency declared by the Turkish state, humanitarian care is impossible. By focusing on the mothering practices of Kurdish women, I reveal

Mothering the Dead • 269

Figure 16.1. • A still from the short movie *7 Days, 7 Nights* by Ali Bozan. Wikipedia Commons, public domain, CC-BY. Screen capture by Mediha Sorma.

how they are stripped from their humanity and therefore their humanitarian subjectivity by the constant state of emergency regime that constructs them as the "breeders of separatist insurgency." An intersectional feminist approach is imperative to create an alternative humanitarian framework that attends to the gendered aspect of internal colonization.

Understanding the behavior of the Turkish sovereign in relation to the Kurdish subject over a span of a hundred years is a matter of understanding "the relationship between politics and death in [the] systems that can function only in a state of emergency."[1] The ongoing racialization of the Kurdish body is a site where the state of emergency becomes the norm. The Kurdish body, individual and collective, as a *colony*, "represents the site where sovereignty consists fundamentally in the exercise of a power outside the law (*ab legibus solutus*) and where 'peace' is more likely to take on the face of a 'war without end.'"[2] In the context of this "war without end" where the Kurdish body is dehumanized, humanitarianism, in the conventional sense of the word, becomes impossible. Therefore, Kurdish women mother and care through a maternal grief register in which neither death is negated as a site of nonexistence nor life is necessarily affirmed as an existence free of death.

The *insurgent care* framework I call for in this chapter is a feminist intervention into conventional humanitarian discourse that reduces women living through a humanitarian crisis to their suffering as victims of war. Kurdish women analyzed in this chapter tell a different story. They not only expose the project of modern nation-state building as a site of racialized violence that creates forms of oppression and displacement that fall through the cracks of international humanitarian law. They also generate forms of insurgency through practices of care and social reproduction that are not recognized by the conventional humanitarian frameworks that emerged out of the global North.

In order to understand the complexity of what happened to Mother Taybet and why the Kurdish reproductive body is so intimately connected to death that she doesn't stand out in the debris of war, we need to decenter two dominant tropes associated with humanitarian care: the unquestioned objective to care for the living, and the binary, hierarchical understanding of humanitarian care that is delivered by international humanitarian organizations to the passive recipients in the war-torn global South.

This chapter tells the story of Kurdish mothers who defy both tropes. This is the story of humanitarian subjects who prioritize resistance and liberation over survival. An insurgent care framework helps us understand care as a form of resistance. It acknowledges the racialized body as a humanitarian subject that practices care in a militant way not only to survive a humanitarian crisis but to actively expose and respond to the state as the primary violator of human rights. I first present a brief historical account of the conflict between the Turkish nation-state and the Kurds to show how state violence against the Kurds strips them of their humanity and therefore their humanitarian subjectivity. Then, I present cases of extreme dehumanization where the line between life and death is blurred. These cases reveal how state violence and subjection create violent, corporeal intimacies between the living and the dead. I show that what emerges out of these violent intimacies is a form of mothering and care that reaches beyond death. Finally, I offer examples of insurgent care that urge us to rethink the human, humanitarian care, and resistance by decentering the living and recognizing forms of care that go beyond death.

The Kurdish Question

The examination of the displacement of Kurds and their humanitarian subjectivity or lack thereof offers a unique opportunity to rethink humanitarian care from a nonstatist perspective. Kurds' exclusion from conventional humanitarianism frameworks attests to the statist stance of these frameworks. The resulting dismissal of violence and human rights violations perpetrated against Kurds by the Turkish nation-state exposes not only the limitations and failures of international humanitarian organizations but nation-states themselves as sites of violence. Kurds stand out as the most populous nation in the world that has not established a nation-state. The majority of the Kurdish population

Mothering the Dead • 271

is living in the Kurdistan region within the borders of Turkey, Iran, Iraq, and Syria. For the purposes of this chapter, I focus on the Kurdish people that reside within the borders of the Turkish nation-state and the state violence they have been subjected to for over a hundred years.

Racialization of Kurds in Turkey began in the 1910s with the decline of the Ottoman Empire and became a significant part of the construction of the newly emerging, ethnically homogenous Turkish identity following the collapse of the empire. This chapter elaborates on how Kurds navigated the "long and bitter process of attempting to transform the state from a decentralized empire, based on negotiated arrangements and loose, local control . . . to a modern state capable of competing economically and militarily with European incursion, while addressing the growing threat of nationalist separatist movements within its own boundaries."[3]

As the only Muslim empire "that survived into the age of modernity,"[4] the Ottoman Empire had to transform itself to survive in a new world order and respond to the project of modernity. With increased pressure and threats from neighbors and the rise of nationalisms in Europe, the Ottoman Empire had to respond to the requirements of running a modern state. Ottoman and Turkish intellectuals and Ottoman statesmen who were under the influence of European thinkers "grew increasingly wary and harshly critical of nomadic tribes and other migrants in the nineteenth and early twentieth centuries."[5]

As part of this modernization competition, the Ottoman Empire embarked on a project of internal colonization of its borderlands. This project brought with it an attack on the heterogeneity of the identity of internally colonized peoples because this heterogeneity was an obstacle in the centralization and homogenization attempts of the empire.

The construction of Kurdishness—with its own language, traditions, and cultural codes characterized as a threat to the integrity of the Turkish nation-state—has created conditions of violent racialization that continue to this day. Since the last two decades of the Ottoman Empire and throughout the history of modern Turkey, nationalist narratives have figured Kurdishness as the biggest threat to the Turkish existence, and state violence against Kurds has since become their normative experience. The cases presented in this chapter focus on state violence against Kurds during the latest state of emergency regime, which started after the 2015 general elections.

In June 2015, after the unprecedented victory of the Kurdish party HDP (People's Democratic Party) in the general elections, which caused Erdogan's party to lose its majority in the parliament, the government reinstated the war against the Kurdish population after five years of ceasefire and peace negotiations.

The state violence that was intensified after the 2015 general elections, however, cannot be explained away with the rising authoritarianism of the Erdogan administration. The current administration has been using the same tools and tactics that date back to the late Ottoman era. The history of the conflict between the Turkish state and Kurds is freighted with mass graves, unsolved murders, and enforced disappearances. The 1990s in Kurdistan was an era of "unmarked white Toros Renault cars," cars everybody knew led to torture and death. Since Kurds are not seen as legitimate war victims or refugees, they have never become humanitarian subjects in their homes or in diaspora. The 1990s saw the largest wave of forced migration; over four thousand Kurdish villages were destroyed by the Turkish army, and approximately four million Kurds were displaced. Between 1990 and 1998, 107 Kurds were extrajudicially executed, 1,683 were killed in unsolved political murders, 179 were "disappeared," 348 were killed in police custody and prisons, 468 died in mine/bomb explosions, 1,053 were executed in shootings against civilians. In total 17,955 people were killed by Turkish security forces in the 1990s. In addition to military violence, Kurds were also kept under 24/7 surveillance, physically and psychologically tortured and stripped of their sources of income, which forced them to migrate to non-Kurdish cities in the south and the west, historically hostile environments for Kurds.[6]

The concept of forced migration usually focuses attention on migrants that cross international borders from a statist humanitarian perspective. The humanitarian framework does not concern itself as strongly with internally displaced people who do not qualify for the refugee status, just as the internal colonization that causes their displacement is not recognized as war or disaster by international humanitarian agencies. The Turkish nation-state displaced Kurds throughout the twentieth century through attempts at "Turkification" of the Kurdish region and the forced removal of Kurds to predominantly Turkish cities in the south and west, where they were expected to assimilate. Similarly, the Erdogan administration attempts to "dekurdify" the Kurdish region by changing the demographics once again, and internal displacement of the Kurds is now further complicated by the fact that external migrants like Syrian refugees are integrated into the process by replacing Kurds in the region. Turkey has been praised for hosting millions of Syrian and Afghan refugees through humanitarian practices. Yet, it would be inadequate and inaccurate to figure Turkey as an alternative genealogy of humanitarianism or as a refugee host country without looking at the ways in which Turkey uses modern categories to grant rights to "external" migrants while denying those it considers "internal" migrants, such as the Kurds. In other words, examination of modern Turkey as a biopolitical settler nation-state that hides its forced migration of Kurdish people and its denial of their political status is crucial to any account of Türkiye's emergent position as a host country.

Analysis of the violent exclusion of the Kurds from humanitarian subjectivity and humanitarian care frameworks requires imagining an alternative frame of care. The insurgent care framework I call for exposes the Turkish nation-state as a site of colonial violence that is not recognized as war by international humanitarian frameworks, and it acknowledges the insurgent and militant forms of care practiced by the racialized maternal body. I locate this alternative framework in the Kurdish women's militant response to state violence through their insurgent mothering practices. The alternative frame of care offered in this chapter is organized into two main manifestations of insurgent care: care beyond death and refusal of care as resistance.

Mothering the Dead, Rethinking Care

To explain how a state of emergency regime where all national and international laws are put on hold makes provision of humanitarian care impossible, I started this chapter with the story of Mother Taybet, whose dead body was left on the street to rot in front of her family and neighbors for seven days. Kurds are already excluded from the international humanitarian framework, and they are also prevented from organizing their own care systems due to constant state violence. Mehmet Inan described what it was like to watch his mother, Taybet Inan, rot right before their eyes.

> She just laid there. She was moving indistinctly first, then hours passed, her movement diminished. She stayed out there for seven days. None of us slept thinking dogs could get to her, birds could chip away at her. She laid out there, we died 150 meters away. Seven days. For 7 days, my mother laid out there in dead winter. And the worst part is that we don't know how many hours of it she was injured. I wish, I hope she died instantly. You killed my mother.

The image was something onscreen that I consumed. A still image that did not rot. I did not observe her cross the border between life and death in real time. Even if I looked at the picture for seven days straight, she would still be the same distance from death or life as she was when this image was captured. It was never a temporality issue for me. I did not think about the exact time of her death, nor was I haunted by the lack of that information. All I know is that she died on 19 December 2015. Her family watched her die all day and still do not know when exactly she did die. To me, it was an image of a past event with a recognizable beginning and an end that happened on a linear temporality. For them, she is still dying out there.

The state violence Kurds have been experiencing for decades has created conditions where traditional practices of care that occur after death—such as funerals, memorial services, collective mourning, and religious rituals—are made impossible. Kurdish funerals have always been a site of conflict due to the politicization of Kurdish death both by the Kurds and the Turkish state. The oppression of the Kurdish people and their resistance movement offer numerous examples of how a racialized body remains a site of conflict after his/her death. In other words, examination of the alternative framework of care Kurdish women create requires seeing Kurdish death not as a physical and temporal end of a life but as a politically charged site of oppression and resistance where racialization and state violence continues. State violence against the racialized body continues beyond death, and so does Kurdish mothering. The following examples reveal the limitations of the conventional frameworks of humanitarian care that focus on rescuing and caring for the living and dismiss the systems and practices of care where the line between life and death is violently blurred.

Mother Emine is one of the mothers who lost a child during the Cizre siege. Her daughter, Cemile (ten), was shot while playing in their garden. Because of the curfew and constant gunfire in the streets, the family could not bury her. Mother Emine had to keep Cemile's body in the freezer for six days (see figure 16.2). Mother Emine lived with the body and the specter of her dead daughter in her kitchen: "We have kids who we keep in the fridge, who died in our basements.... What are we supposed to forget, huh? Our basements, which became our kids' graves? I open the door of the freezer 20 times a day, I see her body every time."[9]

The violent intimacies established between the dead/dying children and their mothers have been a part of the Kurdish history and collective Kurdish memory for decades. A lot of the mothers I interviewed in Istanbul and Amed referred to certain images embedded in this collective memory and constantly reproduced in the present through racialized maternal grief. The image of Ceylan Önkol, a fourteen-year-old girl who was a shepherd and was killed grazing her animals, is one of them. The officials claimed she stepped on a land mine, but her family and local NGOs believe she was hit by a mortar fired from a military base. Upon her death, Ceylan immediately gained historical significance because her death lays bare the violent intimacy forcibly created by the state between Kurdish mothers and their dead children. Her dismembered body was placed in the front yard of the gendarmerie (rural police force) station, not covered, displayed publicly (spectacularized), and her family members were questioned right by her body parts for four hours. After the questioning, Ceylan's mother, Saliha Önkol, picked up the pieces of Ceylan's body, put them in her skirt and carried her home. Kurdish death is a dying without a foreseeable end. The state turns spaces of care and intimacy and reproductive body into sites of conflict. Out of the violent intimacies where death spills into life and dead bodies literally blend with the living emerges a form of care that seems counterintuitive from a traditional humanitarian perspective. Militarization of the private sphere and reproductive body reorganizes Kurdish mothering from being an affective practice into an act of militancy.

Mothering the Dead • 275

Figure 16.2. • A photo of a viewer looking at the online news site *Evrensel*'s coverage of Emine Cagirga standing in front of the freezer where she kept her daughter's dead body for six days, 2022.[8] © Mediha Sorma.

Militant Mothers: Rescuing the Dead and Refusal of Care

Mother Emine and Mother Saliha were/are spatially and temporarily stuck in a coexistence with their dead children. Violent intimacies forged between the dead and the living and the temporal and spatial reorganization of the boundary between life and death in the Kurdish context radically transforms the way Kurdish women mother and relate with death. As demonstrated in the previous section, state violence against Kurds continues beyond death, and so does the resistance to it. This section centers stories of Kurdish mothers whose mothering practices and systems of care in response to state violence are not only affective but also militant. The insurgent care framework I call for challenges the humanitarian care narratives that recognize racialized women only as victims of war and fail to see them as political subjects actively involved in anticolonial resistance movements. In other words, Kurdish women are not only excluded from humanitarian subjectivity; their suffering also falls through the cracks of national and international laws suspended by the state of emergency. They are erased from the imagination of what resistance looks like, as well. The stories in this section disrupt the narrative trope of gendered erasure. The following cases reveal three interconnected practices of insurgent mothering and care that are essential to the imagination of the insurgent care framework I am calling for: rescuing the dead, refusal of care, and mothering toward death.

The first story is about Kurdish women who divorce their grief from the physical body of the lost subject. Dead bodies of the loved ones are deliberately unconsecrated by Kurdish women for the dead to escape further state violence. Sinan Antoon urges us to think about care beyond the living. He says that "material and discursive resources and energies are dedicated to rescue the living and to tend to their wounds," which is never enough; care is always carried out unequally. Indeed, "humans live very unequal lives and the inequalities that structure their lives extend to their deaths and beyond as well."[10] Systems of racialization not only make certain lives expendable but also make certain deaths ungrievable.

The mothers of Cemile and Ceylan know all too well that death of a body does not necessarily stop its racialization and remove it from the state's reach. Antoon aptly argues in his talk that "death is not the total equalizer. It is rather the in-equalizer." Inspired by real-life examples of caring beyond death, the novelist Antoon creates fictional characters such as Jawad, a man who strives to rehumanize the dead by washing the corpses in *The Corpse Washer*, or Wadood, an eccentric bookseller in *The Book of Collateral Damage*, who tries to catalogue everything destroyed by war: from objects, buildings, books, and manuscripts to flora and fauna, even humans. In both books by Antoon, the boundaries between the dead and the living and the human and nonhuman are blurred.

Two Kurdish women who "rescue the dead" employ a different strategy. They do not rescue them by physically tending to the corpses but by freeing their value from the corporeality of their bodies. Indeed, "even the dead will not be safe from the enemy if he is victorious,"[11] and therefore the dead must be rescued.

Kurdish mothers take away the state's power over dead bodies by devaluing the physicality of a dead body and saving it from being a site of power to discipline the living. As Mother Bedia told me:

> My daughter joined the PKK and fell martyr five months later.... When we went there to claim her body, I chanted "Martyrs don't die!" The policeman said they wouldn't give us the body if I kept doing it. I said, "Give her to me or not. It doesn't matter. I saw my kid. I know she is a martyr. You killed her. That's all I need to know. You can feed her to dogs if you want. It doesn't matter whether I bury her, do this or that. You can let the dogs eat her!"

Mother Bedia's approach to her daughter's dead body is almost identical to that of many Peace Mothers I interviewed. After three decades of witnessing extreme dehumanization of the Kurdish body by the state, Kurdish women created an alternative register of care and grief that operates beyond death and does not require a physical body for care to happen. The radical dismissal of the physical connection between the dead and the living as the ultimate condition for the emergence of maternal grief and the insurgency that follows it prevents the state from managing the Kurdish body successfully as a site of intimidation and discipline.

Mother Emine's is another case where DNA connection loses its significance as part of the Kurdish grief register. When I interviewed her, Mother Emine told me that her father and her uncle were taken from their house, executed at the police station, and buried in a mass grave.

To clarify, I asked her, "So your father doesn't have a grave?" And Mother Emine responded:

> He does not, Love. They say he does, but he doesn't. My dad is buried in a hole with ten people. I went there a year ago. I went and had those eleven people dug up. They have a grave now in our village. We buried them all together. They said they could run a DNA test [to identify which bones belonged to her father]. I said I didn't want a DNA test. They gave us the bones. We brought them to the village and buried them together. They say, "Let's do a DNA test." I say, "They all are my father," because our blood became one with those who were killed with my father.

Her account demonstrates that Kurdish women reject the individuality of death and grief and that Kurdish maternal memory operates in a collective and noncorporeal fashion. Death is not about an individual body. It happens to the Kurdish body as a collective.

As the examples above suggest, Kurdish mothers create a unique register of care and rescue the dead by detaching Kurdish maternal memory from the physicality of the subjects it remembers, and by doing so Kurdish mothers neutralize the sovereign's power over death. The state retains its power to kill, but the reach of state violence ends when the body dies, which is also when Kurdish mothers' insurgency through radical practices of care starts. Kurdish mothers not only free the Kurdish body from being a disciplining tool against the living but also create an insurgent memory and a radical grief register that operate in an eternal temporality that is noncorporeal, collective, repetitive, and militant.

The second story is the story of Kurdish women who refuse to care. The conditions of the never-ending war that make it impossible for Kurdish mothers to do care work in traditional ways do not lead to a failure in motherhood but to a refusal of traditional motherhood roles for the sake of militant insurgency. Kurdish mothers acknowledge the fact that the affects, roles, legitimacies, and values that have traditionally been attached to motherhood have never been granted to them in the first place due to their construction as the breeders of separatist insurgency. They are discursively excluded from the nationalist configuration of motherhood in which mothers are recruited as the mothers of the nation who reproduce Turkishness. Kurdish mothers claim an "illegitimate" motherhood role to resist the state and reproduce bodies of insurgency and antinationalist political discourse.

Mother Didem is a Kurdish mother I interviewed in Amed. She is one of the most active members of Peace Mothers with a long history of political activism and incarceration.[12] She told me:

> I was actively involved in Kurdish politics even before I joined Peace Mothers. I would go to the Newroz celebrations, protests, etc. Sometimes my family would ask me why I was going, and I would say, "I feel guilty if I stay home. My conscience would eat me away if I stayed." Luckily my kids took after me. They are involved in the movement. Their dad would blame me for getting them involved. I was arrested twenty-one times. They raided my house twenty times, kept me in police custody for three, four days every time I was arrested.

What her statement demonstrates is that the urge she feels to participate in the Kurdish resistance outweighs her urge to care for and protect her children, which is traditionally the ultimate life purpose of a mother. Mother Didem does not do the care work because, as a political activist arrested repeatedly, she is simply not there to do it. However, her agency as a political subject must be acknowledged here. The arrests are not the reason why she does not do the care work. The fact that she does not do the care work is the reason why she is arrested. Kurdish mothers' consciousness and conscience as a racialized subject to commit to the Kurdish resistance and caring for the Kurdish body as a collective rather than operating in a framework where motherhood is restricted to an affective relationship between an individual mother and her child has been the driving force for the state to mark them as a threat to the Turkish nation. The "illegitimate" mothering practices of Kurdish women criminalize them.

During my fieldwork, I listened to Peace Mothers' self-reflexive accounts of their mothering practices. It is a constant internal conflict for them to reconcile their political identity with their motherhood. As Mother Didem told me:

> My children were never happy. You will ask how I mean. They were never happy because I kept leaving them to go to protests. I was aware what I was doing. I would tell myself to stay home with my kids, but I never did. It was not what they signed up for. They didn't choose that life. Do I have regrets? Definitely not. I was never there for them. I would leave them on their own and run to the streets. I was fighting for peace. I left them alone a lot. . . . They are proud of me, though. They support me. They say, "Mom, you go, we got this." I sometimes tell them, "How unfair it was for me to treat you like that. I would leave you alone when you were little." They would look after each other. The older would take care of the younger. I feel guilty sometimes because I left them alone a lot, but I had to. I am not afraid of the state. I have one life. If it has come this far, it can go wherever from now on. I do not care.

Almost every mother I interviewed made self-reflexive comments like the one presented above, and yet none stated that they regret the way they cared for their children. None of them called themselves a failure as a mother. Moreover, all the children I talked to were unanimously proud of their mothers all the while acknowledging the hardships they went through when they were kids. Kurdish children's appreciation of their mothers despite what they have been put through by them is proof that Kurdish mothers may neglect their daily motherhood duties for the sake of resistance, but they never neglect the social reproduction aspect of their motherhood that instills Kurdish political consciousness into their children.

The third story is the story of women who mother toward death. A common thread in the narratives of Peace Mothers I interviewed is the pride they feel toward their guerilla children, dead and alive. I did not hear a single expression of resentment, anger, or disappointment from Peace Mothers I interviewed toward their guerilla children. On the contrary, three of the Peace Mothers I interviewed in the Istanbul diaspora complained about their children not being politicized enough. They asserted that the perks of modernity and urban life and the diaspora conditions of urban capitalism led to their assimilation. As Mother Emine said:

> Vallah, my dear, I wanted them to go to the mountains, but their dad and his family stopped them. They are not as close to the movement as I am. I cannot lie, they are not. My husband also minds his own business. I went through a lot. I was humiliated, I was beaten. Only those who tasted state violence know how I feel. My children don't know.

Peace Mothers' celebratory attitude toward violence is not only a vicarious one that they develop through their children. As I argued earlier, their role in Kurdish resistance is much more than being peripheral subjects of affective resistance.

When there are only three forms of existence available to Kurdish children (dead, guerilla, or prisoner), there is no point in taking a defensive stance against the state. Therefore, Kurdish maternal politics become militant and offensive. Mother Perihan's account is a clear example of how the Kurdish home operates as a site of counterknowledge production:

> I was expecting my daughter to join the army. I knew it. She was such a patriotic child [*yurtsever*] that she was going to go to the mountains sooner or later. As I mentioned before, resistance [*mucadele*] is all we talk about at home. Resistance is our whole world. We know nothing else. We don't talk about anything else.... I am extremely proud of my daughter who joined the army. I am so happy that a piece of me is fighting in those mountains.... When I see Yazidi women being sold in street markets, or ISIS militants kidnap women and girls or this or that, I tell my other daughter, "I won't stop you, if any of you decide to go to the mountains. I am so grateful that my daughter is fighting against the brutality." I felt so proud when she left. I never cried. Not even once.

Thus, instead of keeping the conflict out of the private space, Kurdish mothers make conflict a constant component of their household. Even when there is no physical conflict at home, they make conflict constantly present at home by not talking about anything but resistance and watching the resistance on TV. They make sure the enemy and its unspeakable actions are known to their children. When she says, "I was expecting my daughter to join the army. I knew it. She was such a patriotic child [*yurtsever*] that she was going go to the mountains sooner or later," Mother Perihan implicitly points at how her mothering practices led to her daughter joining the army and makes explicit reference to the insurgent social reproduction she practices when she says, "When I see Yazidi women being sold in street markets, or ISIS militants kidnap women and girls or this or that, I tell my other daughter 'I won't stop you, if any of you decide to go to the mountains. I am so grateful that my daughter is fighting against the brutality.'" Mother Perihan's involvement in Kurdish politics and her construction of the private space as a site of insurgency is the driving force that led her daughter to join the Kurdish army.

The conditions created by the never-ending state of emergency Kurds have been living in for over a hundred years has transformed their relationship with death. The fact that death has been a constant part of their everyday lives, a physical component of their household, and a specter that dominates their collective memory strips away death's threatening quality. In other words, death stops being the ultimate physical and temporal state that marks the boundary between the dead and the living. There is more to life than life itself. Care work, then, stops being about survival of an individual subject. It is about reproducing resistance in ways that do not necessarily lead to survival.

Leyla Güven, who has been in prison since 2019, is a former member of the parliament affiliated with the Kurdish Party (HDP). I interviewed her during my fieldwork in Amed, and she told me the reason why she went on a hunger strike and almost died when she was in prison:

> When we believe in a cause, we act knowing that we should risk death for that cause. We definitely do not glorify death, though. We do not live to die. We fight to live and ensure our people live. We say everybody has the right to live and live happily. However, sometimes in order to live, you have to walk toward death.

Leyla Guven is a significant figure in Kurdish politics and Kurdish feminism. She follows a legacy of Kurdish women who engaged in practices of violent insurgency such as self-immolation, guerilla warfare, hunger strikes, and suicide bombings. The tradition of self-harm as a form of resistance exemplifies an important trait that characterizes Kurdish resistance where the Kurdish reproductive body stops being an affective subject in the periphery of resistance and becomes a militant political subject that creates violent insurgency through her body.

Conclusion: Daring to Care

After a hundred years of oppression and extreme state violence, Kurds respond to being excluded from the national body and international humanitarian care frameworks by refusing to become humanitarian subjects and instead shifting the focus of resistance from valuing life to radically embracing death both for themselves and their children. They not only mother their children beyond death but also mother them *toward* death. The Turkish state's internal colonial practices have created forms of care and resistance that are not immediately recognizable due to the limitations of statist humanitarian care frameworks. *Mothering the dead*, *refusal of care*, and *mothering toward death* are practices of care that break away from the established norms of mothering and imaginations of resistance that cannot aim beyond the preservation of life. The Kurdish reproductive body has always been situated at the limits of life and death both as breeders of life and makers of death.

Mother Taybet lies "comfortably" in the debris of war. She has always been there. What shaped my mental imagery when I thought she didn't stand out in the picture is, then, the physical and epistemological proximity of the Kurdish reproductive body to death. When you constantly transgress the line between life and death, the line disappears, and you mother in the absence of this line. In other words, the act of care for the racialized body, with her lack of humanity and humanitarian subjectivity, is an act of transgression.

The insurgent care framework I offer in this chapter attends to the complexities of internal displacement, acknowledges racialized women as active members of anticolonial resistance movements, and reveals practices of mothering and care that prompt us to rethink the boundaries of the human and humanitarian care. Exposing life as a form of prolonged suffering rather than the antithesis of death due to constant state violence takes away the sanctity of it and therefore denies the state the power to use death as a deterrent to insurgency.

Mediha Sorma was a predoctoral fellow of Mellon Sawyer Seminar *Humanitarianisms* during 2020–21. Her primary fields of interest are feminist theory, critical race theory, Turkish studies, reproduction and motherhood, queer theory, and transgender studies. Her dissertation, "Militant Mothers of the Kurdish Resistance: Statelessness, Mothering and Subaltern Politics in Contemporary Turkey," examines the ways in which Kurdish women create insurgency through radical/militant practices of mothering that defy the boundaries of global North feminist scholarship on reproduction and motherhood.

Notes

1. Mbembe, *Necropolitics*, 70.
2. Mbembe, 76.
3. Eissenstat, "Modernization, Imperial Nationalism," 432.
4. Deringil, "They Live in a State," 1.
5. Kasaba, *Movable Empire*, 7.
6. Gazi, "Faili Meçhul Cinayetler."
7. Degirmenci, "Bitmeyen Yedi Gunluk Karanlik."
8. The headline in Turkish reads "Cemile Çağırga'nın annesi: Nasıl 'evet' diyelim?" (Cemile Cagirga's mother: How could we say "Yes"?).
9. Muftuoglu and Zozan, "Cemile Çağırga'nın annesi."
10. Antoon, "Rescuing the Dead."
11. Benjamin, "On the Concept of History," 391.
12. Peace Mothers is an organization established by Kurdish mothers in 1997.

References

Antoon, Sinan. "Rescuing the Dead." YouTube. 1 April 2021, 1:07:41. https://www.humanitarianisms.org/spring-2021-rethinking-the-human.html.

Benjamin, Walter. *Selected Writings*. Vol 4: *1938–1940*, edited by Howard Eiland and Michael W. Jennings. Cambridge, MA: Harvard University Press, 2003.

Bozan, Ali, dir. *7 roj 7 şev* (7 Days, 7 Nights). 2018, 3 min., 7 sec. https://vimeo.com/253946851.
Deringil, Selim. "They Live in a State of Nomadism and Savagery: The Late Ottoman Empire and the Post-colonial Debate." *Comparative Studies in Society and History* 45, no. 2 (2003): 311–42.
Eisenstadt, Howard. "Modernization, Imperial Nationalism and the Ethnicisation of Religious Identity in the Late Ottoman Empire." In *Nationalizing Empires*, edited by Stefan Berger and Alexei Miller, 429–59. Budapest: Central European University Press, 2015.
Gazi, Filiz. "Faili Meçhul Cinayetler Niçin Çözülemiyor?" *Bianet*, 13 January 2017. https://m.bianet.org/bianet/siyaset/183584-faili-mechul-cinayetler-.
Kasaba, Resat. *A Moveable Empire: Ottoman Nomads, Migrants, and Refugees*. Seattle: University of Washington Press, 2009.
Klein, Janet. *The Margins of Empire: Kurdish Militias in the Ottoman Tribal Zone*. Stanford, CA: Stanford University Press, 2011.
Mbembe, Achille. *Necropolitics*. Theory in Forms. Durham, NC: Duke University Press, 2019.
Muftuoglu, Dicle, and Fendik Zozan. "Cemile Çağırga'nın annesi: Nasıl 'evet' diyelim?" *Evrensel*, 7 April 2017. https://www.evrensel.net/haber/315142/cemile-cagirganin-annesi-nasil-evet-diyelim.
Ümit Üngör, Uğur. *The Making of Modern Turkey: Nation and State in Eastern Anatolia, 1913–1950*. Oxford: Oxford University Press, 2012.

CHAPTER 17

Unintended Consequences
Debating the Protection of Cultural Heritage during Humanitarian Crises

Stephanie Selover

In the summer of 2010, I arrived in Raqqa, Syria, located on the banks of the Euphrates River in north-central Syria, to begin archaeological excavations at the site of Tell Zeidan. Although I had worked at several archeological sites in the Middle East, this was my first excavation in Syria, and I hoped to complete my doctoral dissertation on this site. I worked for the next six weeks excavating the remains of a Late Chalcolithic (ca. 4000 BCE) settlement and cemetery with amazing preservation and materials. I grew to love the city of Raqqa and its inhabitants, despite the incredible heat and winds. After closing for the season and returning to Damascus, the team excitedly spoke about our planned return the next summer.

Instead, like many of my colleagues, I watched as the country split into factions. The initial response by myself and my colleagues at the start of what became the Syrian Civil War was a combination of confusion and cheer. We did not immediately believe the situation would become violent. In fact, the first few weeks of the Arab Spring period within Syria were nonviolent, with protesters seeking the end of martial law in Syria and new freedoms rather than the fall of the al-Assad regime. I remember and still have emails between colleagues and myself celebrating the first demonstrations, the capture of the city of Raqqa by the Free Syrian Army, and the tumbling of the statue of former president Hafez al-Assad in the central square in Raqqa. Meanwhile, archaeological groups began to plan their 2012 summer excavations seasons, including the site of Tell Zeidan, believing the situation would calm down and work would continue.

However, as the events in Syria turned from peaceful protests to violent responses by the Syrian regime, the archaeological community began to understand the severity of the situation. International media broadcast accounts detailing great losses of life as the cities and monuments of this beautiful country were destroyed through warfare and intentional destruction. We heard even more tragic and personal accounts from our Syrian colleagues, as the city of Raqqa itself eventually became the de facto capital of the Islamic State (IS). The IS created for itself its own ideal version of Islam and Syria, one that did not allow for any dissention or alternative understandings of Islam, or how it was practiced or represented. The IS set about systematically destroying any physical representations and evidence of these alternative versions within its territories. Through a series of well-publicized videos and pictures, the regime simultaneously presented to the world a vision focused more on the annihilation of pre-Islamic materials while obscuring the violence toward Islamic sites.

As the humanitarian crises within Syria raged on, the subject of cultural heritage destruction during times of war became a major topic of conversation among concerned scholars—archaeologists, philologists, historians, and museum workers, both foreign and Syrian. Foreign archaeologists generally are in a unique position from other types of foreign scholars or employees, as we often spend many years working within a country, frequently in rural regions away from larger cities, developing long-lasting ties to local communities. With the rise of violence within Syria, these groups began to try and find ways in which they could help Syrian colleagues who remained within the country.

This situation led to a series of new initiatives across the world of Middle Eastern archaeology. These initiatives were set in place to help from outside Syrian borders, ranging from sending support to archaeologists within the country to surveying the destruction of heritage sites via the continual observation of real-time satellite photography. However, these initiatives, though undertaken with the best intentions in mind, did not always result in the projected consequences. Looking back from 2012 to today, we can now both begin to reexamine what was done by the IS and why it was done, as well as what was deemed worthy of documentation by foreign archaeologists and what were the consequences of our actions. In retrospect, while the intentions of archaeologists were laudable, the actual results have far more often been solely for the benefit of foreign archaeologists, the US State Department, and the creation of new archaeological methodologies rather than any measurable gain or help for the country for which we claimed to care so deeply.

The Televised and Invisible Destruction of Cultural Heritage within Syria

From the beginnings of the Syrian Civil War to the present, destruction of cultural heritage sites and materials have been rampant in Syria and the tolls upon the human population continue to rise. There are two separate forces at play in this destruction, the Islamic State (hereafter IS), also known as the Islamic State of Iraq and Syria (ISIS) or Daesh, and the Syrian government, under President Bashar al-Assad. Though the IS controlled up to one-third of Syrian territory at its height, the al-Assad government continued its campaign against other rebel groups within its borders. These included Al-Nusra, the Free Syrian Army, and a growing movement of united Kurdish groups who hoped to create an independent Kurdish state out of Kurdish territories in Syria, Türkiye, and Iraq.

The continued warfare between the Syrian government and various factions led to the widescale destruction of numerous urban centers, most notably Homs in western central Syria and Aleppo near the northwestern Turkish border. Holdouts of rebel groups in the regions motivated the Syrian government to attack these centers, and both sides used important cultural and archaeological sites as places of refuge. As an example, the Syrian government attacked the Aleppo Citadel against incursions by the rebel Free Syrian Army. This important site dates to as early as the third millennium BCE and is one of the largest remaining and best-preserved medieval castles in the world. The site, located in the Old Town of Aleppo, has been a UNESCO World Heritage Site since 1986 and is one of the best known archaeological and cultural sites within Syria. Much of the site was destroyed between 2012 and 2016 as it was bombed. Both sides accused the other of being responsible for the damage. Elsewhere in Aleppo, the famous Suq (marketplace), and the Umayyad Mosque, one of the oldest mosques in the world, were both critically damaged in the fighting. In these cases, the destruction of the Old City in Aleppo was not intentional but a byproduct of the fight between the Syrian Army and the Free Syrian Army for control of the city. The destruction was often portrayed as an unfortunate casualty of the war by international media coverage. Both Middle Eastern and Western news sources reported widely on the damage of these well-known sites, while considerably less was written, for example, about the destruction of domestic buildings elsewhere in Aleppo, or damage in less prominent locations in Syria, such as Homs.

In the IS territory, destruction of cultural heritage sites was more systematic and focused. Many articles, reports, and books have been written about the rise and fall of IS, though the group still exists and exerts control globally. At the height of the IS power in 2015, the global community watched outraged and sickened as Syrian cities fell to the IS and thousands of Syrian citizens were murdered and engulfed in the violence of the Islamic State. Entire populations were murdered by the regime, with particular violence inflicted upon minority groups such as the Yazidi.

The IS was and remains a politically savvy, twenty-first-century organization. The regime was fully aware that the eyes of the world were watching, and it created slick social media campaigns to bring awareness to its actions, seeking both to outrage and to recruit. The IS used a variety of methods to broadcast messages to the world, including publishing streaming videos, websites, and social media content on Twitter, Facebook, and Instagram. The regime even published a glossy English-language magazine called *Dabiq*.[1] These global campaigns highlighted a variety of the IS's actions, including the conquests of new territory, murders of perceived enemies, and the destruction of cultural heritage located in territories it controlled.

In many ways, the destruction of cultural heritage as it was filmed and presented on IS social media became the global symbol of the IS regime represented to the outside world. This was understandable—as the IS published viscerally violent videos that depicted graphic massacres of civilians, the destruction of a building or a statue was far easier to ingest.

Perhaps the most famous of the IS's publicized spectacles was the destruction of the large guardian *lamassu* (Mesopotamian bulls with human heads) statues that once stood at the gated entrance to the Assyrian site of Nineveh, located in Mosul, Iraq. Other videos featured the wanton destruction of objects in the Mosul Museum, and, within Syria, the destruction of Palmyra.

Palmyra is located in central Syria within the Homs Governate. While this archaeological site has habitation levels dating back to the Neolithic period (ca. 5000 BCE), it is best known for its remarkably well-preserved Roman-era settlement and cemeteries. Palmyra was a major tourist attraction before the civil war began and one of the best-known archaeological sites in the country. The IS took control of Palmyra in 2015 and shortly began destroying important buildings and statues. The IS produced videos flaunting this destruction, including of the famous Lion of Al-Lat, the Temple of Bel, and the Arch of Triumph. These recordings were professionally produced and widely distributed through international sites such as YouTube and Facebook to reach as wide an audience as possible. They were further disseminated through news programs replaying the videos and thus were a highly effective form of propaganda for the IS. In these videos, the IS labeled these objects as forms of idolatry and thus worthy of destruction.

However, these videos did not tell the entire story. While the IS did in fact destroy many artifacts and buildings, the regime often collected anything that could be moved to sell on the black market to collectors, generally in Western countries such as the United States, England, or France. So, while propagandist videos depicted cultural heritage destruction, the IS was simultaneously collecting and selling artifacts to be sold outside of Syria to raise funds for its efforts.

Further, documents later found in former IS territories revealed that the IS was not only systemically excavating archaeological sites but also issuing official archaeological excavation permits to Syrian archaeologists for various sites within its territory. Official documents record IS laws that forbade unofficial looting of archaeological sites without IS permission, stating, "It is prohibited for any brother from the Islamic State to excavate antiquities or give the permit to anyone from the public without receiving a stamped permit issued from the Diwan of Natural Resources and Minerals-Antiquities Division."[2]

It appears that while the IS created a narrative of cultural destruction through its media-released recordings, the regime also facilitated a market for the very materials it claimed to be destroying. It was no coincidence that at the same time the IS controlled vast territories in Syria and Iraq, the international market for Levantine and Mesopotamian material exploded.[3] This market extended from online sales on e-commerce sites like eBay to larger auction houses like Christie's and the creation of larger private collections, such as the Green family's founding collections for the Museum of the Bible.[4] The IS created the crisis and then profited from it.

However, while the above crisis was being exploited, the IS was also actively destroying other cultural heritage sites and materials outside the public eye. These acts of destruction were religiously motivated and not televised or recorded. Any facet of Syrian culture that did not fit into the IS's very narrow concept of Islam were erased. Under the IS's strict conception of Islam, Christian, Jewish, Bahai, and other religions were deemed heretical, prompting the destruction of their buildings and materials. However, the largest category of cultural artifacts targeted was Islamic materials. Shi'a mosques or religious objects, or any mosque or religious building associated directly with a person, were especially endangered. For example, the Nabi Yunus Mosque in Mosul, said to be the final resting place of the prophet Jonah, an important figure in Muslim, Christian, and Jewish faiths, was completely razed. Islamic objects were destroyed rather than sold on the black market.

The IS's publicized destruction of cultural heritage intentionally obscured its own enrichment from the trade of cultural material while creating a new version of Syria that suffocated the true diversity of the region and its connections to diverse forms of Islam. The IS performed a cultural cleansing to recreate the region in its own image. It erased the past through the destruction of both the people and the physical representations of their memories. The IS crafted its agenda with the material wealth gained from international outrage over non-Islamic cultural destruction as it quietly excised large swathes of diverse Islamic culture from the landscape while the media was distracted.

The International Archaeological Response

Throughout this crisis, the archaeological community displayed a range of responses, some more helpful and valuable than others. This was not the first time that archaeologists had been deeply involved in a community at a time when war or violence had broken out. Archaeologists had been in countries during outbreaks of violence within Israel, Iraq, Afghanistan, and Turkey, to name just a few countries where this occurred within the Middle East. However, as the situation worsened, the community sought new ways to help.

Scholars with a connection to the region first sought to directly help their associate communities within Syria. This was largely done on an individual basis through the work of specific archaeological teams who assisted the Syrian community with whom they worked instead of any large, organized effort by archaeological organizations. This was achieved largely through monetary donations sent into the country via various methods to directly aid individuals or families within Syria, allowing them to buy food or supplies. Scholars also used their connections to get individuals who were in danger out of the country altogether. Many of these aid efforts were done outside of official processes, and so details cannot be ethically published here. These direct humanitarian-based efforts by scholars continued throughout the civil war.

Along with their worry over the human cost, archaeologists were also understandably concerned with the cultural heritage of Syria itself; the nature of our profession requires a passion for cultural heritage and the past. As accounts of the destruction of cultural heritage began to mount, archaeologists wondered what could be done from outside the country. This led to several official movements, often spearheaded by professional archaeological organizations, called "conflict archaeologists" by Greenland and Fabiani.[5]

Most of these efforts focused on how to track destruction within the country, creating several new initiatives based in Syria. For example, the America-based Middle Eastern archaeological association ASOR (American Society of Overseas Research) began the ASOR Syrian Initiative, which lasted from 2014 to 2017. Through this initiative, archaeologists knowledgeable in mapping program such as ArcGIS used satellite photography, often in real time, "to document, monitor, and report on cultural heritage damage in Syria."[6] The team published reports of their findings on their website and used information from local colleagues within Syria to ground truth data as much as was possible or safe.[7] Regions were selected for this detailed analysis through a combination of known areas of IS activity, known archaeological sites of importance, and what data was made available by the US State Department. A second American initiative was the UPenn Heritage Stabilization Program, which used similar methods as ASOR to oversee destruction within Syria and Iraq.

A similar international initiative was the Safeguarding the Heritage of Syria and Iraq (SHOSI) Project. Begun in 2014, the SHOSI Project fused the provision of humanitarian aid to locals within Syria and Iraq and the safeguarding of cultural heritage concepts, all through a combination of emergency funding for locals and training within the country and nearby regions for scholars and archeologists.[8] SHOSI worked at first with various groups outside of the Assad regime, such as the Free Syrian Army, in the hope that if they won control over regions they could quickly and effectively work to safeguard cultural heritage within the country through its own people.

SHOSI largely focused on in-country training within Syria and Iraq of what it called "heritage professionals," holding in-person meetings in safe regions for archeological professionals from the United States, Syria, and Iraq for further training. "Its purpose was three-fold: 1) to offer information on how to secure museum collections safely during emergencies; 2) to provide participants with basic supplies for packing and securing museum collections; and 3) to create a dialogue about emergency responses and needs."[9] This project prioritized in-country actions that addressed the specific needs of the local archaeological communities that were impacted by the conflict.

Within Europe, similar initiatives included Heritage for Peace in Spain, the Syrian Heritage Archive Project in Berlin, the Association for the Protection of Syrian Archaeology in Strasbourg, Le patrimoine archéologique syrien en danger in France, Syrian Heritage in Danger in Basel, Switzerland, and Endangered Archaeology in the Middle East and North Africa (EAMENA) out of Oxford University in England, though this is not an exhaustive list. Most often, these projects were able to do little more than observe destruction within the country and publish reports. The goals of many of these organizations were to keep a vigil over the cultural heritage of Syria and Iraq and record what was lost. The hope was that once peace was restored, such data could be returned to local groups to aid in the process of rebuilding as well as saving what was possible to salvage. The archaeologists working on these projects were a mixture of scholars, including graduate students and professors, who had previously worked in Syria and Iraq and scholars with a strong background in GIS programming. Participants, including two of my close colleagues from graduate school, worked both part- and full-time on these projects.[10]

These initiatives were all founded with good intentions and a desperately felt need to do something about the situation within Syria. However, these efforts still bring up questions: What were the priorities set by the archaeological community, and how well did it meet these priorities? It becomes harder as the years pass to know what more could have been done or what a better project would have entailed. However, we can now see that there were detrimental consequences to the well-intentioned aid efforts of foreign scholarly and archeological communities.

First, these groups often focused their efforts on famous archaeological sites, museums, or monuments, for example, the emphasis on the destruction of the site of Palmyra. The atrocities of this site were widely shared across the international archaeological communities and general news outlets. The ASOR Syrian Initiative created five reports in total on Palmyra alone. Other well-documented and well-known archaeological sites, such as Ebla and Mari, excavated in the past by Europe- and America-based archaeologists, received a large share of the coverage. Additionally, significant coverage focused on the destruction of Christian sites and monuments, such as St. Elijah's Monastery in Iraq, the oldest Christian monastery in the country. Destruction of Christian sites often monopolized these foreign aid efforts and the coverage they received.

Far less was published about smaller, lesser-known archaeological sites, especially sites from the prehistoric or Islamic period, Islamic monuments, or modern urban centers, though these were also visible via available satellite photography. The organizations' focus mirrored that of the IS and its propaganda, homing in largely on non-Islamic or pre-Islamic destruction despite the fact that the majority of the destruction targeted Islamic sites and material. The largest loss of cultural heritage went underacknowledged.

A second issue came from how this data was retrieved and stored. To get timely, high-resolution data, researchers depended on government sources. Both the ASOR and UPenn groups received data and funding—$600,000—from the US State Department. This relationship is acknowledged: the ASOR Syrian Initiative website has an American flag posted on the main page, along with text discussing the US State Department's partnership with the initiative.

Funding can be difficult to obtain, and this data was invaluable to these initiatives, but I argue that the ethical implications of this source of data and funding was not entirely well thought out, especially considering how very quickly these initiatives were put together in the early days of the war. As the State Department provided the material support and data for the project, it also set parameters for which geographical areas were allowed to be observed by the archaeological groups and when the data would be received, further limiting what could be monitored by archaeologists. While some members of the archaeological community did express concerns about the projects, they likely reasoned that the State Department money and data were necessary to sustain the project.

Other archaeological groups began efforts to recreate what had been lost. For example, projects like Project Mosul used public-sourced photographs of museums, archaeological sites, and artifacts to generate three-dimensional recreations of destroyed materials. For example, such efforts were used to recreate lost materials from Palmyra, resulting in models of destroyed monuments like the Lion of al-Lat and the Arch of Triumph. While these again seem like worthwhile efforts, what happened instead was a focus on recreating the arch, for example, for display in locations like London and New York, whereas the original in Syria remains absent and destroyed.

Local Responses

As a foreign archaeologist myself, it is harder to evaluate the efforts led by local Syrian archaeologists and communities. These actors made many attempts to communicate the Syrian situation to rest of the world and advocate for their own local-led solutions. The stakes were quite different for Syrians within the country. If they were found to be broadcasting data to outsiders, the punishment could be torture or death.

Many archaeologists worked individually within the country both to monitor destruction of sites and artifacts and to broadcast events within the country to the outside world. For example, Adnan Al Mohamad, an archeologist from Aleppo, worked from 2014 to document the looting and destruction of Aleppo before being forced to flee the country in fear of his life and that of his family.[11]

A far more tragic story concerns the site of Palmyra. At the time that the IS took over Palmyra, the head of antiquities of the site was a Syrian man named Khaled al-Assad, who had worked at the site his entire life and for forty years as the head of antiquities for Palmyra. While he was encouraged to flee as the region fell under IS control, al-Assad instead chose to remain to protect his beloved site. He organized efforts to hide and protect as many artifacts from the Palmyra Museum as possible. At the age of eighty-three, he also believed himself too old to be of consequence to the IS. This was sadly not the case. The IS captured and tortured him in an attempt to learn where many of the smaller antiquities from Palmyra had been hidden. Al-Assad refused to comply and was publicly beheaded by the IS on 18 August 2015. The death of al-Assad, a well-loved figure in Syrian archaeology, shocked the archaeological world.

A final example was the creation of a website by local actors called Raqqa Is Being Silently Slaughtered. This was a consistently updated account from within Raqqa of the atrocities committed against the people of Raqqa, as well as to the city itself and its cultural heritage sites. The authors of this site were remarkably brave, as anyone caught running the site was sure to be executed. The site continued to be updated through the liberation of Raqqa by Syrian forces in 2016.

Unintended Consequences of the Past and Looking to the Future

Here in 2024, it is easy to look back upon the last twelve years and say what could have been done differently or better. It is important to emphasize that this was, and remains, a difficult and stressful situation for all parties involved. Moving forward, we can use these events as a map for future humanitarian crises, asking what the best ways are to support people within a country and make sure they are being heard.

Ultimately, fewer lessons were learned from these events than one might hope. There have been great advances in archaeology and archaeological methodologies in the last ten years, especially in relation to accessibility of archaeological material to the general public. Great strides in digital humanities, 3D modeling of archaeological sites and artifacts, including of sites and artifacts that have been destroyed, and the creation of virtual tours of both existing and demolished locations have changed how the public can interact with archaeology.[12] Many of these new technologies have directly arisen from techniques developed by archaeologists in response to the Syrian crisis. However, the goals first intended by archaeologists back in 2012 have not been met, and the results have been new archaeological methodologies, not necessarily the betterment of Syria, its people, or the preservation of its cultural heritage. What started as a humanitarian response to a horrific situation largely ended advancing the technology of Western archeological organizations, and the loss of life and culture were soon overlooked as time passed and the world moved on from Syria to other crises.

By the end of 2018, the IS had lost nearly all its territorial gains in both Syria and Iraq. However, the group is not dead, and while it no longer controls the numbers of people and territories it once did, it remains a force within the Middle East and North Africa (MENA) and should not be underestimated. The destruction of mosques, shrines, and other Islamic material culture will haunt these regions for decades to come, if not longer. The IS successfully erased large amounts of physical evidence that represented dissenting forms of Islam, and little international money has been raised or provided to date to rebuild Shi'a shrines and mosques. This will be a costly project, as what is destroyed is often difficult to rebuild. The international response that ostensibly cared deeply at one time about the cultural heritage has largely, though not completely, been silent regarding this continued need.

Within Syria, the al-Assad government has regained control of the country, including the regions of Homs and Aleppo; rebel groups have lost most of their gains but remain in parts of the country. The Kurds in northern Syria are still working and fighting toward their goal of an independent Kurdistan and have come up against fierce and violent responses by Türkiye in the north. While the civil war in Syria has changed, the country has not regained the peace from before the war.

Archaeology within the country itself has only haltingly restarted. A small number of Syrian-led excavations have recommenced in various regions of Syria, but foreign excavations remain paused. Within archaeological organizations, there remains hope for the future of archaeology and cultural heritage management within the country, but work remains limited. For example, at the fall 2021 annual meeting of ASOR, only three talks were given in the Archaeology of Syria workshop, only five at the 2022 annual meeting, and the Archaeology of Syria workshop was canceled in 2023, though a small number of talks focused on Syria were presented in other workshops. Before 2012, there would be more than twelve such talks at a single workshop. Of the talks in 2021, two were reports on materials excavated before the war began, and the third featured a Syrian archaeologist speaking about the reconstruction work at a site that had been heavily damaged by recent fighting. In 2022 and 2023, all were reports on materials excavated before the war began or focused on the future of cultural heritage within the country. It is not clear if the ASOR annual meeting will keep its Syrian workshop in future years.

Other organizations formed because of the civil war have pivoted to different projects, either within Syria or in the greater MENA region. For example, the ASOR Syrian Initiative is now known as the ASOR Cultural Heritage Initiative (CHI), focused more generally on in-country training for local archaeologists and combatting trafficking of cultural heritage materials. Nearly the entire staff of the previous Syrian Initiative has since moved on to other projects or jobs; the organization continues with little connection to its original mission. Since there are nearly no original members, there are concerns that the data collected by the original Syrian Initiative is not being preserved. While much was published and remains publicly available on the ASOR site, it remains unclear—even to those who worked for the initiative—where the collected data itself went. The US State Department reclassified much of this information, and so its final uses and results remain unshared and unavailable to archaeological and Syrian communities. This is a major issue for a project whose initial goals were to create publicly available data for the people of Syria. As projects changed scope and focus, personnel left, taking with them the institutional knowledge of a still ongoing problem. Moreover, the data once promised to the Syrian community is now held and controlled by the US State Department.

Endangered Archaeology in the Middle East and North Africa (EAMENA) has also shifted its focus. Now it is no longer focused on satellite work but has shifted toward in-country training across the MENA region. Within Syria itself, the Syrian Directorate-General of Antiques and Museums hosts and updates a website with lists of sites and damage from the last ten years as curated by the Syrian government.

Much of the focus by these groups has now transferred to the training of archaeologists in-country, a meritorious goal, as well as to rebuilding some subsection of what was destroyed. However, which sites and regions are being rebuilt is itself an ongoing question. These projects are often highly reliant upon foreign sources of money for rebuilding, which is then contingent upon the whims of those who are financing the projects—and this presents questions regarding interests not dictated by the preference of the Syrian people. For example, the Russian government has given money for the rebuilding of the site of Palmyra, while the UAE has helped fund reconstruction of the Old Town of Aleppo. However, as these major tourist sites are being revitalized, the living neighborhoods that surround these major landmarks are still rubble. Such projects are of aid to Syria in general but do little to help those who live in these regions.

Overall, a greater number of internationally famous sites are in the process of reconstruction than local Islamic sites, largely due to higher levels of funding for the former over sites and locations of greater cultural importance to contemporary Syrians. Smaller reconstruction projects are completed in-country by heritage groups led by local Syrians or international groups training local populations.

The story of the archaeological response to the Syrian Civil War has laid bare what foreign communities think are important aspects of cultural heritage, what deserves to be preserved, and what does not. The international archaeological community often privileges sites such as Palmyra that are of greater interest to the "Western world" rather than the entirety of the rich cultural heritage of the country, as seen through Syria's strong history of cultural and religious diversity. The IS was able to destroy much of this history while the world focused on other matters.

As a final note, one lasting response to the last ten years, and perhaps a reason for hope for the discipline, is that more archaeologists have moved their focus away from excavation or museum research and now concentrate on the preservation of cultural heritage and studies into the black-market trade of cultural heritage materials.[13] This is a truly emerging field, with a growing number of scholars working in it perhaps to better rectify the shortcomings of the responses by the archaeological community. The future of archaeology is extending further beyond the scope of the trowel and the museum case. The violence of the Syrian Civil War and beyond have taught the archaeological community the importance of this, at great cost.

Stephanie Selover is associate professor of ancient Middle Eastern archaeology at the University of Washington in the Middle Eastern Languages and Cultures and Anthropology Departments, and adjunct curator at the Burke Museum. She has published widely on evidence of violence on ancient human remains, the origins of violence and warfare in the ancient world, and the effects of modern politics on archaeology in the Middle East. She is currently codirector for project logistics and codirector for prehistoric studies at the archaeological excavations at Çadır Höyuk in Türkiye, and field director at Khirbat al-Balua in Jordan.

Notes

1. Koerner, "Why ISIS is Winning the Social Media War," 16; Farwell, "Media Strategy of ISIS," 14; Brooking and Singer, "War Goes Viral," 2016; among many others.
2. Keller, "Documenting ISIL's Antiquities Trafficking."
3. Topçuoğlu and Vorderstrasse, "Small Finds, Big Values," 19.
4. Gerstenblith, *Hobby Lobby*, 22.
5. Greenland and Fabiani, "Collaborative Practices," 21; Greenland, "Pixel Politics," 22.
6. Prescott, "7 Things You Should Know," 14.
7. Dante et al., "American Schools of Oriental Research," 17.
8. Al Quntar et al., "Responding to a Cultural Heritage Crisis," 15.
9. Al Quntar et al., "Responding to a Cultural Heritage Crisis," 15.
10. Greenland and Fabiani, "Collaborative Practices," 21.
11. Flanagan, "Exiled Syrian Archaeologist," 21.
12. Benardou et al., "Cultural Heritage Infrastructures," 18; Early-Padoni, "Spatial History," 17; Harrison, "Computational Research," 20.
13. Brodie et al., "Why There Is Still an Illicit Trade," 22; Greenland et al., "Site-Level Market Model," 19; Mackenzie et al., "Trafficking Culture," 20.

References

Abdelhamid, Tarek Galal. "Digital Techniques for Cultural Heritage and Artifacts Recording." *International Journal on Proceedings of Science and Technology* 2, no. 2 (2019): 72–112.

Al Quntar, Salam, Katharyn Hanson, Daniels, and Corine Wegener. "Responding to a Cultural Heritage Crisis: The Example of the Safeguarding the Heritage of Syria and Iraq Project." *Near Eastern Archaeology* 78, no. 3 (2015): 154–60.

Ali, Hassanein. "The Rise and Fall of Islamic State: Current Challenges and Future Prospects." *Asian Affairs* 51, no. 1 (2020): 71–94. https://doi.org/10.1080/03068374.20 19.1706940.

Benardou, Agiatis, Erik Champion, Costis Dallas, and Lorna M. Hughes, eds. *Cultural Heritage Infrastructures in Digital Humanities*. New York: Routledge, 2018.

Brodie, Neil, Morag Kersel, Simon Mackenzie, Isber Sabrine, Emiline Smith, and Donna Yates. "Why There Is Still an Illicit Trade in Cultural Objects and What We Can Do about It." *Journal of Field Archaeology* 47, no. 2 (2021): 117–30.

Brooking, Emerson T., and P.W. Singer. "War Goes Viral: How Social Media Is Being Weaponized Across the World." *The Atlantic*, 2016. https://www.theatlantic.com/magazine/archive/2016/11/war-goes-viral/501125/.

Danti, Michael, Scott Branting, and Susan Penacho. "The American Schools of Oriental Research Cultural Heritage Initiatives: Monitoring Cultural Heritage in Syria and Northern Iraq by Geospatial Imagery." *Geosciences* 7, no. 95 (2017): 1–12. https://doi.org/10.3390/geosciences7040095.

Earley-Spadoni, Tiffany. "Spatial History, Deep Mapping and Digital Storytelling: Archaeology's Future Imagined through an Engagement with the Digital Humanities." *Journal of Archaeological Science* 84 (2017): 95–102.

Farwell, James P. "The Media Strategy of ISIS." *Survival* 56, no. 6 (2014): 49–55. https://doi.org/10.1080/00396338.2014.985436.

Flanagan, Padraic. "Exiled Syrian Archaeologist Feared His Academic Life Was Over – Until UK Charity Cara Stepped In." *I*, June 4, 2021, sec. World. https://inews.co.uk/news/world/exiled-syrian-archeologist-feared-academic-life-was-over-uk-charity-cara-1033775.

Gerstenblith, Patty. *Hobby Lobby, the Museum of the Bible and the Law; A Case Study of the Looting of Archaeological Artifacts from Iraq.* New York: Routledge, 2022.

Greenland, Fiona A. "Pixel Politics and Satellite Interpretation in the Syrian War." *Media, Culture & Society*, 2022, 1–17. https://doi.org/10.1177/01634437221077169.

Greenland, Fiona A, and Michelle D. Fabiani. "Collaborative Practices in Crisis Science: Interdisciplinary Research Challenges and the Syrian War." *Sociological Science* 8 (2021): 455–79.

Greenland, Fiona A, James V. Marrone, Oya Topçuoğlu, and Tasha Vorderstrasse. "A Site-Level Market Model of the Antiquities Trade." *International Journal of Cultural Property* 26, no. 1 (2019): 21–47.

Harrison, Timothy P. "Computational Research on the Ancient Near East (CRANE): Large-Scale Data Integration and Analysis in Near Eastern Archaeology." *Levant* 52, no. 1–2 (2020): 1–4.

Keller, Andrew. "Documenting ISIL's Antiquities Trafficking: Corresponding Visuals to the Remarks." *U.S. Department of State* (blog), 2015. https://2009-2017.state.gov/e/eb/rls/rm/2015/247739.htm.

Koerner, Brendan I. "Why ISIS Is Winning the Social Media War." *Wired* (blog), April 2016. https://www.wired.com/2016/03/isis-winning-social-media-war-heres-beat/.

Mackenzie, Simon, Neil Brodie, Donna Yates, and Christos Tsirogiannis. *Trafficking Culture: New Directions in Researching the Global Market in Illicit Antiquities.* New York: Routledge, 2020.

Prescott, Kurt. "7 Things You Should Know About ASOR's Syrian Heritage Initiative." *ASOR Blog* (blog), 2014. https://www.asor.org/blog/2014/09/10/6-things-you-need-to-know-about-asors-syrian-heritage-initiative/.

Romano, Andrea. "These 12 Famous Museums Offer Virtual Tours You Can Take on Your Couch." *Travel and Leisure* (blog), 2022. https://www.travelandleisure.com/attractions/museums-galleries/museums-with-virtual-tours.

Starr, Michelle. "Project Mosul to Restore Destroyed Antiquities Using 3D Modelling." *CNET* (blog), 2015. https://www.cnet.com/culture/project-mosul-to-restore-destroyed-artefacts-using-3d-modelling/.

Topçuoğlu, Oya, and Tasha Vorderstrasse. "Small Finds, Big Values: Cylinder Seals and Coins from Iraq and Syria on the Online Market." *International Journal of Cultural Property* 26, no. 3 (2019): 239–63.

Conclusion

Closing Conversation

Lessons in Humanitarianisms from the Global South

Arzoo Osanloo and Cabeiri deBergh Robinson

We began this project in a darkened café one cold, rainy Seattle day in the fall of 2018. We used scraps of paper to chart our ideas. We kept talking until, some hours and many espressos later, we found the thread connecting our interests in Islamic humanitarianism and misperceptions about migrant destinations.

A year and a half later, pandemic lockdowns and travel restrictions hit just as our seminar series was scheduled to begin, and in the end, we had to begin planning anew. At first, it felt like something had been lost. But then we reflected on what we had learned from teaching online for a quarter, and we realized that our work could have enduring and accessible outcomes. This sparked our format of paired conversations—recorded, indexed, and accessibility captioned—and curated endurable teaching resources. Over the years of preparation and production, our idea of the global South transformed; our goals and our conversations shifted from a conference model to global outreach, and we were able to include people from refugee camps and scholars from around the world with limited travel ability. Our multilingual Q&A sessions looked very different from what we had experienced in traditional university lecture halls. Quarterly virtual meetings with our working group members and speakers led to discussions of ongoing research (people writing books, dissertations, articles) and of the courses that many of us teach on related topics. These discussions led to an eventual decision to write this kind of volume.

This conclusion, in a similar vein, is a conversation between the editors, coming together over coffee and tea on an uncharacteristically sweltering Seattle summer day in July 2023.

Arzoo: When we started this project, my main concern was that media outlets—progressive, mainstream, or conservative—as well as people we talked to regularly—whether they were our family and friends, in the sorts of lay communities we inhabit, or students, scholars, and researchers, in our professional lives—had all expressed a sense, almost implicitly, that forced migrants are finding their way to Europe, North America, Australia, and New Zealand, or what we refer to as the global North, when, in fact, both of us knew that to be totally incorrect. And this created a significant misunderstanding about what humanitarian care is, what it looks like, who is involved, what it means in such contexts, and, especially, who provides that care.

So, we set out to do an inquiry into exactly this question of what the understanding of humanitarianism would be if we focused on who is doing the caregiving. And then we thought, if we dared to ask new questions and look at things in new ways, what would we learn?

Cabeiri: I remember, too, that we felt from early in our conversations that another thing that was missing was recognition of historical regional exclusions in the definition of the problem. So, you know, in addition to this idea about where people are hosted, there are problems related to categorization—who even counts at all? I think from there, too, came our commitment to the concept of "the global South." It wasn't just a geographical designation that reflected an empirical reality; it was also a concept that allowed us to question the historical power of hierarchies that made the processes of producing differently valued categories of migration invisible and continue to make them invisible.

Arzoo: Yeah, I love that. And I think you coming at it as a scholar of refugees in South Asia and history and me coming at it more from practicing immigration and refugee and asylum law allowed us to arrive at that question of how categories—particularly, in this case, colonial legal categories—established what we now have as these categories that are denuded of their history, of their politics.

I think the other thing that's important to consider is how some of the stories that we tell help us to see how the Refugee Conventions actually excluded certain categories of forced migrants, particularly those from the global South. We see that with Pam Ballinger's invocation of "patriation" as a project that was in part necessitated by the exclusion from the refugee definition of ethnic Italians displaced by postwar decolonization, or with Emma Meyer's focus on the "evacuee" as a bureaucratic category for managing displacement. That category developed originally in postwar South Asia, also in the absence of an international process of willingness to think of World War II–related or decolonizing displacement as a "refugee" problem.

Cabeiri: Yeah, absolutely. And, as James Pangilinan's chapter shows, other decolonizing nation-states, such as the Philippines, claimed an ability to host refugees as a way of asserting independence within the newly emerging post-colonial and post–World War II world order. So, the relationship between sovereignty and humanitarian care is crucial.

On a related point, I'm thinking about how our early reviewers of the manuscript proposal expressed doubt on whether chapters related to Romania or Bosnia should be included in a collection focused on the global South. We had such a strong instinct that they should, because our understanding of the term wasn't primarily geographical. Yet, including their contributions pushed us to elaborate our understanding of the global South. We understood the term to be connected to colonial and inherited categories, and our sense of the vernacular was also part of this . . . but we also needed to articulate the "in-relation" aspect of it.

Arzoo: That's right. And it's important not to think in purely geopolitical terms, because even in Europe, we saw groups that were caught up in other fraught contexts, such as environmental disaster, and who could not avail themselves of the protections of the Refugee Conventions, given the very limited legal purposes for which they were created. For instance, Cristian Capotescu's chapter explored how people came together in socialist Romania to offer support to others who were dealing with a catastrophic flood, by delivering humanitarian aid through private networks.

Cabeiri: And his concept of "graying" also asks us to think beyond the global North/global South divide. There was something very different about the ways that the Socialist, authoritarian world worked that produced different power imbalances than those that operated in the postcolonial era, engagements that a lot of the global South literature talks about. It was only possible for humanitarian aid to operate by using the gray economy, exploiting private networks, and accommodating social forms on the ground.

Many similar patterns come to the foreground. Kathie Friedman-Kasaba's chapter, for example, examines "a lucky break," to characterize the often chance nature of clearing the legal and other hurdles required to achieve humanitarian protection, which depends so much on personal connections and what relationships are forged. So, humanitarian work operates and expands in these spaces through the labor of caring work done in private networks, by local hosts, often by refugees themselves giving aid and refuge to other refugees.

Arzoo: This was so important to many of our contributors! These include the use of these private interactions, as Amira Mittermaier's chapter explores through the idea of *khidma* (service), which is well-known in many Muslim societies. There is also the fact that these local actors are often circumventing some of the legal structures where there are incompatibilities between the requirements of international relief organizations and the concerns of host states. I am thinking about Gözde Ege's chapter that takes seriously the work that goes on, not just of laypersons in the camps but also of the refugee-turned-manager. It also challenged us to think critically about what it means that such an industry even exists. The world of "development" as ensconced in the context of a refugee camp is juxtaposed by the temporary and supposed emergency nature of humanitarian relief, laying bare layers of contradiction in which people are forced to live or endure, as it were.

Cabeiri: You know, other volumes have tried to address caring traditions outside of the international regime by focusing on charitable organizations and the role they play in caring for refugees in places where humanitarian organizations do not operate. On the other hand, most of the work on how the humanitarian world expanded is really thinking about legal and institutional expansion. This volume makes, I think, an interesting additional contribution by highlighting that, whether it was encountering the regional definitions of "the refugee" or understandings of what giving relationships look like, NGOs had to build on the networks that had been established. This is why, now, looking back, we see that localized vernacular understandings have worked their ways into what we now call "global humanitarianism."

Arzoo: Sure, and more broadly, Ilana Feldman pointed out that practices of refugee management (its legal forms, customs of aid provision, and policies of recognition) influenced contemporary global aid dynamics. That's another important element that we've considered through these chapters because many of our contributors were conducting research in contexts that fall under the UN's definition of a protracted refugee situation. And, as a result, we need to think not just about the vast majority of the world's refugees who are in the global South and never leave it but also about the ample numbers of forced migrants who do not fit within the technical definition of a "refugee."

Cabeiri: And life goes on; they're living in this very weird space that has been historically and legally defined as emergency, temporary, and liminal—for generations. And some of our contributions compel us to think further about what it means to live in liminality for a lifetime. How does that shape a life? I'm thinking about Megan Butler's meditation on what it means to reclaim a kind of psychic sovereignty for somebody who's been incarcerated in a camp for five years or more.

Arzoo: This reminds me of Khathaleeya Liamdee's account of the paradoxes and ambiguities of what she calls "unapproachable histories" of semi-secret or denied so-called "transit camps" that operated in Southeast Asia during the Cold War. This raises the issue, of course, that it's not possible to grapple fully with the impact of how the humanitarian practices of international aid organizations spread unevenly across Asia in so-called refugee-like situations unless one is willing to confront the politics of cultural ideas of refuge and hospitality in local contexts.

Cabeiri: Yes, and Tanzeen Doha raised this as well by invoking the Islamic concept of politically valued forced migration, which unravels the distinctions between migrant and refugee that are so important in international aid practices and legal statuses. His idea of the invocation of "deathworlds" really emphasized the importance of understanding non-Euro-Christian value systems as sources for organizing everyday living among Rohingya refugees in Bangladesh. And Mediha Sorma claimed that Kurdish women mothered the dead and also what she calls "toward death," both in resistance to state violence and in rejection of being seen as appropriate humanitarian subjects. Indeed, for many who consider themselves "refugee-warriors," it is not acceptable to be visual or narrative representatives of the humanitarian community's ability to care for the suffering if it also depends on occupying a space of nonagentive innocence.

Arzoo: This reminds me of your insight [chapter 11] into the importance of "deathwork." Your chapter started with that juxtaposition we were discussing earlier—how international aid organizations view events like earthquakes as "natural," purportedly nonpolitical, disasters, whereas Islamist organizations had a deeply political view of the conditions that contributed to unequal impacts and differences in access to aid. But deep public support for the Islamist groups' work developed from their ritual care for dead bodies, not only from their provisioning of relief to survivors.

Cabeiri: Yeah, you know, this dovetails with something that we thought was really important when we first conceptualized the project and that didn't really work out the way we thought it might, but that also worked out really well in another way. What I'm thinking about is the concept of "rethinking the human," which was a theme in our webinar series. We had challenged ourselves to think about new ways of talking about posthuman phenomena or social actors who are "other-than-human." We thought it might help us to understand the ways in which so many issues, including those that obviously require humanitarian responses—such as climate-change-related displacement and ecological-collapse-induced suffering—are still excepted from institutional and philosophical recognition as "humanitarian" problems. So, we were trying to build on the concept of comparative humanitarianisms to find the language to explore how an expansion of the objects of care might emerge from regional or vernacular care traditions.

Arzoo: Right, in the volume, we see our contributors grappling with "time" and "care" simultaneously, showing, in a sense, that time does not stand still in the liminal state of being a refugee or forced migrant. By the same token, care, we have shown, is not only regionally diverse, but its meaning changes over time. Given the magnitude of the crisis of forced migration, we also have to think about how the political economy and neoliberalism intensify the problems related to these global displacements. The trajectory of the entire series led us to conclude that we have entered an age in which a big transformation is occurring, wherein an entire global regime around care—relief, aid, and repair—is displacing claims to rights. We refer to this new age as the "time of humanitarianism."

Cabeiri: Yeah, that became so important to our final thinking! I thought it was so telling the way that you reflected in your chapter [6] on one of the consequences of the crisis as the enduring quality of benevolence. One of your key points is that with the ubiquity and ever-expanding reliance on charity, mercy, and, yes, care, we see a global shift in which the call to benevolence and care has overtaken the demand for rights. For me, that's a worrisome paradigm to be sure.

Arzoo: Exactly. In the absence of meaningful human rights protections, which were supposed to accrue to refugees but never did, we see more and more people dependent on aid, relief, and other forms of care. In a setting in which people are without rights, living in legal limbo for a protracted period of time, they must make do with charity and handouts—with benevolence. This is not in keeping with the democratic promises of rights, human rights, or civil rights. Our contributors share this critique by highlighting and recognizing the inhumanity of (temporary) care in lieu of rights.

Cabeiri: Speaking on inhumanity, Sinan Antoon, the author of *The Book of Collateral Damage* (2020), didn't write a chapter for the volume, but he gave a wonderful talk in our webinar series that inspired so many of our contributors. Part of that was his challenge to think about an object as something that has a presence in a humanitarian moment, and has an ability to reveal important, maybe unexpected, truths about experiences of violence and the conditions under which humanitarianism ultimately operates.

One of the moments I remember from his talk most vividly was about the "death" of a mosque. I remember when he first said that—"death" ... What? Didn't he mean "destruction"? But he meant "death," and that's really important, because part of what he was talking about is all the ways that wars disrupt, destroy, and kill social connections and cultural inheritance, things that make people human in specific, valued, and important ways that exceed questions of whether they are kept alive. And it was in part because of how inspired our conversations became that we developed our idea to organize our stories around an object, or at least a conceptual object.

So, I guess, in a sense, we tried to take up his provocation.

Arzoo: Speaking of provocations, I remember back in 2002, when I began teaching my course on refugees, there was just a dearth of firsthand accounts of post–World War II refugees in the global South. And apparently, I wasn't alone in thinking this. Edward Said penned his appeal for such narratives in 1984 with "Permission to Narrate," which was inspired by the rich literature of the inter- and postwar experiences of Jewish refugees fleeing Europe. Said was calling on Palestinian refugees to be the narrators of their own stories. Ghada Karmi's *In Search of Fatima* (2002) was one of the earliest published works to take up Said's provocation, and one that highlighted the experience of living a "suspended" life in protracted refugee situations.

Cabeiri: Yeah, and two decades later, we see our contributors fleshing out the sensorial qualities of living in, and with, the experiences of being held in suspension. One of the attributes or qualities of this sensorial world is the importance or attachment to objects. Here, I am thinking about Tiya Miles's incredible *All That She Carried* (2022), which links memory, affect, and social relations through significant and very tangible objects.

Arzoo: Right, in her case, it was about a sack that was passed down through generations that carried with it accretions of meaning; stories of power, too, were embedded and imbued in this object. Such objects contain layers of history and memory. In our case, our contributors also look at objects of care, and we see different ways in which they can offer relief: Jenna Grant's chapter explores how a barrette in a postwar context becomes imbued with meaning and memory. Rawan Arar's story shows how an item of clothing, her mother's embroidered denim shirt, becomes filled with emotion in the context of generational and protracted displacement. Stephanie Selover's chapter widens the lens to examine the macro-socio-political context of heritage objects and the meaning the international community gives to them as it determines which are worthy of saving and which are not. It's really important to acknowledge that people who have experienced long-term displacement have taken up Said's challenge very effectively with the genre of memoir.

Cabeiri: You know, the memoirs that took up those provocations became great teaching tools in addition to being valuable contributions to a global public discussion. I think the authors in this volume—all of whom are scholars and some of whom have also experienced displacement, refugee aid, or asylum processes—were really successful at using the kernel of the story, whether an object, person, place, or idea, as a focal point around which to reveal the iterative processes by which scholars interpret the importance of things that seem ordinary. We really wanted to make it clear to students how we analyze what we discover in our research.

Arzoo: I was thrilled to learn that colleagues around the world are already using the webinars in their teaching. I already felt inspired after my students found the webinars relevant not only to the course but also to their broader education about forced migrants and the wider global political economy.

Cabeiri: I've also been really happy to see how positively undergrad students responded to those videos. I've been using them as integrated modules in courses that are relevant but not focused on the topic of humanitarianism or refugee studies. For instance, I use them in an upper-level undergraduate course on political Islam. The students have had great conversations around a module I created on "Islamic humanitarianism." It got students talking about how an idea of caring that embraces political activity as a part of human well-being challenges Western apolitical conceptions of humanitarian engagement. I've also integrated two modules into an introductory international studies course on social and cultural approaches to political issues—one on "Legal Exclusion from Refugee Recognition" and another on "Manus Island and the 'Humanitarian Solution,'" which paired webinar talks with memoirs. I've found that the diversity of materials approaching the themes and topics from different perspectives and via different mediums really connects with the students and leads to stimulating—and sometimes impassioned—conversations in discussion sections. So now I am looking forward to integrating these story-forward chapters into the course once this volume is out.

Arzoo: This has been a very generative project, and I know we are both looking forward to continuing it by hearing from our readers and adding more teaching materials to our website.

Arzoo Osanloo is professor in the Department of Law, Societies, and Justice at the University of Washington.

Cabeiri deBergh Robinson is associate professor in the School of International Studies and the Department of Anthropology at the University of Washington.

References

Antoon, Sinan. *The Book of Collateral Damage*. New Haven, CT: Yale University Press, 2020.

Karmi, Ghada. *In Search of Fatima: A Palestinian Story*. New York: Verso Books, 2002.

Miles, Tiya. *All That She Carried: The Journey of Ashley's Sack, a Black Family Keepsake*. New York: Random House Trade Paperbacks, 2022.

Said, Edward. "Permission to Narrate." *London Review of Books* 6, no. 3 (16 February 1984): https://www.lrb.co.uk/the-paper/v06/n03/edward-said/permission-to-narrate.

Appendix
Pedagogical Supplement
Thematic Pairings of Chapters for Teaching Modules

As teachers of undergraduate courses for many years, we have sometimes struggled to help our students connect with the research articles that engage the most complex issues related to forced migration and humanitarianism in today's world. In interdisciplinary fields, articles often presume a great deal of background knowledge and use technical language. We were motivated to help educators explore these critical issues of our time with their undergraduate students, as well as with public audiences. This inspiration was the source of our commitment to approach this volume with story-forward chapters that share each author's research and interpretive processes with readers. They are written to be accessible to audiences who are not already familiar with the scholarship.

In this supplemental appendix, we identify eight thematic clusters that we believe may be of use in multiple undergraduate teaching settings and suggest paired additional pedagogical resources. Here, educators will find the chapters organized differently from the grouping offered in the three parts of this volume. This time, we have arranged the chapters in thematic clusters that may be readily incorporated as modules in courses on human rights, refugee and forced migration studies, and peace and conflict studies; this collection will also serve introductory courses in disciplines such as anthropology, cultural studies, history, and critical legal studies, which may integrate topical modules into core survey courses. Each of these eight clusters includes three to four chapters that share a thematic throughline. These clusters run through the parts of the volume:

(1) Legal Exclusions from Refugee and Humanitarian Recognition;
(2) Refugee-to-Refugee Aid;
(3) Humanitarian Governance;

(4) Islamic Humanitarianism;
(5) Private Humanitarianism;
(6) Cultural Production and the Art of Repair;
(7) Incarceration and the "Humanitarian Solution"; and
(8) Humanitarianism's Unintended Violence.

Each cluster identified above includes several story-based chapters, which can be read together and selectively paired with other scholarly articles or with video lectures from our Mellon Foundation Sawyer Seminar, *Humanitarianisms: Migrations and Care through the Global South*, to form a teaching module. We framed the events in that series as sets of conversations that we produced as webinars with accessibility captioning and indexing. They are published on a stable YouTube channel and maintained and archived on a dedicated website (https://www.humanitarianisms.org/), which also offers additional pedagogical resources, such as syllabi.

Legal Exclusions from Refugee and Humanitarian Recognition

Essays in this cluster include chapters 1, 2, and 3. These chapters explore the taxonomies and historical contingency of refugee recognition, including the now-dominant legal framework established by the 1951 Refugee Convention. These chapters go beyond the critique that the postwar refugee definition primarily recognized people displaced in Europe as refugees but also wrote others out of the international regime of protection. Instead, these chapters examine the multiple legal frameworks for refugee recognition that developed during decolonization and the postwar period in the mid-twentieth century and suggest that these definitions left political traces that shape the on-the-ground praxis in the global South. These webinar lectures will supplement the readings for this cluster: Jessica Whyte's *The Opposite of Humanity: Anti-colonial Challenges to International Humanitarian Law*; Ilana Feldman's *Humanitarian Rights and Palestinian Presence*; Pamela Ballinger's *Provincializing the 1951 Geneva Convention on Refugees*; and Emma Meyer's *Managing Migrants, Resettling Refugees*.

Refugee-to-Refugee Aid

Contributors to this cluster include chapters 5, 7, 9, 10, and 12. These chapters examine the importance of refugee-to-refugee aid in humanitarian situations in the global South, which are characterized by protracted living with precarious status often over generations. For refugees hosted in the global South, the ability to access relief and protection is often about intersectional social identities of class, gender, generation, and education status, and aid workers often have a "doubled position" as both refugees and relief providers to other refugees. Elena Fiddian-Qasmiyeh's webinar lecture *Southern-Led Humanitarian Responses to Displacement* provides additional critical perspectives to this cluster's readings.

Humanitarian Governance

Chapters in this cluster include 3, 4, 7, and 9. This theme explores the role that humanitarian organizations, both international and local, play in providing basic services and functions usually considered the purview of the modern state. While the concept of "humanitarian governance" is not new, the chapters here emphasize that it is an essential concept for the global South, especially given the region's history of protracted refugee situations and features of refugee-to-refugee aid work. Ilana Feldman's *Humanitarian Rights and Palestinian Presence* and China Scherz's *Seeking the Wounds of the Gift* webinar lectures are excellent additions to the chapters in this cluster.

Islamic Humanitarianism

Chapters 10, 11, and 15 highlight an alternative humanitarian framework that is grounded in an Islamic ethics that emphasizes service, charity, and mercy and incorporates concepts of a human right to food and shelter and well-being. Islamic humanitarianism emphasizes a relationship with and tethering to others' well-being as a metaphysical as well as a social duty. The chapters also show that Islamic humanitarianism incorporates a critique of the Enlightenment logic of care, which draws from and deepens existing hierarchy and inequality, by presenting an obligation to work toward an equal access to the basic goods of life. Webinar lectures such as Basit Iqbal's *Ambivalence and Askesis in Zaatari Refugee Camp*, Nermeen Mouftah's *The Value of Pakistan's Eid-al-Azha Animal Hide Collection*, and Amira Mittermaier's *God, Humans, and an Islamic Ethic of Care* pair well with readings in this cluster.

Private Humanitarianism

Contributions to this cluster include chapters 5, 8, and 16. These chapters recognize that humanitarianism as an aspect of global political culture is deeply connected to experiences of charitable and private giving in their local contexts. The chapters here explore how cultural orientations and expectations about hospitality, sharing material resources, and alleviating suffering can function either as competitors to global humanitarian care or as a foundation of practice into which global humanitarian actors must work with in entering new contexts, creating hybrid forms. Sienna Craig's *Tibetan Medical Humanitarianisms*, Cristian Capotescu's *Humanity and the Ethics of Giving in Late Socialism*, and Dean Spade's *Mutual Aid* webinar lectures would all be excellent complements to this cluster.

Cultural Production and the Art of Repair

Chapters 2, 6, 13, 14, 16, and 17 explore how material cultural productions such as plays, films, memoirs, and photographs are important in the creation of an archive of a range of forms of humanitarian care and go beyond the emergency relief for humans. They also contribute to the global circulation of knowledge about how humanitarian praxis is experienced. Sinan Antoon's webinar lecture *Rescuing the Dead* provides an inspiring pairing to these essays.

Incarceration and the "Humanitarian Solution"

This thematic cluster includes chapters 6 and 14 in this volume, paired with Anne McNevin's webinar *Sovereignty, Welcome, and Epistemic Hospitality*. Together, these pieces explore the ways that displaced people have experienced the carceral zone of Manus Island in Australia's "humanitarian solution" policy and aboriginal Australians' use of counterclaims to sovereignty to challenge Australia's right to deny entry to asylum seekers. Manus Island is the site of a prison developed to offshore refugees and circumvent Australia's obligations to investigate asylum claims of forced migrants entering Australian territory.

Humanitarianism's Unintended Violence

Chapters 5, 6, 11, 14, and 17 explore diverse examples of the violence of liberal humanitarianism from a global South perspective. They reveal the internal contradictions within a liberal humanitarianism that is concerned with maintaining sovereignty, and thus hierarchy and inequality, rather than with the redistribution of power and agency. Here, grounded experiences of being the object of liberal humanitarianism speak to and reveal the violence inherent in non-redistributive and sovereign expressions of care. Jessica Whyte's webinar lecture *The Opposite of Humanity* provides a historical foundation for understanding these discussions.

Index

Abdullah, Maulana, 185–86, 198
Aboriginal First Nations passports, 250
Afghanistan, 118–22, 272
Africa, 17, 39, 41. *See also specific countries*
The Afterlife of Ethnic Cleansing (study), 110n2
Agamben, Giorgio, 12, 16, 18
agency: ERRA, 200; in ethnic cleansing, 103–6; foreign aid, 93; Genovese on, 39; in global South, 21; humanitarian, 96n9, 261; individual, 89–90; Islamic humanitarianism and, 186; politics of, 278–79; power and, 310; in refugeehood, 23, 99, 103, 107–8; secular, 182; UNRWA, 131–33, 135, 139, 161, 174n1, 174n9, 208–10; vulnerability and, 103–4
Aguinaldo, Emilio, 54, 57–58
AJK Camp Management Organization, 201
AJK State Earthquake Reconstruction and Rehabilitation Agency, 200
Alejandro, Rachel, 52
Algeria, 41, 46–47
Ali, Raza, 73
Allan, Diana, 133
All That She Carried (Miles), 304
Almeida, David, 45
alternate humanitarianisms, 3, 25n14, 147, 269, 272–74, 309
Ambivalence and Askesis in Zaatari Refugee Camp (Iqbal), 309

American Friends Service Committee, 132–33, 139, 142
American Society of Overseas Research, 289, 291, 294
Antoon, Sinan, 276, 303–4, 310
Arabic, 183–84, 187n1, 262
Arab-Israeli War, 163–64
Arab Spring, 284–85
Arar, Rawan, 23, 208, 215, 219, 304. *See also* displacement
archaeology, 284–85, 289–95
Arendt, Hannah, 11–12, 16, 115, 123
arts. *See* benevolent arts
Asad, Talal, 188n8, 262
Asia, 2, 4, 9–10, 13, 17, 19, 302. *See also specific countries*
al-Assad, Bashar, 286, 292
al-Assad, Hafez, 284–85
al-Assad, Khaled, 292
Ateshbari, Javad, 114
Atia, Mona. *See* Palestinian refugee camps; zakāt
Australia, 106, 238–46, 249–51; Papua New Guinea and, 252n12; in theater, 112, 114–15, 118–19, 121
Austria, 58–59, 145, 150–53, 156–57
Azad Jammu and Kashmir. *See* Kashmir
Azam, Maulana, 183–85
Azoulay, Ariella, 225

Bagatsing, Raymond, 52, 54
Ballinger, Pamela, 20, 36–37, 39, 48, 299, 308. *See also* patriation

Banerjee, R. N., 73
Bangladesh, 22, 176–87, 188n14, 302
Battle of Solferino, 8
Becker, Elizabeth: photography by, 223, 229–30; scholarship from, 224–28, 231–34, 235n7
benevolent arts: care in, 122–23; in documentary theater, 119–20; epistolary reception and, 120–22; humanitarian logics and, 112–13; Manus Island Prison and, 23, 125n3; for refugees, 113–18; scholarship on, 123–24
Benhabib, Seyla. *See* Refugee Convention
Benthall, Jonathan. *See* charity; Islamic ethics of care
Bertoletti, Giulio, 45
Bhumibol (king), 88
binary language, 211
Boochani, Behrouz, 23, 114–17, 125n9, 238–42, 244–51
The Book of Collateral Damage (Antoon), 276, 303–4
borderlands, 1, 195, 271
Bornstein, Erica, 264
Bosnia: Bosnian language, 109n1; ethnic cleansing in, 100–9, 110n2; forced migration in, 21; politics in, 98–100. *See also specific topics*
Bozan, Ali, 268–69
Bulgaria, 40, 49, 145
Burma: Burma Evacuees Association, 20; de-Islamization in, 182–83; displacement in, 70–72, 78–80; evacuees and, 68–70, 73–77; Government of Burma Act, 74; India and, 72–73, 80; India-Burma war, 70; Indo-Burma Immigration Agreement, 72–74, 80; Islam in, 178–79; *jihad* in, 181–82; language in, 81n1; *umma* in, 180; violence in, 184
Butler, Megan, 23, 301. *See also* memoir

Cagirga, Cemile, 274–76
Cagirga, Emine, 274–77, 279–80
Caldwell, Malcolm, 226
Calhoun, Craig, 174n3
Cambodia: Cambodian iconography, 236n21; China and, 222–24; civil war in, 226–27; Khmer Rouge in, 84–89, 91–93, 96n6, 96n9, 227–32; Laos and, 96n1; in modernity, 232–34; refugees from, 97n13; repair in, 225–32, 235n7; repatriation in, 86; resistance groups in, 88–89, 94; Thailand and, 20–21, 93–94; UNTAC, 92–93; US and, 225, 231, 234
Canada, 106
"Can the Subaltern Speak" (Spivak), 188n13
Capotescu, Cristian, 22, 300, 310
care: in benevolent arts, 122–23; charity and, 13–14; compassionate, 256, 262; ethics of, 233, 254–55, 260; in forced migration, 17–18; hospitality and, 124; insurgent, 269–70, 272–73, 282; modes of, 120–22; in Pakistan, 189–90; recipients of, 17; repair and, 22–24; in Thailand, 91–93; after World War II, 14–16. *See also specific topics*
care work: care worker, 17; charity and, 197; disaster relief and, 15, 22; in global South, 19, 22–23; humanitarianism and, 6, 21; human rights and, 122–23; intimacy in, 23; with Kurdish mothers, 23, 268–70, 281–82, 302; philosophy of, 123; politics of, 270–75, 278–81; refusal of, 276–81; scholarship on, 3. *See also specific topics*
caring labor, 3, 24
Cartwright, Lawrence, 53–54
categorization, 16, 40, 210, 299
Catholicism, 17
Ceaușescu, Nicolae, 145–48, 150, 157–58
CGDK. *See* Coalition Government of Democratic Kampuchea
charity: care and, 13–14; care work and, 197; Christian Outreach, 90; compassion and, 7; development and, 161–63, 171–74; Islamic, 196–99, 201–2; Islamic Center Charity Society, 175n10; Islamic humanitarianism and, 196–99; in Palestinian refugee camps, 161–70; religion and, 171–72; repair and, 16; secular humanitarian, 177. *See also specific topics*
Chea, Sopheap, 228
Cheam, Bunthay, 228, 231

Chettiar, A. M. M. Vellayan, 73
China: Cambodia and, 222–24; in Cold War, 96n3; Cuba and, 193; Khmer Rouge to, 228; Sino-Japanese War in, 13; US and, 88, 235n7; USSR and, 85
Chouliaraki, Lillie, 224
Christianity, 7–8, 13, 90, 198–99, 255–56, 261–62, 302
Chulabhorn (princess), 88
citizenship law of 1889, 49n17
climate governance, 17–18
Coalition Government of Democratic Kampuchea (CGDK), 86
Cold War: China in, 96n3; Europe in, 150; global South in, 146, 158; Iron Curtain in, 22, 145–47, 150, 153, 158; refugees in, 43–44; religion after, 108–9; Southeast Asia in, 302; Thailand in, 86–87; US in, 84–86
colonialism: decolonization and, 54–55; economics after, 72; in Egypt, 266–4; evacuees after, 73; fascism and, 38–39, 44; France in, 84; in global South, 25n9, 63–64; identity in, 271; in India, 9; by Italy, 39–41; language in, 46–47; Palestine in, 60–61; Portugal in, 43; social justice against, 47–48; in South Asia, 20, 68–70; territories of, 10; to United States, 52–53, 56–57
compassion: in AJK, 190; appeals to, 112–13; charity and, 7; compassionate care, 256, 262; equity and, 197; hospitality and, 122–24; human, 265; in Iran, 118; in *Manus*, 119–20; in Philippines, 62–63; philosophy of, 2, 264; politics of, 5; in society, 14, 122–23
concentration camps, 99
conventional refugees, 3, 9–11
The Corpse Washer (Antoon), 276
COVID-19, 95, 164, 173–74, 232, 260–61, 263–64, 266n19
Craig, Sienna, 310
criminal justice, 116
Croatia, 98, 104–6
Cuba, 193
cultural heritage care work: politics of, 286–89; scholarship on, 24, 303–4; in Syria, 284–85, 289–95

culture: cultural identity, 20; cultural production, 308, 310; cultural tourism, 150–55; religion and, 3, 288
Czechoslovakia, 146, 151

Darroussin, Jean-Pierre, 121
death, 118, 224, 250, 268–70, 274, 282; care beyond death and, 273; deathwork and, 198–99, 302; deathworlds and, 176–77, 184, 302; mothering toward death and, 276, 279, 281, 302; torture and, 272, 292
decolonization: in Africa, 41; colonialism and, 54–55; displacement in, 37; to Europe, 9, 20, 36, 61–62; in global South, 4; for Jewish refugees, 63–64; Libya in, 44, 46; patriation with, 36–41; in Philippines, 51–52, 62–63; politics in, 56–57; refugees in, 48n2; repatriation and, 38–42, 49n13; to United Nations, 46
de-Islamization, 182–83
Deobandi tradition, 22, 186; Islamists and, 179, 181
development aid, 11–12, 58, 161–63, 171–74
dictatorships, 57–58
disaster relief: care work and, 15, 22; displacement and, 138; fundraising for, 151; humanitarianism and, 195; humanitarian jihad and, 189–95; INGOs in, 200; in Kashmir, 22, 189–90, 195–96; politics of, 272; postdisaster reconstruction welfare activism, 199–202; for refugees, 184–85; in Romania, 22
displacement: in Burma, 70–72, 78–80; in decolonization, 37; disaster relief and, 138; forced, 9–10, 99, 104, 107, 196, 216; forced displacement, 9–10, 99, 104, 107, 196, 216; across generations, 207–9; IDP, 2, 11, 16, 37, 99, 196, 272; internal, 6, 272, 282; of Jewish refugees, 52–53, 56–57; of Kurds, 270–73; in Palestine, 23, 209–10; patriation and, 35–36, 47–48; philosophy of, 74–75; precarity in, 136; refugeehood and, 217–19; refugees and, 209–17; repair and,

303; return from, 73–77; scholarship on, 304–5; in South Asia, 68–70, 96n5; in Syria, 214
Doctors Without Borders, 136
documentary theater, 119–20
Doha, Tanzeen, 22, 302. *See also muhajir*
domestic refuge, 58–60
Dragostinova, Theodora, 40, 42
Dudman, Richard, 226
Dugal, R. S., 73
Dunant, Henri, 8

Earthquake Reconstruction and Rehabilitation Agency (ERRA), 200
East Africa, 44
East Asia, 9–10. *See also specific countries*
Eastern Europe. *See* Global East
Eat, Sambath, 228, 236n14
economic migration, 36, 48
Ege, Gözde Burcu, 22, 211, 301
Egeland, Jan, 15
Egypt: colonialism in, 266n4; COVID-19 in, 260–61; *khidma/ khidmat* in, 254–55; NGOs in, 255, 259; Sayyida Zaynab mosque in, 254–55, 257–59, 265, 266n2, 266n19; Sufism in, 23. *See also* Islamic ethics of care
Eisenhower, Dwight, 53
elitism, 63–64
Elizabeth Becker Cambodia and Khmer Rouge Collection, 223–24
emergency relief, 23, 190, 310
Endangered Archaeology in the Middle East and North Africa, 290, 294
epistolary reception, 120–22
Erdogan, Recep Tayyip, 271–72
ERRA. *See* Earthquake Reconstruction and Rehabilitation Agency
ethico-politics, 185–86
ethics of care, 233, 254–55, 260
ethnic cleansing: agency in, 103–6; in Bosnia, 100–9, 110n2; history of, 37–39, 99–103; nationalization and, 42; politics of, 106–7, 109; refugee-centered humanitarianism in, 108–9; scholarship on, 42, 110n2; war refugees from, 106–8; in Yugoslavia, 98–100
ethnography, 22

Europe: Asia and, 19; benevolent arts in, 118; Christianity in, 302; citizenship law of 1889 in, 49n17; in Cold War, 150; decolonization to, 9, 20, 36, 61–62; Endangered Archaeology in the Middle East and North Africa in, 290, 294; Eurocentrism, 36; Euro-Christian humanitarianism, 198–99; European Community, 99; European Enlightenment, 7–8; global South and, 9; hierarchies in, 38; humanitarianisms in, 5–6; Intergovernmental Committee on European Migration, 39; international refugee regimes in, 80; Iran and, 119; Italy and, 48; Jewish refugees from, 304; Nazis in, 58–59; Ottoman Empire and, 10, 40; race in, 56, 59; Refugee Convention in, 100, 300; scholarship from, 12; Ukraine and, 1; US and, 60–61
evacuees: Burma and, 68–70, 73–77; Burma Evacuees Association, 20; evacuee activism, 80; Evacuee Identity Certificates, 76, 78–80; identity of, 76–80, 100; to India, 70–72, 78–80; in prewar migration, 72–73; repatriation for, 75–76. *See also specific topics*
Évian Conference, 60–61

faith-based aid networks, 12–13
Fang (aunt), 91–93
fasad, 176–77
fascism, 38–39, 44
Fassin, Didier, 122–23, 174n3, 262
Feldman, Ilana, 17, 21–22, 142, 211, 301, 308–9. *See also* humanitarian departures
Fiddian-Qasmiyeh, Elena, 17, 211, 309
Filipino-American War, 55–56
Filipino hospitality, 20, 51–54, 62–63
Flanagan, Richard, 240, 244
folklore, 150–55
food. *See specific topics*
forced displacement, 9–10, 99, 104, 107, 196, 216–18
forced migration: in Bosnia, 21; care in, 17–18; economic migration and, 36; education in, 305; to global North, 123–24; in global South, 4–5, 12;

humanitarian care with, 1–2; language in, 183–84; at Manus Island Prison, 23; productive labor in, 10; refugees and, 47; repatriation and, 10, 15, 21, 44–47; scholarship on, 1–2; in theater, 117–18
foreign aid agency, 93–94
forensic humanitarianism, 17–18
form-of-life, 116
Fourth Geneva Convention, 7
France, 41, 46, 84
Frieder, Alex, 53–56, 64
Frieder, Herbert, 53–56, 64
Friedman-Kasaba, Kathie, 21, 300

Gassner, Siegfried, 145–50
Gatrell, Peter, 39, 48n7, 49n8
Gaza. *See* Palestine
gendered migration, 17
Geneva Conventions, 8–10, 35, 40, 109
genocide, 23, 224, 231–32. *See also specific topics*
Genovese, Eugene, 39
Georgescu, Vlad, 148
Germany: Nazis in, 56, 58–59, 63, 119; refugees in, 102; Romania and, 155n10; temporary protection in, 102–3; West Germany, 150–51, 153
ghazals. *See* poetry
Ghost Mountain (documentary), 97–113
Global East: folklore in, 150–55; gray areas in, 155–58; humanitarianism in, 147–50; quiet aid and, 145–47, 158–59
global North: forced migration to, 123–24; Islamic humanitarianism to, 162; Islam in, 25n14; perspectives from, 161; philosophy of, 24; political refugees from, 48; relations with, 158; after World War II, 36
global political matrix, 119
global South: agency in, 21; care work in, 19, 22–23; in Cold War, 146, 158; colonialism in, 25n9, 63–64; decolonization in, 4; development in, 70–71; economic migration in, 48; Europe and, 9; forced migration in, 4–5, 12; humanitarianism in, 298–305; Islamic traditions in, 1; law in, 19–21; meaning of, 4–5; perspectives from,

19; philosophy of, 22; politics in, 36; refugee studies in, 1–2; repair in, 1–3
God, Humans, and an Islamic Ethic of Care (Mittermaier), 309
godforsakenness, 180–81, 186
Government of Burma Act (1935), 74
Grant, Jenna, 23, 304. *See also* repair
gray areas: cultural tourism in, 150–55; graying of humanitarianism, 147–49, 157, 300; quiet aid in, 147–50; socialist, 145–47, 155–58
Greece, 40
Güven, Leyla, 281

Haji, S. N., 73
Hathaway, James, 40
haunting stories, 87–89
al-Ḥayāh volunteers, 161–66
Hekmatnia, Leila, 125n1
Henkin, Louis, 9, 122–23
Hitler, Adolf, 63
homeland, 40, 42, 44, 46–47, 69–70
Homsi, Habib, 132, 134–41
hospitality: care and, 124; compassion and, 122–24; Filipino, 20, 51–54, 62–63; human rights and, 14; with Jewish refugees, 55–56; paradigm of, 123–24; of Quezon, M., 51–52, 56–58; as transitional exchange, 54–56; to UNHCR, 51
human compassion, 265
humanitarian agency, 96n9, 261
humanitarian communication, 235n4
humanitarian departures: humanitarian relations and, 139–41; international aid and, 131–34; persistence with, 141–42; refugees and, 131–35, 137–39; responsibility and, 135–37
humanitarian governance, 17–18, 27n67, 122–24, 174, 307–9
humanitarianisms: in-relation, 4–6, 12–14, 19, 24, 300; scholarship on, 2, 5–6, 261–63, 308–10. *See also specific topics*
humanitarian jihad, 189–95, 199–202
humanitarian logics, 6–7, 112–13
humanitarian praxis, 21–22
humanitarian protection, 21, 37, 99–100, 103, 109, 300

humanitarian recognition, 307–8
humanitarian refugees, 3, 11
humanitarian relations, 139–41
Humanitarian Rights and Palestinian Presence (Feldman), 308–9
Humanity and the Ethics of Giving in Late Socialism (Capotescu), 310
human rights, 14–15, 122–23, 246–49
Hungary, 106, 151
Hunt, Lynn, 120
Hussein (king), 175n10
hybrid humanitarianism, 25n14

ibn Malik, Anas, 187n5
ICRC. *See* International Committee of the Red Cross
identity: building, 42; in colonialism, 271; cultural, 20; Evacuee Identity Certificates, 76, 78–80; of evacuees, 76–80, 100; humanitarianism and, 4, 17; of Kurdish mothers, 270–73; language and, 211–12; manipulation of, 231; in patriation, 40–41; politics of, 44, 105, 249, 279; of refugees, 136, 207–9
IDP. *See* internally displaced persons
Ieng Sary, 226
IFRC. *See* International Federation of Red Cross and Red Crescent Societies
IGOs. *See* international governmental organizations
imaginary, 221, 244, 250–51; emergency imaginary and, 247–48; humanitarian and, 161–63, 173, 246–47; imaginaries and, 240–41; political and, 241
immigration policy, 72–73, 240
Inan, Mehmet, 273
Inan, Taybet, 268, 270, 273, 281–82
incarceration, 301, 308, 310. *See also* Manus Island Prison
independence, 56–58
India: Burma and, 72–73, 80; colonialism in, 9; evacuees to, 70–72, 78–80; immigration policy in, 73; India-Burma war, 70; Indo-Burma Immigration Agreement, 72–74, 80; Kashmir and, 195–96; Pakistan and, 47–48; politics in, 68–70; propaganda in, 75–76; Standing Emigration Committee, 71

individual agency, 89–90
informality, 22, 147–48
INGOs. *See* international nongovernmental organizations
In Search of Fatima (Karmi), 304
insurgent care, 269–70, 272–73, 282
Intergovernmental Committee on European Migration, 39
internal displacement, 6, 272, 282
internally displaced persons (IDP), 2, 11, 16, 37, 99, 196, 272
international aid, 24, 88, 104, 131–34, 190, 193, 302
International Committee of the Red Cross (ICRC), 8, 86–87, 92, 104, 133, 193
international community, 71
International Federation of Red Cross and Red Crescent Societies (IFRC), 132, 140
international governmental organizations (IGOs), 13, 200
international nongovernmental organizations (INGOs), 11, 13, 169, 196–97, 200, 216–17
International Refugee Organization (IRO), 38
international refugee regimes, 80
intimacy, 21–23, 51–52, 62–63; violence and, 274, 276
Iqbal, Basit, 188n14, 309
Iran, 118–22, 238–44
Iraq, 136, 212–13, 217, 286–87, 290. *See also* Islamic State
IRO. *See* International Refugee Organization
Iron Curtain, 22, 145–47, 150, 153, 158
irredentism, 38
Islam: in Bangladesh, 188n14, 302; in Burma, 178–79; de-Islamization, 182–83; education in, 207; faith in, 187n5; *fasad* in, 176–77; history of, 187n4; Islamic Center Charity Society, 175n10; Islamic charity, 196–99, 201–2; Islamic ethics of care, 254–55; Islamic learning, 184; Islamic NGOs, 197, 199–200; Islamic traditions, 1, 199, 255–56; language in, 187n1, 188n13; *muhajir* and, 177–86, 187n4; philosophy of,

186–87; political, 305; politics in, 198; reputation of, 264–65; Sahih Muslim, 178; Sayyida Zaynab mosque, 254–55, 257–59, 265, 266n2, 266n19; scholarship on, 181–82; secularism to, 180–81, 188n14; in Syria, 288; *umma* in, 180
Islamic ethics of care, 265n1; humanitarianisms and, 261–63; religion and, 254–56, 258–61, 263–65; visible/invisible nexus in, 256–58
Islamic humanitarianism: agency and, 186; to global North, 162; humanitarian jihad and, 199–202; in Kashmir, 195–99; scholarship on, 14, 25n14, 196–99, 298, 305, 308–9; in South Asia, 22
Islamic State, 285–88, 292
Islamic State of Iraq and Syria, 280, 286, 288–89
Islamist, 176–77, 181, 186, 187n6, 197, 255–56, 259–60, 302; Islamism, 186; Islamist political parties and, 198; militant organizations and, 189, 197; service and welfare committees and, 199; United Jihad Council, 196
Israel, 64, 163–64, 211
Italy: citizenship in, 41–44; colonialism by, 39–41; in East Africa, 44; Europe and, 48; Intergovernmental Committee on European Migration and, 39; Libya and, 20; propaganda in, 44–45; refugee camps in, 38; Yugoslavia and, 37–38

Japan, 68, 244
Jensen, Katherine, 209
Jewish refugees: anti-Semitism against, 20, 53; decolonization for, 63–64; diaspora of, 54–55; displacement of, 52–53, 56–57; from Europe, 304; in film, 51–52; from Germany, 58–59; hospitality with, 55–56; in Latin America, 60–61; reputation of, 61–62
jihad, 22, 181–82, 189–95, 199–202
Jordan: forced displacement in, 216; foreign aid to, 175n10; INGOs in, 216–17; Iraq and, 212–13; Palestine and, 161–64, 168–74, 208–9; Palestinian refugee camps to, 212; refugee camps in,

22; refugeehood in, 214; Syria and, 131, 217–18

Kampuchean People's National Liberation Front, 86, 96n7
Karmi, Ghada, 304
Kashmir: disaster relief in, 22, 189–90, 195–96; India and, 195–96; Islamic humanitarianism in, 195–99; Pakistan and, 190–95, 199–202; refugees in, 203n5
Khao-I-Dang Transit Center (KID): history of, 87–89; to local hosts, 89–90; refugee camps in, 20–21, 84–86, 91–95, 97n13
khidma/ khidmat: COVID-19 and, 266n19; in Egypt, 254–55; humanitarianism and, 261–63; in Kashmir, 198; Mittermaier on, 187n6; organization of, 193, 198; philosophy of, 177, 257, 260–65; politics of, 259–60; scholarship on, 23, 187n6, 254–61, 300–1; in Sufism, 256
Khmer Rouge: in Cambodia, 84–89, 91–93, 96n6, 96n9, 227–32; Democratic Kampuchea and, 225–26; history of, 222–24, 235n7; propaganda by, 227; to Thailand, 228–29; to US, 234. *See also* Khao-I-Dang Transit Center
KID. *See* Khao-I-Dang Transit Center
Kissinger, Henry, 118
knowledge production, 210, 216, 218, 280
Kowal, Emma, 233
Kristallnacht, 58–59
Kunzru, Hriday Nath, 73
Kurdish mothers: care work with, 23, 268–70, 281–82, 302; identity of, 270–73; philosophy of, 273–75; politics of, 276–81
Kurds: displacement of, 270–73; history of, 268–70, 281–82; in Iran, 238–39; in Syria, 293; terrorism and, 286; in Türkiye, 273–81

labor migration, 6
Land of Shadows (Um), 236n12
Laos, 96n1
Latin America, 17–18, 60–61
law, 7–9, 19–21, 47, 49n17

League of Nations, 10, 136
League of Red Cross Societies (LRCS), 131–33, 136, 138–42
Lebanon, 2, 14, 131–34, 137–38
legal categorization, 210
legal exclusions, 305, 307–8
legal taxonomies, 47
Lek (uncle), 90, 93
Lemkin, Raphael, 42
Liamdee, Khathaleeya, 95, 302. *See also* Khao-I-Dang Transit Center
liberal-secular humanitarianism, 182–83
Libya, 20, 41, 44, 46
Life Lived in Relief (Feldman), 131
Line of Control, 189, 192, 194–95
local development NGOs, 190
local hosts: haunting stories and, 87–89; interviews with, 85–86; perspective of, 89–90; reconciliation and, 95; in refugee camps, 84–86, 91–93; in Thailand, 86–87, 93–94
LRCS. *See* League of Red Cross Societies

Macedonia, 98
Malta, 46–47
Mamdani, Mahmood, 185–86
Managing Migrants (Meyer), 308
Manus (Sahamizadeh), 112–20, 122–24
Manus Island Prison, 23, 125n3, 238–39, 241–42, 244–47, 250, 305, 310
Marxism, 147
Master, M. A., 73
Mayblin, Lucy, 36. *See also specific topics*
McNevin, Anne, 310. *See also specific topics*
McNutt, Paul, 53–54, 56, 64
medicine, in relief camps, 191–92
memoir: from Australia, 240–46, 249–51; philosophy of, 238–40; reception of, 247–49, 301, 305
Mercy Corps, 193
Merleau-Ponty, Maurice, 179–80
Meyer, Emma, 20, 308. *See also* evacuees
Middle East: Asia and, 13; cultural heritage in, 24; gendered migration in, 17; NGOs in, 163; North Africa and, 10, 19, 290, 293–94; Palestine to, 64; religion in, 289–92; volunteering in, 167–74. *See also specific countries*

migration policy: in Australia, 239–41; certification in, 78–79; for evacuees, 80; in India-Burma war, 70; *muhajir* and, 176–86, 302; national, 239; politics of, 71; refugee camps and, 1–2; for refugees, 179–80; travel bans and, 76–80. *See also* forced migration
Miles, Tiya, 304
military-civilian field hospitals, 192–95
military violence, 104
The Missing Picture (Panh), 236n13
Mittermaier, Amira, 23, 187n6, 265, 266n3, 300–1, 309. *See also* Islamic ethics of care
modes of care, 120–22
Mohamad, Adnan Al, 292
Moon, Claire, 17–18
moral values, 7–8
Mostowlansky, Till, 25n14. *See also specific topics*
Mouftah, Nermeen, 309
Mubarak, Hosni, 259, 261
Mückstein, Luise-Margarete, 150
Mückstein, Walter, 150
muhajir: Islam and, 177–86, 187n4; migration policy and, 176–86, 302; philosophy of, 186–87
Mumm, Thiounn, 225–26
Muslim Brotherhood, 170, 175n10, 255–56, 259–60
Mutual Aid (Spade), 310
Myanmar, 22, 176–87. *See also* Burma
myth of difference, 36

Nadwi, Syed Abul Hasan Ali, 181–82
nationalization, 42
national migration policies, 239
National United Front for an Independent, Neutral, Peaceful, and Cooperative Cambodia, 86, 96n7
Nazis, 56, 58–59, 63, 119
necropolitics, 124
neoliberalism, 122, 303
New Zealand, 106, 245
NGOs. *See* nongovernmental organizations
No Friend but the Mountains (Boochani), 238–41, 249–51, 252n12. *See also* memoir

Nol, Lon, 228–29
nongovernmental organizations (NGOs), 17; domestic, 193; in Egypt, 255, 259; ideology of, 116; Islamic, 197, 199–200; local development, 190; in Middle East, 163; Muslim Brotherhood and, 170; in Pakistan, 199; in refugee camps, 88; refugees to, 301; religion to, 182, 260; UN and, 107, 139
nonsecular genealogies, 262
North Africa, 10, 19, 290, 293–94. *See also specific countries*
Norwegian Refugee Council, 15

Odumosu, Temi, 233–34
Önkol, Ceylan, 274, 276
Önkol, Saliha, 274, 276
On Suicide Bombing (Asad), 188n8
Operation Sovereign Borders, 242–45, 247
The Opposite of Humanity (Whyte), 308, 310
Osanloo, Arzoo, 21, 24, 124–25, 219, 298–305. *See also specific topics*
Osmeña, Sergio, 54–55, 57–59
Ottoman Empire, 10, 40, 271–72

Pakistan: care in, 189–90; government of, 199–200; India and, 47–48; Kashmir and, 190–95, 199–202
Palestine: aid work in, 21–22, 136–39, 141–42; in colonialism, 10, 60–61, displacement in, 23, 209–10; Jordan and, 161–64, 168–74, 208–9; Lebanon and, 132–33; to Middle East, 64; Palestinian refugees, 131–35, 139; refugeehood in, 207, 211; Syria and, 216–17; to UNHCR, 210
Palestinian refugee camps: charity in, 161–70; development aid in, 171–74; development in, 171–73; to Jordan, 212; philosophy of, 170–71; resources in, 212–16; statistics from, 209–10; to UNRWA, 174n1
Pangilinan, James, 20, 300. *See also* Philippines
Panh, Rithy, 236n13
Papua New Guinea, 112–13, 125n3, 238–42, 244, 249–50, 252n12

passports, 78–79
patriation: with decolonization, 36–41; displacement and, 35–36, 47–48; philosophy of, 42–44; refugees in, 48n4; scholarship on, 44–47, 49n11
patronage, 62–63
peace activism, 99
Peace Mothers, 277–80, 282
pedagogy, 307–10
"Permission to Narrate" (Said), 304
persistence, 141–42
Philippines: compassion in, 62–63; decolonization in, 51–52, 62–63; Filipino hospitality, 20, 51–54, 62–63; independence in, 56–58; politics in, 54–56; Quezon, M., for, 20, 60–64; refugees in, 58–60, 300; United States and, 55–56
Phnom Penh. *See* Cambodia
Pictet, Jean, 8
poetry, 241–42, 244–45, 247–48
Poland, 151
Pol Pot, 226
Portugal, 43
postdisaster reconstruction welfare activism, 199–202
Prasith, Thoiunn, 228
precarity, 16, 109, 136, 161–63, 172–74, 209–11, 217, 248–49
prewar migration, 72–73
private humanitarianism, 146–47, 149–51, 158, 307, 309–10
productive labor, 10
propaganda, 44–45, 75–76, 227
protection, 62–63
Protector of Emigrants, 79
protracted refugee situations, 17, 22, 122–23, 210, 301, 304, 309
Provincializing the 1951 Geneva Convention on Refugees (Ballinger), 308

Quezon, Aurora, 52, 59
Quezon, Manuel: domestic refuge to, 58–60; hospitality of, 51–52, 56–58; intimacy to, 62–63; legacy of, 53–56; for Philippines, 20, 60–64
Quezon, Manuel L., III, 58–59

Quezon's Game (Rosen), 20, 51–54, 56–64. *See also* Philippines
quiet aid: cultural tourism and, 150–55; Global East and, 145–47, 158–59; in gray area, 147–50; state surveillance and, 155–58
Qur'anic Arabic, 184

Rabbani, Arif, 187n7
Ramadan, 171–73
Rao, A. Narayana, 73
Rath (uncle), 93
Rauf, M. A., 73
reconciliation, 95
Red Crescent, 255–56
Red Cross, 13, 131–33, 136, 138–42. *See also specific Red Cross societies*
Redfield, Peter, 174n3
refoulement, 212
refugee camps: in Italy, 38; in Jordan, 22; in KID, 20–21, 84–86, 91–95, 97n13; local hosts in, 84–86, 91–93; migration policy and, 1–2; NGOs in, 88; precarity in, 161–63; resources in, 107–8; in Thailand, 86–90, 96n9. *See also* Palestinian refugee camps
Refugee Convention: Convention Relating to the Status of Refugees, 8–9, 14; in Europe, 100, 300; history of, 47, 51, 100, 209, 218, 299–300, 308; philosophy of, 7–11, 15, 20; UN Convention refugee rights, 109; UNHCR and, 15–16; after World War II, 7–9
refugeedom, 39
refugee histories, 70–72
refugeehood: agency in, 23, 99, 103, 107–8; displacement and, 217–19; in Jordan, 214; legal categorization of, 210; in Palestine, 207, 211; precarity in, 109; reflections on, 217–18; reflexivity and, 209
refugees: benevolent arts for, 113–18; from Cambodia, 97n13; in Cold War, 43–44; collective memories of, 89–90; conventional refugees, 3, 9–11; Convention Relating to the Status of Refugees, 8–9, 14; in decolonization, 48n2; development aid and, 11–12; disaster relief for, 184–85; displacement and, 209–17; exclusion of, 26n28; in forced displacement, 217–18; forced migration and, 47; in Germany, 102; humanitarian departures and, 131–35, 137–39; humanitarian refugees, 3, 11; human rights of, 14–15, 246–47; identity of, 136, 207–9; international refugee regimes, 80; from Iran, 242–44; in Kashmir, 203n5; migration policy for, 179–80; to NGOs, 301; in patriation, 48n4; in Philippines, 58–60, 300; philosophy of, 16; political, 48; recognition of, 307–8; refugee-centered humanitarianism, 108–9; refugee law, 7, 15; refugee narratives, 238–40, 249–51; refugee studies, 1–2, 209–11, 217, 232–34, 248–49, 305; refugee-to-refugee aid, 307–9; repair for, 5; return migration to, 40; since World War II, 19; from Syria, 163, 172–73; to UN, 13, 218; UN Convention refugee rights, 109; UNHCR, 10–11; to United Nations, 13; to US, 61–62, 103; volunteering and, 22; war, 106–8. *See also specific topics*
relief camps, 191–95
religion. *See* specific religions
repair: art of, 308, 310; in Cambodia, 225–32, 235n7; care and, 22–24; charity and, 16; displacement and, 303; in global South, 1–3; history and, 228; practices of, 222–25; for refugees, 5; in refugee studies, 232–34; stories of, 18–22; work, 234–35
repatriation: asylum and, 21; in Cambodia, 86; decolonization and, 38–42, 49n13; for evacuees, 75–76; forced migration and, 10, 15, 21, 44–47
Rescuing the Dead (Antoon), 310
responsibility, 13, 47, 76, 119, 124, 135–37, 139, 142, 185, 240
return migration, 40
Robinson, Cabeiri, 22, 24–25, 37, 182, 202, 219, 298–305. *See also specific topics*
Robinson, Nehemiah, 9–10
Roll, Jordan, Roll (Genovese), 39

Romania, 22, 159n10; folklore in, 150–55; socialism in, 145–50, 155–58
Roosevelt, Franklin, 60
Rosen, Matthew, 52–53
Rova-Chamroeun, Felicia, 228
Roxas, Manuel, 57–58
Royal Forestry Department, 87
Royal Thai Army, 92
Russia, 295

Safeguarding the Heritage of Syria and Iraq, 290
Sahamizadeh, Nazanin, 112–16, 118–20, 125n1
Sahih Muslim, 178
Said, Edward, 304. *See also* humanitarian departures
Salah, Shaykh, 255–65, 266n19
Santos, Pedro Abad, 58
Sanyassiah, R., 68–69, 71–72, 81n1
Sarreshteh, Keyvan, 125n1
Saudi Arabia, 258
Save the Children, 11, 193
Saxons, 149, 151–53, 155–57
Sayyida Zaynab mosque, 254–55, 257–59, 265, 266n2, 266n19
Scherz, China, 309
Schindler, Oskar, 52
Schöfnagel, Barbara, 145, 150–51. *See also Quiet Aid*
Schöfnagel, Dieter, 150, 156
School of Oriental and African Studies, 226
secularism: humanitarianism and, 7; to Islam, 180–81, 188n14; liberal-secular humanitarianism, 182–83; nonsecular genealogies, 262; secular agency, 182; secular aid, 186; secular civil society groups, 199–201; secular flow, 176; secular historicity, 180, 186; secular humanitarian charity, 177; secular humanitarianism, 22, 186, 254; secular spatiality, 178–79, 184; War on Terror and, 181
Seeking the Wounds of the Gift (Scherz), 309
Selover, Stephanie, 24, 295–96, 304. *See also* cultural heritage care work

Serbia, 100–6, 108
service. *See khidma/ khidmat*
7 Days, 7 Nights (Bozan), 268–69
Sino-Japanese War, 9, 13
slavery, 39
Slovenia, 98
Smith, Andrea, 46
socialist gray areas, 145–47, 155–58
Society of Friends, 13
socioeconomic marginalization, 173–74
Sorma, Mediha, 23, 302. *See also* care work
South Asia, 3, 9, 13, 20, 22, 68–70, 80, 96n5, 299. *See also specific countries*
Southeast Asia, 3, 9, 10, 17, 85–86. *See also specific countries*
Southern-Led Humanitarian Responses to Displacement (Fiddian-Qasmiyeh), 309
Sovereignty, Welcome, and Epistemic Hospitality (McNevin), 310
Soviet Union (USSR), 85, 96n3
Spade, Dean, 310
spatiality, 178, 180, 184, 276; spatial connections, 4, 12
spiritual economy, 254, 259, 263
Spivak, Gayatri, 188n13
Standing Emigration Committee, 71
Stefanescu, Claudia, 157
Stille Hilfe, 151–53, 157–58
story-forward, 18–19, 305, 307
Sufism, 23, 256
Sweden, 106
Syria: Afghanistan and, 272; civil war in, 24, 284–89, 295; cultural heritage care work in, 284–85, 289–95; displacement in, 214; Jordan and, 131, 217–18; Palestine and, 216–17; refugees from, 163, 172–73

temporary protection, 100, 102–3
Thailand: Cambodia and, 20–21, 93–94; care in, 91–93; in Cold War, 86–87; Khmer Rouge to, 228–29; local hosts in, 86–87, 93–94; reconciliation in, 95; refugee camps in, 86–90, 96n9; Royal Thai Army, 92; Vietnam and, 96n10
theater. *See* benevolent arts
Third Indochina War, 84–86, 95, 96n1

322 • Index

Tibetan Medical Humanitarianisms (Craig), 310
Tito, Marshall, 38
Tofighian, Omid, 238–39, 249
Torres, Alfonso, 61–62, 64
Touch, Ammara, 228
transit. *See* Khao-I-Dang Transit Center
transitional asylum, 51–52
transitional exchange, 54–56
Transylvania, 149, 151–53, 155–57
travel bans, 76–80
Tunisia, 41
Türkiye: Iraq and, 286; Kurds in, 273–81; reputation of, 23, 164, 192–93, 200–1; violence in, 268–73, 281–82
Tyabji, S. A. S., 73, 75
Tydings-McDuffie Act (1934), 57–58

Ukraine, 1, 218
Um, Khatharya, 236n12
umma (Muslim community), 180
UN. *See* United Nations
UNBRO. *See* United Nations Border Relief Operation
UNESCO World Heritage, 286
UNHCR. *See* United Nations High Commissioner for Refugees
UNICEF, 216, 255
unintended violence, 308, 310
United Arab Emirates, 295
United Jihad Council, 196
United Nations (UN): civilian convoys, 108; Convention refugee rights, 109; decolonization to, 46; General Assembly, 88; humanitarian communication with, 235n4; ICRC and, 133; intergovernmental agencies of, 37; International Children's Emergency Fund, 216; Israel to, 64; League of Nations and, 136; NGOs and, 107, 139; personnel, 39; reconstruction projects by, 200; refugees to, 13, 218; Security Council, 107
United Nations Border Relief Operation (UNBRO), 87, 92, 96n9
United Nations High Commissioner for Refugees (UNHCR): convoys from, 105; Filipino hospitality to, 51–52;

Global Trends report, 211; hospitality to, 51; humanitarian aid by, 100; ICRC and, 86–87, 92, 193; Iraq to, 212; in Jordan, 214; KID to, 88; Palestine to, 210; politics of, 10–11; Refugee Convention and, 15–16; resources of, 192; temporary protection to, 100
United Nations Protection Force (UNPROFOR), 107
United Nations Relief and Rehabilitation Administration (UNRRA), 38
United Nations Relief and Works Agency (UNRWA), 131–33, 135, 139, 161, 174n1, 174n9, 208–10. *See also* Palestinian refugee camps
United Nations Transitional Authority in Cambodia (UNTAC), 92–93
United States (US): Australia and, 251; Cambodia and, 225, 231, 234; China and, 88, 235n7; in Cold War, 84–86; colonialism to, 52–53, 56–57; disaster relief to, 192; European Community and, 99; Europe and, 60–61; Khmer Rouge to, 234; to Kissinger, 118; Philippines and, 55–56; race in, 59–60; refugees to, 61–62, 103; reputation of, 194; social justice in, 58; State Department, 289–91, 294; Syria to, 289–90; Türkiye and, 164; USSR and, 96n3; War on Terror to, 186
UNPROFOR. *See* United Nations Protection Force
UNRRA. *See* United Nations Relief and Rehabilitation Administration
UNRWA. *See* United Nations Relief and Works Agency
unskilled labor, 71
UNTAC. *See* United Nations Transitional Authority in Cambodia
US. *See* United States
USSR. *See* Soviet Union

The Value of Pakistan's Eid-al-Azha Animal Hide Collection (Mouftah), 309
Vernant, Jacques, 10
Vestergaard, Anne, 224
Vietnam, 84–87, 93, 95, 96n5, 96n10, 96n7, 96nn9–10, 96nn1–2, 226

visas, 78–79
visible/invisible nexus, 256–58
volunteering: al-Ḥayāh volunteers, 161–66; in Middle East, 167–74; refugees and, 22; religion and, 177–78; to UNRWA, 133, 174n9; voluntarism and, 8; voluntary organizations and, 13
vulnerability, 103–4

war. *See specific topics*
War on Terror, 178–81, 185–86, 190, 196
war refugees, 106–8
West Germany, 150–51, 153
WhatsApp, 113
Whyte, Jessica, 308, 310

World Council of Churches, 132–33
World Humanitarian Summit, 140
The World Refugees Made (Ballinger), 36–37, 39–41

Yai Lah, 94
Young Men's Christian Association, 162
Yugoslavia, 37–38, 43, 98–105

zakāt, 197, 260, 262
Zaynab, Sayyida, 255–56, 258–59, 265
Zeidan, Mahmoud, 133
Zionism, 60–61
zone of indifference, 15

www.ingramcontent.com/pod-product-compliance
Lightning Source LLC
Chambersburg PA
CBHW051526020426
42333CB00016B/1798